THE ENGLISH NOVEL
Volume I

1700 to Fielding

LONGMAN CRITICAL READERS

General Editor:
STAN SMITH, Professor of English, University of Dundee

Published titles:

THE ENGLISH NOVEL
Volume I

1700 to Fielding

Edited and Introduced by

RICHARD KROLL

LONGMAN
LONDON AND NEW YORK

Addison Wesley Longman Limited
Edinburgh Gate
Harlow, Essex CM20 2JE
England

and Associated Companies throughout the world

*Published in the United States of America
by Addison Wesley Longman Inc., New York*

© Addison Wesley Longman Limited 1998

First published 1998

ISBN 0 582 08855–0 Paper
ISBN 0 582 08856–9 Cased

Visit Addison Wesley Longman on the world wide web at
http://www.awl-he.com

British Library Cataloguing-in-Publication Data

A catalogue record for this book is available from the British Library

Library of Congress Cataloging-in-Publication Data

The English novel / edited and introduced by Richard Kroll.
    p.   cm. — (Longman critical readers)
    Includes bibliographical references and index.
    Contents: v. 1. 1700 to Fielding
    ISBN 0–582–08856–9 (v. 1). — ISBN 0–582–08855–0 (pbk. : v. 1)
    1. English fiction—History and criticism.   I. Kroll, Richard W.
F.   II. Series.
PR823.E57   1998
823.009—dc21   98–13802
                                                              CIP

Set by 35 in 9½/11½ pt Palatino
Produced by Addison Wesley Longman Singapore (Pte) Ltd.,
Printed in Singapore

Contents

General Editors' Preface

The outlines of contemporary critical theory are now often taught as a standard feature of a degree in literary studies. The development of particular theories has seen a thorough transformation of literary criticism. For example, Marxist and Foucauldian theories have revolutionized Shakespeare studies, and 'deconstruction' has led to a complete reassessment of Romantic poetry. Feminist criticism has left scarcely any period of literature unaffected by its searching critiques. Teachers of literary studies can no longer fall back on a standardized, received methodology.

Lecturers and teachers are now urgently looking for guidance in a rapidly changing critical environment. They need help in understanding the latest revisions in literary theory, and especially in grasping the practical effects of the new theories in the form of theoretically sensitized new readings. A number of volumes in the series anthologize important essays on particular theories. However, in order to grasp the full implications and possible uses of particular theories it is essential to see them put to work. This series provides substantial volumes of new readings, presented in an accessible form and with a significant amount of editorial guidance.

Each volume includes a substantial introduction which explores the theoretical issues and conflicts embodied in the essays selected and locates areas of disagreement between positions. The pluralism of theories has to be put on the agenda of literary studies. We can no longer pretend that we all tacitly accept the same practices in literary studies. Neither is a *laissez-faire* attitude any longer tenable. Literature departments need to go beyond the mere toleration of theoretical differences: it is not enough merely to agree to differ; they need actually to 'stage' the differences openly. The volumes in this series all attempt to dramatize the differences, not necessarily with a view to resolving them but in order to foreground the choices presented by different theories or to argue for a particular route through the impasses the differences present.

The theory 'revolution' has had real effects. It has loosened the grip of traditional empiricist and romantic assumptions about language and literature. It is not always clear what is being proposed as the new agenda for literary studies, and indeed the very notion of 'literature' is questioned by the post-structuralist strain in theory. However, the uncertainties and obscurities of contemporary theories appear much less worrying when we see what the best critics have been able to do with them in practice. This series aims to disseminate the best of recent criticism and to show that it is possible to re-read the canonical texts of literature in new and challenging ways.

RAMAN SELDEN AND STAN SMITH

The Publishers and fellow Series Editor regret to record that Raman Selden died after a short illness in May 1991 at the age of fifty-three. Ray Selden was a fine scholar and a lovely man. All those he has worked with will remember him with much affection and respect.

Editor's Preface

The *Longman Critical Readers* series gives a devotee of the eighteenth century like myself a double opportunity. On the one hand, this volume can draw attention to the sheer interest of an entire literary tradition that has, ever since Wordsworth's Preface to the *Lyrical Ballads*, been relegated (in Arnold's sardonic phrase) to the age of prose and reason, a distinctly unliterary age, or, if literary, certainly unpoetic. On the other hand, in line with the General Editors' aims for this series, I would argue that the particularity of eighteenth-century concerns and methods of representation has resulted in modes of criticism that are theoretically distinct. For one thing – and here Dryden's influence is decisive – eighteenth-century literature has generally assumed the historically and ideologically embedded nature of literary utterances, and therefore did not need to invent new historicism (for example) to redirect criticism onto a road not previously taken.

Second, this volume presents a series of debates about the early English novel that has always been intense. These have gained in intensity and conviction since the 1970s, as the range of possible approaches has proliferated, and as the political implications of different critical positions have come to assume greater significance in the life of literature departments. And – as is not always the case – greater heat seems also to have produced greater light: the reader of the essays collected in this book will, I think agree that, as the debates have opened out, they have been conducted at increasing levels of theoretical and methodological sophistication. I therefore aim in this volume to offer the student a brief overview of the range and style of arguments surrounding the early eighteenth-century novel.

I am grateful to the many colleagues who were willing to provide ideas about books and essays that they found seminal: Paul Alkon, Paula Backscheider, Eve Tavor Bannet, John Bender, Michael McKeon, Max Novak, Ruth Perry, John Richetti, Peter Sabor, and William Warner. My jobs at Princeton and UCI have also provided superb colleagues in my field: Margaret Doody and Earl Miner; Homer Brown, Bob Folkenflik, and Ann Van Sant; as well as Fred Keener during my visiting year at Hofstra. It is a measure of those individuals' caliber that I have, in good conscience, been able to include their work in what follows. Carol Kay, whose work I have found newly inspirational for this project, has remained a friend of heart and head. Most of the preliminary footwork was done with flair and intelligence by Diana Secker. Finally, I have found rigorous readers in Steve Barney, Fraser Easton, Brean Hammond, Fred Keener, Allison Kroll, Jayne Lewis, Mark Phillips, and Victoria Silver. I recognize that there are many fine pieces of criticism I have omitted from this anthology, and that all errors in fact or judgment remain mine.

IRVINE, CALIFORNIA, 1997

Acknowledgements

We are grateful to the following for permission to reproduce copyright material:

the author, Professor John Bender for 'The Novel and the Rise of Penitentiary: Narrative and Ideology in Defoe, Gay, Hogarth and Fielding' from *Stanford Literary Review*, 1984 (the ideas in this essay are argued more fully in *Imagining The Penitentiary: Fiction and the Architecture of Mind in Eighteenth-century England* Chicago: University of Chicago Press, 1987) © John Bender; Cambridge University Press and the author for 'Revelation of the heart through entrapment and trial: Clarrisa's story, Lovelace's plot' by Ann Jessie Van Sant in *Eighteenth-century Sensibility and the Novel: The Senses in Social Context* (Cambridge, Cambridge University Press, 1993); Johns Hopkins University Press for 'The Displaced self in the Novels of Daniel Defoe' by Homer O. Brown in *ELH 38* (1971), extracts from 'The Exact Picture of his Mother': Recognising Joseph Andrews' by Jill Campbell in *ELH 55* (1988) and 'The Elevation of the Novel in England: Hegemony and Literary History' by William B. Warner in *ELH 59* (1992); Oxford University Press Inc. for 'Rise of the Novel' in *Desire and Domestic Fiction: A Political History of the Novel* by Nancy Armstrong. Copyright © 1987 by Nancy Armstrong; the author, John Richetti for an extract from his 'Popular Narrative in the Early 18th Century: Formats and Formulas' in J. M. Armistead (ed.) *The First English Novelists: Essays in Understanding* 1985. Knoxville: Univ. of Tennessee Press; Yale University Press for extracts by Michael Seidel from 'Crusoe's Island Exile' by Michael Seidel in *Exile and Narrative Imagination* (1986).

We have been unable to trace the copyright holder of 'Generic Transformation and Social change: Rethinking the rise of the Novel' by Michael McKeon in *Culture Critique 1* (1985), and would appreciate any information which would enable us to do so.

1 Introduction

This is the first of two volumes that anthologize a series of previously published essays and book chapters about the eighteenth-century British novel. The present collection covers the novel's career from 1700 to Fielding; its companion, the novel's career from Smollett to the end of the century.[1]

My intention is to treat the anthologies as a matching pair, so that my separate introductions will attempt to perform for the student two distinct, but I hope complementary, tasks. The first introduction, more purely 'literary' in manner and method, provides a digest of the major recent critical approaches to the novel of the first half of the eighteenth century. It will also introduce in passing some of the main literary-theoretical approaches that have appealed to critics.

The second introduction will be more historical in scope, responding to what I see as a change in the nature and range of literary expression in the later eighteenth century, and thus in the descriptive challenge confronting the scholar or critic. It seeks broadly to frame the concerns of later eighteenth-century novelists with the pressures and anxieties that distinguish British history between 1745, when the Jacobite cause was decisively defeated, and 1800, when Britain was at war with France in the wake of the French Revolution of 1789. And it connects that analysis to modern debates in intellectual history and political theory about how the eighteenth century as a whole dealt with the effects of a commercial and consumer revolution, and how it developed and articulated cultural ideals of conversation, politeness, and rational debate.

The problem of 'the novel': Ian Watt and his successors

Any responsible commentator on the early eighteenth-century novel must recognize the success and authority of a single book, namely Ian Watt's *The Rise of the Novel: Studies in Defoe, Richardson and Fielding*, published in 1957, the same year in which Northrop Frye

published his *Anatomy of Criticism,* and only four years after the
appearance in translation of Erich Auerbach's *Mimesis,* to which Watt
owes a great deal.[2] Almost none of the essays printed below can
proceed without accounting in some way or another for the impact
Watt's book has had on all later critics of the eighteenth-century
novel. The book has served, for most of us, as a classroom primer.
Qualifying and attacking *The Rise of the Novel* has become the
grounds of a number of books almost as important in their own
right, but Watt's argument is deservedly famous. It takes more or
less as an assumption the view that what we ordinarily recognize
as a novel – a literary artifact aiming, according to Watt, at 'formal
realism' (a term his critics tend to simplify) – first became fully
visible with the publication of Daniel Defoe's *Robinson Crusoe* in 1719.

The success of Watt's book reflected not only its exemplary clarity
and intelligence of presentation, but also the structure of its crucial
opening chapters. Here, Watt argued several things. Above all, he
held that the novel represents a distinct departure in literary aims
and techniques from the former course of European literary history.
Despite an ancient tradition of long prose narratives, of which he
is patently aware, Watt argued that the novel combines a series of
effects reflecting or exploiting the peculiar conditions in European,
specifically English, life that emerged generally after the middle of
the seventeenth century. It is important to see how Watt stresses
that what is new is a question of methods of representation, that
the 'realism' he heralds does not generally in his argument have the
kind of objective, almost ontological status accorded it by many of
his critics. For Watt, 'realism' is itself an artifice: the novel 'attempts
to portray all the varieties of human experience, and not merely
those suited to one particular literary perspective'; its 'realism does
not reside in the kind of life it presents, but in the way it presents it'
(11). Its protagonists are represented not as types but as 'particular
individuals in the contemporary social environment' (19), and its plot
mechanisms are driven by a concern to regard strictly probable and
causal relations among character, motivation, and effects in the
world. Moreover, character is not an allegorical type or bundle of
humors, but is the product of the individual mind's encounter with
numerous particular experiences over time: in fact, it is this pressure
of time on the individual consciousness that distinguishes Defoe from
predecessors such as Sidney or Bunyan (24).[3]

The power of Watt's explanatory mechanism arose primarily not,
I think, from this internalist approach to literary history, where the
emergence of a new literary form becomes visible by contrast to what
literary forms and genres had preceded it. It derived at least as much
from the way Watt elegantly attached it to two different external

forms of explanation. The first, summoning intellectual history, held that Descartes' formulations concerning human identity were indeed as revolutionary as historians of philosophy have thought. Descartes' *Discourse of Method* and *Meditations* were, precisely, intensive investigations of the career of an individual, privatized conscience; and what Descartes revolutionized at the level of high abstract philosophy became profoundly popularized in England with the spectacular success of John Locke's *An Essay concerning Human Understanding* (1690). In this document, Locke argues that personal identity is the accumulation of individual mental experiences through space and time. Though Watt does not explicitly treat it in this way, this aspect of his thesis appealed and still appeals to critics who see the novel as an instrument for forming a new bourgeois conscience or identity in the wake, especially, of the Glorious Revolution of 1688.

The second aspect of Watt's approach is in some ways his most enduring legacy to studies of the novel. For here Watt connected the rise of the novel to the growth of literacy in England, the emergence of different and new kinds of readers – or writers' assumptions that such new kinds of readers existed – the growth of publication, and the creation of such institutions as lending libraries. In short, Watt attended carefully to what is now often called literature's material conditions. In his second chapter, Watt anticipates the outlines of similar lines of inquiry to the present day, especially J. Paul Hunter's excellent amplification of Watt's thesis, *Before Novels: The Cultural Contexts of Eighteenth-Century English Fiction* (1990).[4] He considers the growth of literacy in the early eighteenth century; the relative cost of books, with novels costing less than the expensive folio editions of French romances; the emergence of circulating libraries; a recognition that, increasingly, readers were women, apprentices, and household servants; these classes' aspirations in a society in which upward mobility seemed possible; the overwhelming production of religious literature in an age where tastes nevertheless seem to become increasingly secular; the growth of periodical literature such as the *Gentleman's Magazine* (issued in the 1730s) and the social changes detectable in that journal in the wake of Addison's more gentrified *Spectator* (issued in 1711–12); the rising power of the booksellers in stimulating literary consumption; and the economic conditions of authorship in the literary marketplace which tended to encourage prolixity – one reason that the novel, in the minds of satirists such as Pope, was associated with Grub Street.

There are further reasons why Watt's book has been so successful, ones largely external to his actual thesis and methods. These are inevitably and paradoxically some of the motives for issuing the present volume and its companion. That is, there is a widespread assumption that there is such a thing as *the novel*, accompanied by several other assumptions that Watt's main title (shorn of the important qualifying subtitle) and language tend to foster. We could list them as follows: the novel is about everyday life and the concerns of everyday people; it aims at representational transparency of a kind that can reproduce the texture of quotidian, especially urban, life; its commentary bears quite immediately on social concerns and pressures; and it is both the most popular and most widespread literary form.

The problem is that many of these assumptions either about novelistic form or its social relevance have a nineteenth-century, not eighteenth-century, provenance.[5] Though eighteenth-century writers are conscious that the novel escapes classic generic taxonomies – what are its debts to romance or to epic, to courtesy books or the *novella*? – it was primarily the nineteenth, not the eighteenth century that embarked on programmatic attempts to legitimate the novel as high art (Flaubert, James), following an era in which its social relevance was such that Dickens was cited in parliamentary debates on the poor. Moreover, since the singular power of the novel as a genre goes today unchallenged by and large, and since these assumptions – ideologically pervasive as they are – deeply affect students' views about what they want to read, studies of the eighteenth-century novel often proceed as if the novel as such was as visible and established a category to eighteenth-century readers as it has become to us. Consequently, the tendency has been to assume that the crucial stage in the formation of the novel was the agreement that arose out of the debate between Richardson and Fielding. It is as though all sides were agreed that these writers, between them, had forged a new literary type. And histories of the rise of the novel or the rise of the English novel have often relaxed at this milestone in the 1740s, as if from that point forth, the novel's victory was assured. In some retrospective sense, of course, it was.

I have sketched the significance of Watt's book at some length because it has, positively as well as negatively, determined the course of the major studies to have appeared in recent years, the latest two being Margaret Doody's *The True Story of the Novel* (1996) and Homer Brown's *Institutions of the English Novel from Defoe to Scott* (1997).[6] These studies can, I think, be grouped into three types: studies that effectively accept Watt's thesis about the rise of the novel in England in the first half of the eighteenth century, but seek in significant ways to qualify or extend its terms; studies that argue that the focus on the eighteenth-century English novel as 'new' are essentially mistaken, since the novel has an ancient pedigree of which it has always remained aware; and studies that argue that the shape of the history assumed and encouraged by Watt is itself an outgrowth of highly charged ideological battles fought during the eighteenth century, and decided by the beginning of the nineteenth, about how the novel in English should be recognized, and what values it should be deemed to promote.

Davis, Keener, Hunter, McKeon

Lennard Davis's *Factual Fictions: The Origins of the English Novel* (1983) was one of the first sustained attempts, in the 1980s, to redefine the terms of Ian Watt's book.[7] Davis's book is nothing if not methodologically self-conscious, and interestingly raises the central point of contention of all the major studies since. That is, if the novel has an origin, does it emerge gradually from earlier genres and historical moments, or does it appear rather suddenly as a new form, as Watt implicitly argues? Davis contends that there are essentially three ways of constructing explanations for the emergence of a genre to prominence: the 'evolutionary' model, in which the novel organically develops out of previous narrative forms; the 'osmotic' model, in which the novel rather vaguely responds to, or absorbs, changes in the culture – a position Davis ascribes to Watt; and the 'convergence' model, in which the novel does emerge at a distinct time, but uses everything currently available to it: it is part of a new discursive formation. By citing Foucault, Davis favors the 'convergence' model, but in practice selectively propounds a thesis not unlike that of Watt: the 'osmotic' and 'convergence' models are in practice alike, it seems. This is hardly surprising, since almost all analyses of the emergence of an historical phenomenon tend to fudge the question of whether it was produced by, or helped produce, other, seemingly related, phenomena. For example, did bourgeois expectations help stimulate the novel, which catered to them, or was the novel an essential device for propagating what we might see as distinctively bourgeois values?

Further, and usefully, Davis raises an issue that continues to tease studies of the early novel, and that is its relation to the romance, and by implication specifically the French romances that flowered in the seventeenth century. Since he is thinking in terms of Foucauldian ruptures, whereby the genealogy of historical forces can be dismissed as causal explanations, Davis rejects the connection between the romance and the novel. Rather, the novel emerges from a series of pressures or impulses that are local to Britain, and are marked centrally by an unresolved ambivalence about the difference between fact and fiction. Novels are 'a new and self-conscious genre' (12), Davis argues, precisely because they are fictions that claim to be factual. This doubleness they owe to sixteenth-century ballads and seventeenth-century newsbooks, whereby the Wattian values of immediacy, transparency, and readerly engagement are given a distinct, vernacular genealogy. And what was immediate, though atomized, in the ballad, became more methodical, continuous, though no less engaged, in the newsbooks, especially at that critical juncture in the 1640s when news assumed vital polemical significance for the nation at large, as it lurched toward Civil War. In sum, formal realism has its own history.

In categorically rejecting any affiliation between the romance and the novel, Davis may be overstating his case, but his summary of the opposition is useful, since it so vividly etches the terms that other critics such as McKeon and Doody are themselves trying to negotiate, though in markedly different ways. Thus:

1 The romance is set in the distant, idealized past; the novel is set in a more recent, less heroic, setting.
2 The romance is based on the epic; the novel is modelled on history and journalism.
3 The romance is usually not set in the country of the author but in a remote and exotic location; the novel tends to be set in the locale of the author, that is, the novel tends to be a national form of literature.
4 The romance depicts the life of the aristocracy and is designed for an upper-class reader; the novel tends to be more middle-class in scope and is geared to a slightly less aristocratic readership, although the statement is less true in France of the seventeenth century than in England.
5 Romances tend to be long and episodic; novels are shorter and more compact of plot.
6 Romances value the preservation of virtue and chastity; novels tend to focus on illegal doings and forbidden passions.
7 Novels of the eighteenth century tend to be written in the first person or in letter form; romances are never written in these forms.
8 Romances make clear that they are mixing fact and fiction to create an essentially fictional plot; novels tend to deny that they are fictional.
9 Romances follow the rules of *bienséance* and *vraisemblance*; novelists openly reject these rules since they claim to be writing history or recording life as it is.[8]

Two other important books avowedly develop their cues from Watt, namely Frederick Keener's *The Chain of Becoming: The Philosophical Tale, the Novel, and a Neglected Realism of the Enlightenment: Swift, Montesquieu, Voltaire, Johnson, and Austen* (1983); and J. Paul Hunter's *Before Novels* (cited above).[9] In his subtle and highly original argument, Keener begins with an *obiter dictum* in Watt, namely that realism could apply both to descriptions of the world (its usual connotation), or equally to conveying psychological and moral states and judgments with precision, without necessarily committing itself to rendering the physical world with equal exactitude.[10] It is this latter concern that Keener sets out to elucidate, celebrating the acuity of writers whose texts, such as *Gulliver's Travels* and *Rasselas*, are on the face of it improbable, but which are marked by 'the theme of the main character's psychological self-assessment, at least his need for it, promoting such realism on his part as prerequisite to all other judgments' (14). Keener's argument is unusual in a number of ways, not least in its ability to align philosophy and literature, and in its appreciation of narratives that we don't think of as novels, as well as in its comparative sense of English and French literature. Indeed, Keener remarks that psychological realism is a more central feature of French texts inasmuch as English novels tend to be more determinedly social and moral.

Paul Hunter's *Before Novels* is the most thorough exposition of all the implications of Watt's thesis. In this carefully researched book, Hunter argues that by the 1740s, the novel was indeed thought by contemporaries to have become a defined genre, but that the novel emerged within the context of numerous forces that are particular to the period between the 1690s and the middle of the eighteenth century. It is not to be seen as the necessary outgrowth of the history of narrative forms in literature, least of all the romances. Rather, we must attend phenomenologically to the numerous features that make this period a distinct, and distinctly anxious, moment in the experience of so many British people, especially those in cities. Consequently, he argues, 'the novel did not emerge simply because of the anxieties, but those anxieties produced a climate receptive to a certain kind of texts with particular features. The convergence of these features into a particular kind of text is what the novel, in part, is' (288). Thus Hunter covers more thoroughly much of the territory sketched by Watt: the question of literacy, the emergence of print culture, the importance of journalism, the emphasis on facticity. Hunter's peculiar contribution to the debate, however, comes in two forms. First, he re-emphasizes throughout how the experience of reading the novel, and the forms of address that distinguish it, comprise a peculiar phenomenology, a reaction to the modernity, the speed, the claustrophobia, the loneliness of life from the late seventeenth century on, a life that was by definition distinctively British, just as London played a unique role in the life of the nation. For Hunter, the novel provided a kind of substitute for the lost forms of communality that distinguished an earlier age, as the reader engaged on his own with the world it represented.

Second, Hunter also stresses throughout how the pervasive literature of devotion belongs to the mentalities that the novel also served. That is, more than any other commentator, he shows how the literature of didacticism is endemic to the assumptions of all readers at this time, and that it served purposes that we in the secular West cannot now imaginatively credit, such as the delight readers might have taken in spiritual guides and catechisms. (We should remember the enormous popularity of *Pilgrim's Progress*.) The novel's concern with particularity, on this view, is not merely the reflex of the new empiricism. The attention to minutiae and the urge to interpret them providentially also emerge from theological and confessional habits of mind which are second nature to early readers of the novel.

The most spectacular and ambitious attempt to revise Watt to date is, however, undoubtedly Michael McKeon's *The Origins of the English Novel, 1600–1740* (1987).[11] Although McKeon has been criticized for seeming to argue – like Watt, Davis, Hunter, and many others – that the novel becomes a singular and established category by about 1740, it is important to see that his argument provides the most complex account of the emergence of the novel in the eighteenth century to date. The criticism, if not entirely unfounded, needs considerable qualification. Indeed, the complexity and scope of McKeon's book are almost bound to invite misreadings, since it is comprehensively, closely, and densely argued. Despite appearances, McKeon's thrust is not as teleological as others in this line. He seeks to provide a genealogy which respects what he sees to be the fundamentally dialectical nature of relations among questions of how we know the world (epistemology), how we value ourselves and others (social and political ideology), and how literary artifacts help us mediate among these issues. McKeon focusses primarily, and extensively, on the instability of epistemological and social categories from the late sixteenth century on; and he elaborates a well-established view of the seventeenth century as riven with debates that proved seminal in the formation of modern society. But his dialectical reading of culture has a long view, since he sees the romance as developing at critical junctures from the Greek enlightenment of the fifth century BC, through the twelfth-century Renaissance, and as coming to mediate anxieties that beset aristocratic and feudal culture.

Like the 'emergence' of romance, the 'emergence' of the novel is as provisional as the history and experience of which it is a part. Questions of truth and questions of virtue each have their own dialectical histories, and the relation between literature and common life is also dialectical: the way we tell stories helps us to negotiate the world, and the problems of negotiating the world influence how we speak about it. On this view, literature is a sort of lightning rod for the tensions of lived experience, and at the same time influences how we imagine resolving or sublimating those tensions (238).

Obviously, McKeon's historical scope is vast, since he sees the novel as emerging in part from the kinds of ideological and historical forces that the romance, which stretches back to antiquity, could not adequately confront and explain. Nowhere does McKeon imply that the romance is a lesser form than the novel, or that the novel is the apogee of a progressive literary history; he merely argues that its range of effects were developed over time to negotiate epistemological and social problems that were, by the late seventeenth century, archaic, or had assumed radically new shapes (133; 150). And in peculiar ways romance always potentially returns since it is part of the dialectical process in which both 'romance' and 'novel' participate, along with other kinds of narrative such as 'history.' Thus in the course of the seventeenth century, for example, 'true history' begins to threaten what is perceived as the unrealities of romance, but because that true history involves various epistemological simplifications of its own, it in turn is treated as a species of romance, and must yield to forms that claim that they engage more aptly with the world (88). This aspect of McKeon's argument, it must be admitted, is not always as clear as it might be: McKeon sometimes writes as if these narrative forms objectively embodied distinct descriptive methods, and sometimes as if they were merely perceived and heralded by contemporaries as having different powers of description. This is particularly true of the category 'romance,' since McKeon believes that romance emerged as a distinct mode of representation by the 'early modern' period – only to be subverted – while he also knows that the term was used in the seventeenth century as a polemical means to accuse opponents of *naïveté*.

In short, McKeon's loosely Marxist method is aimed at the general problem of modernity, and the extent to which we can treat the novel as a form of fiction-making whose methods respond to what many see as the distinctive crisis of modernity. Thus the conclusion of the argument is that the novel appears at a specific historical juncture. The methods by which epistemological anxieties and the methods by which social anxieties are resolved become equivalent, even interchangeable, and this doubleness inheres in the ways that the novel represents and negotiates both sets of problems (214; 266).

McKeon is particularly subtle in his refusal to see genre as anything but the cumulative effects of cultural pressures that, by remaining insistent over time, bring a certain set of solutions increasingly to the fore. (In this he agrees with Hunter.) Genre is not a given, but the reflex and mediator solely of historical forces; and it is for that reason that Marx's notion of 'simple abstraction' is so instrumental for McKeon. Marx is warning that our ways of taxonomizing historical actualities are heuristic devices: certain ways of thinking and speaking about given arrangements and regularities become in the course of time increasingly standardized ways of referring to a given phenomenon or set of phenomena. The novel is not some hypostatized entity waiting in the wings, ready to assume its role in the drama of Western literature, but is the effect of the history that produces it.

While McKeon's argument is about instability and flux, conceived through Marxist dialectic, many readers I think find the experience of reading *The Origins* somewhat daunting. One reason is that McKeon's attachment to the dialectical model is both profound and internally rigorous. The author tries to account for virtually every dimension of human and historical experience and subject them to his method. The other reason may be that for all that McKeon celebrates flux through time, he sees epistemological, social, and generic change as occurring in a three-fold synchronic regularity: each category undergoes change as if it were an equivalent of the other. Thus, as in the essay reproduced below (see Chapter 2), we find that three categories undergo change in direct positive ratio (not all these terms are McKeon's):

Questions of truth	Questions of virtue	Genre
Romance idealism	Aristocratic ideology	Romance
Naïve empiricism	Progressive ideology	Novel
Extreme scepticism	Conservative ideology	Satire

Put simply, an archaic aristocratic order (esteeming honor, for example) gives way in the late seventeenth century to a more fluid means of bestowing social value (such as work or virtue), which in turn provokes a conservative reaction. Likewise, romance (an intrinsically improbable mode of narration) gives way to attempts to render the world transparently with empirical precision (*Robinson Crusoe*, for example), whose apparent *naïvetés* in turn invite satirical attack (*Gulliver's Travels*). McKeon finally makes the assertion that such intrinsically dialectical instabilities typify the history of the novel ever since.

Doody

Like its title, Margaret Doody's recent book *The True Story of the Novel* is nothing if not daring. It speaks as though it re-engages the Wattian line that I have described above, but it would be more accurate to say that it comprises such a distinct form and method of criticism that its aims and conclusions operate in completely different ways from the tradition we have been considering. It tends to make even of Watt a straw man, arguing that critics in his tradition have dwelt too exclusively on the English, have dismissed the romance as a paltry genre that had to yield to the more vigorous novel, and that the novel is a camouflage for what Doody calls 'Prescriptive Realism.' There are some grounds to her criticisms. But the plain fact is that, for all she wants to take us back to classical 'novels,' Doody, by her own admission, is not really interested in history, or at least the kind of historical account that frames Hunter's and McKeon's projects.[12] Since ultimately Doody is celebrating The Novel, an organism in its own right, with its own often subversive desires that unconsciously govern individual novelists and novel readers, and for whom the distinction between romance and novel is empty, the focus is finally on what Doody herself calls 'a timeless continuum' (164).

There are several arguments at work in this book. Doody argues that we need to remember our most profound debts to the Greek romances; that those stories encapsulate what is most significant about The Novel as an utterance; that The Novel so defined is essentially religious in origin and still in purpose; that it brings certain pleasures validating the personal and the erotic; and that it confirms the yearnings, the desires, the pains of those outside official culture, primarily the poor and women. The roots of The Novel in Eastern, African, and Greek culture make it inevitably multiform and encompassing, and connect it symbolically to an apprehension of the feminine as a mode of being, and the indefinable *satura* as a form which expands or dilates almost *ad infinitum*. Inspired in part by Bakhtin's celebration of the novel's polyglot subversiveness, and in part by a German tradition of archetypal criticism from roughly the same inter-war period, Doody aligns The Novel's fecundity against the emergence of interest in civic values – which prefers the manly, the rule of law, the purely public, the elite, and the narrowly disciplined – from the Renaissance on, culminating, in her view, in the Whiggish and ideologically patrolled world of the early to mid eighteenth century (e.g. 229). Novel criticism in the seventeenth century celebrated its Eastern and Greek origins. By the mid eighteenth century, however, the novel was treated as native and recent, and subject to the prescriptions of realism that privileged the domestic scene, and forever distanced it from the indiscipline and associated barbarisms of romance.

In sum, I think it fair to say that there are two predominant kinds of arguments at play in Doody's book. First and foremost, an ontological argument assigns permanence and even a definite agency to The Novel as a 'force,' to use Doody's term. Second, Doody's discussion of the seventeenth and eighteenth centuries views the English 'novel' as the creation of an ideological back-formation. That is, what we see as 'the novel' in the standard versions of Watt and company, the argument goes, itself reflects cultural pressures that emerged some time after Defoe and especially Richardson and Fielding wrote. The novel, whose 'beginnings,' 'origins,' or 'rise' we see almost encapsulated in those three authors, is much less a reflection of what those authors did or thought they were doing, than a reflection of what became, in the course of time, a set of narrow prescriptions for the genre we now denominate 'the novel,' often falsely in contradistinction to the romance. In Doody's version of this story, the insidious Whiggishness of the early eighteenth century on ensured that only certain literary utterances were respectable, and those utterances had to be safe and sanitized.

Warner and Brown

Two critics have developed a similar insight more fully. William Warner has asked why it is that we have difficulty accounting for Behn's, Haywood's, and Manley's productions, and has proposed that Richardson's and Fielding's claims to have invented a new kind of writing was so credited that they successfully blocked all subsequent critics and readers from seeing anything other than the genealogy they approved. In two important essays – one reprinted below (see Chapter 3) – Warner argues that Behn, Haywood, and Manley both created and fulfilled the demands of the new literary marketplace from the 1690s on, in which readers indulged their imaginative pleasures in lurid, salacious, and often improbable ('romantic') tales.[13] Richardson and Fielding set out to inoculate their readers against the morally pernicious influence of these stories; but rather than displacing such stories wholesale with entirely new kinds of narratives – as they claimed to do – they refashioned many of the key topoi they inherited from this literature, in an effort to redirect their moral impact. Consequently, both Richardson and Fielding's own narratives suffer a kind of instability inherited from this project, since the very kinds of narrative pleasures that disturb them most about their predecessors return to infect the experience of their own readers. Their greatest success seems not to have been truly to sanitize literature, since imaginative experience often releases asocial desires, but to create a fiction about their originality that determines the course of most critical histories of the novel ever since, and has prevented us from valuing Behn's, Haywood's, and Manley's achievements for what they are.

The most thorough and sophisticated version of this argument to date appears in Homer Brown's *Institutions of the English Novel from Defoe to Scott* (1997). Brown's argument has several dimensions that combine debts to traditional literary history, to post-structuralism, and to the most contemporary interests in national identities. First, a proper assessment of the actual achievements of Defoe, Richardson, and Fielding will reveal how unlike they are, how each thought of his achievement differently (in the case of Defoe, insisting oddly that his stories were true), and how the subsequent fortunes of each fluctuated over time and relative to the others.[14] At no point through the eighteenth century were any of these authors taken to represent 'the novel,' and at no point did they become a triad signifying the novel synecdochically, as they might seem to do in Watt's and McKeon's theses – certainly not, Brown insists, by 1750.

Second, it is the emergence of collections of novels prepared for the late-eighteenth- and early-nineteenth-century marketplace that gropingly began to make a canon of sorts; and it was paradoxically and fatefully Scott's assessment of the history of the English novel for just such an anthology in 1814 that created something we might call 'the English novel' as a recognizable entity – what Brown calls an 'institution,' which then requires recursive validation.[15]

Third, however, for Scott, what was being made at this juncture was the British, not narrowly the English novel, at a time when 'literature' as an idea was also being invented (and significantly a year before Waterloo). For the paradox of Scott's success involves the role of romance in Scott's reading of the history and nature of the novel. The romance, we discover, belongs to the story of the novel, a fact that bears directly on Scott's status as a Scottish Anglophone writer: in incorporating the romance into his genealogy, and indeed already in *Waverley*, 'Scott aimed to create . . . a truly *British* identity' (xvii). For the Scots, as for the Anglophone North Americans, romance could be conscripted as a means to reveal the indebtedness of a gradually hardening 'Englishness' or 'Britishness' to ethnic traditions which it had absorbed and was in danger of obscuring. Brown's close readings of Defoe's narrative equivocations have the flavor of high deconstruction, but are uncharacteristically yoked to strictly historical ends, since they reveal that to treat Defoe as a representative 'realist' is to see something that is hardly there: Defoe

becomes the ultimate litmus test of the demand to legitimate
institutions after the fact.

One might remark in conclusion that Brown's methodological
precision is impressive, since he puts on hold the question of what,
if anything, happened in the history of literary genre in the 1720s
or so. The specific genre of the novel only comes into view, that is,
when it is named by powerful literary historians such as Scott, so that
the scholar's task is to chart the relationship between past literary
histories and the ideological purposes they served. Nevertheless, we
should consider two unresolved complexities within this position.
First, Brown vigorously disagrees with McKeon, as if McKeon were
merely ossifying Watt. But Brown's analysis requires something
not unlike McKeon's Marxist 'simple abstraction.' The difference
is that Brown can point to a date when that abstraction becomes
institutionalized. McKeon's tack requires a double strategy. The critic
or scholar must adjudicate when such an abstraction can be spoken
of as an analytic or cultural reality by observing the history of
literary history. But he or she must also measure the point at which
habit and usage demand that we recognize and name a constellation
of effects which we can no longer ignore as arbitrary or unrelated.
In fact, McKeon's method recalls something like Wittgenstein's
'family resemblances,' whereby groups of regularities call attention
to themselves and require description.

Second, Brown cannot entirely escape behaving as if something like
'the novel' emerged in the 1720s, if only because he admits that
something was happening in literary history when the works of
Defoe, Richardson, Fielding, and Sterne were published, and if only
because he writes about them so passionately. For him the
phenomena are plural and have no ontological status as such, so that
to speak of 'the novel' is a mistake. Nevertheless, Brown is worrying
at a problem articulated somewhat differently by Thomas Kuhn in
The Structure of Scientific Revolutions when he describes how oxygen
was discovered.[16] Retrospectively, we now think the gas was
first isolated in the early 1770s by C. W. Scheele, but this had no
contemporary impact, since the fact was only published when the
discovery of oxygen had been independently announced. Thus, in
some ways, in 1774–75 Joseph Priestley was the first to discover
oxygen, but he didn't fully know it: the language of eighteenth-
century chemistry prohibited him from recognizing the substance
fully for what we now hold it to be. It was only when Lavoisier,
possibly prompted by Priestley's experiments, recognized the new
gas as a distinct substance that we can say that oxygen could be said
to have been discovered. Nevertheless, because we only now know
that Scheele had isolated oxygen, and because we only now know

Priestley's theories involving 'phlogiston' pointed to oxygen, does not mean that Scheele's and Priestley's discoveries were entirely empty of ontological meaning until Lavoisier's experiments permitted others to appreciate their efforts. That revolutions are hidden from those who help cause them doesn't necessarily show that they aren't in some real sense taking place.

The ideology of the eighteenth-century novel: Bender, Castle, and Kay

Some important books are not exercised about the problem of defining the eighteenth-century novel, or the novel *tout court*, but concentrate rather on what ideological role novels played in the culture.[17] Here we have three basic models: the Foucauldian view that the novel participates in the increasing regulation and disciplining of personality and consciousness; the Bakhtinian view that the novel's playfulness and fecundity release energies that allow characters and readers in some sense to remake themselves; and what I would see as a liberal model which takes eighteenth-century social and political theory largely in its own terms. The last combines the view that social institutions are indeed constitutive (and can be oppressive), with the view that to recognize the artifices of those institutions allows us to imagine – or at least to debate – the effectiveness of individual choice and reform.

John Bender's *Imagining the Penitentiary: Fiction and the Architecture of Mind in Eighteenth-Century England* (1987) and Terry Castle's *Masquerade and Civilization: The Carnivalesque in Eighteenth-Century English Culture and Fiction* (1986) are among the most successful and widely received books on the eighteenth-century novel in the last dozen years.[18] Perhaps because both authors are colleagues of Ian Watt, Watt's basic view of the 'rise' of the novel goes unchallenged, even though Bender and Castle pursue very different theses. For both critics, the fact of the novel as a distinct genre is more or less untroubled and axiomatic. Indeed, Bender's thesis – however indebted to thinkers such as Foucault or E. P. Thompson – actually requires Watt's view of the emergence of a new kind of realism in Defoe, and elaborates at length on the specifically post-Cartesian and post-Lockean concepts of identity that Watt emphasized exactly thirty years before.[19] Bender's argument is a carefully worked-out and historicized version of the thesis of Michel Foucault's *Discipline and Punish*. Both authors regret the passing of a feudal, theatrical, and customary culture before the onslaught of more alienated, more regimented, and more impersonal social and political relations in the course of the eighteenth century.[20] For Foucault, there is something both splendid and theatrical in the public torture of a mid-eighteenth-century assassin which contrasts with the insidious world of bureaucratic surveillance epitomized in Jeremy Bentham's panopticon. Bender tells a similar story by describing the world of early-eighteenth-century prisons, which comprised a social world in themselves and were porous to everyday relations being played out in the world outside their gates: they were an institutional expression of the world of reciprocity that, E. P. Thompson argues, the new bourgeois values ruthlessly ignored or suppressed. In contrasting earlier with later institutions, Bender implicitly adopts a contrast between a spatial and a temporal way of imagining human relations. Bender appeals to Victor Turner's anthropological models of marginal stages, and argues that to occupy one of the earlier prisons was to occupy a liminal place, in which cultural rituals could redeem individuals. By contrast, the newer prisons that accompanied prison reforms from the middle of the century on were constructed on a narrative model: the prisoner was not available for ritual redemption but was rather the depersonalized object of reform, which was imagined as the effect of a series of narrative stages which would bring the prisoner to the desired point. Bender challenges the view that these reforms were originally motivated by industrial necessity, and proposes instead that the ideological revolution embodied in novelistic notions of identity, sequence, time, and guilt were both the precondition and corollary of new prison designs that were governed by the same attitudes towards the individual and his capacity for inner change.

Castle's argument opposes a liberationist reading of novelistic action to what I would call this paranoid model (Foucault is, above all, allegorizing the rigidly centralized nature of French life). Bakhtin's response to the Stalinist regime was to see in the novel a form of resistance to Soviet tyranny. Somewhat mysteriously, for Bakhtin, the polyglot nature of the novel gives it a special connection with the truly dialectical process of history, such that it escapes the regulatory motives of imposed ideologies. Like Bender, Castle localizes this argument for the eighteenth-century English novel by describing the actual culture of masquerades as they became institutions in the early eighteenth century. These she sees as the secularized and commercialized vestiges of popular traditions of misrule, which accordingly sustain many of their playful, fantastic, erotic, grotesque, and subversive possibilities. As her analysis of the masquerades proceeds, Castle's own language becomes increasingly infused with the febrile enthusiasm and the utopian promise that they seem to have offered a wide variety of eighteenth-century participants. For they freed both women and the lower classes to mingle intimately and without restriction with all sorts, the whole event inverting or descanting on the normal symbolic economies of sex and class, and suspending the usual sartorial codes that show us that people know their place in the moral and social order. Similarly, eighteenth-century novels are drawn to scenes of masquerade that on the face of it would play havoc with their didactic ends. But Castle argues that precisely because masquerade presents us with a world which suspends conventional laws, releases strange fantasies, and exudes sexual danger, novelistic plots find in masquerade a powerful device to catalyze all kinds of transformations, ones which are particularly useful for comic resolutions.

Bender and Castle share one important characteristic that tends to mark academics whose political sensibilities were deeply affected by the 1960s: for them both, modern governments and forms of social governance have sacrificed a world we have lost – in fact the one imagined by Bakhtin and Foucault as an alternative to Stalinism and French bureaucratic control. Their common nostalgia for some alternative is evoked by appealing to Victor Turner, and by their evident pleasure in speaking of a pre-bourgeois world in anthropological and celebratory tones.

Carol Kay's *Political Constructions: Defoe, Richardson, and Sterne in Relation to Hobbes, Hume, and Burke* (1988) constitutes an altogether more hard-headed appraisal of why human life should be conceived of as political life, guided by an admiration for Hobbes's *Leviathan* as a deeply sardonic but practical approach to managing human affairs.[21] Kay calculatedly avoids discussing the nature of the novel as such. She argues that the question of how political societies are made is an informing concern of all genres in the period between the English and French Revolutions. The focus on genre tends to create intellectual barriers that do not exist, and tends to ignore the fluid nature of eighteenth-century utterances of all kinds. In some sense, the choice of Defoe, Richardson, and Sterne is a matter of taste, as well as a means to register the shifts in how the changing emphases in moral and political philosophy through the century are registered in the wider literate culture. Thus Defoe repeats Hobbes's concern with the need to make a viable political entity under extreme circumstances – the Civil War, Crusoe's island, Moll's economic exigencies. Richardson reveals how the Hobbesian and Lockean attention to express contracts by which to bond people into political relation has relaxed in Hume, who can now trust that social habit, custom, and opinion can regulate morality and behavior: *Pamela* is a positive example of this principle; *Clarissa* reveals how mere custom fails without recourse to express legal and political structures, which

in the novel never adequately respond to the heroine's distress, and
to which Clarissa never appeals. And Sterne represents a further
stage in the process, by which the foundations both of politics and of
social mores are so secure by the end of the century that Sterne can
indulge a politics of play that cannot threaten the body politic, and
indeed becomes instrumental in ensuring that men of sensibility can
cordon themselves off from the distractions of female society. Sterne
in some ways anticipates Burke's reverential view of inherited
institutions in his outburst against French barbarism.

The end of Kay's book happily introduces some of the concerns
that are presently very much engaging critics of the eighteenth
century, in particular two. First, as the world of commerce becomes
an obvious place where large numbers of English men and women
conduct extensive exchanges – both social and material – the question
becomes increasingly urgent: are such potentially venal relations
sufficient means by which individuals can imagine mutual
obligations? This question pits itself potentially against two major
European political traditions: either classical republicanism, or
contract theory as developed especially by Hobbes and Locke. Put
another way, is commerce an alternative or supplement to these ways
of discussing our roles in the polity? It is possible to say that it reenacts the contractarian view on a daily basis; or it is possible to say
equally that the consumer's degree of self-possession can foster the
political disinterestedness required of autonomous citizens on the
republican model. And further, since consumerism is associated with
a new world of leisure and taste, it is also possible to think that men
– as well as women – are increasingly refined by their engagements
in the marketplace: the fading of honor gained in combat threatens
the rigid differentiation of gender codes it demanded.[22] Kay argues
that in this economy, we see a determination by men to exclude
women from the exchanges of sensibility that earlier only women
were thought to possess – a process she calls 'remasculinization.'

Second, Kay writes that 'the move from Hobbes to Burke is to
trace the development of nationalism – the deliberate organization
of veneration and identification with the nation – out of arguments
about the necessity and authority of states' (268). Here Kay helps to
construct a narrative about the eighteenth century that (especially
since the appearance of Benedict Anderson's *Imagined Communities*[23]
and Linda Colley's *Britons*[24]) has become a virtually canonical
approach. The major question seems to be, what does the emergence
of British national self-confidence after the Act of Union in 1707 tell
modern Anglo-Americans about the anxieties that seem at present to
beset them on two fronts: how do we imagine ourselves to possess
mutual benefits and obligations, both relative to one another and

relative to the state (however conceived)? And how do we imagine ourselves – whether American citizens or British subjects – as perhaps different from, yet as owing something to, the wider world with which we are inevitably connected, and of which Great Britain officially ruled about half until the end of the Second World War?

Women and the early novel

A collection like this is faced with something of a quandary when it comes to discussing early women novelists or writers of fiction. There are several problems. First, most critics agree that it is only in the second half of the century that we see significant numbers of women novelists writing in an increasingly respectable genre, and producing works that are, to our eyes, technically accomplished.[25]

Second, most accounts of early women writers begin in the seventeenth century – before 1700 – with figures such as Margaret Cavendish, Katherine Phillips, and Aphra Behn, before proceeding to those highly successful contemporaries of Defoe such as Eliza Haywood and Delarivière Manley. The search here is for a distinct genealogy of female authorship which is taken to culminate in Jane Austen, so that Haywood and Manley are embryonic versions of what we readily acknowledge to be superbly finished novels (in Doody and Richetti, we merely have to wait for Richardson).[26]

Third, most of the by-now standard books on these authors are largely descriptive in nature, and also tend to rehearse aspects of Watt's thesis about the rise of the novel, with the aim of accounting for the role of women authors in that story.[27] A common approach is to emphasize those notions of consciousness, of privacy, and of feeling that appear in Watt's analysis as if to imply that women by nature were – and indeed are – especially fitted to be both the subjects and writers of novels. An additional twist occurs when critics point to the paradox by which women gain literary respectability in direct inverse proportion to the increasing loss, after the late seventeenth century, of women's economic and social viability outside the home.

Three arguments have recently sought to sophisticate this more or less standard model and in various ways take issue with it. Partly what we are witnessing is the attempt to replace thematic and biographical forms of criticism with methodological arguments. The first, William Warner's, I have already described. What is significant here is that Warner rather rudely interrupts the line of continuity from Behn either to Richardson or Austen, in order to suggest that we will never understand the narratology of early fiction until we resist teleological models: we should rather credit the local reasons behind its appeal, without expecting them to obey 'novelistic' standards.

Almost conversely, in *Nobody's Story: The Vanishing Acts of Women Writers in the Marketplace, 1670–1820* (1994), Catherine Gallagher argues that the position of women writers from Behn on is a special (that is, an entirely typical) case of authorship in a literary marketplace increasingly defined by credit and exchange value.[28] In arguing that various categories emerge in the early eighteenth century, Gallagher self-consciously complements Ian Watt's account rather than challenges it: what is new (what 'rises') are concepts of authorship, of femaleness, of credit, and of fiction per se.[29] Beginning with Marx's notion that exchange value tends to rob commodities of substance, and make them increasingly impalpable, Gallagher argues that all authors after the late seventeenth century became conscious of the extent to which their literary reception depended on creating reproducible and fungible fictions of authorial identity. If only because they proliferate – especially in a print culture – such fictions point to yet disguise the 'real' author behind them, a conundrum that for obvious reasons speaks to the particular problems of women, and especially women authors. In their different ways, Behn and Manley enact that *difference* by various devices: Behn by appealing to the analogy between the author and the whore, and by exploiting the doubleness inherent in the image of the monarch (the 'monarch' is never really himself); and Manley by self-consciously and almost parodically aligning herself with her own narrative excesses, as if to suggest, like Swift, that the literary system is purely nominal and self-referring. Gallagher additionally observes that political history from the Restoration to the early eighteenth century evidences increasing dismay at the loss of social as well as fiscal value in a credit economy; and proposes that the very complexities of authorship produce the idea of fiction proper in the course of the eighteenth century.

Finally, Nancy Armstrong's *Desire and Domestic Fiction: A Political History of the Novel* (1987) has had a considerable impact on eighteenth-century studies.[30] Inspired by Foucault's *History of Sexuality*, Armstrong argues that what we now call 'the novel' was part of an emerging ideology of gender during the course of the eighteenth century which culminated in the privileging of domesticity in the nineteenth century. The novel was the chief instrument by which older notions of social value such as genealogy and hierarchy were displaced in favor of the idea that the core value of human life – for men as much as for women – rested on the satisfaction of romantic and domestic desires. And it was the chief instrument by which the politics of the home gained ultimately greater prestige than the discourse of high politics: by appearing to eschew politics and directing attention to sexual desire, the novel played a powerful political role in its own way. Thus, in the mid eighteenth century, the framing of domestic desire served to secure bourgeois values against an older aristocratic system; and in the nineteenth century, the same fiction served to disable alternative views emerging from the proletariat. Armstrong reverses the thesis that the domesticating of women offers a politically regressive story, since the feminization of values has, according to her, been so constitutive of modern life that we can only see history through that lens. Indeed, because feminine and domestic values were what the novel especially mediated for the entire culture, women became singularly empowered as novel writers, and thus as arbiters of pervasive social ideologies. Further, the novel and modern sexuality are dialectically related, so that we cannot tell a history of the novel without telling the story of the construction of a new form of sexuality, and vice versa. By the same token, the 'novel' as such only comes into view once the process of domestic ideology has come to fruition – that is, in the nineteenth century or even after – and here Armstrong draws on Brown. But ironically, Armstrong in her own way repeats one of the standard topoi of Watt's *Rise of the Novel*, since for her one of the turning points in her story coincides with a key turning point for Watt, for McKeon, and for many others: with the publication and astounding success of *Pamela*. In the history of criticism or the history of fiction, perhaps there is an inescapable power in those who first told the story or, more pertinently, in those who we believe first told the story.

Notes

1. I am grateful to a number of readers of earlier drafts of this introduction: Steve Barney, Fraser Easton, Brean Hammond, Fred Keener, Allison Kroll, Jayne Lewis, Mark Phillips, Victoria Silver. There are two other recent general books that seek to introduce the reader to newer approaches to the eighteenth-century British novel. These are John Richetti *et al.* (eds.) *The Columbia History of the British Novel* (New York: Columbia University Press, 1994); and Richetti (ed.), *The Cambridge Companion to the Eighteenth-Century Novel* (Cambridge: Cambridge University Press, 1996). These are both collections of commissioned essays.

2. Ian Watt, *The Rise of the Novel: Studies in Defoe, Richardson and Fielding* (1957; rpt. Harmondsworth: Pelican, 1976); Northrop Frye, *Anatomy of Criticism: Four Essays* (Princeton: Princeton University Press, 1957); Erich Auerbach, *Mimesis: The Representation of Reality in Western Literature* (1946; trans. Princeton: Princeton University Press, 1953). William Warner points out that an earlier book than Watt's helped establish the canon we see in Watt, namely Alan

Dugald McKillop, *The Early Masters of English Fiction* (Lawrence: University of Kansas Press, 1956). See William B. Warner, 'The Elevation of the Novel in England: Hegemony and Literary History,' *ELH* 59 (1992): 594 n. 1. (Reprinted below.)

3. Watt interestingly expands on his view of realism in 'Realism and the Novel' in S. P. Rosenbaum (ed.), *English Literature and British Philosophy* (Chicago: University of Chicago Press, 1971), 65–85. In this essay, he makes even clearer that realism is a question of representational method that responds to profound changes in European conceptions about the relation between particulars and universals – a position few philosophers would deny – and which can itself amount to a convention of its own.

4. J. Paul Hunter, *Before Novels: The Cultural Contexts of Eighteenth-Century English Fiction* (New York: Norton, 1990).

5. This is Homer Brown's central point. See the discussion below, pp. 161–87.

6. Margaret Anne Doody, *The True Story of the Novel* (New Brunswick: Rutgers University Press, 1996); Homer Brown, *Institutions of the English Novel from Defoe to Scott* (Philadelphia: University of Pennsylvania Press, 1997). A lucid exposition of this point appears in Robert Folkenflik, 'The Heirs of Ian Watt,' *Eighteenth-Century Studies* 25 (1991–92): 208–17.

7. Lennard Davis, *Factual Fictions: The Origins of the English Novel* (New York: Columbia University Press, 1983).

8. Davis, *Factual Fictions*, 40.

9. Frederick Keener, *The Chain of Becoming: The Philosophical Tale, the Novel, and a Neglected Realism of the Enlightenment: Swift, Montesquieu, Voltaire, Johnson, and Austen* (New York: Columbia University Press, 1983).

10. Brean Hammond points out (personal communication) that this argument is also well developed in criticism of the theatre.

11. Michael McKeon, *The Origins of the English Novel, 1600–1740* (Baltimore: The Johns Hopkins University Press, 1987).

12. Many of Doody's arguments about the sheer variety of prose narratives from the Renaissance on, of which the eighteenth-century English novel is only one aspect, are anticipated in Ioan Williams, *The Idea of the Novel in Europe, 1600–1800* (New York: New York University Press, 1979). Williams writes that in the early eighteenth century, something did in fact happen to the English novel: 'What happened was essentially a change in focus, which brought the novel closer to the texture of the individual and social experience and widened its range to include new areas of both. I want to suggest, however, that this change did not amount to the development of a new literary form but rather the evolution of an existing one, and that the development of the novel through the previous two hundred years in Europe as a whole may be seen as continuous though irregular' (ix–x). Unlike Doody, however, Williams argues for the view that the novel is distinctively modern, conceding that any definition of the novel in public terms is inadequate, and that studies often articulate what they assume the novel to be in the choice of the periods and texts they focus on.

13. William Warner, 'The Elevation of the Novel in England'; Warner's other essay ('Licensing Pleasure: Literary History and the Novel in Early Modern Britain') appears in Richetti *et al.* (eds.), *The Columbia History*, 1–22.

14. Brown writes, 'the novels of Defoe, Fielding, and Richardson actually change in meaning as they are historicized at later vantage points' (*Institutions*, x).

15. For similar views, see Doody, *True Story*, 262; 288.

16. See Thomas S. Kuhn, *The Structure of Scientific Revolutions*, 2nd edn (Chicago: University of Chicago Press, 1970), 53–6.

17. In the second volume, I will discuss J. G. A. Pocock's and Jürgen Habermas's arguments about political economy as alternatives to the Foucauldian and Bakhtinian models I discuss here.

18. John Bender, *Imagining the Penitentiary: Fiction and the Architecture of Mind in Eighteenth-Century England* (Chicago: University of Chicago Press, 1987); Terry Castle, *Masquerade and Civilization: The Carnivalesque in Eighteenth-Century English Culture and Fiction* (Stanford: Stanford University Press, 1986).

19. Similarly, Castle summarily refers to 'the new genre of eighteenth-century realistic fiction' (*Masquerade and Civilization*, 144).

20. Michel Foucault, *Discipline and Punish: The Birth of the Prison* (1975; trans. New York: Vintage, 1979).

21. Carol Kay, *Political Constructions: Defoe, Richardson, and Sterne in Relation to Hobbes, Hume, and Burke* (Ithaca: Cornell University Press, 1988). For a more detailed description of Kay's book, see my review of Kay in *Eighteenth-Century Studies* 23 (1989): 103–7.

22. This position is epitomized in J. G. A. Pocock's very influential series of essays in *Virtue, Commerce, and History: Essays on Political Thought and History, Chiefly in the Eighteenth Century* (Cambridge: Cambridge University Press, 1985). Catherine Gallagher discusses it well in *Nobody's Story: The Vanishing Acts of Women Writers in the Marketplace, 1670–1820* (Berkeley: University of California Press, 1994), 108–10.

23. Benedict Anderson, *Imagined Communities: Reflections on the Origin and Spread of Nationalism* (1983; rev. edn. London: Verso, 1991).

24. Linda Colley, *Britons: Forging the Nation, 1707–1837* (New Haven: Yale University Press, 1992).

25. This issue I address at greater length in the second volume.

26. See Margaret Doody, *A Natural Passion: A Study of the Novels of Samuel Richardson* (Oxford: Clarendon, 1974); and John Richetti, *Popular Fiction before Richardson: Narrative Patterns, 1700–1739* (Oxford: Clarendon, 1969).

27. Examples are: Caroline Gonda, *Reading Daughters' Fictions, 1709–1834: Novels and Society from Manley to Edgeworth* (Cambridge: Cambridge University Press, 1996); Ruth Perry, *Women, Letters, and the Novel* (New York: AMS, 1980); Mary Anne Schofield, *Masking and Unmasking the Female Mind: Disguising Romances in Female Fiction, 1713–1799* (Newark: University of Delaware Press, 1990); Jane Spencer, *The Rise of the Woman Novelist: From Aphra Behn to Jane Austen* (Oxford: Blackwell, 1986); Dale Spender, *Mothers of the Novel: 100 Good Writers before Jane Austen* (London: Pandora, 1986); Janet Todd, *The Sign of Angellica: Women, Writing and Fiction, 1660–1800* (London: Virago, 1989). Two of the earliest accounts remain two of the best, namely Margaret Doody's chapter, 'Novels, Fables, and Letter-Books: The Approach to *Pamela*,' in *A Natural Passion*, 14–34; and John Richetti's *Popular Fiction before Richardson*.

28. Gallagher writes that her study 'takes [women] to be special in their extreme typicality and describes the metamorphosis of authorship as seen through the magnifying glass of women's careers' (*Nobody's Story*, xv).

29. 'Far from being the descendant of older overtly fictional forms, the novel was the first to articulate the idea of fiction for the culture as a whole . . . what Ian Watt called "formal realism" was not a way of trying to hide or disguise fictionality; realism was, rather, understood to be fiction's formal sign' (*Nobody's Story*, xvi–xvii).

30. Nancy Armstrong, *Desire and Domestic Fiction: A Political History of the Novel* (New York: Oxford University Press, 1987).

Part I

Models and Beginnings

2 Generic Transformation and Social Change: Rethinking the Rise of the Novel

MICHAEL McKEON

Michael McKeon is one of the foremost neo-Marxist and cultural critics in late-seventeenth- and early-eighteenth-century studies. His work is distinguished by its connections between literary texts and political actualities, as well as by its emphasis on archival sources. In this essay, he digests the main thesis of his book *The Origins of the English Novel, 1600–1740*, whose aims and methods I also discuss in the Introduction (pp. 8–10). He makes clear his relationship to Ian Watt's *The Rise of the Novel* (see Introduction, pp. 1–5), and argues that as the novel emerges from the seventeenth into the eighteenth century, it responds simultaneously to a series of crises, social, epistemological, and literary (or 'generic').

Twenty-five years after its first appearance, Ian Watt's *The Rise of the Novel* continues to be the most attractive model we have of how to conduct the study of this crucial literary phenomenon.[1] The phenomenon is crucial because it is modern. If the novel originated in early modern Europe, it should be possible to observe and describe its emergence within a historical context whose richness of detail has no parallel in earlier periods. But of course this is no coincidence: it is the rise of an unprecedented historical consciousness, and of its institutional affiliates, that has both encouraged the preservation of historical detail, and legitimated contextual methods of study which use that detail as a mode of understanding. Watt's book is attractive because it is fully responsive to the call for a historical and contextual method of study that seems somehow implicit in his subject. Thus his concern with the rise of a distinctive set of narrative procedures – 'formal realism' – is informed by a concern with a parallel innovation in philosophical discourse, and these he connects, in turn, with a set of socioeconomic developments at whose center are the rise of the middle class, the growth of commercial capitalism, and the concomitant eclipse of feudal and aristocratic modes of intercourse. The analogy between these historical strands is most succinctly accounted for in their

shared 'individualism' – that is, in their common validation of
individual experience – a term that allows Watt at various points
to argue the importance to his subject of a fourth major strand of
historical experience, the Protestant Reformation.

Watt's account of the unity of the historical context in which the
novel arose is far more subtle, as all readers know, than this bald
outline can suggest. And its general persuasiveness is evident in the
fact that the sort of criticism to which it has seemed most vulnerable
has aimed not to refute the relevance of historical context, but to
complicate Watt's version of it. The problem is perhaps most
notorious in the social strand of his context. Where is the evidence,
critics have asked, for the dominance of the middle class in the early
eighteenth century? How is it distinguished from the traditional
social categories of the nobility and gentry, which clearly survive the
rapid social mobility of the seventeenth century and persist into the
eighteenth with considerable power and prestige? Don't the novels
of Henry Fielding, an indispensable figure in the rise of the novel,
evince a social attitude much closer to that of a middling gentry than
to that of a putatively flourishing commercial middle class? But even
in the literary realm, critics have also been preoccupied with a
problem of persistence. The narrative procedures of Daniel Defoe,
Samuel Richardson, and Fielding may explicitly subvert the idea
and ethos of romance, but they also draw, without apparent irony,
on many of its stock situations and conventions. Although Watt pays
little attention to it, and then only as a superseded genre, romance
can be seen to inhabit both the form and the content of these early
eighteenth-century narratives. And once again it is Fielding who
points the problem most acutely, since he has little use for several
of those narrative procedures that have been advanced as the *sine qua
non* of the new form.

From this brief summary it is clear that the two central problems
with Watt's account of the rise of the novel are versions of each
other. His treatment of the early modern historical context, because
of its very richness, has sensitized us to what has been left out: the
romance and the aristocracy. By the end of the eighteenth century,
the conceptual categories of 'the novel' and 'the middle class' will
be sufficiently stable to enjoy the stability of that nomenclature. But
it is of course precisely in the period that we wish most definitively
to understand – the period of crucial transformation – that such
categories are most unstable and most resistant to being strictly
identified either as what they are going to be, or as what they once
were. What is required, then, is an understanding of how conceptual
categories, whether 'literary' or 'social,' exist at moments of historical
change: how new forms first coalesce as tenable categories by being

known in terms of, and against, more traditional forms that have thus far been taken to define the field of possibility. We must begin, in other words, with the very fact of categorial instability in the later seventeenth century.

Let me pause for a moment before entering my argument, in order to summarize it. What I have to say is based on a set of terms and relations that will recur from time to time throughout the essay. They are not particularly complicated, but I think it will be helpful to lay them out as quickly and clearly as possible. I plan to describe the two great instances of categorial instability that are central to the rise of the novel. The first sort of instability has to do with generic categories; the second, with social categories. The instability of generic categories registers an epistemological crisis, a major cultural transition in attitudes toward how to tell the truth in narrative. For convenience, I will call the set of problems associated with this epistemological crisis, 'questions of truth.' The instability of social categories registers a cultural crisis in attitudes toward how the external social order is related to the internal, moral state of its members. For convenience, I will call the set of problems associated with this social and moral crisis, 'questions of virtue.' Questions of truth and questions of virtue concern different realms of human experience, and they are likely to be raised in very different contexts. Yet in one central respect they are closely analogous. Questions of truth and virtue both pose problems of signification: What kind of authority or evidence is required of narrative to permit it to signify truth to its readers? What kind of social existence or behavior signifies an individual's virtue to others?

As we will see, the instability of generic and social categories is symptomatic of a change in attitudes about how truth and virtue are most authentically signified. But for both questions, we can observe the process of change only if we break it down into its component parts. Let me summarize this break-down: first, for questions of truth. At the beginning of the period of our concern, the reigning narrative epistemology involves a dependence on received authorities and a priori traditions; I will call this posture 'romance idealism.' In the seventeenth century, it is challenged and refuted by an empiricist epistemology that derives from many sources, and this I will call 'naive empiricism.' But this negation of romance, having embarked on a journey for which it has no maps, at certain points loses its way. And it becomes vulnerable, in turn, to a counter-critique that has been generated by its own over-enthusiasm. I will call this counter-critique 'extreme skepticism.' As we will see, in refuting its empiricist progenitor, extreme skepticism inevitably recapitulates some features of the romance idealism which it is equally committed to opposing.

29

For questions of virtue, the terms alter, but the two-part pattern of reversal is very much the same as for questions of truth. We begin with a relatively stratified social order, supported by a reigning world view which I will call 'aristocratic ideology.' Spurred by social change, this ideology is attacked and subverted by its prime antagonist, 'progressive ideology.' But at a certain point, progressive ideology gives birth to its own critique, which is both more radical than itself, and harks back to the common, aristocratic enemy. I will call this counter-critique 'conservative ideology.'

Needless to say, contemporaries did not articulate these several positions as consciously formulated and coherent doctrines. I have abstracted these ideologies and epistemologies from a large body of early modern discourse, in order to isolate the principal stages in the process of historical change that we refer to when we speak of 'the rise of the novel.' By this means, I think, we may come closer to conceiving how change occurs: how the past can persist into the present, and help to mediate the establishment of difference through the perpetuation of similarity. Let me now proceed to fill in the spaces in my argument.

I

I will begin with questions of truth and the instability of the system of narrative genres in the seventeenth century. Evidence for the unstable usage of terminology lies everywhere, but it is most striking in explicit attempts to categorize the several genres of narrative. In 1672, the bookseller John Starkey advertised his list of publications in a catalogue divided into the following categories: Divinity; Physick; Law; History; Poetry and Plays; and Miscellanies. Under the heading of 'history' he includes Suetonius, Rabelais, what he calls the 'Novels' of Quevedo, biographies, travel narratives, and a contemporary work that we would be likely to see as a popular romance.[2] By modern standards, the most pressing problem raised by such usage is the absence of any will to distinguish consistently between 'history' and 'literature,' 'fact' and 'fiction.' But on the other hand, the catalogue of William London, printed fifteen years earlier, obligingly separates 'History' from 'Romances, Poems and Playes.'[3]

What is most significant about this sort of usage is that it is not entirely foreign to us. Unlike traditional generic taxonomies, it evinces a real, but markedly inconsistent, commitment to comprehend its categories within a basic discrimination between the 'factual' and the 'fictional.' Indeed, it is the inconsistent imposition of this recognizably 'modern' concern on a more traditional system that makes the usage of this period look so chaotic. What it represents,

I think, is a movement between opposed conceptions of how to tell the truth in narrative. Another sign of this movement is the transformation which the term 'romance' has undergone in the past hundred years. Despite the neutral usage that I have just quoted, by the end of the seventeenth century the ascendant meaning of 'romance' is both far broader, and far more pejorative, than before. Increasingly the idea of romance dominates the thought of the Restoration and early eighteenth century as a means of describing, and most often of discrediting, a particular, idealist way of knowing. Romance comes to stand for a species of deceit that undiscriminatingly includes lying and fictionalizing; and the category to which it is most often opposed is not 'the novel,' but 'true history.'

Many cultural movements contributed to the naive empiricist championing of 'true history.' Three of the most important are also closely intertwined: the scientific revolution, the typographical revolution, and the Protestant Reformation. Moreover in all three of these movements we can see both the dominant influence of naive empiricism, and the stealthy emergence of a subversive, extreme skepticism. I will begin with the new science. In his history of the founding institution of the new science, Thomas Sprat compares unfavorably the ancient mode of natural history with that of his fellow moderns: it 'is not the true following of *Nature* . . . It is like *Romances*, in respect of *True History* . . .'[4] The new science was dedicated, of course, to objective observation, experiment, and related principles of empirical method. And it was deeply interested in trying to embody these principles in literary technique and form. According to the *Philosophical Transactions* of the Royal Society, 'we have more need of severe, full and punctuall Truth, than of Romances or Panegyricks.'[5] To this end, the Society even undertook to instruct foreign travellers in the best literary techniques for ensuring what we might call the 'historicity' of their journals. It enlisted the aid of Robert Boyle and the mathematician Lawrence Rooke to formulate directions not only for how to keep a travel journal, but also for how to turn it into a narrative without diluting its crucial historicity.[6]

It is not too much to say that these directions amount to one of the most important, explicit bodies of literary theory composed in conjunction with the origins of the English novel. They prescribe a preferred style and rhetoric that correspond to a new type of the man of letters, the ethically and socially humble recorder of reality who is enabled to master the new knowledge by his very innocence of the old. In Sprat's words, the new breed are 'plain, diligent, and laborious observers: such, who, though they bring not much knowledg [sic], yet bring their hands, and their eyes uncorrupted:

such as have not their Brains infected by false Images . . .'[7] One such observer is described by the editors of the multi-volume collection of travel narratives in terms that might collectively be called the convention of the claim to historicity: 'This Narrative has nothing of Art or Language, being . . . deliver'd in a homely Stile, which it was not fit to alter, lest it might breed a Jealousy that something had been chang'd more than the bare Language.'[8] According to another, equally conventional, traveller, 'it would be no difficult Matter to embellish a Narrative with many Romantick Incidents, to please the unthinking Part of Mankind, who swallow every thing an artful Writer thinks fit to impose upon their Credulity, without any Regard to Truth or Probability. The judicious are not taken with such Trifles; . . . and they easily distinguish between Reality and Fiction.'[9]

At the heart of the claim to historicity is the assertion that what one is describing really happened. And it is not hard to hear in these sober claims the naive empiricism of Defoe and Richardson, both of whom pretend to be only the editors of authentic documents whose plain and artless truth is above question. But if we permit the sobriety of the voices slightly to extend into self-parody, we also can detect the extreme skepticism of Swift and Fielding, subverting the claim to historicity by carrying it to absurdity. This is one example of how naive empiricism generates its own, radically skeptical, critique. Let me turn now to another example, one related not to the new science but to the new typography.

To a certain extent, we owe the very notion of comparative and competing accounts of the same event to the opportunity for comparison uniquely provided by print. Printing produces documentary objects that can be collected, categorized, collated, and edited. Like science, it promotes the norm of 'objective' research, and it favors criteria of judgment that are appropriate to discrete and empirically apprehensible 'objects': singularity, formal coherence, and self-consistency. Finally, print encourages a test of veracity that accords with the process itself of typographical reproduction: namely, the exact replication of objects or events in their external and quantitative dimensions.[10] Contemporaries were conscious of the epistemological powers of print. William Winstanley describes 'some I have known (otherwise ingenious enough) apt to believe idle Romances, and Poetical Fictions, for Historical Varieties [i.e., verities], . . . and for this only reason, *Because they are Printed*.'[11] But only a slight extension of this awe brings us to the satiric stance of Cervantes, who has a great deal of fun at the expense of characters – including Sancho Panza – who naively believe everything they see in print. In fact much of the self-reflexive pleasure of Part II of *Don Quixote* lies in watching its characters compare the documentary objectivity of Part I (which has already been printed) with the more fallible standard of truth upheld by private memory and experience.[12] Cervantes himself naively claims that his book is a 'true history' dedicated to the critique of chivalric romance. But we know to read this affiliation, as well as his playful attitude toward print, as at least in part a skeptical critique of naive empiricism.

My third and final example concerns the contribution of Reformation thought to naive empiricism and its subversion. Protestantism, like the standard of 'true history,' elevates individual and closely observed experience over the a priori pronouncements of tradition. But Protestantism is also the religion of the Book, of the documentary object, and as such it inevitably tends to elevate the truth of Scripture as the truth of 'true history.' This documentary and empiricist emphasis is clear in the great works of the Protestant tradition. The central aim of John Foxe's *Acts and Monuments* (1563, 1570) is the documentation of the Protestant martyrs, and the task is achieved in an aura of scrupulous historicity and with a battery of editorial procedures that are dedicated to the critical authentication of every historical detail.[13] Such authenticating procedures may also be found in John Bunyan's *Life and Death of Mr. Badman* (1680), even though its protagonist is a palpable fiction. Bunyan claims that it is based on 'True stories, that are neither *Lye*, nor *Romance* . . . All which are things either fully known by me, or being eye and ear-witness thereto, or that I have received from such hands, whose relation as to this, I am bound to believe.'[14] By the same token, Protestant spirituality encouraged individual saints to a scrupulous documentation of their own 'true histories.' When Ralph Thoresby first went up to London, his father sent him a typical directive: 'I would have you, in a little book, which you may either buy or make of two or three sheets of paper, take a little journal of any thing remarkable every day, principally as to yourself . . .'[15]

So from the beginning, Protestantism was deeply invested in the materialistically oriented techniques of naive empiricism as a useful means to its spiritual and otherworldly ends. The potential contradiction between worldly means and otherworldly ends is most apparent in writings like the 'apparition narratives' of the later seventeenth century; Defoe's *A True Relation Of the Apparition of one Mrs. Veal* (1706) is the best-known of them today. These narratives use the evidence of the senses in order to prove the extra-sensory world of spirit. They deploy an extraordinary arsenal of authenticating devices – names, places, dates, events, eye- and ear-witness testimony, etc. – in order to prove the reality of the invisible world. Richard Baxter explained his own important contribution to the form in terms that poignantly convey the

dilemma of a culture divided between two competing standards
of truth that still seem somehow reconcilable: 'Apparitions, and
other sensible Manifestations of the certain existence of Spirits of
themselves Invisible, was a means that might do much with such
as are prone to judge by Sense.'[16] But it is a very short distance from
Baxter's earnest and spiritualizing dependence on the evidence of the
senses to the realm of conscious satire. Consider those moderns in
Swift's early satires who mistake their own bodily wind for the spirit
of intellect and divinity.[17] Once again, that is, the counter-critique of
extreme skepticism is involuntarily extruded by naive empiricism
itself as a form of subversive self-parody.

But over time, extreme skepticism emerges as a self-conscious and
autonomous stance in its own right. Its premises are the same as
those of the naive empiricism which it undertakes to negate. It is
equally critical, that is, of 'romance,' but it is so thoroughly skeptical
as to discredit empiricist skepticism itself as nothing more than a
new, and artfully modernized, species of the old romance. It is this
counter-critique that will issue eventually in Fielding's narrative
form. Along the way we may observe certain milestones, narratives –
like William Congreve's *Incognita* (1691) – which elegantly achieve
the double negation that is characteristic of the form: first, of the
fictions of romance, and then of naive empiricism itself. But like its
antagonist, the counter-critique of extreme skepticism undergoes a
considerable development; I have space only to offer several
exemplary quotations.

Richard Steele is an important figure in the attack on naive
empiricism. Echoing pamphleteers of the mid-seventeenth
century, for example, he argued in one of his periodical letters that
newspapers were to England what books of chivalry had been to
Spain.[18] Steele was also critical of the claim to historicity in the genre
of the secret memoir, which was especially popular among what
he called 'some merry gentlemen of the French nation.' The secret
memoir claimed, as Steele observed, to give the true history of
military campaigns or court intrigues even though their mendacious
authors had really been cowering behind the lines or scribbling in
a drafty garret.[19] Writing of the same phenomenon, Pierre Bayle
observed that thus 'the new romances [that is, these supposedly
historical memoirs] keep as far off as possible from the romantic way:
but by this means true history is made extremely obscure; and
I believe the civil powers will at last be forced to give these new
romancers their option; either to write pure history, or pure
romance . . .'[20] Henry Stubbe compared the natural histories of the
Royal Society to 'the story of *Tom Thumb*, and all the *Legends* or
falsifications of History, which the *Papists* obtrude upon us.'[21] The

language is striking: whether implicitly or explicitly, over and over true history is discredited as the new romance. The skeptical critique of travel historicity was similarly acerbic. The dubious reader of a typically authenticated travel narrative of 1675 confuted the pamphlet's overheated claims by coolly writing on its title page: 'By a new fashion'd Romancer.'[22] The most thorough and trenchant critique of travel historicity was made by the Third Earl of Shaftesbury, who began, as Steele did, with the remark that 'these are in our present Days, what *Books of Chivalry* were, in those of our Forefathers.'[23] As the critique of naive empiricism gained momentum toward the end of the century, parodic impersonation seemed to offer itself as the most likely means of subversion. Another dubious reader of travel narratives wrote the following parody of a rival's fashionably plain style of objective narration: '*We cast Anchor: We made ready to Sail. The Wind took Courage* Robin *is dead. We said Mass. We Vomited.* [Then he continues in his own, sarcastic voice.] Tho' they are poor Words any where else, yet in his Book, which is half compos'd of them, they are Sentences, and the worth of them is not to be told.'[24]

But if this kind of extreme skepticism was to become more than an (admittedly liberating) act of subversion, it was obliged, like the subversive stance of naive empiricism before it, to elaborate an alternative, positive, and coherent conception of how to tell the truth in narrative. And here its position was quite as unstable as that of its opponent. For if the claim to historicity is naively posited as the negation of the negation of romance idealism, how tenuous must be that secret sanctuary of truth, distinct both from romance and from too confident a historicity, which is defined by the meta-critical act of double negation? With hindsight we might want to say that the counter-critique of extreme skepticism was groping toward a mode of narrative truth-telling which, through the very self-consciousness of its own fictionality, somehow detoxifies fiction of its error. But the ingenuity of this maneuver could itself look more like a mask for the stealthy recapitulation of romance lies. Consider Fielding's ostentatious indulgence in romance conventions, or Swift's obviously parabolic narratives. Indeed the sheer defensiveness of this counter-stance makes it parasitic upon, and reproductive of, the errors of the enemy. If naive empiricism is too sanguine regarding its own powers of negating romance fiction, its critique is too skeptical about that possibility, and it risks, through its reactive method of parodic impersonation, the effectual affirmation of what it is equally committed to replacing.

Both epistemologies, in other words, are unstable. I would argue that they attain stability not in themselves but in each other, in their dialectical relationship, as two competing versions of how to tell the truth in narrative, which, in their competition, constitute one part of the origins of the novel. The paradigmatic case is *Pamela* (1740) vs. *Shamela* (1741), since it is then that the conflict emerges into public consciousness and is institutionalized as a battle over whether it is Richardson or Fielding that is creating the 'new species of writing.' My argument is that it is, rather, the conjunction of the two. But I would also point out that the logic of our progress through the seventeenth century into the middle of the eighteenth argues against trying to pinpoint 'the first novel,' or even its first dialectical engagement. Before *Pamela* and *Shamela*, for example, there is the tacit but crucial confrontation between *Robinson Crusoe* (1719) and *Gulliver's Travels* (1726), a confrontation to which I will return. The novel rises not in the isolated emergence of a great text or two, but as an experimental process consisting of many different stages.

II

So far our attention has been focussed on epistemological instability, and the series of critiques by which questions of truth are propounded. We must now turn to the analogous questions of virtue, to the instability of socioeconomic categories, and to the interaction between what I have called the aristocratic, progressive, and conservative ideologies. In the seventeenth century, the traditional imprecision in the use of status categories is complicated by an unprecedented rate of social mobility. The effects of this mobility are suggested by the fact that it is at this time that attempts begin to be made to assess the population not according to a traditional, status stratification, but by annual income and expenditures. This amounts to the first, systematic emergence of the modern impulse to classify society according to the fundamentally economic criteria of class.

The form taken by these population tables is quite relevant to our purposes, because they provide the sort of evidence of instability, on the subject of social categories, that we found in publishers' book lists on the subject of generic categories. Gregory King's celebrated table of the 1690s ostensibly aims to give a continuous financial, and therefore quantitative, progression from the top to the bottom of English society. But he is obliged to work with both honorific and occupational categories, and around the middle of his table the two sorts of category become intermixed in a way that undermines the purpose of the project. For in several cases, King lists status categories above occupational ones, even though the crucial standard of average yearly income should reverse the orders. In other words, King's abiding respect for the traditional status hierarchy momentarily

overrules his modernizing aim to create a hierarchy of incomes.
The qualitative criteria of status infiltrate and disrupt the effort at
a quantitative categorization.[25] Half a century later, in 1760, Joseph
Massie carried over King's six traditional categories of elevated
status to the top of his own table. But they repose there aloof and
untouched, a kind of honorific gesture that has nothing to do with
the real work of economic discrimination, for which Massie uses
completely different categories in the rest of his table. In other words,
status categories persist here as a vestigial remnant of a mode of
thought which, however useless in the definitive description of
contemporary English people by class, still appears indispensable.[26]

In both men, the instability of social categories owes to a
discrepancy between two standards of classification, that of 'status'
and that of 'class.' It reflects what we might call a crisis of 'status
inconsistency,' a divergence of power, wealth, and status widespread
and persistent enough to resist the methods by which stable
societies traditionally have accommodated the instances of non-
correspondence that occasionally must arise. One such method
is the traditional granting or selling of honors to newly enriched but
ignoble families. To speak of 'traditional' societies is also to speak of
societies dominated by what I have called an 'aristocratic' ideology.
In aristocratic culture, it is not only that power, wealth, and honorific
status most often accompany each other; honor also is understood to
imply personal merit or virtue. Thus the social hierarchy is a great
system of signification: the outward forms of genealogy and social
rank are taken to signify an analogous, intrinsic moral order. The
seventeenth-century crisis of status inconsistency therefore strikes
at the moral foundations of aristocratic ideology. The sale of honors
became, in Lawrence Stone's phrase, an 'inflation,' and the latent
tension between honorific and monetary criteria became a glaring
contradiction for contemporaries.[27] The word 'honor' itself acquired
a more complicated import. As a neutral term of description, its
meaning was, in effect, internalized, changing from 'title of rank' to
'goodness of character.'[28] But 'honor' in the more traditional sense of
the term, like 'romance,' had fallen on very hard times.

We can hear this in the genial contempt expressed by Bernard
Mandeville. For Mandeville, honor 'is only to be met with in People
of the better sort, as some Oranges have kernels, and others not,
tho' the outside be the same. In great Families it is like the Gout,
generally counted Hereditary, and all Lords Children are born
with it. . . . But there is nothing that encourages the Growth of it
more than a Sword, and upon the first wearing of one, some People
have felt considerable Shutes of it, in Four and twenty Hours.'[29]
The aristocratic system of signification held no illusions for Stephen

Penton, either. For 'if Merit were to be the Standard of Worldly
Happiness, what great desert is there in being born Eldest Son
and Heir to several Thousands a Year, when sometimes it falls out,
that the Person is hardly able to Answer Two or Three the easiest
Questions in the World wisely enough to save himself from being
Begg'd?'[30] William Sprigge plausibly argued that 'the younger Son
is apt to think himself sprung from as Noble a stock, from the loyns
of as good a Gentleman as his elder Brother, and therefore cannot but
wonder, why fortune and the Law should make so great a difference
between them that lay in the same wombe, that are formed of the
same lumpe; why Law or Custome should deny them an estate,
whom nature hath given discretion to know how to manage it.'[31]
And Defoe draws the versified conclusion:

> What is't to us, what Ancestors we had?
> If Good, what better? or what worse, if Bad?
> . . . .
> For Fame of Families is all a Cheat,
> *'Tis Personal Virtue only makes us great.*[32]

In the realm of social change, the idea of 'personal virtue' occupies
the place that 'true history' does in epistemology. For progressive
ideology, elevated birth is an arbitrary accident which should not
be taken to signify worth. If it is, it becomes a fiction, an imaginary
value, like 'honor' a mere 'romance.' Thus Defoe observes that when
gentlemen 'value themselves as exalted in birth above the rest of the
world . . . ,' it is upon the basis of a strictly 'imaginary honour.'[33]
Real honor, honor of *character*, attaches to personal virtue. And
Defoe heartily approved of the assimilationist practice whereby
the meritorious and newly risen crowned their merit through the
purchase of titles of rank.

But what were Swift's views on questions of virtue? Swift was as
caustic as Defoe on the subject of aristocratic pretension. But he was
far more inclined to see the ideas of inherited honor and gentle birth
as useful fictions that had an instrumental social value. 'Suppose
there be nothing but *Opinion* in the Difference of Blood,' he wrote.
'Surely, that Difference is not wholly imaginary. . . . It should seem
that the Advantage lies on the Side of Children, born from noble and
wealthy Parents . . . [And] Ancient and honorable Birth[,] . . . whether
it be of real or imaginary Value, hath been held in Veneration by
all wise, polite States, both Ancient and Modern.'[34] It may seem
puzzling that men like Swift should return to half-embrace the
very fiction they have rejected. But we already have seen this sort
of movement in the return of extreme skepticism to a form of self-
conscious romancing. For progressives like Defoe, aristocratic

ideology was subverted and replaced by a brave new view of
social signification. Virtue is signified not by the a priori condition
of having been born with status and honor, but by the ongoing
experience of demonstrated achievement and just reward. Thus the
status inconsistency endemic to aristocratic culture is rectified, in this
progressive view, by upward mobility through state service, private
employment, or any other method of industrious self-application.
To conservatives like Swift, this progressive model of the career open
to talents was deeply repellant, as we will see. But the negation of
both aristocratic and progressive ideology left conservative ideology
without a positive and stable view of how the social injustice of
status inconsistency ever might be overcome.

From the conservative point of view, progressive ideology only
replaced the old social injustice by a new and more brutal version
of it, unsoftened now by any useful fictions of inherited authority.
At the heart of this new system was the naked cash nexus. For the
conservative, the archetypal progressive upstart rose by exploiting
the capitalist market, and especially the new mechanisms of financial
investment and public credit which were established at the end of
the seventeenth century. For men like Swift, only landed property
had real value. All other property was, as he put it, 'transient and
imaginary,' but most of all that of exchange value.[35] Defoe also
recognized that the modern world of exchange value was ruled by,
in his phrase, 'the Power of Imagination.'[36] And he perceived that in
some mysterious sense, capitalist credit was only a secularization of
aristocratic honor. But Defoe was convinced that the circulation of
money and the opportunity for capital accumulation were essential
if individual merit were to be dependably signified and rewarded.
For Swift, the market exchange of commodities only established a
new elite of the undeserving on the grounds of a new, and far more
dangerous, species of corruption. That is, it only institutionalized a
new form of status inconsistency: namely, wealth and power without
virtue. As for honorific status, the situation had become hopelessly
confused. To the conservative mentality, there was an obvious
corruption in those progressive upstarts who sought to legitimate
their rise by the purchase of a title. But the system of honors was
itself corrupted, and many ancient landed families were as thoroughly
indebted to the capitalist market for the improvement of their estates
as anyone.

Here, as on questions of truth, the doubly critical posture of men
like Swift left very little ground for the affirmation of any positive
social signifier of merit and virtue. With the triumph of Whig
oligarchy in the eighteenth century, the aristocratic order seems
to regain its stability after the rapid social mobility of the previous

century. But the status category of 'aristocracy' has altered considerably, even if the terminology has remained the same. The status orientation itself has been complicated by a class orientation – by individualistic and monetary criteria and by capitalist practices. The rise of the middle class, in other words, was not the rise of a discrete and determinate social entity, but a historical process in which traditional status groups were altered as much from within as from without. And the rise of the middle class is inseparable from the rise of a class orientation toward social relations. Men like Swift knew this; they knew that the enemy was not so easily distinguished as an ungentle, upstart invader from without. Nevertheless, for lack of a more dependable signifier, they retained in their minds the possession of land and gentle status as a self-consciously conventional signification of what seemed an increasingly embattled virtue.

Why should narrative, in particular, be suitable for the representation of progressive and conservative ideologies? The term 'ideology' often is used to suggest a simplistic reduction of human complexity. But as I intend the term, 'ideology' is discourse whose purpose is to mediate and explain apparently intractable social problems – in this case, the problematic questions of virtue. To explain the condition of status inconsistency is not to explain it away, but to render it intelligible. In fact, the very plausibility of ideological explanation depends on the degree to which it appears to do justice to the contradictory social reality that it seeks to explain. In the present context, ideological explanation works by telling stories. The question of how virtue is signified has an inherently narrative focus because it is concerned with genealogical succession and individual progress, with how human capacity is manifested in and through time. This concern can be seen in the 'macro-narrative' of seventeenth-century history itself, which provided writers with an important model for their novelistic micro-narratives. Seventeenth-century England was vitally concerned with the problem of political sovereignty and its sources. At the beginning of the century, sovereignty seemed to rest with the king and to be validated by, among other things, his genealogical inheritance of royalty. In 1642, Charles I warned that parliament's challenge to royal sovereignty threatened the very continuity of the historical succession. The great danger, he said, was that at last the common people would 'destroy all rights and proprieties, all distinctions of families and merit, and by this means this splendid and excellently distinguished form of government end in a dark, equal chaos of confusion, and the long line of our many noble ancestors in a Jack Cade or a Wat Tyler.'[37] Charles was not entirely wrong in this apocalyptic prophecy: seven years after it he was decapitated. And before the end of the century, the nation had joined together to depose another rightful monarch and to exclude the next fifty-seven prospective heirs to the throne. In their place was crowned a foreigner, and in the place of sovereignty by genealogical inheritance was affirmed sovereignty by achievement: the simple and pragmatic fact that a peaceful and stable settlement had been achieved.[38]

In the language of questions of virtue, the fall of Charles I is the most infamous instance of status inconsistency in the century. And after the Battle of Worcester in 1651, prince Charles wandered the land in disguise like nothing so much as a romance hero destined, after much travail, to be discovered and restored to his aristocratic patrimony.[39] But to readers of a progressive persuasion, the triumphs of Oliver Cromwell and William of Orange showed, in different ways, the superiority of industrious valor to mere lineage. Progressive ideology even entered into the making of Cromwell's New Model Army. In 1643 he declared: 'I had rather have a plain russett-coated captain that knows what he fights for, and loves what he knows, than that which you call a gentleman and is nothing else . . . Better plain men than none, but best to have men patient of wants, faithful and conscientious in the employment . . .'[40]

Cromwell's language here reminds us that Calvinist Protestantism has an important relevance to progressive ideology, for God's mark of inner nobility was superior to any external social elevation. Speaking of divine election, Cromwell asked: 'May not this stamp [of God] bear equal poise with any hereditary interest . . . ?'[41] And, as a coreligionist affirmed, 'It is not the birth, but the new birth, that makes men truly noble.'[42] If Calvinist election argued a new aristocracy alternative to that of birth, Calvinist discipline dictated a spirit of service and reform that worked both to glorify the works of God and to signify one's possession of grace. But what are the narrative implications of this dovetailing of Protestant belief and progressive ideology? As early as Foxe's *Acts and Monuments*, the apocalyptic battle between the Roman Catholic hierarchy and God's saints is colored by the progressive contest between corrupt noblemen and industrious commoners. Foxe's 'Story of Roger Holland, Martyr,' for example, is the tale of an apprentice who is idle and licentious until the moment of his Protestant conversion. Thereafter he prospers wonderfully as a merchant tailor. So when the reformed apprentice is finally called up before his papist inquisitor, he is able to manifest, through a spirited resistance and a serene martyrdom, that spiritual grace which already has been apparent in his labor discipline and his material prosperity.[43]

Calvinist doctrine encouraged in progressive narrative the self-serving conviction that divine grace could be internalized as virtue, and externalized once again as worldly achievement. But Calvinism also counselled against the proud sufficiency of human desire, and it sharpened the conservative critique of enthusiasm and the Protestant ethic. The adventures of Robinson Crusoe exemplify both the ethical obstacles to progressive ideology, and the power of that ideology to drive all before it. Robinson Crusoe is an industrious younger son whose worldly success at first signifies nothing more than acquisitiveness and ambition. But once he is shipwrecked, his island turns out to be a progressive utopia. Because it excludes all human society, it provides an arena in which the anti-social passions of avarice and domination can be indulged without suffering the consequences. Thus Robinson can accumulate goods without creating exchange value. He can exercise absolute sovereignty without incurring the wrath of a greater authority. And when human society finds him, and it comes time to leave the island, he is able to naturalize the artificial, laboratory conditions of his utopia because he has learned to internalize divinity, to identify his own passions with the will of God. A slighter version of this progressive, utopian plot is given by Henry Neville, whose George Pine is an industrious city apprentice who happens to stumble into a travel narrative.[44] Stranded with four women on an Edenic desert island where productive labor is unneeded, Pine resourcefully proceeds to manifest his merit through reproductive labor, populating the island with offspring who then constitute a new genealogy and social order, of which he is the unquestioned sovereign.

But the progressive battle between aristocratic corruption and industrious virtue could of course be waged in a setting closer to home. Often it was embodied in plots that pitted aristocratic seducers, rapists, and dunderheads against chaste and canny young women of the middle and lower orders. The obvious exemplar is Richardson's *Pamela* (although it is by no means the rule that virtue should be so ostentatiously rewarded as hers is). Behind Pamela lies a succession of Pamela-like heroines, including the sister of Gabriel Harvey (Spenser's college friend), who left a manuscript account of her pert resistance to seduction.[45] The most important development of this particular progressive plot model was achieved by Aphra Behn, whose ingenious variations include a female aristocratic oppressor who is pathologically fixated on nobility of birth as the trigger of sexual desire, and who is finally reformed by falling in love with an apparent nobleman who turns out to be the son of a Dutch merchant.[46]

Whatever their differences, progressive plots have in common the aim to explain the meaning of the current crisis of status inconsistency, and, in the symbolic realm of fictional action, to overcome it. How do conservative plots manage this explanation so as to subvert progressive ideology itself? One method is by making the oppressor an aristocrat not by birth but by purchase, and his ruling corruption not sexual desire, but the lust for money and power. But the villains of conservative plots need not be aristocrats at all. Fielding's undeserving upstarts, like Shamela and Jonathan Wild, show an obvious debt to the assorted rogues, highwaymen, and pirates of criminal biography. When Charles Davenant undertook to describe the fall of English virtue under the Whigs, he cast his macro-history in the pseudo-autobiographical form of a micro-narrative about the rise of the rogue figure Mr. Double, 'now worth Fifty thousand Pound, and 14 years ago I had not Shoes on my Feet.' Mr. Double's story is that of a bad apprentice whose vice is not idleness but too much industry, and he ends his allegorical autobiography by comparing himself to 'most of the Modern Whigs . . . Did they rise by Virtue or Merit? No more than my self.'[47]

When conservative protagonists are sympathetic, they are victims of the modern world – either comically ingenuous innocents, or sacrifices to its corrupt inhumanity. One of the striking achievements of *Gulliver's Travels* is that its protagonist is able to fill both of these conservative roles. Like Robinson Crusoe, Lemuel Gulliver begins as a naive and industrious younger son, a quantifying empiricist and an upwardly mobile progressive. In Lilliput he falls into the role of the obsequious new man, hungry for royal favor and titles of honor (recall his assimilationist vanity at being made a Nardac, the highest honor in the land). But Gulliver in Lilliput is also a hardworking public servant who ruefully learns, like Lord Munodi later on, the conservative truth about modern courts and their disdain for true merit. However in his final voyage Gulliver so successfully assimilates upward that he goes native, believes he is a Houyhnhnm, and is forced to endure the comic rustication of an unsuccessful upstart, bloated with pride and uncomprehendingly indignant at his failure to make it.

In this final character of Gulliver (or in that of Shamela) we see the industrious virtue of the progressive protagonist pushed to its limits, so that it breaks open to reveal an ugly core of hypocritical opportunism. This technique of parodic impersonation is typical both of conservative ideology, and of its epistemological counterpart, extreme skepticism. It is the mark of a stance so intricately reactive as to be hard to pry loose, at times, from what it opposes. Moreover unlike progressive narrative, conservative plots are far from hopeful about the overcoming of the social injustice and status inconsistency which they explain with such passion. Their frequent pattern is a retrograde series of disenchantments with all putative resolutions, and conservative utopias tend to be, as Houyhnhnmland is and as Robinson Crusoe's island is not, hedged about with self-conscious fictionality, strictly unfulfillable and nowhere to be found.

Let me now briefly summarize this attempt to rethink the rise of the novel. In order to overcome some deficiencies in the reigning model of what this movement amounted to, I have isolated, as its central principle, two recurrent patterns of 'double reversal.' Naive empiricism negates romance idealism, and is in turn negated by a more extreme skepticism and a more circumspect approach to truth. Progressive ideology subverts aristocratic ideology, and is in turn subverted by conservative ideology. It is in these double reversals, and in their conflation, that the novel is constituted as a dialectical unity of opposed parts, an achievement that is tacitly acknowledged by the gradual stabilization of 'the novel' as a terminological and a conceptual category in eighteenth-century usage. But we have also been concerned with a pattern of historical reversal that is of broader dimension than this movement, and from whose more elevated perspective the conflicts that are defined by our double reversals may even appear to dissolve into unity. For as we have seen over and over again, the origins of the English novel entail the positing of a 'new' generic category as a dialectical negation of a 'traditional' dominance – the romance, the aristocracy – whose character still saturates, as an antithetical but constitutive force, the texture of the category by which it is in the process of being replaced.

Of course the very capacity of seventeenth-century narrative to model itself so self-consciously on established categories bespeaks a detachment sufficient to imagine them *as* categories, to parody and thence to supersede them. And with hindsight we may see that the early development of the novel is our great example of the way that the birth of genres results from a momentary negation of the present so intense that it attains the positive status of a new tradition. But at the 'first instant' of this broader dialectical reversal, the novel has a definitional volatility, a tendency to dissolve into its antithesis, which encapsulates the dialectical nature of historical process itself at a critical moment in the emergence of the modern world.

I have argued that the volatility of the novel at this time is *analogous* to that of the middle class. But it is clear that in a certain sense, the emerging novel also has *internalized* the emergence of the middle class in its preoccupation with the problem of how virtue is signified. From time to time we can observe the distinct questions of virtue and truth being raised simultaneously by writers of the most diverse aims and formal commitments. At such times we sense that writers wish to 'make something' of the analogous relation between these questions, if only through their tacit juxtaposition. And occasionally the analogy will even be explicitly asserted. In this way, questions of truth and virtue begin to seem not so much distinct problems, as versions or transformations of each other, distinct ways of formulating and propounding a fundamental problem of what might be called epistemological, sociological, and ethical 'signification.' And the essential unity of this problem is clear from the fact that progressive and conservative positions on questions of virtue have their obvious corollary positions with respect to questions of truth. What this means is that epistemological choices come to have ideological significance, and a given account of the nature of social reality implies a certain formal commitment and procedure. Moreover we may conceive these correlations of truth and virtue also in terms of narrative form and content, so that the way the story is told, and what it is that is told, are implicitly understood to bear an integral relation to each other.

But I do not mean to suggest that the conflation of questions of truth and virtue occurred easily or quickly. On the contrary, it is the result of much thought and experimentation, a very small portion of which I have described here, expended over a considerable period of time. And the conflation itself begins to occur when writers begin to act – first gingerly, then systematically – upon the insight that the difficulties of one set of problems may be mediated and illuminated by the reflection of the other. This insight – the deep and fruitful analogy between questions of truth and questions of virtue – is the enabling foundation of the novel. And the genre of the novel can be understood comprehensively as an early modern cultural instrument designed to confront, on the level of narrative form and content, both intellectual and social crisis simultaneously. The novel emerges into consciousness when this conflation can be made with complete confidence. The conflict then comes to be embodied in a public controversy between Richardson and Fielding – writers who are understood to represent coherent, autonomous, and alternative methods for doing the same thing. At this point – in the mid-1740s, after the first confrontation between Richardson and Fielding – the novel has come to the end of its origins. And it begins then to enter new territory.

Notes

1. *The Rise of the Novel: Studies in Defoe, Richardson and Fielding* (Berkeley: University of California Press, 1957). The following essay summarizes one central argument of my forthcoming book, *The Origins of the English Novel, 1600–1740* (Baltimore: Johns Hopkins University Press, 1987).

2. *The Annals of Love, Containing Select Histories of the Amours of divers Princes Courts, Pleasantly Related* (1672), sig. Dd7^v–Ee4^v. Except where noted, place of publication of early modern works is London.

3. *A Catalogve of The most vendible Books in England* . . . (1657).

4. *The History of the Royal-Society of London* . . . (1667), 90–91.

5. *Philosophical Transactions*, 11 (1676), 552.

6. See *Philosophical Transactions*, 1 (1665–66), 141–43, 186–89. Boyle's instructions are excerpted from his *Some Considerations of the Usefulness of Experimental Natural Philosophy* (1663).

7. *The History of the Royal-Society of London* . . . 72.

8. Awnsham and John Churchill, eds., *A Collection of Voyages and Travels* . . . (1704), I, viii.

9. Edward Cooke in *ibid.*, II, xix.

10. See in general Elizabeth L. Eisenstein, *The Printing Press as an Agent of Change: Communications and Cultural Transformations in Early Modern Europe* (Cambridge: Cambridge University Press, 1979), Chap. 2 and *passim*.

11. *Histories and Observations Domestick and Foreign* . . . (1683), sig. A5^v, A6^r.

12. E.g., see *Don Quixote*, II (1615), ii-iv.

13. See the discussion of William Haller, *The Elect Nation: The Meaning and Relevance of Foxe's Book of Martyrs* (New York: Harper & Row, 1963), 122, 159–60, 213–14.

14. Bunyan, *Life and Death*, 326, sig. A4^v.

15. *The Diary of Ralph Thoresby, FRS, Author of the Topography of Leeds (1677–1724)*, ed. Rev. Joseph Hunter (1830), I, xv, quoted in George A. Starr, *Defoe and Spiritual Autobiography* (Princeton: Princeton University Press, 1965), 10.

16. *The Certainty of the Worlds of Spirits* . . . (1691), sig. A4^r.

17. E.g., *A Discourse concerning the Mechanical Operation of the Spirit* . . . (1704).

18. *Tatler*, No. 178, May 27–30, 1710.

19. *Tatler*, No. 84, Oct. 22, 1709.

20. *The Dictionary Historical and Critical of Mr Peter Bayle* (1697), 2nd ed. (1734–38), IV, 'Nidhard,' n. C, 366.

21. *The Plus Ultra reduced to a Non Plus* . . . (1670), 11.

22. See the copy of [Richard Head,] *O-Brazile, or the Inchanted Island* . . . (1675) reproduced in *Seventeenth-Century Tales of the Supernatural*, ed. Isabel M. Westcott, *Augustan Reprint Society*, No. 74 (1958).

23. 'Soliloquy: or Advice to an Author' (1714), in *Characteristicks of Men, Manners, Opinions, Times*, 2nd ed. (1714), I, 344.

24. [François Misson,] A *New Voyage to the East-Indies, by Francis Leguat and His Companions* . . . (London and Amsterdam, 1708), iv. The rival is the Abbot of Choisy.

25. See the discussion in David Cressy, 'Describing the Social Order of Elizabethan and Stuart England,' *Literature and History*, No. 3 (March, 1976), 29–44.

26. See Peter Matthias, 'The Social Structure in the Eighteenth Century: A Calculation by Joseph Massie,' in *The Transformation of England: Essays in the Economic and Social History of England in the Eighteenth Century* (New York: Columbia University Press, 1979), 176, 186, 188.

27. See Lawrence Stone, *The Crisis of the Aristocracy, 1558–1641* (Oxford: Clarendon Press, 1965), Chap. 3. For a discussion of 'status inconsistency' and reference-group theory in the context of seventeenth-century historiography, see Stone's *The Causes of the English Revolution, 1529–1642* (London: Routledge & Kegan Paul, 1972), Chap. 1.

28. A generalization based on the use of the term in dramatic contexts: see C. L. Barber, *The Idea of Honor in the English Drama, 1591–1700*, Gothenburg Studies in English, 6 (Göteborg: Elanders, 1957), 330–31.

29. *The Fable of the Bees* (1714), ed. Phillip Harth (Harmondsworth: Penguin, 1970), 'Remark (R),' 212–13.

30. *New Instructions to the Guardian . . .* (1694), 135–36.

31. *A Modest Plea for an Equal Common-wealth Against Monarchy . . .* (1659), 62–63.

32. *The True-Born Englishman. A Satyr* (1700), 70–71.

33. *The Compleat English Gentleman* (written 1728–29), ed. Karl D. Bülbring (London: David Nutt, 1890), 171.

34. *Examiner*, No. 40, May 10, 1711; (Irish) *Intelligencer*, No. 9 (1728).

35. *Examiner*, No. 34, Mar. 29, 1711.

36. *Review*, III, No. 126, Oct. 22, 1706.

37. 'Answer to the Nineteen Propositions,' June 18, 1642, in J. P. Kenyon, ed., *The Stuart Constitution, 1603–1688: Documents and Commentary* (Cambridge: Cambridge University Press, 1966), 23.

38. See Gerald M. Straka, *Anglican Reaction to the Revolution of 1688*, State Historical Society of Wisconsin (Madison, Wi.: University of Wisconsin Press, 1962).

39. See *Charles II's Escape from Worcester: A Collection of Narratives Assembled by Samuel Pepys*, ed. William Matthews (Berkeley: University of California Press, 1966), 40, 42, 44, 50, 74, 96.

40. To Suffolk County Committee, Aug. 29, Sept. 28, 1643, in *The Writings and Speeches of Oliver Cromwell*, ed. Wilbur C. Abbott (Cambridge, Ma.: Harvard University Press, 1937), I, 256, 262.

41. Quoted in Michael Walzer, *The Revolution of the Saints: A Study in the Origins of Radical Politics* (Cambridge, Ma.: Harvard University Press, 1965), 266.

42. Thomas Edwards, 'The Holy Choice,' in *Three Sermons* (1625), 63–64, quoted in *ibid.*, 235.

43. See *Acts and Monuments*, ed. S. R. Cattley (London: Seeley and Burnside, 1839), VIII, 473–74.

44. See *The Isle of Pines* . . . (1668).

45. See 'A Noble Mans Sute to a Cuntrie Maide,' in *Letter-Book of Gabriel Harvey, 1573–1580*, ed. Edward J. L. Scott, Camden Society, N. S. 33 (London: Nichols and Sons, 1884), 144–58.

46. See *The Fair Jilt: or, the History of Prince Tarquin, and Miranda* (1696), in *The Histories and Novels Of the Late Ingenious Mrs Behn* . . . (1696).

47. *The True Picture of a Modern Whig* . . . , '6th ed.' (1701), 14, 32.

3 The Elevation of the Novel in England: Hegemony and Literary History

WILLIAM B. WARNER

William Warner has engaged with a number of different theoretical and critical models, including psychoanalysis and deconstruction. He is currently involved in a project to describe the ideological significance of women's writing in the late seventeenth century and early eighteenth century, focussing on such figures as Behn, Manley, and Haywood. His interests are distinctly sociological, and he alludes to the work of the French sociologist Pierre Bourdieu. In this essay, he argues that early writers of fiction should not be judged by novelistic criteria established after they wrote, and established by powerful male writers – especially Richardson and Fielding – who were responding to different market conditions, and who had little understanding or regard for the peculiar concerns of earlier writers, even though their success depended on them (see Introduction, pp. 12–13; 19–20). In this, he takes issue with Michael McKeon's implication that we can speak of the novel as embodying a distinct genre.

In the last few years the question of the novel's rise in England has felt all the shocks and complications of theoretical and political critique. Although traditional literary histories of the early 'masters' of English fiction have been rewritten by marxist and Foucaultean literary histories, in at least one regard, the more things change, the more they remain the same. Even the most theoretically sophisticated and politically progressive of these recent literary histories return to familiar canonical texts to stage the formation of 'the' English novel.[1] These literary histories extend an idea dear to Richardson and Fielding: of the cultural novelty of their novels, of their radical and unheralded break with earlier novels. One of the most efficient ways to break the spell of this *grand récit* of the novel's rise is to ask: when and why does it begin to be told?

Modern attempts to tell the novel's rise follow in the wake of Richardson's and Fielding's efforts to introduce 'new species' of

English novels by displacing the popular novels written, in the six decades before 1740, by Aphra Behn, Delarivière Manley, and Eliza Haywood. The rationales offered by Richardson and Fielding for their novelistic practice are first drafts for what will later be told, within literary studies, as 'the rise of the novel.' By allowing Behn, Manley and Haywood to emerge out of the footnotes and margins of literary history, recent feminist literary history – written in very different ways by Jane Spencer, Mary Ann Schofield, Paula Backsheider, Laura Brown, Judith Kagan Gardiner, Janet Todd, and Catherine Gallagher – offers chances for a fundamental revision of the novel's elevation in England. In their literary historical narratives, Spencer, Schofield and Todd place Behn, Manley and Haywood at the beginning of a tradition of women's novel writing which develops through Sarah Fielding, Charlotte Lennox, Frances Burney and Jane Austen. But this elaboration of a separate, semi-autonomous domain of 'women's writing' serves to obscure what my own more inclusive literary history seeks to apprehend: the specific role played by the novels of Behn, Manley and Haywood in the novel's elevation in the 1740s.[2]

Neither traditional nor Marxist nor feminist literary histories allows one to grasp what is sudden or brutal, odd or unexpected or contingent about the novel's elevation into a new cultural legitimacy. Nor do they allow one to understand how, when it comes to the rupture in the reading and writing of novels in England in the 1740s, it is, as John Frow writes, 'not so much the old that dies as the new that kills.'[3] Only with this perspective on the rhythms of cultural strife can one understand how it came to be that the novels of Richardson and Fielding, rather than novels by others, won a unique combination of popularity and cultural importance. In other words, given the popularity of Behn, Manley, Haywood and Defoe, given the aesthetic 'finish' of novels by Behn and Congreve, given the coherent ethical design of novels written by Penelope Aubin and Jane Barker, how is it that Richardson's and Fielding's novels are the ones that were countersigned in the eighteenth century as exemplary models for future novels? The ethical program, mimetic coherence and aesthetic ambition claimed by Richardson and Fielding for their novels were 'countersigned' by many of their early readers, as well as early critics like Samuel Johnson in his *Rambler* #4 essay. This positive reception of their novels functioned as a 'contingent decision' in favor of their novels, and against the novels of Behn, Manley and Haywood they supplanted. Like the 'decision' in a legal proceeding or sporting event, it establishes a hierarchical relation of one term or agent over another; the decision is 'contingent' because it did not have to happen the way it did.[4]

Re-articulating the novel: Richardson and Fielding in the 1740s

Well over two hundred years of novelistic and critical practice
has sustained itself upon a certain fable of origins. This fable
casts Richardson and Fielding as the first coherent, self-conscious
practitioners of what would become the modern novel, as rival
inventors of two diametrically opposed, yet complementary types of
novelistic writing, one that explores psychic depths, and another that
narrates the diverse forms of the social: in short, as the two fathers of
the novel. Such a fabulous double paternity for the novel helped do
what genealogies always do, to produce a pedigree for a literary genre
with very dubious origins. The bipolar simplicity of this fable has
helped produce the pulsive force to promote the novel as a 'serious'
and intelligible option for subsequent writers. But, as I have already
suggested, this fable has stood in for, and thus helped to efface, a
much more plural and complex history of early novel writing.

The complex cultural event I am calling 'the elevation of the novel'
depends upon two events: first, the operation of the market as it
facilitates the popular circulation of the novel, and supports shifts
in novel reading; and second, a hegemonic articulatory 'moment'
expressed in the 'programs' to elevate the novel pursued in parallel
but different ways by Richardson and Fielding. The 'decision' in
favor of the elevated novel of Richardson and Fielding is reached
by a broad group of readers, who express themselves through 'the
market,' as well as those readers who claim and exercise special
critical and moral authority. How does the market come to play
a decisive influence in this 'turn' in the history of culture and
literature? The novel of the late seventeenth and early eighteenth
centuries is one of the first instances of popular culture circulating
as a commodity within a system of production and consumption
that approximates that which we know today. Literary historians
have noted the break this entailed with the patronage system that
had encouraged a catering to the taste of a coterie audience. But it
also entailed a fundamental break with the literary ideal that had
informed Western print culture: the assumption that by writing
according to classically ordained models, authors should aspire to
produce works that would have timeless value. By contrast, writers
of early novels in England, perhaps influenced by the rationale for
the new and modern developed by both Protestantism and the New
Science, scandalize the high cultural expectation that a book be
written to endure.[5]

The early novelists wrote the first 'disposable' books – books
written in anticipation of their own obsolescence, and in acceptance
of their own transient function as part of a culture of serial

entertainments. Only as replaceable elements in a series could the early novel negotiate the market's contradictory double demand: to produce the effect of the latest hit, yet appear enticingly new, to be, quite paradoxically, *recurrently new*. The compositional strategies that issue from this marketing imperative are familiar from Hollywood film production: a recourse to adaptations, translations, sequels. The special rigor with which Pope lampoons Haywood in *The Dunciad* results in part from her particularly successful deployment of this new, more market-oriented concept of the book in her short novels of the 1720s.

By using the market as a compass for interpreting the directions of popular taste, early novelists could bring their writing into increasingly intimate exchange with that taste. In such a commodified cultural system, events at the site of consumption engender a feed-back loop that modifies activity at the site of production. To understand the elevation of the early novel, we need to bring everything that is usually comprised under the word 'production,' – writing, authorial intention, audience address, publication, conscious and unconscious models, etc. – into relation with what primes and directs this productivity – the tug of consumption and popularity. The market orients Richardson and Fielding toward those novels of Behn, Manley and Haywood which offered the dominant prior instance of the sort of popularity and atavistic pleasure Richardson and Fielding wished to mobilize for different ends. If the popular success of novels by Behn, Manley and Haywood had defined 'the novel' as a racy, immoral story of love, Richardson and Fielding rearticulate the novel so as to win a contingent decision in favor of what is claimed to be a 'new species' of writing. This 'decision' is not punctual but gradually unfolding: it begins with the spectacular popularity of *Pamela* (1740) and the imitations and refutations it provoked; the decision becomes confirmed over the course of the decade, with the popularity of *Joseph Andrews* (1742) as well as the critical and popular success accorded *Clarissa* (1747–48) and *Tom Jones* (1749). By the end of the decade the possibilities of this terrain of production and consumption, the set of cultural practices called 'reading novels,' had been remapped.

Because the novels of Richardson and Fielding in the 1740s focus upon the topic the earlier novels of Behn, Manley and Haywood had told – the adventures of the protagonist as developed through a story of love, passion and (sometimes) marriage – it is entirely appropriate that *Pamela* was called a 'dilated novel' when it was published.[6] But there is a pointed reason why the exchange between Richardson's and Fielding's novels of the 1740s and the novels of amorous intrigue they sought to supplant is obscure, complex and vexed.

The exchange between these two very different species of novels is antagonistic. Neither Richardson nor Fielding offers his writing as another discrete narrative practice to be consumed alongside the novels of Behn, Manley and Haywood, like different columns on a Chinese menu. Nor does either envision his writing as a simple inversion or negation of a wayward novelistic writing that can be subsumed, either logically or dialectically, into their own more enlightened practice. Instead, by claiming to inaugurate an entirely 'new' species of writing, Richardson and Fielding both seek to assert the fundamental difference of their own projects from [those of] these antagonists – the notorious trio of Behn, Manley and Haywood – who continue to circulate in the market as threatening rivals in a zero-sum struggle to control a common cultural space and activity.[7] If Behn's and Haywood's novels flourish, then their popularity drains Richardson's and Fielding's projects of their cultural efficacy. This antagonism is most difficult to define because it is an unstable, nonrelation between two terms and subject positions that the antagonists have every interest in obscuring, and is only graspable from a later analytical perspective.

The antagonism of the reformed novel to the popular novel is legible wherever Richardson and Fielding polemicize on behalf of their new practice: on the title page, in prefaces, and chapter headings; in private and public letters, advertisements and critical essays. Thus in the title page of the first edition of *Pamela*, the reader is promised that we are offered a narrative that 'at the same time that it agreeably entertains, [by a Variety of curious and affecting Incidents,] is entirely divested of all those Images, which, in too many pieces calculated for Amusement only, tend to inflame the Minds they should instruct.'[8] Is this, as it seems to be, the first 'G' rating ever offered for popular culture? Notice that in this fleeting title-page allusion to the 'bad' early novel, opponents are not named. The 'novel' is so disreputable a cultural terrain, that merely naming a specific novelist could compromise the whole project to reform the novel.[9] The antagonism between the reformed novel and the popular novel never becomes a fair fight or open relationship, dialogue or debate. The earlier novel of amorous intrigue is not a legitimate precursor, but the alternative in popular entertainment that is being put out of play by ethically enlightened novels. The popularity of these earlier novels functions less as an 'influence' upon Richardson and Fielding than a plague-like 'influenza,' against the uncontrolled spread of which Richardson and Fielding produce their novels as warning, antidote and cure. Antagonism is the pulsive force in the event my secret history seeks to interpret: the sudden violent shift in the cultural credit from an earlier species of writing to one proclaimed to be an-other.

Through their novel-writing practice in the 1740s, as well as their polemical critical statements in support of that practice, Richardson and Fielding successfully hegemonize the novel through a series of articulatory moves that reshape what their culture takes the novel to be. First they annul the significant differences between prior instances of novel writing. Thus under the opprobrious terms 'romance' and 'novel' they include: the artificial, idealistic, and long out of fashion French 'grand romance' of Honoré d'Urfé, La Calprenède and Madeleine de Scudéry; the short novel, adapted out of Italian, Spanish and French novellas by Aphra Behn in the late Restoration and turned into a formula for popular fiction in the 1720s by Eliza Haywood; and finally the 'secret history,' adopted from French models by Behn, and practiced with enormous notoriety and scandal by Manley, who was imitated by Haywood and Defoe. Now lumped together in shadowy caricatures, these early novels are often condemned for diametrically opposed reasons: for offering implausibly idealistic accounts of love (what Richardson calls 'romantic fustian'), or inappropriately literal depictions of sex. What renders these early novels essentially equivalent is their tendency to induce mental delusion and moral corruption.

Now placed on the other side of a boundary drawn by a new hegemonic practice of narrative, the (old) novel appears as beyond the pale, appropriately relegated to the curious heap of surpassed cultural forms. What lies on this side of a newly drawn frontier of cultural legitimacy acquires identity and value as the new species of (utterly un-novelistic) writing, consistently tagged by Richardson and Fielding with the term 'history.' Within this new 'province' of writing, the divergent practices of Richardson and Fielding now evidence significant differences of narrative form or representational strategy. Thus Sarah Fielding chose to write the first part of *David Simple* in the third person narrative used by her brother in *Joseph Andrews*, but published its second part as a novel in 'familiar letters,' under the influence of Richardson's practice.[10] In *Rambler* #4 (1750) Johnson defended Richardson's attempt to offer his heroines as exemplars of virtue against Fielding's effort to deploy 'mixed characters' as the more realistic protagonists for fiction. The lively and contentious debates about the proper form for fiction after 1740 makes the novels of Richardson and Fielding appear to be what literary history has made them ever since: a horizon for critical reflection upon 'the novel.' But this horizon is not a natural or stable boundary; it only appears as one from where literary history has put us. The interplay of presence and absence this horizon secures is predicated upon a certain forgetting of those earlier novels of Behn, Manley and Haywood which evidence characters both mixed and

ideal, narratives in both the first and third person. It is only from
the vantage point of Richardson's and Fielding's effort to give the
novel a higher cultural calling that the novels of Behn, Manley and
Haywood are made to appear 'low' or immoral. In other words, 'the
elevation of the novel' performatively produces 'high' and 'low' as
judgments about what constitutes coherent ethical design. Since this
repositioning of the novel results from a quite conscious attempt to
hegemonize or lead a culture's practice of reading, it has little of the
spontaneity suggested by the phrase the 'rise the novel.' Only by
eroding the cultural legitimacy of earlier novels could Richardson
and Fielding later come to appear as 'the first' 'real,' that is
legitimate, novelists.

Richardson and Fielding disavowed rather than assumed their debt
to those popular novels whose cultural space they would redefine,
and whose narrative resources they incorporate. Their rearticulation
of the novel depends upon appropriating terms from the earlier
novel – such as the female libertine, or the intricate seduction scheme
– and articulating (by connecting together, and thus 'speaking') these
elements in a new way, with new meaning, as part of a new form
of novel. To produce an antidotal substitute to the earlier popular
novel, Richardson and Fielding must swallow those racy novels of
love by Behn, Manley and Haywood, divest them of their offensive
tendencies, [and] feed on their popular subject matter. So, hidden
within the plot lines and scenes of the healthy reformed novel, the
old discredited novel can help bring popularity to Richardson's
and Fielding's texts. If the early novels were, in Richetti's words,
'machines for producing pleasurable fantasies,'[11] the influence
of those novels that 'merely amuse' comes to be expressed in the
reformed novel's obsession with the problem of how readers read.
Because his characters are destined for more than fantasmatic
identification, Richardson deploys extraordinary vigilance about the
way his characters are 'consumed': he embeds responses to Pamela
and Clarissa within the novels; extends each text long after the basic
action is complete, so their story may be haggled out before the
reader finishes the text; adds revisions that foreclose false readings,
and so on. In all these ways Richardson seeks to forestall a tendency
built into those aspects of the early novel he would adopt: stories
of love, written in first person letter/narratives, that encourage
spontaneous reader identification and thus tend to lose their way.
Richardson becomes a postman intent upon delivering his 'letter/
novel' to its correct (that is, ethical) destination.

It is difficult to reform and elevate the novel because Richardson's
and Fielding's moral fiction is founded upon the volatile, undecidable
ground of the early novel. By this I mean that the moral telos of their

new novels is not 'given' or decided in advance, by their wish to write ethical novels. Quite the contrary. Both authors not only must contend with the errant readings encouraged by the earlier novels and reading habits, but counter the dangerous tendencies of those novelistic themes and motifs they embed in their novels. In a letter of 13 August 1741, to Dr. George Cheyne, who had worried that Pamela and B do too much 'fondling' before their marriage, Richardson defends, at the same time that he defends against, the erotic currents in *Pamela*. They are indispensable if Richardson is going to interpose his novel as a replacement for 'such Novels and Romances, as have a tendency to inflame and corrupt'; only through a calculated and controlled incorporation of the popular novel can Richardson take readers at that 'Time of Life, in which the passions will predominate' and direct those passions to 'Laudable meanings and Purposes.'[12]
In Fielding we find a very different strategy for incorporating the popular novel. In the first interpolated story in *Joseph Andrews*, entitled 'The History of Leonora; or, the Unfortunate Jilt,' we get the story of a young woman whose values and manners seem to have been perverted by a too literal identification with certain heroines of Behn, Manley and Haywood. Fielding tells Leonora's story so as to dissipate the cultural credit of the early novel. What gets pulled into the body of Fielding's writing is a popular novel that, parodied and interrupted, rewritten and recontextualized, supports a new species of ethical fiction.

Overwriting the intertexts

The articulatory moment by which Richardson and Fielding founded their species of writing upon an earlier one has justified, at least since the later eighteenth century, relegating the novels of Behn, Manley, Haywood to a marginal 'pre-history' of 'the novel.' Most subsequent literary histories have concurred with the critical judgment that the novels of these three writers lack the coherent subjectivity (character), cohesive structure (plot), and consistent ethics (theme) that Richardson and Fielding would bring to the novel. If we are to open that 'pre-history' of the novel to historical investigation, we must reread Behn, Manley and Haywood as more than precursors to the texts to follow; we must concede them differences and autonomy as part of another earlier cultural terrain. We can begin to do this if we attend to the implications of the way Richardson and Fielding *overwrite* the novels of Behn, Manley and Haywood. From the vantage point of their conscious project to elevate the novel, such an overwriting means writing above and beyond them, toward higher cultural purposes. But overwriting the earlier novel involves a paradoxical double relation: the earlier novel becomes an intertextual support and that which is to be superseded, that which is repeated as well as revised, invoked as it is effaced. Thus 'the elevation of the novel' is founded in an antagonistic, but never acknowledged or conscious intertextual exchange with the earlier novel. This overwriting, in the special sense I am using it, offers chances for reading against the grain of earlier literary histories.

To interpret the unacknowledged exchanges working within a text like *Pamela*, one must reverse the procedures of that sort of literary history that goes back to earlier noncanonical texts to find the 'sources' for canonical texts. Thus one should not read the novels of Behn, Manley and Haywood, or Penelope Aubin, Elizabeth Rowe and Jane Barker, in hopes of finding the closest possible resemblance to the stories, characters, or ethos of Richardson's novel.[13] Such an assemblage of single sources, supposed to operate as causes or influences upon the single author of the privileged text, fails to develop a general profile of those antithetical novels circulating among readers before 1740. Nor will I be focusing upon the intertextual networks of explicit or implicit allusion subservient to the conscious intentions of the author: evident, for example, when Fielding announces on the title page to *Joseph Andrews* that the 'history' is written in 'the manner of Cervantes.'

To read the general cultural antagonism between Richardson and the novelists he would displace, one might more fruitfully begin with a rather perverse question: Where does one find a character who could not be more *different* from Pamela? Although there are many plausible candidates, my choice is the erotically inventive central character of Eliza Haywood's *Fantomina; or, Love in a Maze* (1725). Let me remind you of her story. Fascinated with the erotic freedom of prostitutes at the theater, Fantomina changes her upper class dress for the garb of these ladies. When she is approached by the charming Beauplaisir, one who has long admired her, but always been in awe of her reputation, she decides to follow the dictates of her own passion and indulge his solicitations. Through a gradually escalating series of half-steps she loses her virtue and finds herself entangled in [a] secret amour with him. When his desire for her begins to languish she contrives an original solution: by changing her dress, hair color, accent, and manner, she transforms herself into a series of erotic objects to engage Beauplaisir's fascination: Celia, the 'rude' 'country lass' who serves as the maid in his guest house in Bath; Mrs. Bloomer, the charming widow in distress, who begs his assistance on the road back to London from Bath; and finally, an upper class enchantress called Incognita, who carries him through an

erotic encounter in her London apartments, while staying masked
and anonymous. This chain of erotic intrigue is brought to an abrupt
close with the sudden return of Fantomina's mother, and the
discovery that the heroine is pregnant.

Pamela incorporates and displaces the narrative and thematic
elements we find in *Fantomina*. Near the end of Pamela's tenure as
a servant in Mr. B's estate at Bedfordshire, there is a scene that offers
a telling contrast to Haywood's novel. By way of preparing for her
return to her father's modest home, Pamela has 'trick'd' herself out
in 'homespun' country clothes. This metamorphosis from the silks
she had been wearing is so striking that the housekeeper doesn't
recognize Pamela when she appears in her new outfit. Mrs. Jervis
prevails upon Pamela to be introduced anonymously to Mr. B,
who calculatedly (Pamela thinks) uses the chance to kiss her. Pamela
narrates: 'He came up to me, and took me by the hand, and said,
Whose pretty maiden are you? – I dare say you are *Pamela*'s sister,
you are so like her. So neat, so clean, so pretty! . . . I would not be so
free with your *Sister*, you may believe; but I must kiss you' (61). This
provokes Pamela's emphatic assertion of her true identity. After her
escape she is called back to receive Mr. B's accusation: since he had
recently resolved to give Pamela no 'Notice,' now 'you must disguise
yourself, to attract me.' She offers this defence: 'I have put on no
Disguise. . . . I have been in Disguise indeed ever since my good
Lady, your Mother, took me from my poor parents' (62). After
Pamela leaves the room, a servant overhears Mr. B say, 'By God I
will have her!' This scene has decisive consequences. Rather than
letting Pamela return home to her parents, Mr. B makes plans to take
Pamela, against her will, to his Lincolnshire estate. There the heroine
finds herself removed from the ordinary everyday reality of modern
England, and thrown into a fantasy-laden, erotically charged setting
more compatible with the romance and the early popular novel,
where B pursues, with unrestrained passion, his plots on her virtue.
After the disguise scene, B becomes the active prosecutor of the
romance coordinates of the action, a possibility suggested early on
in the text, when he says to Pamela, 'we shall make out between us,
before we have done, a pretty Story in Romance, I warrant ye!' (42).[14]

Pamela rearticulates the resources for fantasy and pleasure working
in a novel like *Fantomina*. In both stories the heroine's disguise works
in parallel ways: as a stimulus to a male desire that is in danger
of fading, and as a way to carry the narrative forward to a new
phase of the action. In both a transformation of life, and a romantic
plasticity and mobility of the self, is catalyzed by the heroine's
artistry in changing her dress. By putting this empowering fantasy
into practice, Fantomina can control the desire that would control

her: by appearing as a succession of beautiful women, Fantomina
fulfills an impossible male demand for infinite variety; by tricking
the male gaze that would fix her, she cures that gaze of its tendency
to rove; by taking control of the whole *mise en scène* of the courtship
scenario, Fantomina directs the spectacle of courtship that would
subject her. In all these ways, Fantomina achieves a temporary
reprieve from that whole courtship system as described by Paula
Backsheider: a discursive system that positions women as the one
'on trial,' subject to the 'attack of spectacle,' always in danger of
becoming grotesque, threatened with the loss of love.[15] But the
critique and transgression of the courtship system in Haywood's
Fantomina, developed from the vantage point of a female heroine's
achievement of erotic mastery, encounters its limit when the fruits
of her licence become the occasion for her mother's determined
investigations and harsh measures – a secret lying-in, and retirement
to a convent.

By contrast with Haywood's novel, Richardson's *Pamela* represents
the heroine's participation in disguise as problematic, an issue open
to reflection in the novel by the strenuous debate it provokes
between the heroine and B. From the moment Pamela puts on
her outfit in her bedroom, Pamela's pleasure in her new appearance
is presented in a risky and morally equivocal light: looking in 'the
Glass, as proud as any thing . . . I never lik'd myself so well in my
Life.' Pamela's conduct-book self-assessment of her impending
social decline – 'O the Pleasure of descending with Ease, Innocence
and Resignation!' – is qualified by the way the scene echoes the
narcissism of Eve's look in the pool in Paradise, or Belinda's 'rites of
pride' before her mirror in *The Rape of the Lock*. Pamela's complicity
in acquiescing to the masquerade staged by Mrs. Jervis – Pamela
admits 'it looks too free *in me*, and *to him*' – means Pamela must
submit to the kiss which she does not consciously seek. But what
starts out in the naive frolics of the teenaged heroine turns, through
the intensity of B's desire, into the violence of B's accusations, and
his subsequent plots. Pamela's defensive insistence that her new
dress is her truest clothing and her recent dress, a kind of disguise,
does not make Pamela's clothing the reliable sign of a stable social
position. Instead, her clothes, manner and language become equally
arbitrary and non-natural, the instruments for dressing across and
between classes. This problem of truth and error in dress – as it
denotes or confuses class position, bars or provokes sexual exchange
– complicates that aspect of the scene that offers the surest anchor
of the ethical conduct-book agenda of Richardson's novel: Pamela's
presentation of self. When Pamela says, 'O Sir, said I, I am *Pamela*,
indeed I am: Indeed I am *Pamela, her own self!*' (61), the very

repetition of the first person pronoun, the double chiasmic assertion, the intensifiers 'indeed, indeed,' the emphasis and overemphasis of this circular enunciation of identity betrays the difficulty of stabilizing identity. The precariousness of this incipient selfhood results from factors operating elsewhere in the scene, the shifts of dress, class and language that enable the mobile erotic exchange Pamela and B are having such a difficult time controlling.

My reading of Richardson's novel in parallel with Eliza Haywood's is offered as an alternative to conventional studies of the 'influence' of one text or writer upon the 'author' of an other. Richardson does not have to have read Haywood to have his text receive the shaping force of the 'influenza' of her popularity. Reading the stories of Fantomina and Pamela together suggests how motifs typical of numberless early novels – disguise, an erotic agon, and fantasies of self-transformation through change in dress – become indispensable to the reformed novel Richardson writes. Thus production of Pamela's exemplary self depends upon the way dressing the heroine, in new clothes as well as the clothes of her language, produces effects of truth or unveiling out of the ruses of disguise. This masquerade may be ethically risky, but it is essential to the comic denouement of *Pamela*. It also serves as an apt metaphor for what may be entailed in Richardson's attempt to elevate the novel: redressing the novel with clothes that are paradoxically at once more modest and truthful, not a covering but the naked truth. The critical storm that *Pamela* provoked suggests that writers like Fielding, in his *Shamela* (April 1741) and Haywood, in her *Anti-Pamela; or, Feign'd Innocence Detected* (July 1741), immediately understood and exploited the constitutive tensions in Richardson's revision of the novel: between Richardson's conduct-book agenda – to represent a paragon of virtue, to represent her pathway to reward – and the intricate and eroticizing modes of the earlier novel he incorporates, but never fully controls.

Reading over the vortex of the novel's elevation

Although reading *Pamela* alongside the short novel *Fantomina* suggests the difference and antagonism between the writings of Richardson and the early Haywood, it only offers a tantalizing hint of the possible alternative coherences of the novels of Behn, Manley and Haywood. To understand disguise in *Fantomina* as a positive constituent of a novel and culture radically different from that projected by *Pamela*, one would need to carry out a sustained reading of a long, ambitious and influential novel like Behn's *Love Letters Between a Nobleman and His Sister* (1684–87).[16] I write 'possible' 'coherence' because the very success of Richardson's and Fielding's rearticulation of the novel for their own culture, and every subsequent English literary history, has made it most difficult to read these early novelists outside the generic conceptions that proliferate with the novel's elevation in the 1740s. *Love Letters* may be oriented toward collective cultural obsessions – like following the dialectical interplay of love and honor, self-interest and public virtue, disguise and truth – markedly different from those that concern the novel writers and readers after 1740. But to remark these differences does not return *Love Letters* to a historicist primal ground for knowing the text as history. Nor can we ground literary history by reading *Love Letters* 'in itself,' as a virtual identity, free of history. Literary history can only produce its explanatory framing narrative by interweaving each text into a significant intertextual context. But a self-reflexive literary history understands that one can never do this for the first time. A historically sensitive literary history will inhabit rather than refuse the ironies and displacements produced by the history of novel writing and reading that precedes and complicates its efforts.

The elevation of the novel in the 1740s operates like a vortex within every subsequent effort to read the early novel in England. Appearing as a rupture, disturbance, or gap in the history of novel reading and writing, it throws some of the functions and ideas of novelistic writing down into obscurity, and throws others up into prominence; as a feature of the cultural land(sea)scape, it reiterates the influence of certain texts (like *Pamela*), and is an abyss for others (like *Love Letters*); as a mobile field of force, it enters subsequent critical contexts to direct the reading and assessment of early novels. To read across the vortex left by the elevation of the novel means reading in terms of shadowy origins and indelible destinations, prospectively and retrospectively, facing both forward and back. One can emphasize the paradoxical relation of history and text this entails by casting the problem in terms of intentionality. Aphra Behn did not write *Love Letters* so it could be overwritten sixty years later by Richardson, but this did happen. To read *Love Letters* over (in spite of, in view of) the vortex of the novel's elevation, one needs to attempt a double reading of *Love Letters*. On the one hand, one must seek to grasp those now mostly illegible ways Behn's writing rearticulates the literature of love she inherits; on the other, since the texts of Richardson and Fielding inaugurate the concept of the elevated novel we find ourselves thrown into, we need to read *Love Letters* with an eye to how they and others overwrite that text. To write a literary history that includes *Love Letters*, the text must be read for itself (as enunciation, in relation to precursor texts), but also as a novel swirling toward that 'other' reformed novel that engulfs it.

Space does not here permit a detailed reading of Behn's novel within the alternative literary history this essay advocates. However, a very brief discussion of this novel will allow me to suggest how it might displace our literary history of the novel's rise. Published in three installments (1684, 1685, 1687), *Love Letters* is a disguised secret history loosely based upon the scandalous elopement of Henrietta Berkeley with her brother-in-law Forde, Lord Grey of Werke, captain of Monmouth's horse. The novel's extended fictional exploration of infidelity in love, published during the height of the succession crisis, develops a political allegory strongly critical of the infidelity of the English people to the Stuart line. More comprehensively, *Love Letters* is about *love*: its different species, social positionalities, ideal realizations and bathetic collapse. *Love Letters* is also about love *letters*: thus, about the chance for etching (young) love (new), for the first time, and its impossibility; about a rhetoric of the love letter that encompasses both singular inventions and fatal repetitions; about the letter and the spirit of the letter(s) of love; and thus about how a lettered lover's discourse entangles its communicants. Finally, *Love Letters* is about the between that befalls love and its letters. What comes between a 'nobleman' called Philander, and his 'sister'-in-law, Sylvia, is first of all the social law that proscribes their incestuous love. But more significantly there is the gap, space and slippage between love letters that produces tricky contaminating effects. Lovers, to remain lovers, must constantly be sending and receiving, emitting and transmitting the letter and spirit of their love. But in doing so, they are also habitually putting love's arrival at risk. In part 1 of the novel, the fold in their letters results from a recourse to diplomacy (from 'di-ploma,' a folded paper) necessitated by a desire that must disguise itself to survive and achieve its ends. But when the ruses of the diplomatic subject, and its pursuit of its self-interest, become habitual, then that climactic moment of truth – when lovers were to take off all disguises for each other – may never arrive, may be interminably deferred . . . as it is in *Love Letters Between a Nobleman and His Sister*.

How does Behn write a novel that realizes the utopian promise and abysmal possibilities entailed in the three terms: 'love' 'letters' 'between'? Behn braids together two generic types of love narrative, the first-person novel in letters and the third-person low comic novella, into a more capacious third-person narrative that can enclose and critique them both. What results is a dialogical and implicitly intertextual exchange between the grounding assumptions of the two earlier generic types of love narrative, issuing in a more sophisticated and 'modern' interpretation of sexual relations. Like the two most famous novels of letters of Behn's time – the *Letters from a Portuguese*

Nun to a Cavalier and the letters of Heloise and Abelard – part one of Behn's *Love Letters* displays insistently personal interpretations of an excessive self-lacerating passion.[17] Part one of *Love Letters* receives a piquant counterpoint in the novella written by Philander to Octavio in three long letters scattered through parts two and three of the novel (164–72; 232–46; 315–20). This novella within the novel, telling of Philander's seduction of Calista, the wife of the lecherous old Count of Clarinau, resembles the novellas of Boccaccio or Chaucer. The whole is delivered as an entertaining 'sport,' in that urbane style of muted, tongue-in-cheek self-glorification, appropriate to bragging between men about their seduction of women.

The early love story of Philander and Sylvia and the tale of Philander's seduction of Calista confront each other as equally suspect narratives of love: one implausibly exalted, the other comically debased; one naively innocent, the other jaded experience, and both with the same hero – the philandering Philander. By contrast, the third-person narrator who emerges in parts two and three of *Love Letters* produces a story that appears less artfully fictive, and thus more historically plausible. Between parts one and two of *Love Letters* action moves from France to Holland, and love becomes politics pursued by other means.[18] What is called 'love' increasingly entails diplomacy, the assertion of one's self-interest through negotiations, which in its turn requires disguise, a veiling of one's motives and intentions so as to win one's object at the expense of the other. By carrying the novel of amorous intrigue to its logical limit, *Love Letters* opens a coherent ethical critique of earlier genres of love narrative, as well as its own action. Sylvia's use of disguise becomes less instrumental and more habitual; diplomatic maneuvers appear less witty than treacherous, and Octavio's climactic renunciation of the ruses his passion for Sylvia had entailed is cast in an ideal light.

Even this cursory overview of *Love Letters* resituates a theme central to the most influential literary histories of the novel's rise. Thus from Watt to Armstrong to Bender it has been argued, in different terms, that 'the novel' plays a crucial role in the constitution of 'the' modern subject. For example, Armstrong locates in Richardson's *Pamela* the moment when the invention of a certain discursive construct – the 'domestic woman' as the object of Mr. B's desire – established the paradigm for 'the' modern subject, as divorced in some fundamental way from political life. Although this thesis proves useful for the study of later culture, it produces the impression that there is no subjectivity realized in the novel before Richardson. A reading of Aphra Behn's *Love Letters* makes such a hypothesis seem unacceptably modernist in its bias. In fact those selves that come to the reader of *Love Letters* – diplomatic subjects thrown into the 'fatality' of their passion, and making ceaseless use of disguise – elucidate precisely the issue that Armstrong finds Richardson occulting: the politics of subjectivity, its implication in the play of power, the battle of the sexes, the defiles of representation.

The counter-articulations of love, diplomacy and disguise effected by Richardson and Fielding in the 1740s, and later comprehended under the term 'sentimental' and the 'ethics of the good heart,' become part of a fictional program that would do much to change the way early novels like *Love Letters* appear to us today. How this happens is a long story, but I can sketch a few of the ways that Richardson, in his role as an 'organic intellectual,' overwrites the kind of fiction he abhorred.[19] Richardson reinterprets the cardinal terms of the novels of Behn, Manley and Haywood: 'love,' subject to a new critical ambivalence, is devalued, diplomacy is interpreted as selfishness, disguise as deceit. Richardson's method of doing this is quite ingenious. By incorporating the vicious tendencies of the earlier novel within his own male characters and opposing them to his own virtuous, and finally victorious, heroines, Richardson offers an antidote within his own fiction to the poisonous influence of the female novelists.[20] Thus B and Lovelace are possessed by an extravagant morally irresponsible love, a diplomatic pursuit of their self-interest, and a penchant for intrigue and disguise. By contrast, Pamela and Clarissa write a discourse of conduct that develops an explicit critique and alternative to the social values and ideas of the novels of Behn, Manley and Haywood. Their love is not a mighty, autonomous force, but a quite manageable 'inclination,' subordinated to rational estimations of the worth of the beloved; Pamela and Clarissa eschew those who act from self-interest and propound an ethos of strict honesty and spontaneous directness. This program sharply restricts – though, as we have seen, Richardson cannot completely eliminate – the heroine's recourse to disguise.[21] Though Richardson stays with the seduction plot he inherits from the novels and dramas of the Restoration and early eighteenth century, he works a decisive shift in perspective and sympathy. While the novels like *Fantomina* and *Love Letters* are told from the vantage point of the worldly and inventive seducer, the novels of Richardson and Fielding exfoliate around those characters – virtuous, innocent, and often naive – who become the objects of others' plots.[22]

Hegemony and literary history

Although what Homer Brown has called 'the institution of the novel' has passed through a full two and a half centuries, my account of

Richardson's and Fielding's role in rearticulating the novels of Behn, Manley and Haywood suggests that the cultural position of the novel is not fixed, it still pivots within an unstable vortex.[23] Because the elevated novel habitually refers to the popular novel it overwrites, there is a fundamental instability about Richardson's and Fielding's 'program' to elevate the novel. In his recent work, the Marxist theorist Ernesto Laclau offers valuable ways to describe the antagonistic (non)relation of forces that only seem to reach a stable form at moments of cultural and political hegemony. He notes that antagonistic forces have a radical nonrelational alterity to one another, and thus cannot 'know' one another.[24] The privileged first term – here Richardson's and Fielding's novel – can 'violently subordinate' a second term – here, 'the early novel of Behn, Manley and Haywood' – so this contingent 'decision' constitutes an identity ['the novel'] which carries within it the destablizing negativity of this contingent founding instant. But this very application of 'power' – the reformed novel's ability to repress the earlier novel it invokes but disavows – functions also as a limitation on power. The subordinated term is never simply abolished, but is in fact carried forward, in ghostly secondary traces, in the hegemonic cultural formation. This repression is shadowed by certain limits, and the possible breakdown or reversal of this hierarchy of two terms.

In other words, the contingent decision in favor of the reformed novel, once apparently final, is subsequently opened to appeal and repeal, in the light of new contingencies. Richardson's and Fielding's decisive victory for the high-toned morally responsible novel continued to gain consensus into the nineteenth century, and became one of the implicit criteria for a novel's inclusion in the canon. It received no systematic challenge (that I know of) until the polemics of Hardy and D. H. Lawrence on behalf of more realistic 'modern' treatments of sex and love. The recent feminist revaluation of the women novelists of the early eighteenth century seems to depend upon a change in contemporary reinterpretation of what is happening in the novels of Behn, Manley and Haywood: explicit treatments of gender, sexuality and power that have critical currency in our own time. The 1970s also saw the return of 'the romance' – in Harlequin guise – to centrality in popular culture. But you won't find the contemporary romance in the bookstore under a section entitled either 'novel' or 'literature'; you have to look under 'romance' or 'fiction.' It seems the 'elevation of the novel' is still bearing its effects into the contemporary mapping of culture; it is a decision still undergoing review.

Notes

Special thanks to several especially astute critics of early drafts of this article: John Bender, Rick Bogel, Jill Campbell, Bonnie Hain, Deidre Lynch, Paula McDowell and John Richetti.

1. The classical study of eighteenth-century English novelists is Alan Dugald McKillop, *The Early Masters of English Fiction* (Lawrence: University Press of Kansas, 1956), a delimitation of authors accepted and consolidated by Ian Watt in his *The Rise of the Novel* (Berkeley: University of California Press, 1957). These studies have received revision in marxist and Foucaultean studies: Michael McKeon, *The Origins of the English Novel, 1600–1740* (Baltimore: Johns Hopkins University Press, 1987); J. Paul Hunter, *Before Novels: The Cultural Contexts of Eighteenth-Century English Fiction* (New York: W. W. Norton & Co., 1990); Nancy Armstrong, *Desire and Domestic Fiction: A Political History of the Novel* (New York: Oxford University Press, 1987); John Bender, *Imagining the Penitentiary: Fiction and the Architecture of Mind in Eighteenth-Century England* (Chicago: University of Chicago Press, 1987). Hunter, McKeon, Armstrong, and Bender mark the caesura between 'the novel' and its contextual origins in very different ways. Hunter focuses upon the various constituents of culture 'before novels' appeared. McKeon devotes the first two of three parts of his book to the ideological strife that originated 'the Novel,' before leaping to consideration of six canonical novels in the third and final part of the book. While Armstrong focuses the beginning of the novel and the modern self in Richardson's writing of *Pamela*, Bender distributes invention for the 'imagining of the penitentiary' and the subjectivity it entails to Defoe, Fielding and others. In an essay important for my own study, Judith Kegan Gardiner has demonstrated how different currently prevailing conceptions of 'the novel' are used by critics like Michael McKeon to disqualify Aphra Behn's *Love Letters* from consideration as a novel, perhaps the 'first English novel,' and by Jane Spencer to qualify the feminist tendencies of the same novel. See Gardiner's 'The First English Novel: Aphra Behn's *Love Letters*, The Canon, and Women's Tastes,' *Tulsa Studies in Women's Literature* 8 (1985): 201–22.

2. Recent feminist literary histories of the early novel include Jane Spencer, *The Rise of the Woman Novelist: From Aphra Behn to Jane Austen* (Oxford: Blackwell, 1986); Janet Todd, *The Sign of Angellica: Women, Writing, and Fiction, 1660–1800* (London: Virago, 1989); Mary Ann Schofield, *Masking and Unmasking the Female Mind: Disguising Romances in Feminine Fiction, 1713–1799* (Newark: University of Delaware Press, 1990). These feminist reinterpretations of the novel's beginnings in England have many of the qualities of a 'monumental history' (in Nietzsche's sense): they revalue and reappropriate early modern novelistic writing in view of inventing a new women's culture. But there are limits and liabilities entailed in this alternative feminist history. Firstly, the strategies for the lifting of the old repression changes the leading players rather than reconceiving the form of literary history. The history of women's writing is given the same progressive, dialectical shape as canonical and Marxist literary histories, but where male writers were, there shall women writers be – not as the fathers but [as the] mothers of the novel, with not Richardson but Behn as the first English novelist. Secondly, reading anachronistically for precursors of feminism in early modern texts produces a new set of obstacles for understanding the distinct qualities of a novelist like Aphra Behn. Judith Kegan Gardiner (note 1) demonstrates how the various concepts of women's writing invoked by Ruth Perry, Jane Spencer and Nancy Miller produce problems for reading Behn's novel with any sympathy. Gardiner acknowledges various problems with proclaiming any one novel the

'first' novel – it is 'necessarily fallacious' (201) – but she does precisely this for Behn's *Love Letters* as part of an effort to revalue 'women's erotic "formula" fiction' (202).

3. John Frow, *Marxism and Literary History* (Cambridge: Harvard University Press, 1986), 110.

4. John Guillory has offered a powerful critique of attempts, whether from the right or the left, to defend or recast 'the canon' in terms of reified, transhistorical conceptions of value, predicated upon democratic protocols of fair representation. See 'Canonical and Non-Canonical: A Critique of the Current Debate,' *ELH* 54 (1987): 483–527. Rather than ground my revisionary literary history in twentieth-century claims about the value of women's writing, my study seeks to understand why the men and women of the early modern period devalued the many novelists before Richardson. Such a remapping of the terrain of the early novel complicates the 'exclusion' of early popular women novelists from subsequent literary histories. My own study of the early novels of Richardson and Fielding suggests ways in which Behn, Manley and Haywood, although seldom named, are still 'there,' woven into a (secret) affiliation, as the antagonistic 'other' of Richardson and Fielding's novels.

5. On the commingling of the influence of Protestantism and the New Science see McKeon (note 1); for the strife around divergent concepts of reading and the book, see Martha Woodmansee, 'Toward a Genealogy of the Aesthetic: The German Reading Debate of the 1790s,' *Cultural Critique* 11 (1988–89): 203–21.

6. See *A Literary History of England*, ed. Albert C. Baugh (New York: Appleton-Century-Crofts, 1967), 803.

7. Behn's most significant novel, *Love Letters Between a Nobleman and His Sister*, was published in seven editions over the course of the first five decades of the eighteenth century: 1708, 1712, 1718, 1735 (serialized in the *Oxford Journal*), 1736, 1759, 1765. Haywood's collected novels of the 1720s and 1730s were published as *Secret Histories, Novels, and Poems* in four volumes in 1742.

8. Samuel Richardson, *Pamela*, ed. T. C. Duncan Eaves and Ben D. Kimpel (New York: Houghton Mifflin, 1971). All citations of the novel will be to this edition.

9. Richardson follows the same strategy in the anonymous introduction he apparently wrote for the collected novels of Penelope Aubin in 1739. See Wolfgang Zach, 'Mrs. Aubin and Richardson's Earliest Literary Manifesto (1739),' *English Studies: A Journal of English Language and Literature* 62 (1981): 271–85.

10. See Martin C. Battestin, *Henry Fielding: A Life* (London: Routledge, 1989), 414–15.

11. John Richetti, *Popular Fiction before Richardson: Narrative Patterns, 1700–1739* (Oxford: Clarendon, 1969), 8.

12. *Selected Letters of Samuel Richardson*, ed. John Carroll (Oxford: Clarendon, 1964), 46–47.

13. This is the kind of strategy pursued most convincingly for Richardson's *Pamela* in valuable chapters devoted to literary and cultural backgrounds of the novel in McKillop's *Samuel Richardson: Printer and Novelist* (Chapel Hill: University of North Carolina Press, 1936), and Margaret Doody's *A Natural Passion* (Oxford: Clarendon, 1974).

14. Ronald Paulson has pointed out to me the strong resemblance between the scene of Pamela's disguise, and the first plate of Hogarth's *The Harlot's Progress* (1732).

15. The phases are those used by Paula Backscheider in an unpublished manuscript she was kind enough to let me consult, entitled 'The Resisting Text: Women Writing Women.'

16. Like *Love in Excess* (1719–20) and *Clarissa* (1747–48), *Love Letters* was published in three parts, and only subsequently published as a single novel.

17. [Titles vary in English] See the French *Portuguese Letters from a Nun to a Cavalier* (1669) and the English *Five Love-Letters from a Nun to a Cavalier*, trans. Roger L'Estrange (1678). The letters of Heloise (d.1164) and Abelard (d.1142) were first published in France in 1616, and were followed by many imitations and free translations, including John Hughes's translation (1713) and Pope's 'Eloisa to Abelard' published in the 1717 *Works*.

18. Thus during the short time where Sylvia and Philander live together in Holland, Sylvia falls sick, and Philander is forced into exile in Germany. Over the first sixty pages of the novel's second part, [however,] circumstances have changed so a set of political imperatives invade and explode the love dyad, into a fantastic proliferating geometry of no less than eight overlapping love triangles. Octavio becomes friend of Philander and (secret) lover of Sylvia; Brilliard, the tame instrument of Philander, and clandestine husband of Sylvia, emerges as a secretly aspiring lover of Sylvia, and torments himself by listening through the wall to their love-making; Brilliard seduces Sylvia's lady in waiting Antonet, who harbors a secret admiration for Octavio; Philander seduces Calista, sister to Octavio, away from the Count of Clarnau, while continuing to profess his love in letters to Sylvia; later, after Octavio becomes a successful lover to Sylvia, his Uncle Sabastian becomes his rival for Sylvia. To complicate these heterosexual love triangles, there is a strong homoerotic entanglement, quite explicitly addressed by the text, between women (Antonet and Sylvia) as well as between men (Octavio and Philander).

19. Gramsci's term, 'organic intellectual,' is applied to Richardson by Terry Eagleton in *The Rape of Clarissa* (Minneapolis: University of Minnesota Press, 1982), 2–6.

20. The metaphor is Richardson's own. In a letter to Sara Chapone he remarks that three contemporary women writers of scandal are enough to make 'the Behns, the Manleys, and the Heywoods' look white, and calls upon Chapone to develop an 'antidote to these Women's poison.' *Selected Letters*, ed. Carroll, 173.

21. The whole tortured history of the reception of Richardson's work suggests the way it exceeds the ethical program that motivated its writing. Thus, for example, the sentimental program to reform love, and dispense with diplomacy and disguise, has the effect of displacing the self-divisions it would overcome. Thus in order to weave a veil of representation to cover the body of virtue, Richardson develops the blush of modesty, as a privileged, gendered term by which the female heroine may signify her virtue in a divided and contaminated social sphere, without falling prey to its divisions. The blush veils the heroine at the moment where her complicity, guilt, or desire might become readable. But this blush implies the very self-dividedness it would annul.

22. Charlotte Morgan notes that Penelope Aubin seems to be one of the first to work this shift in the use of the seduction scenario. See her valuable early

study, *The Rise of the Novel of Manners: A Study of English Prose Fiction Between 1600 and 1740* (New York: Russell & Russell, 1963). In French literature of the eighteenth century, as late as Laclos and Sade, there is a persistent privileging of the seducer's standpoint. That Richardson gives so much weight and space to the seducer's narrative in *Clarissa* helps to produce the struggle of interpretations around this most ambiguous, and historically conflicted, of the novels of the 1740s.

23. See Homer Brown's essay, 'Of the Title to Things Real: Conflicting Stories,' *ELH* 55 (1989): 917–54.

24. Ernesto Laclau, lecture given at SUNY, Buffalo, Spring 1991.

4 Popular Narrative in the Early Eighteenth Century: Formats and Formulas

JOHN RICHETTI

Two of the most hard-headed and complex assessments of the nature of early narrative fiction before Richardson remain John Richetti's *Popular Fiction before Richardson: Narrative Patterns, 1700–1739* (Oxford: Clarendon Press, 1969), and Margaret Doody's discussion of the early fiction in *A Natural Passion: A Study of the Novels of Samuel Richardson* (Oxford: Clarendon Press, 1974). In his more recent essay from 1985, Richetti presents a general account of this fiction. Richetti combines his sense that it suffers from a certain artistic crudeness, with his view – shared by other critics such as William Warner – that it responds to a number of issues of great cultural and ideological importance to the period during which it was published.

Like most narrative, literary history is drawn to an organic metaphor, the useful analogy whereby literary forms can be thought of as engendered, nourished, and developed toward strength and eventual maturity by just those circumstances historians seek to delineate. Perhaps more than other genres, the eighteenth-century English novel seems especially well served by such an analogy, since the qualities often said to define it – social and psychological realism, moral complexity, narrative self-consciousness – represent for modern criticism a sort of evolutionary pinnacle of narrative achievement.[1]

At the same time, however, the evolutionary analogy has been accompanied by another, almost contradictory, emphasis in literary history that stresses the uniqueness of the major eighteenth-century novelists and identifies their work as a radically new beginning for narrative, recognized as such by the novelists themselves.[2] On the one hand, the eighteenth-century novel seems best and most fully understood within a rich complex of generating circumstances, and literary history like other sorts of history is committed to genetic explanations. And some of the narratives published in England in the late seventeenth and the early eighteenth centuries do resemble in themes and techniques the works of the masters. On the other hand, as modern readers of those narratives have generally agreed, there are no meaningful precursors in them of those same masters. In a now discarded exercise, literary historians used to sift patiently through such material, looking hopefully for small signs of development toward the social and psychological realism, moral complexity, narrative control, and technical sophistication achieved by Defoe, Richardson, and Fielding.[3] They found so pathetically little evidence of evolution that it now seems safe to assert that there are no missing links and that the major English eighteenth-century novelists, in effect, created the genre *ex nihilo*, by sheer force of genius and imagination. Or, to put the case less dramatically and to give the literary historian something to do, Defoe, Richardson, and Fielding transcended their predecessors, not simply refining, extending, or adapting but transforming the narrative themes and techniques available to them. Their crude contemporaries and immediate predecessors, then, serve chiefly to dramatize the force and profound originality of the major novelists.[4]

But these crude materials also acquire from this perspective two kinds of related significance. First, they represent an essential stage for the eruption (if not the evolution) of the eighteenth-century novel, a set of forms (or at least formats) and possibilities that the major novelists could transcend, a necessarily inferior provocation to their genius. Second, and more specifically, these books are evidence of an emerging, crucial shift in the nature and purpose of narrative that affects and indeed promotes the appearance of the major novelists themselves. Minor eighteenth-century narratives point by their very features to a new sort of audience and a changing set of social circumstances surrounding the production and consumption of narrative literature.

Artistically insignificant, then, the forgotten fiction that precedes and surrounds the eighteenth-century masters has at least a sociological relevance for a genre whose emergence is inseparable from changing social conditions. During the early decades of the eighteenth century, certainly, there is a busy, expanding market for prose fiction, and that bookseller's product provokes in different ways, as the century continues, the works of Defoe, Richardson, Fielding, and other novelists: Defoe to serve or exploit some of the market's needs; Richardson to improve, refine, indeed exalt some of those needs; and Fielding to parody and then to transform some of them. What, then, was that market like? What sorts of needs did it serve? Did those needs represent something new for prose fiction? Is the presence of such needs a significant factor in the emergence of the novel in something like its modern form in the early eighteenth century?

To ask such questions and to grant a limited genetic importance to the minor fiction of the early eighteenth century should not obscure the simplified artificiality of our scheme. Then, as now, a variety of narrative formats and purposes competed for attention and served different audiences, and it is a mistake to think in terms of the clear dominance of one particular form of narrative. For example, as Ian Watt points out, the popularity of religious narrative continued unabated. By 1792, Bunyan's *Pilgrim's Progress* had gone through 160 editions, and religious and didactic works remained hugely popular throughout the century.[5] At the other end of narrative possibility, Sidney's *Arcadia* appeared in its fourteenth edition in 1725 and in the same year in a rewritten modern English form.[6] Popular religious allegory and aristocratic romance such as these books represent, however, were both giving way in the early years of the eighteenth century, or at least sharing the stage with a number of other narrative types – some just as traditional, others newer, some modified and modernized versions of romance and religious allegory.[7] To some extent, popular narrative in the early eighteenth century can be said to veer away from the extremes represented by religious allegory and aristocratic romance toward a center of secular factuality, although generalization of this sort is risky and needs immediate qualification. Obviously, Bunyan's enduring popularity stems from his grounding of Christian allegory in the felt experience of that rural working-class life he lived in all its difficulty.

What seems undeniable is that overt fictionality or artificiality ceased to be an attractive or profitable feature, at least in narratives that claimed to be current. In his bibliographic survey of prose narratives published in England from 1700 to 1739, W. H. McBurney found only one *new* English work deliberately labeled a romance. However improbable or conventionally fictional the events within a book might be, McBurney notes, booksellers favored descriptive titles that claimed factuality: history, memoirs, life, voyage (trip, travels, discovery), adventures, tale, letters, and account (journal, relation). Most such books seem patently fictional to a modern reader, and the ones labeled 'novels' were really only shorter, often crudely simplified versions of the elaborate plots of romance.[8] For whatever cultural reasons, many readers seem to have wanted at least the claim of factuality attached to narrative.

In part and at times, this claim was valid; a good deal of narrative from the first half of the century has at least some documentary validity. Given the absence of modern newspapers and other information media, there was a traditional market for news of a sensational sort, notably the lives of criminals, including pirates and prostitutes. Pamphlets, broadsides, even topical ballads for spreading

sensational news or rumors are as old as the hills, but the expansion
of the English printing industry in the early eighteenth century and
the accompanying growth of a reading public (whether cause or effect
of the former) enabled more elaborate publication of such 'news.'[9]
Following a practice stretching back to the late sixteenth century,
short pamphlet accounts of sensational crimes and domestic violence
were still popular in the early decades of the eighteenth, reflecting
the perennial fascination of tabloid journalism. Three examples will
illustrate not just the lurid attractions of these pamphlets but the
journalistic particularity that is an important part of their appeal:

*An Account of a most Barbarous and Bloody Murther Committed on
Sunday last, by Mr. James Smith . . . on the Body of one Mr. Cuff . . . With
an Account of how he mangled his Body in a most Barbarous manner, Cut
off his Left Hand, and Stabb'd him in several places of the Body, leaving
him Dead upon the place, with other particulars relating to the occasion of
that Inhuman Action* (1703).

*The Tryal and Conviction of several Reputed Sodomites, before the Right
Honourable the Lord Mayor, and Recorder of London, at Guild-Hall, the
20th Day of October, 1709.*

*The Cruel Mother. Being a strange and unheard-of Account of one
Mrs. Elizabeth Cole, a Childs Coatmaker in the Minories, that threw her
own Child into the Thames on Sunday Night last, a Girl of about Five Years
of Age. With the manner how the poor Child begg'd of her Mother not to
drown her. . . . Also, an Account of one Sarah Taylor a Maid-Servant, near
Ratcliff-Cross, that Hang'd her self on Tuesday last at her Masters, for the
Love of a Young Man* (1708).

Much of the material in such pamphlets came from more sober
accounts of criminal trials at the Old Bailey, published in the Sessions
Papers. The most popular and presumably authentic accounts of
notorious criminals were the pamphlets issued by Paul Lorrain,
the ordinary (chaplain) of Newgate prison from 1698 to 1719, whose
office made him privy to the last, normally repentant, hours of the
condemned. These pamphlets had an immediate appeal, issued as
they were at eight in the morning following the execution.[10] *The
Ordinary of Newgate's Account of the Life, Conversation, Birth and
Education, of Thomas Ellis, and Mary Goddard. Who were Executed
at Tyburn, on Wednesday, the Third of March, 1708. With the most
Remarkable Passages of their whole Lives and Wicked Actions, from
the time of their Birth, to their untimely Death; as also their Tryal,
Examination, Conviction and Condemnation, at the Old-Bayly, their
Behaviour in Newgate, their Confession, and True Dying-Speeches, at the
Place of Execution* (1708) is a typical sample of Lorrain's apparently
popular enterprise. Sensational and pious, circumstantial and
evangelically generalized, such pamphlets exploited the traditional

drama of sin, repentance, death, and salvation and intensified the appeal of that spectacle by local details, yesterday's events, and ordinary folk caught in the eternal struggle between good and evil.[11]

By 1730, according to F. W. Chandler, the popularity of such crude pamphlets had declined, giving way to more sophisticated criminal biographies (*Moll Flanders* is the most well-known example, but there were various lives of actual offenders like Jonathan Wild and Jack Sheppard) and to more elaborate collections of criminal biography, like the very popular *History of the Lives and Robberies of the Most Noted Highway-Men, Foot-Pads, House-Breakers, Shop-Lifts and Cheats of both Sexes in and about London and Westminster* (1713) by one Captain Alexander Smith.[12] As Chandler pointed out long ago, much of this criminal 'journalism' is rooted in traditional rogue stories, the local and sensational details supplemented or indeed guided by patterns inherited from the myth of the 'trickster' figure and passed on through various subliterary and literary embodiments like Elizabethan ballads and chapbooks, Spanish picaresque fiction, and its French imitators such as Paul Scarron.[13]

And yet in spite of such sources, in spite of the perennial appeal of criminal heroes, it can be argued that the increasingly detailed and specific interest in criminal narrative in the late seventeenth and early eighteenth centuries is significant for the emergence of the novel. Perhaps the criminal increasingly represented an apt expression for many readers of certain feelings of isolation and marginality to which they could respond; perhaps the criminal's attractiveness lay in his or her subversive individuality, an exaggerated or simplified version of what many readers presumably admired or feared. Certainly, such possibilities are exploited in Defoe's pseudo-memoirs of Moll Flanders and Colonel Jacque and in his monumental compilation, *A General History of the Robberies and Murders of the most notorious Pyrates* (1724), where many of the buccaneers are hugely attractive, glamorous, and powerful figures, quasi-mythic embodiments of a ruthless acquisitive individualism.[14]

At the least, criminal narrative, from Paul Lorrain's brief pamphlets to Defoe's extended narratives, suggests a preoccupation with the patterning of individual lives, the connections between individuals and various forms of social environment. Criminal narrative tends to balance two contradictory explanations of behavior: the criminal, a prisoner of circumstance, has either been led astray, or has consciously and horribly deviated from moral norms. Such a life can highlight dramatically both the coercive force of circumstance and the individual's self-defining freedom. Although later fiction is more self-conscious about these issues, some version of such ideological ambiguity is at the heart of most novels.

Lennard Davis has recently underlined and complicated the significance of criminal narrative for the emergence of the novel. Following Michel Foucault's view, Davis sees the criminal, at the moment of execution or in the truthful rendering of his life in print, as a figure of what he calls the novel's 'double discourse.' This is to say, the novel 'is a reaction against social repression' (depicting free and self-defining individuals who are of interest to narrative precisely because of their deviation from social norms), but the novel 'also authorizes that very power of repression at the same time' (the criminal tells his story only because he is about to be executed or is repentant, or his story assumes its meaningful shape only in the moment of capitulation to a necessity greater than himself).[15] Davis's 'double discourse' is a provocative notion, pointing to other contradictions at the heart of the novel that are highlighted by criminal narrative. For example, the novelist in the early eighteenth century claims to tell the truth but in fact invents a lie to bring the reader to some sort of moral truth. Like the criminal, says Davis, the novelist is both an 'example and dis-example'; the novelist's lies are like the criminal's transgressions, immoral preconditions to a moral end.[16]

To be sure, such critical paradoxes have their limitations, since the early eighteenth-century literary marketplace includes other sorts of popular narrative featuring less controversial characters. The traveler, like the criminal, is a figure of perennial interest and, like the early novelist, something of a liar. The loose mixture of fact, exaggeration, and plain invention in the enormous mass of travel literature from the seventeenth and early eighteenth centuries has been charted by various scholars, notably P. G. Adams.[17] The pirate, of course, is the traveler as criminal, and the popularity of Defoe's *History of the Pyrates*, a book that effectively establishes the buccaneer as a mythical figure who is still a part of the popular imagination, points to the force of the combination. Defoe surrounds his pirates with impressive documentation – biographical details, statistics, casualties, judicial proceedings, etc. – but the accounts of some of them, like 'Blackbeard' (Captain Edward Teach), Bartho Roberts, and Captain Misson, serve purposes that run counter to historical realism. They provide, for example, exotic locales, stirring adventure, daring exploits, thrilling cruelties, and moral-satiric commentary on ordinary society. In short, pirate biography can be both real and fantastic; it is defined much of the time in Defoe's book by a combination of carefully documented actuality and an imaginative rendition of the extraordinary.[18]

Something like that combination animates other apparently fictional narratives featuring travelers who stay within the law. *Robinson Crusoe* (1719) is the most subtle and well known of such

narratives, and it provoked various imitators throughout the
eighteenth century. A convenient example is William Chetwood's
*The Voyages, Dangerous Adventures, and imminent Escapes of Captain
Richard Falconer: Containing the Laws, Customs, and Manners of the
Indians of America . . . Intermix'd with the Voyages and Adventures of
Thomas Randal, of Cork, Pilot: with his Shipwreck in the Baltick . . .
Written by Himself, now alive* (1720).[19] Titles like this advertise the
complementary satisfactions of travel adventure narrative: educational
and informative, providing facts about other cultures gathered first-
hand by an actual person, the book is also exciting and unusual, full
of 'imminent Escapes' and 'Dangerous Adventures.' Falconer's story
is an adventure-travelogue, a series of near-disasters (shipwrecks,
encounters with hostile natives and pirates, captivities, ingenious
and daring escapes) and commercial transactions. Like *Robinson
Crusoe*, on which it is clearly modeled, it features regular affirmations
of providential design in the middle of all this tremendous variety
of incident and locale, the religious moments acting as a sort of
ideological check to the ingenuity, daring, and self-reliance of
the heroes.

The Voyages of Captain Falconer is a clumsy book, clearly a hasty
attempt to exploit the pattern of adventure stories just made popular
by Defoe. But it is also an energetic, entertaining narrative, hardly as
penetrating psychologically as Defoe's best work but less pious than
Crusoe and immensely readable. Martin Green has seen in Defoe's
adventure novels (and he could have included spirited imitations
like *Falconer*) a rival tradition to what he calls the 'novel of courtship'
or domestic realism that came to dominate the English narrative
tradition. Green proposes an elaborate cultural theory to account
for the demotion of the adventure novel to the rank of popular or
children's literature, the essence of which is that the adventure novel
expresses rather too overtly a myth of European imperialism that
literary intellectuals felt uncomfortable with, preferring an opposite
'myth' of domestic order and an interiorized psychological-moral
adventure in place of the crudely external travel adventure story.[20]
Part of Green's thesis makes good sense if we look at one sequence
in *Falconer*.

Near the end of his adventures, Falconer is separated from his
shipmates while on shore getting wood and water. Captured by
Indians, he is made a member of the tribe and given a wife. 'But I
had no great Stomach to my Bride, although a young, well-featur'd
Woman, yet her Complexion did not like me.' She proves lovable,
however: 'Loving and Courteous, and nothing like the rest of the
Savage Crew, who were prone to all manner of Wickedness . . . I
really began to love her and only wish'd she had been my Wife in

the usual Forms.' One day when Falconer wanders into a vale that his wife has warned him he must not enter, he is seized and bound to a stake by Indians from a rival tribe. In a scene depicted on the frontispiece of the first edition, these Indians 'set fire to the Wood which enclos'd me' and dance around him in various grotesque and threatening postures as he looks up past palm trees and high mountains to a dark sky, confident and untrembling, an English St. Sebastian. A storm breaks and extinguishes the flames; another group of Indians appears and defeats Falconer's captors; his wife rushes in and frees him, but she is killed as they attempt to run away. In the end, Falconer escapes, taking an Indian who has been his friend and guide and who becomes his servant when they settle in England.

This sequence offers solid emotional and ideological satisfactions to willing readers: action in an exotic locale, a brave and resourceful hero who also trusts in providential pattern, the titillation of miscegenation with a racist solution in self-sacrificing love, suspense and pleasing dread in the presence of the savage non-European 'other,' and the eventual defeat and rejection of the exotic culture we have sampled. Unlike Swift's parodic reversal in *Gulliver's Travels*, travel adventure like this implicitly confirms the superiority of home; it validates the ordinary by allowing its readers to exhaust and indeed to domesticate the extraordinary. In its confused variety of scene and action, *Falconer* has little time for psychological development. The emphasis in travel adventure tends naturally away from seeking the depths of personality in experience to depicting breadth and extent of experience. Even Defoe's *Colonel Jacque*, a rather more specific and historical and less melodramatic narrative, promises its readers the same sort of pleasures as *Falconer*; witness its charming title page: *The History and Remarkable Life of the Truly Honourable Col. Jacque. . . . Who was Born a Gentleman, put 'Prentice to a Pick-Pocket, was Six and Twenty Years a Thief, and then Kidnapp'd to Virginia. Came back a Merchant, married four Wives, and five of them prov'd Whores; went into the Wars, behav'd bravely, got Preferment, was made Colonel of a Regiment, came over, and fled with the Chevalier, and is now abroad, compleating a Life of Wonders, and resolves to dye a General* (1722).

A review of the English fiction that survives from 1700 to 1739 yields only a few examples of such extended and unified travel adventure narratives.[21] Variety of scene and action was, however, an advertised feature of more traditional anthologies of shorter narratives. Charles Gildon's *The Golden Spy: or, A Political Journal of the British Nights Entertainments of War and Peace, and Love and Politicks: Wherein are laid open, The Secret Miraculous Power and Progress of Gold, in the Courts of Europe. Intermix'd with Delightful Intrigues, Memoirs, Tales, and Adventures Serious and Comical* (1709) initiates a narrative tradition of using an inanimate object to tell a story.[22] But as the title page makes clear, these stories have more in common with Chaucer or Boccaccio than Defoe. The 'golden spy' is a French gold coin (a *louis d'or*) who was part of Jove's golden shower in the rape of Danae, is now in the author's purse, and relates all the scandalous events he has seen. Various other coins, including an English guinea, take part in telling lascivious satirical tales, mostly of comic adultery and other sexual escapades. Supervising these rough-and-ready entertainments is a satiric leveling and comic reduction of rank and pretense. The narrator asks the golden spy for news of 'the *Camp* and the *Court*, which were places I had but little acquaintance with.' The coin invokes the comic inevitability of the ordinary, a theme repeated in many of the stories:

> You must not [replied he] expect to find Princes and Great Men
> such Gods as their Flatterers and Idolaters make 'em, or so exalted
> in Wisdom and Virtue as in Riches or Degree. Alas! their Failings
> and Follies, as well as Vices, are as numerous as those of other
> Men: Nay, I who have been admitted into their closets, have
> been Witness of such Transactions as the meanest of their Subjects
> would have blush'd at. These Demi-gods, whom some Men
> reverence as things of a superior nature in many particulars, in
> all Ages, have discover'd themselves to be much less than Men.
>   (pp. 31–32)

The old satiric attitude that all men, seen up close, are morally equal can also point to a newer interest in the ordinary or the domestic or the grossly material and biological as the only valid categories of experience. At first glance, this newer domestic or reductive realism is more prominent in Gildon's other narrative anthology, *The Post-Man Robb'd of his Mail: or, the Packet broke open* (1719).[23] The author-editor, Sir Roger de Whimsey, echoes Addison and Steele's Sir Roger de Coverley and claims in his preface to follow in their wake: 'I find most Readers are of my Mind, and love not to dwell long on any thing. This gave Success to the *Tatlers*, the *Spectators*, the *Lay-Monk*, and the like, which are a Sort of Epistles to the Publick, such as I now present, tho' not in the same Form.' The book consists of commentary on letters stolen by the members of the club, a series of essayistic, generalized discussions of set satirical situations illustrating moral topics such as the lewdness of women, the avarice of old men, the cupidity of lawyers, the intellectual pride of irreligious wits, and so on. Behind their jocular pretense to journalistic veracity, Gildon's energetic collections exemplify an older, less intense, less specific mode of narration, overtly committed to moral and satiric patterns and taking pleasure in the priority of exemplary moral types over particular personages. Popular as this mode of narration remained (it is, of course, preserved in novelists like Fielding), its essayistic moral manner is less prominent in the popular market of the time than the amatory novella, a much more involving and less sophisticated sort of narrative.

In terms of numbers, at least, the market for fiction in the first forty years or so of the eighteenth century was clearly dominated by amatory fiction, narratives (mostly short, novella length) often subtitled histories or secret histories or memoirs, sometimes original English productions, often translations of foreign authors. 'A small tale, generally of love,' is Johnson's definition of 'novel' in his *Dictionary of the English Language* (1755), and he was thinking of the short amatory narratives that seem to have replaced as main purveyors of this theme the enormous and elaborate French heroic romances of the seventeenth century. The latter had enjoyed a considerable vogue in the late seventeenth century, but even then their English translators felt it necessary to defend them against 'the charge of unreality.'[24] Indeed, a recurring theme in various early eighteenth-century comments on fiction is the need for rejecting an unreal artificiality, represented by just these French romances, and for developing a native truthful simplicity and naturalness.[25]

In the preface to her *Secret History of Queen Zarah and the Zarazians* (1705), Mary Manley notes that the French romances have been replaced by books such as 'the little Histories' she offers for sale. The virtue of such 'histories,' she says, lies essentially in eliminating those features of the romances that have 'given a distaste to persons of good sense,' their 'prodigious length . . . the mixture of so many extraordinary adventures, and the great number of actors that appear on the stage, and the likeness which is so little managed.'[26] Manley goes on to recommend a moderate realism, involving consistent and probable characters with 'passions, virtues, or vices, which resemble humanity' and a moral neutrality in which the author 'ought neither to praise nor blame those he speaks of . . . contented with exposing the actions, leaving an entire liberty to the reader to judge as he pleases' (pp. 24, 25).

Manley's preface is not entirely consistent, for she also emphasizes two sorts of authorial manipulation. First, she tends to stress the reader's involvement when the author achieves characters and actions that are familiar. The result is a 'curiosity and a certain impatient desire to see the end of the accidents, the reading of which causes an exquisite pleasure when they are nicely handled' (p. 24). At the same time, Manley pays lip service throughout to conventional eighteenth-century didactic notions, and she concludes her preface by reaffirming her commitment to recommend virtue and discourage vice. But the reader she evokes is caught up in events and personalities, instructed by a powerful involvement in the narrative.

'Tis an indispensable necessity to end a story to satisfy the disquiets of the reader, who is engaged to the fortunes of those people whose adventures are described to him; 'tis depriving him of a most delicate pleasure when he is hindered from seeing the event of an intrigue which has caused some emotion in him, whose discovery he expects, be it either happy or unhappy. The chief end of History is to instruct and inspire into men the love of virtue and abhorrence of vice by the examples proposed to them; therefore the conclusion of a story ought to have some tract of morality which may engage virtue. Those people who have a more refined virtue are not always the most happy, but yet their misfortunes excite the readers' pity and affects them. Although vice be not always punished, yet 'tis described with reasons which shew its deformity and make it enough known to be worthy of nothing but chastisements.

(pp. 26–27)

This passage deserves quotation because, in spite of Manley's attempt to voice a modest moral realism, she points to the central and significant confusion behind a good deal of the amatory fiction of the early eighteenth century. The reader's excited participation ('pleasure' is Manley's recurrent term) is in fact what matters for her in such fiction; didactic clarity is subordinated in practice to the emotional needs of the reader, who learns about virtue and vice chiefly by inspiration and engagement rather than 'moral reflections, maxims, and sentences' – which are 'more proper in discourses for instructions than in Historical Novels' (p. 26). In the fiction Manley and others actually wrote, the traditional literary ideal of moral instruction shifts strongly away from a combination of edifying scene and moralizing discourse toward a proto-sentimentalism that is in practice as morally confused as it is emotionally intense and ideologically coherent. By and large, the popular amatory novella quickly disregards its claims to domestic moral realism and constructs a world of sexual fantasy and thrilling moral melodrama, a world where persecuted female innocence is exploited by male corruption, sexual and financial. As we shall see, there are a few exceptions, witty and well-shaped moral tales, but they prove the popular rule.

Manley's preface is totally inconsistent in its defense of sense, clarity, and probability, for *Queen Zarah*'s characters are monsters of vice, their language rhetorically swollen, and the scenes and actions wildly exaggerated. In fact, the book is not a collection of 'little Histories' but a *chronique scandaleuse* attacking Sarah, Duchess of Marlborough. As a narrative format, the scandal chronicle has a long, dishonorable pedigree.[27] Collections of rumor, libel, and scandal about prominent people, these 'secret histories' began to be especially popular in England during the late seventeenth century. Manley achieved special notoriety and tremendous popularity a few years after *Queen Zarah* with *Secret Memoirs and Manners of several Persons of Quality, of Both Sexes from the New Atalantis, an Island in the Mediteranean* [sic] (1709).[28]

Like *Queen Zarah*, *The New Atalantis* is a collection of scurrilous, often nearly pornographic, incidents involving Whig nobles and politicians, notably the Duke and Duchess of Marlborough. The stories have some small basis in fact, and the book was designed as Tory propaganda to undermine public confidence in the Whig ministry, which fell from power in 1710. Manley's enormous success is easy enough to explain: her scandals were mostly sexual (usually false or grotesquely exaggerated), and she had a talent for vividly rendering what the eighteenth century often called 'warm scenes.' Like other such narratives, *The New Atalantis* has an elaborate moral structure and claims to be an outraged satiric attack on the corruption of the times. It is actually a lubriciously delighted version of life at the English court from the Restoration to the early years of the reign of Queen Anne. Manley begins Part II by calling her book a satire 'on different Subjects, Tales, Stories, and Characters of Invention, after the Manner of Lucian, who copy'd from Varro.' For a modern reader, the best parts of the book are precisely the satiric ones, those recurring energetic denunciations that add up to a lively, often grotesque panorama of intrigue, lust, betrayal, and even crime. *The New Atalantis* was reprinted several times until 1736, long after its scandals had faded, suggesting that Manley's real achievement was the effective imagining of a mythical world of corruption and immorality in which readers found satisfactions that were neither satiric nor political.

One incident from the book will serve as an example of how Manley's gossip is accommodated to the imaginative world of the melodramatic amatory novella. Near the end, we are introduced to Lady Diana, married to the old and rich Conde de Bedamore but desired by Don Tomasio Rodriquez (the 'Key' to the book identifies these characters as Lady Diana Cecil, Lord Scudamore, and Lord Coningsby). Manley's description of Lady Diana is a set piece, an almost abstract and totally formulaic evocation of female desire.

Her Person lovely, as the most lovely Imagination could form it.
The darting Lustre of her Eyes, were like the Lightnings Flash,
so awful and so piercing. But having cast the dazling Death, they
roul'd into a rest from Fire, and gave the Gazers an Alternative
of pleasing Pain, with leave to wonder at their various Beauty,
for Languishments would take their turn, and show the Mine of
Love within. A mine which threw abroad such Sparkles of desire,
as spoke the amorous Temper of the Fair: She was the Queen of
Love herself, in all her Attributes! so bright, so soft, so warming,
so enviting, so envited, as if she languish'd for a part of that
Delight, which her Beauties must necessarily inspire into the
Hearts of her Beholders.[29]

Such writing is deliberately indifferent to anything but the reader's
capacity for erotic fantasy; indeed, it presupposes an eager reader
able to construct a picture of desire from this formulaic sketch. The
'power of love' (which was Manley's title for a collection of amatory
novellas she published in 1720) is irresistible, and this outline of the
signs and effects of desire prepares readers for the inevitable warm
scene between Diana and Don Tomasio. He, naturally, is also married,
but 'no sooner did he see the Day of Madame de Bedamore's Eyes;
but he thought to himself he had hitherto wander'd in unaccountable
Darkness!' (p. 221).

Since the Conde de Bedamore has agreed to rebuild his country
house to suit his wife's continental taste, Tomasio offers part of his
house to the couple, and to Diana he offers his passion. She resists,
and resolves not to see him. He feigns departure, but returns on a
day when her husband is away and finds Diana in the garden. What
follows is Manley's recurrent erotic moment, the soft-core rape-
seduction extravaganza that was her signature as a popular narrator.

It was the Evening of an excessive hot Day, she got into a shade
of Orange Flowers and Jessamine, the Blossoms that were fallen
cover'd all beneath with a profusion of Sweets. A Canal runs by,
which made that retreat delightful as 'twas fragrant. Diana, full of
the uneasiness of Mind that Love occasion'd, threw her self under
the pleasing Canopy, apprehensive of no Acteon to invade with
forbidden Curiosity, her as numerous perfect Beauties, as had the
Goddess. Supinely laid on that repose of Sweets, the dazling Lustre
of her Bosom stood reveal'd, her polish'd Limbs all careless and
extended show'd the Artful Work of Nature. . . . [Tomasio] vow'd
he wou'd not make himself possessor of one Charm without her
willing leave; he sighed, he look'd with dying! wishing! Soft-
regards! The lovely she grew calm and tender! The Rhetorick of

one belov'd, his strange bewitching Force; she suffer'd all the
glowing pressures of his roving Hand; that Hand, which with
a Luxury of Joy, wander'd through all the rich Meanders of her
Bosom; she suffer'd him to drink her dazling naked Beauties at
his Eyes! to gaze! to burn! to press her with unbounded Rapture!
taking by intervals a thousand eager short-breath'd Kisses. Whilst
Diana, lull'd by the enchanting Poison Love had diffus'd
throughout her form, lay still, and charm'd as he! – she thought
no more! – she could not think! – let Love and Nature plead the
weighty Cause! – let them excuse the beautous Frailty! – Diana
was become a Votary to Venus! – obedient to the Dictates of the
Goddess.

(pp. 227–29)

Tomasio's wife discovers them *in flagrante* and vows to reveal all, and
at last Tomasio returns to her, leaving Diana to the forgiveness of her
husband. This resolution is quite tame. Many of Manley's swollen
anecdotes are much more violent and melodramatic, involving
outright rape, incest, fake marriages, and suicide. But sensational
violence is always subordinate to voyeurism, to pseudo-elegant
evocation of sexual fantasy like the one above. *The New Atalantis*
is necessarily indifferent to narrative values such as individuality
and depth of characterization, complexity of scene and plot, and
linguistic self-consciousness. Characters and narrator inhabit without
embarrassment a stylized world of moral and emotional simplicity,
indeed a narrative world in which the chief attraction is the utterly
predictable repetition of character, scene, and language.

That there is always a large and eager audience for formula fiction
of this sort is evident from the career of Eliza Haywood, Manley's
successor in the 1720s as the chief purveyor of sensational amatory
fiction. Haywood produced a highly successful imitation of Manley's
secret history in her *Memoirs of a Certain Island Adjacent to the Kingdom
of Utopia* (1725). The satiric occasion for the book's denunciations
of the rich and powerful was the so-called 'South-Sea Bubble'
financial disaster of 1720, but the book's main appeal was the
near-pornographic intensity and lurid melodrama of its recurring
sexual scenes. Unlike Manley, Haywood was not a political writer,
and her tremendous output of popular narrative during the 1720s
repeats tirelessly the formulas of the amatory novella, occasionally
extended to novel length (several hundred pages).

Haywood began her career in 1719–20 with *Love in Excess; or,
the Fatal Enquiry*, a novel in three parts, a great success that reached
a seventh edition in 1732. During the decade that followed she
published some thirty-eight original works, translated a number of

French novellas, and wrote three plays.[30] In stories such as *Idalia: or, the Unfortunate Mistress* (1723), *Lasselia; or, the Self-Abandon'd* (1723), *The Injur'd Husband: or, the Mistaken Resentment* (1723), *The Fatal Secret; or, Constancy in Distress* (1724), *The Force of Nature: or, the Lucky Disappointment* (1725), *The Distress'd Orphan; or, Love in a Mad House* (1726), *Philidore and Placentia: or, L'Amour trop Delicat* (1727), and *Love-Letters on All Occasions Lately passed between Persons of Distinction* (1730), Haywood rehearsed with unfailing energy and only slight variations the popular formula promised in her titles: a format highlighting genteel, euphemistic but effectively pornographic descriptions of female passion and male lust, and featuring most of the time aristocratic elegance and corruption.[31] Typically, a young girl is pursued by a treacherous suitor in a complicated social or moral situation that sometimes includes incest as well as adultery. Seduction or outright rape is standard, and terrible consequences invariably follow, even violent death and sometimes grim revenge on the seducer. At the center of all this operatic melodrama is the 'power of love,' an irresistible but, for women, a destructive urge whose thrilling, forbidden intensities and pathetically satisfying tragic aftermath Haywood's stories were designed to elaborate. A prefatory poem in her 1732 collected *Secret Histories, Novels and Poems* identifies her methods and certifies her success: 'Persuasion waits on all your bright Designs, / And when you point the Varying Soul Inclines: / See! Love and Friendship, the fair Theme inspires, / We glow with Zeal, we melt in soft Desires!'

A scene like this one from her first novel, *Love in Excess*, is entirely representative of her style and method and recalls the scene I have quoted from *The New Atalantis*. The virginal heroine, Melliora, is asleep: her 'Gown and the rest of her Garments were white, all ungirt, and loosely flowing, discover'd a Thousand Beauties, which modish Formalities conceal.' Melliora dreams of her guardian (to whom she was entrusted by her dying father), the handsome Count D'Elmont, and he enters to steal a chaste goodnight kiss. But the scene erupts with Haywoodian eroticism complicated by the moral melodrama of near-incest. D'Elmont hesitates as he gazes on the luscious but innocent Melliora; he thinks 'it pity even to wake her, but more to wrong such Innocence.' But as he stoops to her, she embraces him as part of her dream, and we are off:

> He tore open his Waistcoat, and joyn'd his panting Breast to hers, with such a Tumultuous Eagerness! Seiz'd her with such a Rapidity of Transported hope Crown'd Passion, as immediately wak'd her from an imaginary Felicity, to the Approaches of a Solid one. Where have I been? (said she, just opening her Eyes) where

am I? – (And then coming more perfectly to her self) Heaven!
What's this? – I am d'Elmont (Cry'd the O'erjoy'd Count) the
happy D'Elmont! Melliora's, the Charming Melliora's D'Elmont! O,
all ye Saints, (Resum'd the surpriz'd Trembling fair) ye Ministring
Angels! Whose Business 'tis to guard the Innocent! Protect and
Shield my Virtue! . . . Come, come no more Reluctance (Continu'd
he, gathering Kisses from her soft Snowy Breast at every Word).
Damp not the fires thou hast rais'd with seeming Coiness!
I know thou art mine! All mine! And thus I – Yet think (said she
Interrupting him, and Strugling in his Arms) think what 'tis you
would do, nor for a Moments Joy, hazard your Peace for Ever.
By Heaven, cry'd he: I will this Night be Master of my Wishes,
no matter what to Morrow may bring forth.[32]

The simple structural principle in *Love in Excess* is delayed rape,
a protracted eroticism or extended foreplay intensified by the crudest
sort of moral melodrama. But one detail in this scene is especially
revealing. Melliora finds to her confusion no clear distinction between
dream and reality; in fact, the latter is even more compelling and
confusing for her than the former. Haywood's novels of the 1720s are
virtually unreadable nowadays, but they are an important expression
of a vigorously insistent sort of the crisis of subjectivity that becomes
in due course the central theme of much serious fiction. Women
in eighteenth-century popular fiction, as Ruth Perry observes,
are 'imprisoned, seduced, abducted, raped, abandoned, and their
passively outraged responses to these developments are carefully
detailed.' By and large, Perry suggests, the only act granted women
in this fiction is self-examination, bewildered observation of
their own psychological instability and social marginality.[33] Even
(or perhaps especially) in Haywood's formula fiction, women are
symbolic figures who enact in melodramatic fashion the marginal
status and limited basis of female identity that many eighteenth-
century readers seem to have found truthful and moving (or perhaps
simply reassuring). The popularity of formula fiction like Haywood's,
in short, points to a definition of psychosexual differences that is
of profound importance in the development of the novel with its
particular notions of personality. Women in the psychological novel
that develops eventually, as Myra Jehlen shrewdly proposes, 'define
themselves and have power' only in the 'interior life,' and androgyny
becomes 'a male trait enabling men to act from their male side and
feel from their female side.'[34]

However pathetically helpless she made her heroines, of course,
Haywood herself seems to have been an independent, successful
writer, and there is an implicit feminist awareness in her works that

flares out occasionally: in *The British Recluse* (1722), two women find they have been violated by the same man and resolve to live together in the country, 'happy in the real friendship of each other.'[35] But even a plot resolution like this bears out Jehlen's point that psychological interiority is *the* defining female trait in such fiction, a source of strength but simultaneously a capitulation to and affirmation of the division of psychosocial reality along the patriarchal lines that generate in the first place the harrowing plots of female formula fiction.

Contemplative rejection of the male world rather than defiance of it, then – self-absorption and examination as the defining and compensatory female acts – is what Haywood dramatizes here and makes explicit in, for example, the dedication to *The Fatal Secret* (1724). This is a defiant sort of apology for the subject matter of the novel that makes a virtue of her limitations: 'But as I am a Woman, and consequently depriv'd of those Advantages of Education which the other Sex enjoy, I cannot so far flatter my Desires, as to imagine it in my Power to soar to any Subject higher than that which Nature is not negligent to teach us.' To write about love, she continues, 'requires no Aids of Learning, no general Conversation, no Application; a shady Grove and purling Stream are all Things that's necessary to give us an Idea of the tender Passion.' But this sleep of reason that female authors like Haywood allow to possess them produces monsters, male and female, whose active/passive sadomasochistic intertwinings look forward to Richardson's intense dramatization of a similar relationship in *Clarissa*.

Consider in this regard Haywood's *The Mercenary Lover: or, The Unfortunate Heiresses. Being a True, Secret History of a City Amour* (1726). The story looks interesting at first glance for its nod to local realism, its attention to money as well as love. Clitander, a 'Trader' but a 'Master of Accomplishments rare to be found in a Man of his Station,' marries a rich country heiress, Miranda.[36] Quickly tiring of her and anxious to secure the other half of the family fortune, which her sister holds, he sets out to seduce Althea, plying her with 'certain gay Treatises which insensibly melt down the Soul, and make it fit for amorous Impressions, such as the Works of *Ovid*, the late celebrated *Rochester*, and many other of more modern Date' (p. 17). Ludicrous enough, such a strategy for seduction points to an interesting contradiction in the standard amatory plot. Otherwise intelligent female characters like Althea are manipulated by seducers like Clitander, who exploit their helpless ignorance of psychosexual fundamentals obvious, one would think, to anyone past puberty. When female passion explodes, it is mysterious and irresistible, grounded in this disabling female ignorance. Haywood defers to Althea's inexpressible confusion:

But with what Words is it possible to represent the mingled
Passions of *Althea's* Soul, now perfectly instructed in his Meaning;
Fear, Shame, and Wonder combating with the softer Inclinations,
made such a wild Confusion in her Mind, that as she was about
to utter the Dictates of the one, the other rose with contradicting
Force, and stop'd the Accents e're she cou'd form them into
Speech; in broken Sentences she sometimes seem'd to favour, then
to discourage his Attempts, but all dissolv'd and melted down by
that superior Passion, of which herself till now was ignorant she
had entertain'd, never had Courage to repel the growing Boldness,
with which he every Moment encroach'd upon her Modesty . . .
Action was now his Business, and in this Hury of her Spirits, all
unprepared, incapable of Defence, half yielding, half reluctant, and
scarce sensible of what she suffer'd, he bore her trembling to the
Bed, and perpetrated the cruel Purpose he had long since contriv'd.
(pp. 23–24)

Eventually, Clitander poisons Althea, who dies in agonies physical
and spiritual, 'Ravings so horrible and shocking, that they imprinted
a Terror on the Minds of those present, which for a great while they
were not able to wear off' (p. 54).

The Mercenary Lover is a painful book to read, as melodramatic as
anything Haywood wrote but convincing as an image of female
hopelessness in the face of male power and guile. Popular eighteenth-
century female fantasy seems drawn to elaborated self-hatred and
destruction, fascinated evocations of rape and murder. Although
happy endings and imposed moral symmetries are often employed
to negate the pain of such imagining, Haywood's artless dreaming
of what 'Nature is not negligent to teach' reveals a sort of cartoon
version of women's psychological complicity in their double
oppression: exploited sexually and economically by men, and
betrayed into that exploitation by their own irresistible, wayward
sexuality.[37]

Haywood's successful formula, then, is not simply a careless,
thrilling blend of sex and violence; rather, it is thrilling precisely
because it is a balance of erotic effects and psychological consolations
with profound cultural implications. This conclusion is reinforced
by brief consideration of some representative examples of similar
amatory tales that appeared during the period of her great
popularity. Some are variations from the Haywoodian norm that
seem to have been relative failures. Others conform more exactly
to the pattern and were slightly more successful.

The audience for the amatory novella seems not to have been
attracted by the bluntly sensational brutality that sold so well in

some criminal biographies. A collection of uncompromisingly brutal stories, *Lovers Tales: In Several New Surprising and Diverting Stories* (1722), apparently did not reach a second edition, in spite of what is to a modern view a fairly concise and realistic presentation and a refreshing lack of moral posturing: 'The relations are concise, and 'tis hoped will prove diverting to the Reader, which is the only Aim of the Author.'[38] Some of these are rough-and-tumble stories, fairly free of the pathetic, full of violence and sex of a straightforward, traditional kind. In the first of them, for example, a rich old man marries a young girl. She acquires a lover, her husband's nephew, who not only tricks the old man but manages to inherit his fortune. Similar in its rough cuckold baiting is 'The Pleasant Adventure of the Doctor and the Scholar, about the Art of making Love,' in which the clerk receives lessons on seduction from the doctor. The woman on whom this quick scholar practices the art turns out to be the doctor's wife. The old doctor is not only cuckolded but beaten and bound in chains. Perhaps all this is too close to the simple amorality of the folk-tale for the pseudo-sophisticated audience that bought Haywood's hugely moralistic love tragedies.

Haywood's persecuted maiden is nowhere in sight in the next story, 'The Cruel Revenge of a young Lady on a Gentleman who promised her Marriage, but deceiv'd her.' Hector, a young Venetian nobleman, promises Leonice that he will marry her and is, on the strength of this, admitted to her bed. After a time, Hector reconsiders; it is soon announced that he is to marry Clelia, a lady of suitable wealth and position. Leonice persuades Hector to visit her again, drugs him, ties him up, and then dismembers him with ritualistic cries, a female avenging angel of a horrible sort:

> Infamous Man, said she, it is now that at the Peril of my own
> Life I come to revenge the Affront thou hast done me. Thou hast
> ravished from me my Honour, and I will take from thee thy
> Life. . . . I will begin thy Punishment with that deceitful Tongue,
> which hath been one of the first Instruments of my Disgrace. No
> sooner had she pronounced these words, but she took a Razor and
> slit his Tongue in the middle.
>
> (pp. 42–43)

She then pulls out his eyes, cuts off his genitals, and stabs him in the heart. To complete the story, she takes poison and denounces Hector with her dying breath before the Venetian court.

Having read Haywood, we know that this spectacular vengeance violates the central moral precept of the formula story. Leonice begins as a pragmatist who agrees to marriage and, worse, to premarital sex before she loves Hector. Only after she gives herself to Hector does she come to love him, which may be psychologically accurate but is past forgiveness within the ideology of the amatory novella. The ritual murder, obviously, is a further violation, offending as much by its shocking aggressiveness as by its extravagance. Heroines may kill seducers occasionally, but only by an involuntary reflex when fate provides the circumstances.

This collection looks like an uncertain attempt to please a public taste that in 1722 could confer enormous success on both *Love in Excess* and *Moll Flanders*. The sensationally specific journalistic titles and the gory crimes depicted point to an attempted compromise between the novella and the criminal pamphlet or novel. But the brutality must have been excessive for the audience that bought love tales. As the third decade of the century wore on, Haywood's dominance continued; her amazing production held steadily until about 1727, and her influence and popularity were plain until well after that.[39] Two anonymous novellas from the late 1720s will serve to illustrate the persistence of her formula and, by comparison, the special skill with which she exploited it.

All of the moral simplifications of the Haywoodian tale are packed into a novella short enough to be an epitome of the fable of endangered innocence, *The Treacherous Confident; or, Fortune's Change* (1728). Allegorical simplicity and moral melodrama are the main values here, as innocence is threatened and rescued miraculously within twenty-two pages. We are in Castile, where Syphon, an eminent nobleman, has retired to the country with his only daughter, Almiana. She is a paragon of 'Virtue, Sense and Beauty,' and is in love with Thetes, himself a 'generally belov'd and admir'd' noble youth now in exile owing to the king's unjust displeasure with him. Almiana continues to love and even glories in misfortune, 'to make her Love the more apparently Great and Constant; and resolv'd to persevere in her Affection, or wait the Event of Time, and sink with her Love.'[40] Further afflictions and a specific adversary are provided in the person of Scomes, a treacherous courtier who petitions the king for Almiana's hand. She declares that she loves Thetes, and Scomes resolves to murder Thetes. The latter is saved when he deviates from his route to save a lady from a ravisher. This lady turns out to be the king's niece. The narrator pauses to remind us of the moral implications of these fortunate accidents: 'How omnipotent is the Preservation of the Almighty Being! which protects the Innocent and Meritorious from the Snares of the Envious and Cruel' (p. 16). Scomes does shoot a traveler he mistakes for Thetes and announces his death to Almiana and her father. Then Thetes arrives, and the divine purpose in all this is evident. Syphon draws the tale to a close with still another reminder of the unique perfection and distinction of the match: not just a happy marriage but the triumph of virtue. 'Since the Gods have thus countenanced the Loves of this joyful Pair! and have thus declar'd themselves instrumental in preserving this noble youth! to the Joy of us all, and the Rescue of my Daughter's Life: Let us give 'em Thanks, and join the Couple, which is miraculously distinguish'd to be their Will' (p. 22).

Such transparent simplicity is foreign to Haywood's novels, and this is a simple-minded provincial imitation. By her standards, the heroine's distress is too artificial and open to charges of superficiality because it is so deliberate and articulate. The quasi-physiological details of passionate awakening are missing. The plot lacks intricacy; there are no complications and subplots. The style is too clear and simple, lacking those swellings of anguish, pain, and confused desire that should accompany love and provide sexual excitement. In other words, this novella has a moral simplicity and bare unreality foreign to Haywood's tangled narratives, where endless moral complication and elaborate fantasy are the rule.

But even exaggeration can be overdone. Using Haywood's novels as a norm, we can see that an extravagant novella like *The Forced Virgin; or, the Unnatural Mother* (1730) goes too far perhaps. Written in a style even more tumid than Haywood's, it describes a sexual encounter and an ultimate disaster that make Haywood's big scenes look decorous and staid. Here, for example, is the heroine, Lominia, kidnapped out of the arms of her lover, Arastes, by the minions of his spurned rival, Lysanor. She is taken to a secret cave where Lysanor awaits her.

> Thus they dragg'd the beautiful Innocent in; forcing her thro' many dark Turnings to a Room, in Appearance, more like a Palace, than a Place of so villainous a Retreat; where she again saw, seated on a Purple Couch, the hated Lysanor. . . . Lysanor, impatient of Delay, already prepared for the direful Act, came hasty in; from forth his burning Orbs the destructive Light'ning flew; – His whole Frame shook with boiling Joy; Lust, not Love, sway'd his Soul, and nothing less than Lominia's Ruin possessed his Brain. The Door at his first Entrance he secured, when with a sudden Turn he seized the trembling Maid; – The beautous Fair, press'd in his rough and harden'd Arms, by more than manly Force he bore with Pleasure to his stately Bed: in vain she prayed, his Lust had shut his Ears to such Intreaties. – In vain she strove to stay his raging Flames; regard to her Virtue, or Fear of future Punishment, could make no room for a Moment's Delay; he had her now in full Possession, and was resolved to use the wished-for Hour; with one Hand

intangled in her Hair, he held the Maiden down; while the other furthered him to compleat his hellish Purpose. . . . 'Nor Heaven nor Hell, (cry'd he) shall share my Joy, or participate with me in my good Fortune. – I'll make one continual Riot of the much-desired Feast, nor shall fear of any Punishment rob my swelling Love. – My Soul's on the Wing! O Enjoyment! unable for Expression, – I melt, – I die, – I live, – I feel your Charms; the balmy Bliss revives my dropping Soul, and I'm all Ecstacy!'[41]

This passage has a ponderousness missing in Haywood's lubricious cadences. 'In full possession' and other similar phrases are almost clinical descriptions when we recall Haywood's breathless euphemisms. The picture evoked by the foaming assailant holding Lominia down with one hand in her hair, 'while the other furthered him to compleat his hellish Purpose,' has a crude graphic directness she never allows herself. Moreover, there is an unequivocal violence about this rape that she carefully avoids, preferring seducers who are ambiguously attractive, constructed to encourage the participation and identification that are the key values of formula fiction. Lominia's distress lacks the erotic subtlety Haywood evokes in the cornered maiden; there is no reciprocal and tangled complication of masculine force and reluctant feminine desire. There is too much simple terror here for the special kind of pity Haywood delivered.

The rest of the plot seems, as well, an unsuccessful variant of stock tragedy. Lominia escapes but soon grows pregnant from 'Lysanor's filthy embraces.' She has already shown her capacity for action by stabbing Lysanor with his own knife just as he finishes raping her. She now resolves to abort and does. Such strength of purpose is a bad sign. Heroines usually do abort ill-begotten babes but because of involuntary agitation. Lominia seeks the abortion actively and, without actually submitting to a medical operation, causes it – wills it we are assured. There follows a series of complications, at the end of which Lominia kills her child, fathered she thinks by Lysanor (but actually by Arastes). About to be tried for this crime, she kills herself.[42] All these details are merely horrible rather than pathetic; the author has miscalculated and allowed his heroine to go past distress into criminal insanity. As the Haywoodian novella makes clear, it is quite correct to have the heroine possessed by mysterious impulses, but these should render her passive and helpless. In *The Forced Virgin* the standard combination of sex and violence is unbalanced, tilted toward an unacceptable explicitness and aggressiveness.

There can be little doubt that Haywood's blend of these ingredients was the most popular recipe. Even after her vogue was past, we can see a clear attempt to market the same confection in an elaborately presented and expensive book published in 1732, *The Happy Unfortunate: or, the Female Page* by Elizabeth Boyd.[43] This book concerns not one but a series of unhappy heroines, tied together by simple narrative links that lead to endless interwoven complications and relationships between their various stories. But such variety is superficial. The stories are all the same; the masculine world makes every woman's story tragic, and Boyd uncovers the expected facts relentlessly, with no hesitation or embarrassment at the repetition.

The central female character is Amanda, who is posing as a page (Florio) in the Duke Bellfond's household. In this sort of formula fiction, country houses burst at the seams with amorous intrigue and hiss with illicit desires; this book is clearly no exception. Amanda-Florio is in love with the Duke but is loved by the Duchess and her maid. The Duke has come to the country in order to pursue still another lady, Amira, whose tragic story is the first of several we are told. Although betrothed to a rich old man who died and left her his fortune, Amira had been in love all along with Marcus La-Motte, declared unsuitable by her father, who preferred the avaricious Zemo. In what reads almost like a parody of Haywood's overheated style, we hear how Zemo parted the lovers just as they were to marry:

> Zemo, observant, watch'd the cautious Lovers, and on the very Day assign'd for Hymen, parted them, far [*sic*] obliging La-Motte to hasty leave the Shore; the Hour unnotic'd, nor a Cause declar'd, nor ever made La-Motte the Cyprian Isle [the setting is Cyprus], whilst three long Annals roll'd their yearly Circuit, the Time he found Amira at the Duke's.
>
> (p. 90)

Meanwhile, the Duke seems especially friendly to the young page, and Amanda-Florio is set ablaze by his seemingly innocent intimacies. He bids the page lie with him that night for warmth and there reveals his knowledge of Amanda's identity. Readers are invited to imagine the specific erotic turbulence of a situation rendered in very general terms: 'Let those who know a fierce unbounded Passion, smothered by Awe, Respect and Modesty, a long, long Term, and but imagin'd found, judge of her Thoughts' (p. 48). Repression of and extended resistance to desire are the prerequisites for intensity, and Amanda runs away the next day, pursued by the Duke (who surrenders Amira – remember her? – to La-Motte). Bellfond plies Amanda with sophistical arguments for free love as opposed to sordid marriage, but she hesitates virtuously, clinging to a purer vision of 'the Nuptial State' as 'the State of Angels' (as she calls it later in this long novel when she is still unmarried). A sort of rescue from these torments comes when Bellfond's mistress – by whom he has two sons – dies, and he sails off to find forgetfulness. Amanda retires to the country with her brother Felix and his new bride, Elaira. Then Luvania comes along and tells them the most involved and incredible of all the female tragedies in the book.

Predictably, Luvania has been married at fourteen to a man of fourscore and got with child by Carlo, a young courtier. Her husband forgives her and accepts the child. When he dies, however, she is imprisoned by her husband's relatives, escapes, and is then restored to her former privileges. She resolves to return to Spain where she was born and enter a convent. As she bids farewell to her son and to the world, the narrator pauses and asks familiar questions:

What now could injure the All-happy Fair, divinely beautiful, divinely good: but what is certain in a Mortal State? This lower world, govern'd by unseen Springs, bears nothing perfect, lest it become a God. From the bold Vigilance of one fallen Star, how many weep, even old in Bitterness: Thus well-inclin'd, thus as all thought past Fate, the lovely new-made Nun, form'd to be wretched (for Beauty is but rare sublimely bless'd) was in a surly Minute robb'd of Peace.

(p. 164)

Her old seducer, Carlo, arrives; he fires the convent, and ravishes Luvania. Unlike Haywood's novels, *The Happy Unfortunate* is sparse in erotic details, and the assault is rendered in general terms. It is worth noting, however, that even as Carlo violates her amid the flames of the convent and she pleads with him to cease, 'a thousand Terrors made the Villain hated, whilst yet a thousand Softs pleaded within: So true it is, where once we love, 'tis difficult to hate' (p. 164). But worse follows. Easily sated, Carlo ships her off to Persia in the hands of an infidel captain, who makes her his slave and concubine. She is saved by Osorio, a young Neapolitan who has loved her ever since he saw her enter the convent and who happens to be on the voyage to redeem his brother from slavery. He persuades the 'Sophy's' vizir to buy her, and when the Sophy dies, she and Osorio run away.

The indefatigable Carlo is soon at her again, but when she threatens to expose his crimes, he turns his attention to Amanda and to Elaira, Felix's wife. Treachery and countertreachery too complicated to summarize ensue, and Carlo is finally captured and tried for his crimes in Spain. He confesses but implicates Luvania falsely. This perjury, the last of his assaults on the long-suffering fair (and I have omitted a number of her ordeals), proves fatal. Shipwrecked, she lands back in Spain, where she is put on trial and convicted of the crimes of which Carlo has accused her. Her execution is truly spectacular, a tragic apotheosis beyond anything Haywood ever contrived, a *via dolorosa* for the persecuted maiden that in its quasi-blasphemy comes close to making explicit the buried analogy in this sort of fiction between the female victim and the Christian martyr.

> Distrest Luvania, was condemn'd to walk wrapt in a Sheet, branded with the vile Name of an Apostate, with lighted Tapers, naked legg'd and footed, three tedious Miles, by the Priest's rigid Sentence, o'er snowy Mounts and Bars of burning Steel, but that the Royal Goodness would not suffer; in Lieu of which, she was adjudg'd to walk thrice three Times slowly on snow-cold Irons, and repeat her Crimes, the Circuit of the Courts of Judicature, from thence was to be led to the left Convent Altar [i.e., the convent Carlo set afire and kidnaped her from], there to be stript and excommunicated, then to be drest as an Apostate Nun, in Black and Veil'd, which as a Hieroglyphick of her Choice, was stain'd with Blood of the most Salvage-Wolves, then to be drove in a black open Chariot, to a retir'd Palace of the Kings, there on a Scaffold hung with mournful Sables, with a Sharp Axe to lose her Head; and Being; after which her Body was destin'd to be burn'd to Ashes, and mingled with inhumane Carlo's Dust, scatter'd over some wide, unfathom'd Sea, and be deny'd the sacred Rites of Burial.
>
> (pp. 326–27)

Amanda hears of this in a letter from Luvania's son, also named Carlo. She herself is suffering intolerably, besieged by would-be seducers on all sides. Bellfond's brother, married unhappily, has resorted to violence in his attempts at her, and she has just heard that the Prince of Cyprus is enamored of her. This prince, having listened to calumnies, has banished Duke Bellfond, but not before Amanda finds herself pregnant by the still-married Duke. Luvania's spectacular expiation changes the course of the novel abruptly. No explicit connection is made, but the relationship is clear: the gods can now relent, for Boyd's readers have had their tragic catastrophe and can proceed to the happier possibilities of the story of persecuted female innocence.

The Duchess dies suddenly, and Bellfond is free to marry, the prince having discovered his innocence. The marriage is prefaced by Amanda's denial that this is the end of love, the end of intensity and excitement. She warns Bellfond not to marry her out of a sense of duty; this is to be a free act and to continue the bliss of love without the guilt.

> If ever I am wedded to Bellfond, let Love alone make up the
> solemn Contract, it is that Doubt, my Lord, makes me uneasy;
> I would be Bellfond's Wife, but for the Dutchess would not lose
> the Lover. . . . But if you love like me this Moment wed me, and
> let us be the Wonder of gay Cyprus, for it is now almost a Miracle
> to see a Great Man marry her he loves, or she that loves him, tho'
> mutual Love is all we know of Heaven.

(p. 337)

Such trenchant separation from the world of lust and avarice is a satisfying if abrupt and implausible conclusion to a series of events that has demonstrated the impossibility of escape from that world's complicated networks of disaster. Love descends and rewards its faithful devotees by its magic simplifications.

Simplicity, in fact, is the key to the erotic-pathetic formula. The trick in such fiction is to twist events, characters, and scenes into a tightly tangled mess whose unravelling is accomplished by the recurring simplicity of personality and motive in characters who are rigidly confined to psychosexual stereotypes. The audience assumed by *The Happy Unfortunate* expects and enjoys disaster, and the author's skill as a popular entertainer is in playing heightened variations upon that convention of danger and disaster or near-disaster. Complexity of character, particularity of scene, or narrative self-consciousness has no place in such fiction, because any of them would interrupt the immediate pleasure of formula recognition. Character, especially, conforms to the preexisting pattern, and the reader's pleasure is precisely in tracing the narrative's quick assertions of the inevitability of the pattern, which invokes an unavoidable, often destructive psychosexual destiny for all concerned. It is difficult to say exactly what the popularity of such fiction tells us about its audience, especially since something very like that formula is still a part of contemporary pulp romances. In any event, as I have suggested above, the emergence and insistence of the formula in the early eighteenth century must signify something about the way readers responded to the issue of female identity and destiny.

But is this mass of popular amatory narrative nothing but humorless pulp, interesting perhaps for the literary historian but virtually unreadable otherwise? Not quite. Within the repetitive sameness of amatory formulas there are, after all, a small number of genuine minor precursors of the masters.[44] 'Precursors' is, however, a misleading term that appears to justify the untenable evolutionary model of literary history. Instead of looking forward to what did not yet exist, these books refined or rejected existing narrative formulas, modifying their extravagance and unreality, adding especially a certain consistency of character that avoids the melodramatic moral and psychological simplicities of the amatory novella. One obvious importance thus granted to formula fiction is that it provoked these refinements, dramatizing by its popularity the significance of its themes and challenging some writers to appropriate those themes for audiences more attuned to sophisticated narrative values. To be sure, there were other ways of rejecting or improving the Haywoodian formula. Pious female writers like Jane Barker, Penelope Aubin, and Elizabeth Rowe produced stories that shifted the thematic emphasis of the novella toward virtuous and ultimately victorious resistance to the power of love, providing most of the thrills of watching beleaguered virtue but avoiding the violence and lubricity that usually supplemented them.[45] What separates early eighteenth-century fiction still worth reading from these moral tales is technique, management of narrative so that it yields a truthful complexity – moral, psychological, or social.

Robert A. Day calls *The Perfidious P* (1702) 'the best epistolary novel before Richardson.'[46] By such praise he means that its epistolary technique is an expressive form rather than merely a format, that its letters serve to differentiate and define characters, that the reader is made aware of individualized characters writing letters rather than simply being made to speak through them. In formula fiction, as a strict rule, language is transparent, a vehicle for whatever emotional and ideological satisfactions are being delivered by the narrative: hence the unembarrassed repetition and eager reception of clichés that are crucial to its effects. More sophisticated narration tends to stress the functionality of language for revealing character and describing setting and action. That stress on language as a medium, manipulated openly by characters or by authors, points at times to its inadequacy for rendering the truth, the latter emphasis helping to establish the mode of narration we call 'realistic.' *The Perfidious P* in one sense is a banal tale of amorous betrayal, but it is redeemed by moments when such manipulation is highly visible, when characters implicitly reveal their uneasiness with amatory language and the world it invokes.

Corydon, a nobleman, has sent his mistress, Clarinda, to the country while he is at court in London. Writing to Corydon, Clarinda reminds her lover of his extravagant promises. She finds his previous letter written in 'too loose a Stile for my Heroick Love; with more Care and greater Study you made your first Approaches to my Virgin-Heart.'[47] Clarinda's suspicion, then, begins in textual alertness, as a modern critic might like to put it – in an analysis of her lover's writing that causes her to extend that analysis back to his seductive speeches. In its protestations, Corydon's response verifies Clarinda's suspicions, as he denies his old rhetoric even while affirming his feelings. For amatory hyperbole, Corydon substitutes homely and potentially reductive analogies, turning his letter into a self-conscious display of verbal virtuosity, preferring his own wit to meaningful reassurance for Clarinda.

Why all these Doubts and Fears, my Love? Why this needless Repetition? Does my *Clarinda* think I am grown so stupid, so lifeless, for so I must be when I forget the least Particular of what has past between us, those soft Embraces, moaning Sighs and melting Tears, which were too precious to fall unobserv'd, are still fresh in the Memory of *Corydon*. What shall I say more? I think there is nothing more of consequence to say, except I entertain you with Truths obvious to every eye; as, that 'tis Day when the Sun shines, and when he's gone 'tis Night; or, that I love you dearer than all the Women in the World, as great a Truth as either of the former, and ought to be as well known to you. For my part, I think the telling of this over and over, as some Men do their Passions, ought to be tiresome to Women of your Nicety, and as nauseous to the Mind, as Meat often drest to the Stomach: for to be always in the high Road of making Love, a Man must Bake, Boil, Roast, Hash, and Mince his Love, to find Variety for his Mistress, who perhaps does not think, because 'tis brought warm to her, it has so often been cool'd by another, and only tost up again for her Palate. . . . I am now in haste, being just going to wait upon the King; yet you see I prefer Love to all, and stay to write this long Letter, when it might be easie for me to tear what I have done, then tell you wittily, this Letter is an Emblem of my Heart rent and torn for you – Meer trifling, and ought no more to pass for Love than Childrens Toys for Riches, or a gilded lump of base Metal for true Sterling.

(pp. 13–16)

Corydon visits Lucina, Clarinda's friend and confidante, and soon falls in love with her. Knowing this, the reader can see revelations in Corydon and Lucina's letters to Clarinda that she cannot, and again the book's interest turns on the simultaneous duplicity and truthfulness of language. After the betrayal is known to her, Clarinda writes in conventional ranting fashion, calling herself a dreadful warning to her sex not to listen to man's 'bewitching Tale, for if you hear like me, you surely are undone' (p. 132). Melodramatically

97

desperate enough, Clarinda is still aware just how rhetoric did her in and begins her sad summary with a specific warning against listening to love's language rather than falling in love. Especially in the context of Clarinda's passion, such awareness marks the technical sophistication of *The Perfidious P.*

There is another kind of self-consciousness about language and another sort of protorealism in the novels of Mary Davys.[48] *The Reform'd Coquet* (1724), to my mind her best work, stands nearly alone in early eighteenth-century domestic narrative for its humor. Numbering among its subscribers Martha Blount, Alexander Pope, and John Gay, *The Reform'd Coquet* is a genuinely witty book about the education through experience of a young lady, her conversion into a woman of good sense as well as a happy wife.

Amoranda's father is a nobleman whose estate has been eaten up by the excesses of his father. His younger brother, a rich East India merchant, redeems the estate; when her father dies without male issue and her mother soon after, Amoranda becomes an orphan heiress, much sought after, spoiled and self-indulgent but essentially strong and sensible rather than weakly pathetic and quiveringly susceptible like the typical heroine of the Haywoodian novella.

The ensuing complicated plot has a richly theatrical inventiveness, as Davys manages an ironic, controlled distance from actors and events, her narrative a balance of the standard entanglements of the amatory novella and witty moral observations. In a stylish anticipation of Fielding's manner, Davys invites her readers to the contemplation of ironically inevitable moral complications and the enjoyment of the twists of fictional artifice required to resolve them, rather than to the amatory novella's excited participation in events and enthralling identification with characters. From the beginning, Davys displays a narrative control that balances events and witty moral observation. Here, for example, is her rendering of the financial and sexual excitement that threatens the newly orphaned heiress before her uncle can send a substitute guardian.

> During this Interregnum, *Amoranda* was address'd by all the Country round, from the old Justice to the young Rake; and, I dare say, my Reader will believe she was a Toast in every House for ten Parishes round. The very Excrescencies of her Temper, were now become Graces, and it was not possible for one single Fault to be joined to three thousand Pounds a Year; her Levee was daily crowded with almost all sorts, and (she pleased to be admir'd) tho' she lov'd none, was complaisant to all.[49]

Amoranda's various suitors provide occasion for a comic version of the novella's melodramatic sexual aggression, and Davys' bantering dialogue shows her knowledge of stage models. When Lord Lofty swears he is entangled in her charms, Amoranda pretends to misunderstand him:

> Well, I'll swear, my Lord, said Amoranda, that's a pity; methinks a Man of your Gallantry should never marry. Marry! said my Lord in great Surprize, no, I hope I shall never have so little love for any Lady as to marry her: Oons! the very Word has put me into a Sweat, the Marriage-Bed is to Love, what a cold Bed is to Melon-Seed, it starves it to death infallibly.
>
> (p. 26)

As on the eighteenth-century stage, such bantering easily turns brutal and sordid. Two of Amoranda's other suitors, Callid and Froth, plot to kidnap her and force a marriage. Pleased and amused even by foolish admirers who prove dangerous, Amoranda is saved by Formator, a middle-aged friend sent by her uncle to protect her. Formator and a footman, disguised as Amoranda and her maid, thrash Callid and Froth soundly. (They quarrel subsequently, and in Davys' wicked summary, 'tho' they liv'd like Scoundrels, they went off like Gentlemen, and the first Pass they made, took each other's Life' [pp. 52–53].) Formator then institutes a program of moral improvement for Amoranda. 'His constant Care was to divert her from all the Follies of Life, and as she had a Soul capable of Improvement, and a flexible good Temper to be dealt with, he made no doubt but one day he should see her the most accomplish'd of her Sex' (p. 53).

A stranger appears soon after and reveals herself as Altamira, a woman driven out of her home by her incestuously minded brother, only to be seduced by Lord Lofty, who has tricked her with a written contract of marriage. Amoranda is as quick as her new guardian; she arranges to meet Lord Lofty for a secret wedding and to substitute for herself the wronged Altamira. Matters seem to be resolving themselves with perfect romantic symmetry, as Altamira's brother marries Lofty's sister, when Amoranda is kidnaped by one Biranthus, a visitor who has arrived in female disguise. Lurid melodrama takes over: Amoranda strikes the poses of the persecuted maiden, and her virtue hangs by a thread:

> No, base Biranthus, said she, if Providence had design'd me a Prey for such a Villain, I should have fallen into your first Snare, but I was delivered from you then, and so I shall be again. Before I would consent to be a wife to such a Monster, I would tear out the Tongue by the roots that was willing to pronounce my Doom. I would suffer these Arms to be extended on a Rack, till every

Sinew, every Vein and Nerve should crack, rather than embrace, or so much as touch a Viper like thyself. Then hear, said he, and tremble at thy approaching Fate. This minute, by the help of thy own Servant, I will enjoy thee; and then, by the assistance of my Arm, he shall do so too. Thou lyest, false Traitor, said she, Heaven will never suffer such Wickedness.

(pp. 112–13)

And heaven, of course, does not. A passing gentleman, Alanthus, rescues her and becomes her suitor, Formator informing her that this in fact is the man her uncle has selected for her. But there is one last revelatory twist to the plot. Alanthus and Formator turn out to be one and the same, and both are actually Lord Marquis of W, who was unwilling to force Amoranda into marriage by her uncle's command and has resorted to elaborate subterfuge to improve her and win her love.

The Reform'd Coquet strikes a balance, clearly, between the extravagance of the amatory novella and the moral realism of stage comedy, but it does not renounce the lurid thematics and moral melodrama of the novella. Although the theory can hardly be proved, it seems as if the emergence of what we now recognize as novelistic narrative in these early years of the eighteenth century takes place precisely because of the force of those crude, popular thematics. What this survey of the market for fiction in the century's first four decades or so may suggest is that the popularity of the amatory novella expresses or responds to the radical separation of middle- and upper-class women from public economic life. That is Ruth Perry's point when she insists that the novel as a crucial literary form coincides with the separation of urban literate women 'from the active concerns of life into a pretend world of romantic love and fantasy relationships.'[50]

I would prefer a slightly broader conclusion. Suffering and confused female characters in eighteenth-century popular fiction enact, we may say, a cultural crisis and enormous ideological transition, the privatization and fragmentation of experience for men and women. This is a theme the major writers both accept and attempt to revise by means of the technical control and moral coherence they bring to bear on the formulas of popular fiction.

Notes

1. The evolutionary analogy has been challenged by many critics lately. Henry K. Miller, for example, ridicules it elegantly by speaking of the 'gloriously self-serving' teleology of nineteenth-century literary history. Miller also

admits that the last two hundred years really have produced something new and remarkable in narrative, 'and this has made the invocation of an evolutionary or teleological pattern considerably more plausible' ('Augustan Prose Fiction and the Romance Tradition,' in *Studies in the Eighteenth Century*, ed. R. F. Brissenden and J. C. Eade [Toronto: University of Toronto Press, 1976], 241–42).

2. And modern criticism has simply followed the eighteenth-century view of Richardson's and Fielding's originality. As William Park summarizes it ('What Was New about the "New Species of Writing"?' *Studies in the Novel* 2 [1970], 113–14), Richardson and his coterie stressed three factors in his work that were without real precedent: 'writing to the moment,' by which a new intensity and realism were added to romance; the depiction of a 'familiar' everyday life rather than the unrealities of 'high' life (as in romance) or the sordid details of 'low' life (as in criminal and picaresque narrative); a moral control and coherence whereby moral values were actually exemplified in characters and events rather than merely stated at the beginning or the end of the narrative. In his preface to *Joseph Andrews*, Fielding claimed to be introducing a new narrative genre into England, 'the comic epic in prose,' and in *Tom Jones* he speaks of himself as the founder of a 'new province of writing.' Eighteenth-century readers, Park points out, awarded the two novelists different kinds of originality but saw their works 'as but two versions of the "modern romance," a familiar, natural, and moral species which had "exploded" the old improbable one.'

3. In *Factual Fictions: The Origins of the English Novel* (New York: Columbia University Press. 1983), 7, Lennard Davis rejects what he defines as three 'models' literary historians have used to account for the English novel: evolution, osmosis, and convergence. While most traditional literary history has employed the first of these, Davis calls Ian Watt's *Rise of the Novel* (Berkeley: University of California Press, 1957) 'osmotic' because it posits a connection between cultural change and the emergence of the novel, a sort of osmosis in which shifts in philosophical perspective and social structure permeate narrative structures. Watt's attempt fails, says Davis, because the 'micro connection between, say, a larger, middle-class reading public and a structural change in narrative' is missing. In the 'convergence' model, the novel is simply the result of all the narrative forms that preceded it, 'taking on the best features of disparate forms such as the essay, the history, and so on.' In the place of such models, Davis proposes Michel Foucault's notion of 'discourse'; that is, the novel should be understood as part of a 'larger ensemble of written texts,' including not only novels and literary criticism but 'parliamentary statutes, newspapers, advertisements, printer's records, handbills, letters, and so on.' Like Foucault, Davis boldly rejects the question of origins, since the shift to that 'discourse' of which the novel is a part is a 'rupture' or a 'transformation' rather than part of a linear progression in which one can properly speak of causes and effects. The novel, in this latest attempt to account for it, is part of the effort by seventeenth- and eighteenth-century European man to dominate and administer the world. Just how superior such a formulation is to the older ones that Davis rejects is an unresolved issue.

4. Ernest A. Baker (*The History of the English Novel*, 10 vols. [1929; rpt. New York: Barnes & Noble, 1959], III:107) made the case for the minor novelists very clearly: 'The service they rendered was to have kept up a supply of novels and stories, which habituated a larger and larger public to find their amusement in the reading of fiction, and which poor in quality as they were, provided the original form for the eighteenth-century novel of manners.

Defoe, for the most part, took a line of his own; yet he was not entirely out of their debt. Richardson and Fielding were less innovators than is usually supposed; in turning to novel-writing, they entered upon an established and thriving business, and they adopted many tricks of the trade from these humble precursors.'

One of the problems students of the novel have faced is the difficulty of reading what posterity has willingly let die. Eighteenth-century popular narrative of the sort that precedes and surrounds the major writers has hitherto been available only in major research libraries. That situation has been remedied lately by the Garland Press series, Foundations of the Novel, 'a collection of 100 rare titles reprinted in photo-facsimile in 71 volumes,' compiled and edited by Michael F. Shugrue (New York: Garland, 1973). Most of the works discussed in this essay are reprinted in that series.

5. Watt, *Rise of the Novel*, 50.

6. Maurice Evans, Introduction to *Arcadia* (New York: Penguin, 1977), 9.

7. Earl Wasserman pointed out that the prose fiction of the Renaissance enjoyed steady popularity through the eighteenth century, as did medieval romances and other traditional narratives adapted into popular and modern idiom as chapbooks for the barely literate (*Elizabethan Poetry in the Eighteenth Century* [Urbana: University of Illinois Press, 1947], 253). Henry K. Miller recalls for us that Sterne's Uncle Toby remembers 'when Guy, Earl of *Warwick*, and *Parismus* and *Valentine* and *Orson*, and the *Seven Champions of England* were handed around the school' (*Tristram Shandy*, VI, xxxii) ('Augustan Prose Fiction,' 249).

8. W. H. McBurney, comp., *A Check List of English Prose Fiction, 1700–1739* (Cambridge, Mass.: Harvard University Press, 1960), vii–viii.

9. Marjorie Plant, *The English Book Trade*, 2d ed. (1939; rpt. London: Allen and Unwin, 1965), 56–58.

10. See the article on Paul Lorrain by Thomas Seccombe in the *Dictionary of National Biography* (XXXIV: 140).

11. See my *Popular Fiction before Richardson: Narrative Patterns, 1700–1739* (Oxford: Clarendon Press, 1969), 27–29, for more detailed discussion of the issues raised by these pamphlets.

12. For an extended discussion of this and other similar works, see ibid., 45–59. 'Smith' produced several other collections like this one, as well as one devoted to female offenders: *The School of Venus, or Cupid restor'd to Sight; being A History of Cuckolds and Cuckold-makers* (1715–16).

13. F. W. Chandler, *The Literature of Roguery* (New York: Houghton Mifflin, 1907), 173–74. For a discussion of *The Scotch Rogue: or, the Life and Actions of Donald Macdonald A High-Land Scot* (1706) and *Tom Merryman* (1725) as works that exemplify this combination of criminal journalism and folktale features, see *Popular Fiction before Richardson*, 41–43.

14. Manuel Schonhorn has edited Defoe's work and provided a full and illuminating introduction. His conclusion summarizes Defoe's achievement and the importance of the book: 'In its narrative vigor, its emotional balance, and its creative reconstruction of dim events elevated at times to a dramatic universality, it has remained the indispensable record of English piracy in the first quarter of the eighteenth century and a classic in the literature of the sea' (*A General History of the Pyrates* [Columbia: University of South Carolina Press, 1972], xl).

15. Davis, *Factual Fictions*, 136.

16. Ibid., 132.

17. P. G. Adams concludes his study by emphasizing the inellectual importance of travel writing for an age of expanding enlightenment, and he points to the philosophical and scientific implications of travel narratives that, collectively, 'taught that each nation had a distinctive, even appropriate, way of life.' But Adams also notes that the improbability of many accounts of foreign parts was apparent from the beginning: 'That travelers were eyed askance is proved not only by the hesitant acceptance accorded them, but ironically by the great necessity they all – truthful and untruthful – felt to profess their innocence, as if they had been caught in a company of shady characters' (*Travelers and Travel-Liars 1660–1800* [Berkeley: University of California Press, 1962], 224, 228).

18. For a discussion of some of these pirate lives, see my *Popular Fiction before Richardson*, 64–84.

19. Like so many other producers of early eighteenth-century popular narrative, Chetwood was a member of the subculture referred to as 'Grub Street,' part of a number of struggling 'hack' writers and publishers associated with the neighborhood around that now vanished London street. He was the publisher of many of Eliza Haywood's works, and she and Chetwood are numbered among the dunces in Pope's *Dunciad*. Bookseller, dramatist, and miscellaneous writer, he was the prompter at Drury Lane theater for many years. See James Sutherland's biographical appendix to his volume of the Twickenham edition of Pope's *Dunciad* (London: Methuen, 1943), 433. On Grub Street, see Pat Rogers, *Grub Street: Studies in a Subculture* (London: Methuen, 1972).

20. Taking a broad historical overview beginning with the seventeenth century, Martin Green sees a 'moral revolution' in England sponsored by the 'merchant caste' that appropriated literature and culture. 'This moral revolution redirected spiritual intensity toward home life, marriage, and sex; away from older objects of devotion, like the liturgical life of the church, and the cults of the aristomilitary caste. When the spiritual religion came out of the monastery, to adapt a famous phrase, it settled in the home as well as in the market place, making its altar the bedroom and the bed. Indeed, as far as the serious novelists were concerned, it was the home and *not* the market that was important' (*Dreams of Adventure, Deeds of Empire* [New York: Basic Books, 1970], 63).

21. McBurney's *Check List* shows sixteen original English narratives published during those years that qualify in my judgment as travel adventure stories. I exclude the novels of Penelope Aubin, who combines the pattern of the amatory novella with the geographical diversity of the adventure story. For an account of her works, see *Popular Fiction before Richardson*, 216–29, and W. H. McBurney, 'Mrs. Penelope Aubin and the Early Eighteenth-Century English Novel,' *HLQ* 20 (May 1957), 245–67.

22. Malcolm Bosse, Introduction to the Garland edition of *The Golden Spy*, 5.

23. Gildon's original version of this anthology dates to 1692, when John Dunton printed *The Post-boy rob'd of his Mail: or, the Pacquet Broke Open. Consisting of Five Hundred Letters to Persons of Several Qualities and Conditions.* As Robert A. Day notes, this was partly translated from Italian and French models (*Told in Letters: Epistolary Fiction before Richardson* [Ann Arbor: University of Michigan Press, 1966], 243).

24. J. B. Heidler, 'The History, from 1700 to 1800, of English Criticism of Prose Fiction,' *University of Illinois Studies in Language and Literature*, no. 13 (Urbana: University of Illinois Press, 1928), 17.

25. For a discussion of these and other issues surrounding the romance tradition in the early eighteenth century, see Miller, 'Augustan Prose Fiction,' 245–46.

26. 'To the Reader,' in *Eighteenth-Century British Novelists on the Novel*, ed. George L. Barnett (New York: Appleton-Century-Crofts, 1968), 22. References in the text are to this edition.

27. According to A. J. Tieje, the *chronique scandaleuse* became a formal type in 1660 with the appearance of Bussy-Rabutin's *Histoire amoureuse des Gaules* ('The Theory of Characterization in Prose Fiction Prior to 1740,' *University of Minnesota Studies in Language and Literature*, No. 5 [Minneapolis: University of Minnesota Press, 1916], 54). An English translation of Bussy-Rabutin's book appeared in 1725, and such translations were popular and frequent during the early decades of the century. As James Sutherland points out in *English Literature of the Late Seventeenth Century* (Oxford: Clarendon Press, 1969), 209–10, English secret histories began to flourish in the climate of partisan politics after James II's abdication.

28. See *Popular Fiction before Richardson*, 119–52, for a discussion of Manley's popularity.

29. *Secret Memoirs and Manners of several Persons of Quality, of Both Sexes from the New Atalantis, an Island in the Mediteranean* [sic]. *Written Originally in Italian* (London: Printed for John Morphew and J. Woodward, 1709), 217. References in the text are to this edition.

30. See G. F. Whicher, *The Life and Romances of Mrs. Eliza Haywood* (New York: Columbia University Press, 1915); Mary Anne Schofield, *Quiet Rebellion: The Fictional Heroines of Eliza Fowler Haywood* (Washington D. C.: University Press of America, 1982).

31. *The Force of Nature, Lasselia*, and *The Injur'd Husband* have been reprinted in facsimile recently by Mary Anne Schofield (*Four Novels of Eliza Haywood* [Delmar, N. Y.: Scholars' Facsimiles and Reprints, 1983]). *Philidore and Placentia* can be read in W. H. McBurney's *Four before Richardson: Selected English Novels, 1720–1727* (Lincoln: University of Nebraska Press, 1963). Many of Haywood's novels are also available in facsimile reprints in the Garland series, Foundations of the Novel.

32. *Love in Excess* is divided into three parts, the first two published separately in 1719, the third in 1720. This passage is from Part II, pp. 48–49 (Garland edition). For an extended analysis of the book, see *Popular Fiction before Richardson*, 183–207. Melliora, it is worth noting, escapes D'Elmont here, and consummation of their love is delayed through many ordeals and temptations until the happy ending in Part III.

33. Ruth Perry, *Women, Letters and the Novel* (New York: AMS Press, 1980), 22–23.

34. Myra Jehlen, 'Archimedes and the Paradox of Feminist Criticism,' in *The Signs Reader: Women, Gender and Scholarship*, ed. Elizabeth Abel and Emily K. Abel (Chicago: University of Chicago Press, 1983), 90.

35. See *Popular Fiction before Richardson*, 210, for a discussion of this work.

36. Garland edition, p. 10. References in the text are to this edition.

37. In some ways, eighteenth-century amatory formula fiction resembles what John G. Cawelti calls 'social melodrama,' which he defines as a synthesis of the archetype of melodrama 'with a particular set of current events or social

institutions.' The result looks like social criticism but is in fact an affirmation of the status quo. 'The appeal of this synthesis combines the escapist satisfactions of melodrama – in particular, its fantasy of a moral universe following conventional social values – with the pleasurable feeling that we are learning something important about reality' (*Adventure, Mystery, and Romance: Formula Stories as Art and Popular Culture* [Chicago: University of Chicago Press, 1976], 261).

38. It had rather stiff competition in 1722. Defoe's *Colonel Jacque* appeared then, and *Moll Flanders* reached a third edition in the year of its publication. Haywood's *The British Recluse* went through two editions, and Penelope Aubin published two of her novels that year.

39. In 1727, Haywood published six books, including the notorious secret history *The Court of Caramania*, which is one of the books borne by the donkey in the frontispiece to Pope's *Dunciad* (along with 'Haywood's Novels'). A collected edition also appeared that year, bringing together *Secret Histories, etc. Written or translated by Mrs. Eliza Haywood. Printed since the Publication of the four Volumes of her Works* (see McBurney, *Check List*, 74). Those four volumes referred to were reissued in a third edition in 1732.

40. *The Treacherous Confident* (Dublin: Printed by S. Powell, for Sylvanus Pepyat and Thomas Benson, 1728), 8. Page references are to this edition.

41. *The Forced Virgin; or, the Unnatural Mother. A True Secret History* (London: printed for W. Trott, 1730), pp. 11–16. References in the text are to this edition.

42. To summarize briefly: Lominia does abort Lysanor's child, but is then made pregnant again by Arastes, who drugs her wine and takes her in her sleep. As far as she knows, then, the child she feels in her must be Lysanor's. She has her maid expose the child when it is born, but Arastes is watching; he takes the child into the country and has it cared for. Arastes and Lominia come upon the child by accident while walking in the country some years later, and Arastes reveals that he saw her maid expose this child but does not say he is the father. Lominia comes back later and kills the child.

43. According to Robert A. Day, Elizabeth Boyd issued in 1732 a proposal for printing her novel by subscription. Day cites these interesting figures: 328 subscribers, 188 men and 140 women; 92 subscribers belonged to the nobility (*Told in Letters*, 74). The bound book cost five shillings but was obtainable in quires for three shillings. It was reissued in 1737 as *The Female Page: A Genuine and Entertaining History, Relating to Some Persons of Distinction*. All references in the text are to the 1732 edition.

   The Happy Unfortunate is prefaced by some verses exalting Boyd as Haywood's successor:

> Yield Haywood yield, yield all whose tender Strains,
> Inspire the Dreams of Maids and lovesick Swains,
> Who taint the unripen'd Girl with amorous Fire,
> And hint the first faint Dawnings of Desire:
> Wing each Love-Atom, that in Embryo lies,
> And teach young Parthenissa's Breasts to rise.
>
> A new Elisa writes – by her the Young
> Instructed, shall avoid the busy Throng,
> Retire to Groves, by murmuring Fountains sigh,
> Expire in Vision, and in Emblem die.

The hint of humor in the last line is confirmed by lines that predict the novel's effects on its male readers:

> Rough Country 'Squires, the Glory of our Isle:
> Soft Billet-doux, shall in kind Accents write,
> And wafted Vows from Cornwall wing their Flight.
> No more on Dunkirk, or the Nations Debt,
> Old Hackney'd Themes, our Senators shall meet,
> But o'er a gilt Romance enamour'd hang,
> Sit on a Leer, or on a Sigh Harrangue:
> And Love's own Monosyllables apply
> To their due Province restor'd, No, and Ay.

Such genial humor disappears in the novel itself.

44. Robert A. Day finds four epistolary novels that 'represent the highest development of letter fiction before Richardson': *The Perfidious P* (1702), *Lindamira* (1702), *Olinda's Adventures* (1693), and Mary Davys' *Familiar Letters Betwixt a Gentleman and a Lady* (1725). Day praises these 'highly promising experimental' books for their varying degrees of technical competence and for the resulting verisimilitude of scene and character but calls them 'fragmentary and tentative,' lacking the 'significance and depth' of Richardson and later novelists (*Told in Letters*, 177, 191). On the issue of technical achievement, see Benjamin Boyce's introduction to his edition of *The Adventures of Lindamira* (Minneapolis: University of Minnesota Press, 1949) and my discussion of *Lindamira* in *Popular Fiction before Richardson*, 170–73.

45. For an extended analysis of the works of these three writers, see ch. 6, 'The Novel as Pious Polemic,' of *Popular Fiction before Richardson*, 211–61.

46. *Told in Letters*, 178.

47. Garland edition, p. 9. References in the text are to this edition.

48. W. H. McBurney sees Mary Davys as Fielding to Haywood's Richardson and traces a number of interesting similarities between her novels and Fielding's. He praises her humor and her restraint, contrasting her with the 'typical woman novelist of her day who sought rather to rouse the reader's mind "to (till then) unknown Pleasures or generous Pity."' McBurney concludes that Fielding probably never read her works but that she 'is interesting as one of the few writers before 1740 to formulate a conscious theory of the novel, to show how realistic comedy might be adapted to the new genre, to place emphasis upon characterization and setting rather than upon simple variety of action, and to bring sturdy commonsense and humor to a literary form which had been dominated by the extravagant, the scandalous, and the sensational' ('Mrs. Mary Davys, Forerunner of Fielding,' *PMLA* 74 [1959], 351, 355).

49. Garland edition, p. 10. References in the text are to this edition.

50. Perry, *Women, Letters, and the Novel*, 137.

5 The Novel and the Rise of the Penitentiary: Narrative and Ideology in Defoe, Gay, Hogarth and Fielding

JOHN BENDER

John Bender's *Imagining the Penitentiary* is influenced by Michel Foucault's *Discipline and Punish*. In this essay, Bender presents the main thesis of his book. He argues that the narrative devices embedded in the psychological novel, as it was developed from Defoe onwards, created the imaginative terms which guided the construction of prisons in the later eighteenth century. Earlier prisons were liminal spaces, peculiarly open to the wider society around them. Later prisons isolated prisoners absolutely, and sought to manipulate the prisoners for the purpose of characterological reform – an idea summarized in Jeremy Bentham's infamous panopticon. The ideas about how individual character was formed which drove the new penology were the ideological outgrowth of the new forms of narrative. (See Introduction, pp. 15–16.)

'Subjectivity,' as Clifford Geertz has said, 'does not properly exist until it is . . . organized; art forms generate and regenerate the very subjectivity they pretend only to display. Quartets, still lifes, and cockfights are not merely reflections of a pre-existing sensibility analogically represented; they are positive agents in the creation and maintenance of such a sensibility.'[1]

This essay outlines an analysis that aims to exemplify the subtle process of generation, representation, and regeneration that Geertz attributes to works of art in their cultural context. Above all I want to reach beyond the assumption that literature and art merely reflect institutions and attitudes. I want to consider 'motives' in Freud's sense of their multiplicity, and in Kenneth Burke's sense of categories or material conditions through which we can understand 'language and thought primarily as modes of action.'[2] Of course culture shapes art, but this essay explores the correlative that art may shape culture.

I shall argue that attitudes toward prison which were formulated between about 1720 and 1750 in narrative literature and art – most especially in fiction – enabled the conception and construction of actual penitentiary prisons later in the eighteenth century. Fabrications in narrative of the power of confinement to reform personality contributed to a process of cultural representation whereby prisons were themselves reconceived and ultimately reinvented. The new penitentiaries, whose geometric disposition of individual cells and rigid daily routines we now take as inevitable, sprang suddenly into being about 200 years ago, first in England and then across the whole of Europe and America. These penitentiaries assumed novelistic ideas of character and re-presented the sensible world to their inmates with the aim of altering motivation and, ultimately, personality.

Before continuing, I need to describe the old prisons in contrast with the new penitentiaries. Then I will outline my argument, while introducing some theoretical terminology. Next comes the heart of my case insofar as it must be argued here on a merely exemplary basis: that Defoe's representation of the old prisons fictionally implied the conception of a new kind of imprisonment structured along narrative lines. Of course, the old prisons too could be construed by the fabulist, but they were not internally ordered by narrational rules. Defoe took two crucial steps toward the full novelization of confinement in the penitentiary: (1) He subjected experience to a detailed grid of narrative articulation and thereby revealed the high degree of control latent in the novel as a representational form (even if he himself did not attain it); (2) He showed how the internal forces of psychological motivation fuse dynamically in confinement with the physical details of perceptual experience. Here is the penitentiary imagined as the meeting point or nexus between the individual mind and material causes. This central section lays the foundation for some large-scale assertions which limitations of space force me to illustrate sketchily by way of a conclusion. There, I shall discuss how Gay and Hogarth regenerated the new structure of feeling in overtly paradoxical artistic forms, and, finally, how Fielding adapted these paradoxes into intellectually accessible narratives that opened onto the explicit, reformative phase of the penitentiary movement.

I

The old prisons were not intended, in themselves, as penal instruments but as places of detention prior to judgment or disposition. Death was the common penalty, though often commuted to transportation abroad. At mid-century in England, petty offenders were hanged or transported for any simple larceny of more than twelve pence or for any robbery that put a person in fear. The typical residents of eighteenth-century prisons were debtors and people awaiting trial, often joined by their families like Hogarth's Rake or

Goldsmith's Vicar. Their society might include convicts awaiting transportation or execution as well as innocent witnesses held by the court. Most prisons were not built purposely for confinement, but all were domestically organized and the few specially constructed ones resembled grand houses in appearance (e.g. York Prison, c. 1705). Prisons were temporary lodgings for all but a few, and the jailer collected fees from prisoners for room, board, and services like a lord of the manor collecting rents from tenants. Still, documentary inquiries indicate that life inside the old prisons spontaneously derived its own structure and its own rather exacting methods of governance.[3] As Smollett observed, these prisons microcosmically condensed the society which created them. They were mirrors of social and economic class, though like coffee houses they brought a cross section of society together on special terms that suspended the ordinary rules.

The Enlightenment reimagined these old, domestically ordered prisons, conceiving instead the penitentiaries later perfected by industrial society. This occurred in stages. As impulses to reform became intellectually focused during the 1760s and critics attacked the old practices, prison *exteriors* were reimagined, although their *interiors* remained much as before. While the old contract system based on jailors' fees sturdily resisted change, prisons during this decade outwardly assumed a fearful, awesome, sublimely intimidating aspect – imagery envisioned in the graphic arts by Piranesi and in architecture by George Dance's 1768 design for London Newgate.

Then, beginning in England during the 1770s and culminating throughout America and Europe in the 1840s, the reformers, guided by a Utilitarian analysis of human nature, envisioned prison as a highly refined instrument. They aimed to reshape the life story of each criminal by the measured application of pleasure and pain within a planned framework. Each convict was assigned upon entry to live out a program or scenario which took as its point of departure a generic classification based upon age, sex, type of offense, and social background. Beginning in the 1780s, English prison buildings underwent huge changes in interior plan. Each structure was contrived as the physical setting implied by a narrative – or series of narratives – of criminal reformation. Governmental authorities began to pay all expenses and to dictate every detail of penitentiary architecture along with every movement in the prisoner's carefully specified daily regime. Confinement itself became the punishment, and by the mid-nineteenth century, penitentiary sentences had virtually supplanted other criminal punishments except execution for murder or treason.[4]

II

In thinking about the old-style prisons that preceded penitentiaries I have found Victor Turner's anthropological terms useful. I would like to introduce one of them now as the hinge on which many particulars of the analysis in this essay will turn.

Certainly one of the most explicit motifs in seventeenth- and eighteenth-century prison accounts is the identification of the experience of imprisonment with the point of view of the initiate or neophyte in a ritual.[5] And so I have come to see the old-style prisoners as subjects who, to use Turner's word, undergo the 'liminal' experience characteristic of rites of passage. I believe that the application of this term to prisons gains a credence beyond that of suggestive metaphor since, as Turner says, 'often the indigenous term for the liminal period is . . . the locative form of a noun, meaning "seclusion site".' Indeed, the English word 'jail' derives ultimately from the medieval Latin diminutive of 'cavea' meaning 'hollow', 'cavity,' 'dungeon,' 'cell,' or 'cage.'[6]

The 'liminal' rite of passage enacts symbolic demise and takes for granted a randomness that, quite unpredictably, can bring about real death. 'The essential feature of these symbolizations is that the neophytes are neither living nor dead from one aspect, and both living and dead from another. Their condition is one of ambiguity and paradox, a confusion of all the customary categories' (p. 340). Incessant complaints by eighteenth-century reformers that the old prisons were confused in tone – sites at once of misery and hilarity, punishment and immorality, death and generation – serve, in this context, to affirm their liminality. The old prisons neither told stories nor assigned roles. Rather, the 'coincidence of opposite processes and notions in a single representation characterizes the peculiar unity of the liminal: that which is neither this nor that, and yet is both' (p. 341). In the larger perspective taken by formal analysis and interpretation, liminal space has a double structure visible only in part to the passenger who acts within it and who experientially finds it out during initiation.

In the old prisons the real, if transient, danger to the liminal passenger depended, as in carnival, upon losing control within a demarcated arena where new patterns of life could be formulated. 'Initiation,' at the threshold (*limen, liminis*) separating one role in the larger social structure from another, 'is to rouse initiative at least as much as to produce conformity to custom.' Randomness was one of the rules in the old prisons: the squalor; the disease; the possibility of escape; the periodic jail deliveries voted by Parliament; the chance that creditors might relent, courts miscarry, judges commute death to transportation, patrons gain a reprieve, or friends revive one's corpse after hanging. This rule of randomness of course adopts the point of view of the 'passenger' – or that of the carnival spectator temporarily subject to misrule – one who engages in 'liminal forms of symbolic action, those genres of free-time activity, in which all previous standards and models are subjected to criticism, and fresh new ways of . . . interpreting . . . experience are formulated.'[7] Finally, however, liminality does not posit change in personality, but change in status; it fosters the outlook appropriate to a new social standing (p. 345).

Perhaps the best way to understand how the old prisons could embody all of the different aspects of liminality is to fragment the experience of entering them, first into temporal sequence and then into architectural space. The passenger in the old prison encountered first and last the jailer and his aides, who exacted fees at entry and exit and who applied or struck off irons according to the fees the prisoner could muster: the lighter the irons, the higher the price. The jailer's chief responsibility was to secure the perimeters; his chief right, to gain fees for every service supplied the prisoner. Legal authority waited at the gate. Within the geographic and economic boundary defined by the jailer, most prisoners came and went through lodgings and yard, pub and coffee house, as fancy and their fellows guided them.

The liminal boundary was perhaps sharpest at the moment when the prisoner stepped clear of the keeper and his turnkeys into the yard or public rooms where he was subjected to the custom of 'garnish.' This was not a keeper's fee, but a charge levied by the associated prisoners. As the hackneyed poet put it in verse on the frontispiece to the *Humours of the Fleet*:

> Welcome Welcome Brother Debtor
> To this poor but merry place
> Where no Bayliff, Dun, or Settor,
> Dare to show his horred Face
> But kind Sir as you'r a Stranger
> Down your Garnish you must lay
> Or your Coat will be in danger
> You must either Strip or Pay.[8]

Though Paget's verse catches the jocular tone typical of hazing rites, reformers universally deplored this as the most degrading moment of the prisoner's initiation into his new life: if upon entry he could not pay a rather large set fee or 'garnish' to purchase drinks all around, his clothes were stripped off to be sold for the purpose. Such is one of Booth's first indignities in Fielding's *Amelia*.

For all its randomness, the rite of passage is governed and contained by the relation among neophtyes, on the one hand, and between them and their instructors, on the other. 'There exists a set of relations that compose a "social structure" of a very simple kind: between instructors and neophytes there is often complete authority and complete submission; among neophytes there is often complete equality' (p. 341). Thus it is consistent with the character of the old prisons to view them, simultaneously, as arenas of randomness and as structured microcosmic versions of society. They were at once the site of individual rites of passage and the collective embodiment of liminality in institutional and topological form. They physically expressed the liminal paradox through their enclosure of classless liberty. But since by the seventeenth and eighteenth centuries the rite of passage was becoming residual, the authority of the instructors or elders, which Turner describes as independent of legal sanctions, had been institutionalized in the keeper who served as an agent of the legal system though not as one of its officers. Still, the old prison keepers could function because they represented 'the self-evident authority of tradition . . . the absolute, the axiomatic values of society in which are expressed the "common good" and the common interest' (pp. 341–42).

Three facts about the old prisons – all surprising from a modern point of view – demonstrate the force of traditional authority in their maintenance. First, the easy traffic in visitors – which sustained familial communication and enabled supply by franchised tradesmen – depended upon consensual boundaries. Second, the guard was strikingly light even at Newgate, the chief jail for felons, where one official to each 100 prisoners sufficed during the 1760s to secure the walls and gateways.[9] Third, the old prisons literally penetrated life in surrounding neighborhoods by extending outside their own walls into legally drawn sectors known as the Rules, where less dangerous prisoners might be detained in private buildings called sponging houses. Like the prison itself, these were businesses run for profitable fees by keepers, bailiffs, and landlords. In short, the boundaries were at once fixed and fluid, legally set and socially enacted: to the prisoner, opaque as a wall; to the visitor, transparent as a veil.

Perhaps the strongest sign of the reciprocal relation between the old prisons and the culture which produced them is that the structure which was 'found' during the rite of passage was a version of the surrounding social order. The requirement of garnish is a case in point. In fact, a newcomer's compulsory purchase of drink for his entire company or shop enjoyed widespread acceptance as a rite of passage into trades and occupations – even at the higher levels of the magistracy – right through the eighteenth century and beyond.[10] This is not surprising since, according to Turner, rites of passage 'are not restricted . . . to movements between ascribed statuses. They also concern entry into a newly achieved status, whether this be a political office or membership of an exclusive club or secret society' (p. 339). Similarly, the old prisons signified liminal equality among initiates by the freedom, above all, of the coffee house – that egalitarian innovation among eighteenth-century institutions where, according to Habermas, lord and commoner could converse on equal terms in the 'public sphere,' outside the rules of status governing the period's usual social intercourse.[11] At the same time, the system of fees for lodging and services imposed by the jailer transparently reduced social standing to the terms of a purely economic code, demystifying it and rendering it apparent. As Turner says, 'Liminality may be partly described as a stage of reflection. In it those ideas, sentiments, and facts that had been hitherto for the neophytes bound up in configurations and accepted unthinkingly are, as it were, resolved into their constituents' (p. 345).

The old prisons visibly situated the transient structures of liminality in the topography of the early modern city. They were representational no less than the new penitentiaries; the difference lay in the principles governing their form. The old prisons were loose structures bounded by authority yet out of its reach, while, reciprocally, their randomness sustained tradition by clarifying its elemental value. Structurally articulate, yet unpenetrated by systematic governance or precisely formulated rules, the old prisons maintained an account of reality which had informed earlier religious, governmental, and narrational practice and which continued to permeate much of eighteenth-century popular culture.

Conversely, the new penitentiaries banished Chance and Fortune – the Providential order of things – in favor of human planning and certitude imagined in material terms. Our very words make the case: 'rebirth' through initiation or baptism implies mysterious recreation, whereas 'reform' assumes rationally ordered causal sequence and conceives human invention as capable of reconstructing reality. Penitentiaries have regimes, schedules, disciplines; their inmates progress or regress, and they have stories not to be told upon release or just prior to execution (like the subjects of the *Newgate Calendar*), but to be lived out in the penitentiary itself. Much of the history of penology subsequent to the establishment of penitentiaries in England during the last quarter of the eighteenth century can be described as an attempt to order the prison story generically with divergent classifications of story for each age, sex, and type of convict. This idea is, then, at the heart of my argument: the form prisons took when they were subjected to consciousness was narrative form of a distinctively novelistic kind.

I believe that we must look outside the legal sphere to English narrative between Defoe and Goldsmith to trace the cultural formulations that endowed the penitentiary idea with its ultimately dominant force. For, as Durkheim observed in arguing that legal systems are themselves symbolically constituted,

> A representation is not simply a mere image of reality, an inert shadow projected by things upon us, but it is a force which raises around itself a turbulence of organic and psychical phenomena . . . it arouses images, sometimes excites beginnings of illusions and may even affect vegetative functions. This foothold is as much more considerable as the representation is itself more intense, as the emotional element is more developed.[12]

Or, as Frederick Jameson has suggested more recently, 'fantasy or protonarrative structure' is 'the vehicle for our experience of the real.'[13]

When the form of story telling now called the 'novel' emerged in the 1720s, it at once evinced an intimate self-consciousness concerning prison and confinement. The pervasive link between the novel and the subject of confinement strongly indicates the presence of some cycle of generation and regeneration such as Geertz proposes. Defoe's narratives, for example, subtly introduce time, sequence, and developing consciousness of role into the liminal prison. According to my analysis, Defoe, Hogarth, Fielding, and Smollett all predicate the new prisons in the very act of depicting the old. Under novelistic conditions, even when the social function of prisons is not explicitly at issue, the old practices begin to split apart and become subject to a corrosive irony that sets the stage for their rejection and reformulation.

The old prisons socially inscribed the principle that the true order of things had to be discovered through discord (*discordia concors*), and that final causes lay hidden beneath appearances. Romance narratives – by their magical strategies and implicit causes – bore this cultural fiction in literary form. The novel bears another fantasy entirely: that of a reality constituted from material causes. The novel articulates reality within a fine grid of visible, observationally discoverable causes which are the motor factors of the narrative itself: among others, the internal forces of psychological motivation, the details of perceptual experience, the 'natural' requirements of physical survival, the social demands of law and decorum. The reader experiences this complex grid as 'reality' by accepting the fiction of a governing consciousness in narrator and characters alike.

The very notion of a penitentiary sentence assumes ideas of time and determined sequence. Before the rise of penitentiaries, the 'sentence' was a judicial decision on guilt versus innocence, or it was a determination of punishment – both absolute, instantaneous pronouncements that referred themselves and their objects of judgment to principles outside time.[14] But linguistically a sentence unfolds in time like a plot, and its elements have grammatical roles to play; narratives are made of such sentences. Indeed, as Roland Barthes has argued, narratives are properly viewed as expanded sentences with their own distinctive grammatical rules and syntactic structures. The novel is a special kind of narrative that arose when sentences became accepted as surrogates of reality.[15] The liminal prison became the penitentiary when, through a conflation of the legal and grammatical notions of a 'sentence,' randomness gave way to narrative order and 'sentences' came to be served rather than executed. Punishment – previously the simple binary pronouncement 'innocent/guilty,' followed by its consequence 'life/death' – was reformed into a programmatic course of events with the end of shaping personality according to controlled principles.[16]

The balance of this paper elaborates the significance I find in the conjunction of an emergent narrative form with a subject matter previously limited to broadside accounts, penny pamphlets, and popular court reporters.

III

In Moll Flanders' fictional world, 'Newgate,' as a word and as a place in general, appears to signify liminality at its most concentrated. At the denouement of her story, Moll is cast into Newgate for stealing two pieces of brocaded silk:

> 'tis impossible to describe the terror of my mind, when I was first brought in, and when I look'd round upon all the horrors of that dismal Place: I look'd on my self as lost, and that I had nothing to think of, but going out of the World, and that with the utmost Infamy; the hellish Noise, the Roaring, Swearing and Clamour, the Stench and Nastiness, and all the dreadful croud of Afflicting things that I saw there; joyn'd together to make the Place seem an Emblem of Hell itself, and a kind of an Entrance into it.[17]

Moll conceives of her imprisonment emblematically, as if she were an allegorical figure, whereas Defoe's narrative requires us to situate her in a much more immanent, 'naturally' motivated narrative structure. Moll describes life in prison as a death of her old self, again emblematically, in terms of the old psychological category of *acedia*, the sin of spiritual sloth:

> I degenerated into Stone; I turn'd first Stupid and Senseless, then Brutish and thoughtless, and at last raving Mad as any of them were; and in short, I became as naturally pleas'd and easie with the Place, as if indeed I had been Born there.
>
> (p. 278)

Moll has forgotten (in a famous lapse) that she has just previously decried Newgate as 'that horrid Place! . . . where my Mother suffered so deeply, where I was brought into the World' (p. 273). The lapse, whether Moll's or Defoe's, characterizes her status as a liminal passenger. As Turner says,

> In so far as a neophyte is structurally 'dead,' he or she may be treated, for a long or short period, as a corpse is customarily treated . . . they are allowed to go filthy and identified with the earth . . . often their very names are taken from them . . . The other aspect, that they are not yet classified, is often expressed in symbols modeled on processes of gestation and parturition. The neophytes are likened to or treated as embryos, newborn infants, or sucklings by symbolic means which vary from culture to culture.
>
> (p. 340)

So far, so good. Moll appears to be undergoing a symbolic rebirth which displaces her sense of first origins. Next should come either death or new social placement.

But suddenly the account splits. Defoe interposes Moll's retrospective judgment in her description of 'the compleatest Misery on Earth' – which is a mind weighed down with immense guilt, yet unrelieved by remorse or repentance. Now we hear two stories. The first is of collapse and failure in face of the liminal challenge presented by the rite of passage:

> I was become a meer *Newgate-Bird*, as Wicked and as Outragious as any of them; nay, I scarce retain'd the Habit and Custom of good Breeding, and Manners, which all along till now run thro' my Conversation; so thoro' a Degeneracy had possess'd me, that I was no more the same thing that I had been, than if I had never been otherwise than what I was now.
>
> (p. 279)

The second story ensues at once with Moll's trauma of seeing her Lancashire husband brought into Newgate under arrest as a highwayman, combined with her own indictment by the grand jury:

My Temper was touch'd before, the harden'd wretched boldness
of Spirit, which I had acquir'd in the Prison abated, and conscious
Guilt began to flow in upon my Mind: In short, I began to think,
and to think is one real Advance from Hell to Heaven; all that
Hellish harden'd state and temper of Soul, which I said so much
of before, is but a deprivation of Thought; he that is restor'd to his
Power of thinking, is restor'd to himself.

(p. 281)

Defoe employs the model of spiritual autobiography and decisively
breaks with it, for self-consciousness here replaces the ascent from
hell to heaven, thought replaces salvation, and private awareness
rather than emblematic public expression defines meaning.[18]
Repentance, reunion with a husband she always had loved,
transportation to Virginia in lieu of execution, and ultimately a new
life of prosperous gentility ensue. Narrative predicates have subtly
introduced time, sequence, and causation into the liminal place.

At the simplest level we notice that Moll's conversion leads to
wealth, not to any spiritual sustenance. Were there no attempt on
Defoe's part to explicate this arbitrary denouement in spiritual terms,
it would follow easily from Moll's rite of passage in the old Newgate.
But Moll asserts that she has undergone a revolution of conscience,
and Defoe's use of conventions drawn from Puritan spiritual
autobiography leads us to expect one. Although Defoe depicts the
old type of prison, when his imagination reforms it into narrative,
it splits apart into different stories that register to us as irony and
paradox. Thus, while the social role of prisons is not explicitly at
issue, we can see the unselfconsciousness of the liminal prison
slipping away in the juxtapositions that occur in *Moll Flanders* (1722).

No doubt what I have called Moll's second story (the spiritual one)
could be told from a purely liminal perspective, for with that lucid
simplicity possible only in fantasy or fiction, Moll's account outlines
the cultural significance of the old prisons. Their filth, their
dangerousness, their mysterious randomness, their carnival
subculture, their absorption of the divine and otherworldly imagery
of hell into a secular and social context all point to their liminality;
that is, to their provision of transformational experience on privileged
ground where both festivity and profound danger are structurally
central. This is precisely my argument: that Defoe takes the material
surfaces of an institution that operates according to one set of
principles and from those surfaces constructs a mentality that views
the world quite differently. This may appear to be no more than the
simple notion that his narrator holds a recognizable point of view.
But really this is not the case since Moll is the sole narrator, and

she undergoes *both* experiences. Finally, let me underline that change itself is not the essence of the penitentiary as opposed to the liminal prison; change may occur in both, but the rite of passage is merely an occasion, while the penitentiary experience seeks out reasoned causes, driven, on the one hand, by physical circumstance in all its detail and, on the other, by the assumption that human behavior is – to use Moll's term – governed by thought acting in response to circumstance.

The point is that, at the very same instant when Defoe's plots represent the liminal prison in all its externally arbitrary, emblematic circumstance, he is reimagining punishment causally and sequentially as the reformation of inner thought. The peculiar quality of the novel as Defoe conceived it enabled ideas, which in themselves were not new, to be inserted culturally through their enactment in a minutely particular mental world. The mere presence of ideas is not enough. The reception of early tracts such as Dr. Thomas Bray's *Essay Towards the Reformation of Newgate and Other Prisons in and about London* (1702), which remained unpublished until the nineteenth century, underscores this fact. Intellectual history is but one strand in the skein of cultural history. The modern scholarly picture of Defoe as an eclectic, intellectually informed writer who purposefully drew upon a wide range of literary traditions – spiritual autobiography, casuistry, pilgrim allegory, exempla in the 'guide' literature aimed at youth, criminal narratives, and so forth – obscures the intuition with which he placed the general and the particular in a wholly new structural relation.[19]

Defoe's 'realism' ensues from his masterstroke. It comprises his unwavering focus on an individual character's mental world and his construction of each character's mentality out of the minute particulars, the very superficies, of physical objects.[20] But the condition of possibility that enables Defoe's 'realism' lies in a structural innovation at once peculiar to his moment and so fundamental to our own world view that ordinarily we pass over it.

Let me characterize it as clearly as I can. Defoe's narratives foster the belief that ordinary everyday experience is meaningful. This he achieves by constructing apparently true life stories, the plots of which purport to accord with established paradigms of moral significance even though these plots contain a discordant profusion of thought and incident. The quality in Defoe's narratives that reminds us of allegory comprises their conformity to discernible meaning, while the urge to read them allegorically corresponds to our wish to find significance in diversity. Because Defoe leads us to ascribe meaning to a tangible fictional world that includes recognizable attributes, we come to think of human destiny as intentional or preconceived. But only the inconsistencies and contradictory materials that belong to our idea of realism, or even of reality itself, enable this meaning to emerge and validate the proposition that the flux of ordinary experience signifies. This is profoundly paradoxical, for the nature and function of novelistic realism lie in its ability to produce meaning by containing its own contradiction and thus to leave the impression that consciousness and subjectivity are stable across time.[21]

One way to describe Defoe's contribution is to note that he took the traditional Puritan methods of reading the world allegorically and ran them backwards. Before, divinely validated stories had been sought in actual lives (as in spiritual autobiography), but he contrived fictional lives that could be construed as material validations of spiritual order. With Defoe, salvation becomes a matter of self-confirmation through psychological insight. This is not merely to propose a commonplace: that Defoe started with meanings and constructed a fictional world out of which they could be extracted in turn. Every classically oriented theory I know of claims some such constructive essence for fiction. Herein lies much difficulty, for even during the Renaissance the theory of fictional meaning continued to be argued in a remarkably stable terminology while narrative procedures were shifting radically.[22] Indeed, my own description of Defoe's innovation appears to fail in this respect, for how can it distinguish between the sort of moral fable envisioned by Sidney's *Apology for Poetry* and typified by great exemplary fictions such as the *Aeneid*, *The Faerie Queene*, or Sidney's own *Arcadia* and works such as Defoe's? Obviously these earlier stories also construct worlds out of which meaning can be extracted; the vital difference is that they presume their entire contents to be homologous with the moral prototypes they represent. This may not always in fact be so (for a variety of reasons, including failures of execution) but the presumption of both author and reader of these works is that all elements and details refer themselves ultimately to moral significance, even if only as devices to delight the reader and keep hold of his attention.[23]

Defoe describes his own enterprise in the very traditional terms I have been discussing when, in the preface to Robinson Crusoe's *Serious Reflections*, the third and least often read volume of his most famous work, he says:

> I come now to acknowledge to my reader that the present work is not merely the product of the two first volumes, but the two first volumes may rather be called the product of this. The fable is always made for the moral, not the moral for the fable.[24]

This terminology is retrospective, and it forces Defoe's greatest work into traditional categories that grant priority to invention over execution and deem fictional events valid when they can be seen to correspond to moral prototypes. Defoe says his *Idea* preceded its mere fictional exposition. At the same time, however, he asserts the temporal precedence of the fable – that is, he wrote it first. He seems at pains to deny his innovation, the essence of which had been in finding a new way to validate fictional meaning.

The way is so simple that we assume it: Defoe constructs fictions whose contents are not consistent with reference to any moral, but only with reference to a central consciousness. His idea of 'just history' and of 'fact' is such that, in order to convey his moral, he has to recreate the very predicament of finding meaning in the world at large. The truthfulness to fact which, in Defoe's view, grants credence to his moral can exist only under materially realistic conditions that erode or even contradict it. Moll's repentance is but one of the more obvious examples. His archetypal plot represents a central consciousness constructing a moral world in face of this contradiction. His fiction purveys the myth – or ideology – that such representational constructions are real and material in themselves. Defoe formulates this myth most powerfully in *Crusoe*, where he constitutes the course of discovery and change that his castoff undergoes as stages in the fabrication of an island estate. (It is worth noting, as an aside, that well before his death, Defoe's brief novelistic career ends with *Roxanna*, a work whose heroine never assembles a morally coherent world and whose consciousness splits off into Amy, her servant-double.)

Defoe's reversal of the traditional method of reading the world allegorically becomes a radical innovation because he takes it so realistically; that is, with such material literalism. Defoe's very conception of personality derives from materialistic ideas of how the human mind and character are constructed from sense impressions. These ideas, on which Locke had founded his theories of personality, education, and government, have been cited by Maximillian Novak as formative to Defoe's intellectual world and by Ian Watt as instrumental to the rise of the novel.[25] They presage the Utilitarian analysis of pleasure and pain as motive forces, on which the narrative penitentiary depends for its theoretical impetus. In these institutions the sentence consisted of a reformation according to a narrative sequence of rewards and punishments over time. The sudden clarity of liminal conversion does not figure in these clean, well-ordered places.

We have now returned to the center of my argument. The narrative penitentiary, which uses the material instruments of architecture and daily regime to recreate the convict, who has been sentenced for a crime which signifies tangible failure to extract moral order from experience, parallels the novel in which a facsimile of the material world is shaped by a central consciousness discovering ordering principles among contradictions. It is worth recalling here that penitentiaries were constructed as narratives in the tracts of reformers long before the institutions were built. The idea of starting with categories of prisoners divided according to age, character, nature of crime, or the like and ending with a facsimile of an 'ordinary' person is fundamental to the reformist arguments. Since no one had ever seen these things done in prison, every reformer's account of what would ensue once the penitentiaries were built was a fiction.[26]

At the simplest level, Defoe made the link I have been discussing when, in the Preface to the *Serious Reflections*, he said:

> All these reflections are just history of a state of forced confinement, which in my real history is represented by a confined retreat in an island; and it is as reasonable to represent one kind of imprisonment by another, as it is to represent anything that really exists by that which exists not.
>
> (p. xii)

But representation alters as it preserves, creates as it maintains, and Defoe, for all his defensiveness here, cannot forestall the generative power of his narrative. Because Defoe writes in new forms where crosscurrents are available to analysis, he accommodates during the 1720s structures of feeling that will not be institutionally constituted for decades and that are available to consciousness at this moment in history only in fictional modes.

The marginal place of confinement where liminal experiences of transformation can occur also figures centrally in *Robinson Crusoe* (1719); at the same time, even as in *Moll Flanders*, the work presents materially realistic delineations of consciousness shaped through the narration of imprisonment.

Here is Crusoe's situation liminally considered. Prior to the wreck, Crusoe lays stress on the unceremonious break with his parents and on the immaturity of obeying 'blindly the Dictates of my Fancy rather than my Reason.'[27] After the wreck, invoking the metaphor of condemnation and reprieve, he hovers at the boundary between life and death:

> I believe it is impossible to express to the Life what the Extasies and Transports of the Soul are, when it is so sav'd, as I may say, out of the very Grave; and I do not wonder now at that Custom, *viz.* That when a Malefactor who has the Halter about his Neck,

is tyed up, and just going to be turn'd off, and has a Repreive brought to him: I say, I do not wonder that they bring a Surgeon with it, to let him Blood that very Moment they tell him of it, that the Surprise may not drive the Animal Spirits from the Heart, and overwhelm him.

(p. 46)

Crusoe's thinking here catches the primitive doubleness of marginal symbolism in the notion of bloodletting at the moment of reprieve: the wound that heals. His overarching metaphor assumes the liminal prison because Newgate launched the condemned onto the infamous road terminating at Tyburn gallows, and held the fortunate few who returned with reprieves until their transportation abroad. Indeed, we later discover that Crusoe has been simultaneously alive and dead throughout most of the book, for legally he has undergone '*Civil Death*' (pp. 283–84). During the island confinement he subjects his entire previous standard of life to criticism; his initiative rises to the recreation, often in parodic forms, of virtually every craft or social comfort known in England. Time becomes conjectural after he loses track during a delirious, nearly fatal, illness, and its value becomes immeasurably small during his ceaseless labors to shape the island into a microcosm of European life. Having undergone his own rite of passage, Crusoe undertakes Friday's instruction and eventually institutes a facsimile of civil society on the basis of truths he has discovered about human nature. Finally, Crusoe, as Governor himself reprieves certain mutineers and commutes their sentences to a form of transportation: the colonization of the island. He thus closes the liminal cycle with full acceptance of axiomatic social values, including the use of reprieves as tokens in the system of patrician patronage through which the gentry exercised authority.[28] Although Crusoe never settles down to realize them, the social prospects implied by his entry into the class of substantial landholders have been enacted prospectively on the island through his journeys from sea coast fort to inland country seat, as well as by his exercises in governance. In the end, however much greater his fortunes might have been had he remained in Brazil instead of undertaking the fateful voyage, Crusoe does achieve a new economic status well above his father's 'middle state.'

Yet the liminal account, like Crusoe's metaphor of reprieve, seems artificial – not false, but insufficient or old fashioned – because Defoe centers the work on Crusoe's obsession with finding an account of his mental life that coheres sequentially, causally, and spiritually. Solitude is the occasion, narrative the medium, and prison the overarching figure:

Now I began to construe the Words mentioned above, *Call on me, and I will deliver you*, in a different Sense from what I had ever done before; for then I had no Notion of any thing being call'd Deliverance, but my being deliver'd from the Captivity I was in; for tho' I was indeed at large in the Place, yet the Island was certainly a Prison to me, and that in the worst Sense in the World; but now I learn'd to take it in another Sense: Now I look'd back upon my past Life with such Horrour, and my Sins appear'd so dreadful, that my Soul sought nothing of God, but Deliverance from the Load of Guilt that bore down all my Comfort: As for my solitary Life it was nothing; I did not so much as pray to be deliver'd from it, or think of it.

(pp. 96–97)

Here, as in the wreck, Crusoe's terms are more directly religious than in Moll's turn to *thought*. But in context the theological referents are wholly subordinate to the machinations of Defoe's narrative as it struggles – repeatedly retelling the early phases of the story – to trace the reformation of Crusoe's conscience. We move from 'just history of fact,' to straight journal, to journal interrupted and dissolved by reflection. Defoe uses the 'real' words of Crusoe's chronicle to certify the truth of reflections that break into the texture of the critical pages surrounding the delirium and eventually overtake them entirely. Narrative in its relation to consciousness is the actual subject here: accounts of the self *are* the self, and fuller, more circumstantial, accounts placed in a reflective context are more true than mere chronicles or journals. This section of *Robinson Crusoe* stands at a vital juncture in the history of the novel because of its literal quest through generic types for some material equivalent to the formation of thought. This quest structures Defoe's 'realism' as a mode of representation that incorporates and subordinates the others into what Bakhtin calls polyglossia. The new, reflective, consciousness-centered form literally displaces the genres it has subsumed – a state of affairs traced in Defoe's text by Crusoe's progressive dilution of his ink until the journal fades into gestural illegibility a few pages following the passage quoted above.

During Crusoe's 'solemn' observance of the second anniversary of his shipwreck, the prison metaphor recurs, again yoked with solitude. Here, the two terms fall into clear opposition, signifying states of mind before and after Crusoe's correct understanding of deliverance some two months earlier. To be imprisoned is to be subject to random misery:

I was a Prisoner lock'd up with the Eternal Bars and Bolts of the Ocean, in an uninhabited Wilderness, without Redemption: In the

123

midst of the greatest Composures of my Mind, this would break
out upon me like a Storm, and make me wring my Hands, and
weep like a Child: Sometimes it would take me in the middle of
my Work, and I would immediately sit down and sigh, and look
upon the Ground for an Hour or two together; and this was still
worse to me; for if I could burst out into Tears, or vent my self
by Words, it would go off, and the Grief having exhausted it self
would abate.

(p. 113)

But to comprehend solitude is to be spiritually and mentally whole,
as well as to function materially:

I spent the whole Day in humble and thankful Acknowledgments
of the many wonderful Mercies which my Solitary Condition was
attended with ... I gave humble and hearty Thanks that God had
been pleas'd to discover to me, even that it was possible I might be
more happy in this Solitary Condition, than I should have been in
a Liberty of Society, and in all the Pleasures of the World. That he
could fully make up to me, the Deficiencies of my Solitary State,
and the want of Humane Society by his Presence ... supporting,
comforting, and encouraging me to depend upon his Providence
here, and hope for his Eternal Presence hereafter.

(p. 112)

Meanings outnumber terms here as the notion of prison slides from
the liminal, arbitrary, openly public realm into the private realm of
reflective thought.

Several things are happening. (1) The liminal experience, while
present, is losing its tangibility and its outer forms are assuming
a negative tinge. (2) The outcome of punishment is now being
represented as mental reformation. (3) Errant personality is
reconstituted as self-consciousness by solitary reflection. (4) And the
ability to function materially is specifically attributed to the proper
inner comprehension of life as a story, each circumstance of which
is meaningful. We see the mythology of reform taking shape here.
Prison, now equated with solitary reflection, is first viewed as
negative, liminal, random, punitive, vengeful; but it slides into
another thing entirely – a notion of something salubrious, beneficent,
reformative, and productive of wealth and social integration.
Crusoe's illness can be read, in this light, as a prospective allegory
of the move from the old, fever-ridden jails to the clean, healthy,
contemplative solitude of the penitentiaries.

Crusoe equates having a self with being able to account for his crime, and his story literally enacts a quest for some narrative equivalent to personality. Just as his construction of material surrogates of European civilization is indistinguishable from the narration of his story, so is novelization inseparable from the reformation of his consciousness. Friday's advent enables Crusoe to test the power of narrative to constitute the self. Crusoe must teach him the causes and raise him up into the crafts before Friday is recognizable as human and Crusoe is validated as a person. Crusoe ends by forcing the mutineers into his own cave prison by creating the personage of the Governor of the Island as a pure fiction. The self and the authority it projects are shown as narrative constructs that effect material ends.

IV

John Gay's *Beggar's Opera* (1728) changed the way in which the idea of Newgate signified and the level of awareness at which it did so. Gay explicitly enacts the rejection of the liminal prison implicit in the opposing structures of feeling delineated by Defoe's narratives. Instead of the place of marginality, Newgate becomes the place of contradiction. Of course contradictory symbolisms had long assumed their place deep in the nature of liminal marginality and were tacitly subsumed in rites of passage that subordinated paradox to larger social truths. But with Gay, contradiction becomes an issue at the level of discourse. The old acceptances become untenable because in Gay's Newgate every meaning is contradicted by some other. All categories cancel one another out. Peacham is warmhearted and predatory; Polly is innocent and rapacious; Macheath is hero and highwayman, husband and adulterer, hanged and reprieved, great man and scoundrel – a pure paradox. Gay's 'total irony,' as Ian Donaldson has called it, dissolves all boundaries, whether between criminals and prime ministers, or between gentlemen and highwaymen.[29] These total ironies sap liminality of function by discrediting the very distinctions and delineations that its randomness worked ultimately to sanction. *The Beggar's Opera* was genuinely subversive not because it exposed authority to temporary ridicule, as festive comedies had done for thousands of years, but because it depicted all moral authority as permanently corrupted by self-interest. The virtues that survive are the strictly personal ones that adhere exclusively to Polly and Macheath. Here, as implicitly in Defoe, the world is ordered by personality, not personality by the world. Although Polly and Macheath are far from ideal human beings, we tend to imagine human nature on their terms and to exaggerate their virtues as antidotes to the sardonic world they inhabit.

One index of the radical nature of *The Beggar's Opera* is that its treatment of villainy as a profession horrified Defoe, who condemned its jocular pardon of Macheath as the highwayman-hero.[30] Gay's Newgate, compared with Defoe's, becomes a place of cynicism in terms of character, sarcasm in terms of tone (note the dance of prisoners in chains), and arbitrariness in terms of plot (note the rescue of Macheath).

Although I cannot now argue the issue of how realism in *The Beggar's Opera* links Gay's work to the novel and goes hand in hand with its reach across accustomed generic boundaries, I can stress the point by noting some suggestive facts. Rich, the producer of the work, had specialized in pantomimes which, in the vogue of the 1720s, contrasted with plays and operas by their elaborate scenery showing real places. A few years before, a pantomime of the famous prison breaker Jack Shepard had been shown at Drury Lane with scenery 'painted from the real Place of Action.'[31] The earliest versions of Hogarth's canvases of *The Beggar's Opera* on stage at Lincoln's Inn Fields indicate that Rich probably used realistic pantomime scenery.[32]

As a second instance of Gay's realism, let me emphasize the specific material conditions epitomized in his construal of Swift's idea that he write a 'Newgate Pastoral.' Gay takes Newgate's ancient marginal standing as a gateway or place of passage and reformulates it into a generic contradiction between terms drawn from pastoral and those drawn from heroic drama and opera. From this germ, Gay built the inspired edifice of contradictions in genre, character, plot, and tone that make up the total irony of *The Beggar's Opera*. Both Swift and Gay had to have had the literal place in mind. Everyone was familiar with Newgate's location neither inside nor outside the City, but literally in and part of its walls. Everyone feared the rural terrain surrounding London, where one was much more likely to encounter highwaymen than swains. (In the 1720s, Jonathan Wild's luxurious house stood outside the wall, across the street called Old Bailey.) Swift and Gay probably would have noticed that the old Newgate, as rebuilt after the Great Fire, was ornamented in the Tuscan order. In the Vitruvian and Palladian architectural vocabulary, this order signified the strength called for in prisons, arsenals, and treasuries; and also the rusticity and rural simplicity appropriate to farmhouses, stables, grottoes, and dog kennels. These qualities had signified opposite potentials of civic enclosure and rural freedom, both latent in the liminal perspective and both personified at the old

Newgate with statues that included not only Severity, Justice, Fortitude and Prudence, but Peace, Plenty, and Liberty.[33]

The simultaneity of liminal and penitential views of prison found in Defoe's narratives no longer is possible after *The Beggar's Opera*. Gay's total irony discredited the very fabric of established order by using Newgate and its mysteries as a central metaphor. Gay acted at precisely the moment Hogarth and Fielding were establishing themselves independently in London. Both take up their public careers with works closely affined to Gay's. Fielding opened his first London play two weeks after *The Beggar's Opera*, and his plays thereafter explored generically mixed forms such as Gay had introduced in *The What d'Ye Call It* and perfected in *The Beggar's Opera*. Later, Fielding took up Peacham's original, Jonathan Wild, as the subject of one of his first novels. Hogarth, one of whose earliest commissions in oil yielded a series of paintings showing the climactic scene of *The Beggar's Opera* on stage, confronted Gay's contradiction in his two great sequences, *The Harlot's Progress* (painted 1730/31, published 1732) and *The Rake's Progress* (painted 1734, published 1735). He turned, in short, to the visual equivalent of the narratives in which Defoe had shaped the penitentiary idea out of the material of the liminal prison. With Hogarth, as with Defoe, we are considering the reformulation of existing genres into a new mode – this time taking Gay into account. Hogarth claimed the invention and dubbed it, paradoxically, 'comic history painting.'

In the visual arts, Hogarth's series of 'comic history paintings' repeat Defoe's innovation in verbal narrative of more than a decade earlier. Defoe had posed an alternative to liminal confinement by representing it causally and sequentially as an individual quest for meaning. Gay enacted the contradiction of the liminal prison that had been implicit in the structure of feeling Defoe reveals, and he dissolved all meaning derived from social institutions. Hogarth's narrative plates accept Gay's rejection of liminal transformation and the social structure it implies. The Harlot and the Rake both die pursuing passion in the predatory social world Gay set forth. His endings are the kind found in bourgeois tragedy, not the arbitrary heroic sort Gay ridiculed in his comic conclusion to *The Beggar's Opera*. Hogarth's visual narratives reject the liminal prison, but in so doing they reintroduce sequence and moral causation. In *The Rake's Progress*, for example, the liminal prison splits into the Fleet and Bedlam, which appear sequentially in the series as stages of development in the plot. In the Fleet scene Hogarth represents the farcical aspect of the old prison, but rejects its comic potential by ending the series tragically in Bedlam. The Fleet in its carnival aspect has become a step on the way to insanity and death, not an arena of free play from which any outcome can issue. The rite of passage, outside of ordinary time and full of potential for either rebirth or sudden death, now splits into the opposites of caprice and terror seen in sequence. The life of caprice leads to a death of terror. Finally, Hogarth's Progresses, not to mention the explicit captions on his plates, imply alternative stories in which the victims might prosper. The plates spur us to consider social institutions that might foster rather than destroy such youths. Later, Hogarth's double progress, *Industry and Idleness* (1747), actually tells both stories at once and, though recognizing the difficulty of restraining passionate natures, veers toward the workshop as a social model.[34]

Fielding's *Jonathan Wild* (1743), like Hogarth's earlier Progresses, takes Gay's 'total irony' as its point of departure. Fielding directly imitates *The Beggar's Opera* in his use of Jonathan Wild, the thieftaker, as a surrogate for Walpole, the Great Man. But where Hogarth implied an alternate story shaped by reasoned and human institutions, Fielding's plot supplies it. Fielding underscores his rejection of the liminal prison and the society of which it was a structural part by introducing Heartfree, the good man who is nearly hanged because of Wild's perversion of the old system. Further, Fielding's story never slips from the control of his omniscient, heavily ironic narrator who, at the denouement, declares that his story will not be marred by a rescue like that in *The Beggar's Opera*. Instead, Fielding saves Heartfree by bringing forward a conscientious magistrate whose inquiries have unraveled the willful case of mistaken identity upon which Wilde had founded his denunciation of the innocent man.

A crucial step has occurred. Fielding has introduced authoritative moral control rather than leaving it implicit – as it is in the novels of Defoe. These novels had shaped consciousness through narrative specification of the material world. But consciousness needed governance, in Fielding's view, and so did narrative. From this belief arose both his attack on the moral ambiguity of Richardson's *Pamela* and his derivation of the 'comic epic in prose' as a narrative form.

Fielding's literary innovation signals, in my analysis, a major stage in the emergence of structures of feeling that enable the narrative penitentiary because he moves from the use of consciousness contrived as a narrative of the material world to the inclusion of omniscient authority in that world. In *Amelia* (1751), Fielding's last novel, these structures are at their most available. The hero's every move takes place in literal prisons or in the sanctuary of 'rules' and 'verges' pertaining to them. The novel opens with an overt rejection of the old-style prison as a source of every possible corruption from fraud to adultery. In this extended prison sequence, Booth, the hero, falls under the seductive spell of a protracted narrative told, in the consciousness-centered mode of Defoe, by the remarkable Miss Williams. At the end of her story, Booth commits the adultery upon which the balance of the central plot hinges. Thereafter, Booth and Amelia are kept under watch by the beneficent, all-knowing authority, Dr. Harrison. Much later in the novel, when Dr. Harrison has Booth committed for debt, this good man controls every detail. He enacts an exemplary narrative with Booth as the main character and creates a fictional surrogate of the narrative penitentiary. Harrison's procedure stands in the sharpest possible contrast with that of the jailer in the opening scene. In the same year as *Amelia*, Fielding wrote his *Enquiry into the Causes of the Late Increase of Robbers*, and two years later he produced *A Proposal for Making an Effectual Provision for the Poor* (1753). In this latter work he called for supplanting executions with intermediate punishments that combined 'correction of the body' with 'correction of the mind.' One of the punishments he conceived was solitary confinement – which was to become one of the leading notions among the reformers.[35]

With the late works of Fielding, we reach the moment when the structures of feeling I have been tracing in narrative forms emerge with full force in reformist discourse and then, during the 1760s, in the external form of prisons. Now the fictional materiality of the novel gives way to the physical materiality of the architectural facade. The old prisons would continue side by side with the new, but they could never again be looked upon as places of liminal passage. Perhaps this fact can be grasped most clearly by juxtaposing George Dance, Sr.'s 1751 project for a New Newgate, which would still have been a gateway using the Tuscan order, with his son's horrific facade of 1768.[36] An enormous change has occurred. Now, prison buildings will be shaped into exemplary symbols that face the outside world and serve to regulate crime by *illustration*. The new prisons will not only shut criminals in; they will shut out the citizen, whom they stop, grip, and frightfully engage almost as if he has become a criminal. They will inspire narrative creation by the viewer. The final stage will take the narrative inside the penitentiary.

Notes

1. *The Interpretation of Cultures* (New York: Basic Books, 1973), p. 451.

2. Sigmund Freud, Clark University Lectures, *Standard Edition of the Complete Psychological Works of Sigmund Freud* (London: Hogarth Press, 1953), XI, 38: 'Psychoanalysis prepared to find *several* motives for one and the same mental occurrence, whereas what seems to be our innate craving for causality declares itself satisfied with a *single* psychical cause.' Kenneth Burke, *A*

Grammar of Motives (Berkeley: University of California Press, 1969), p. xxii. Burke shows how language bridges the spheres of culture and social action which, as Geertz suggests, are merely analytic categories: 'One of the more useful ways – but far from the only one – of distinguishing between culture and social system is to see the former as an ordered system of meaning and of symbols, in terms of which social interaction takes place; and to see the latter as the pattern of social interaction itself. On the one level there is the framework of beliefs, expressive symbols, and values in terms of which individuals define their world, express their feelings, and make their judgments; on the other level there is the ongoing process of interactive behavior, whose persistent form we call social structure. Culture is the fabric of meaning in terms of which human beings interpret their experience and guide their action; social structure is the form that action takes, the actually existing network of social relations. Culture and social structure are then but different abstractions from the same phenomena' (*The Interpretation of Cultures*, pp. 144–45).

3. See W. J. Sheehan, 'Finding Solace in Eighteenth-Century Newgate,' in J. S. Cockburn, *Crime in England, 1550–1800*, (Princeton: Princeton University Press, 1977), pp. 229–45, especially pp. 233–34; and Joanna Innes, 'The King's Bench Prison in the Later Eighteenth Century: Law, Authority and Order in a London Debtors' Prison,' in John Brewer and John Styles, eds., *An Ungovernable People: The English and Their Law in the Seventeenth and Eighteenth Centuries* (New Brunswick, N.J.: Rutgers University Press, 1980), pp. 250–98.

4. For detailed accounts of eighteenth-century prisons, see John Howard, *The State of the Prisons* (Warrington: William Eyres, 1777); rpt. ed. Martin Wright (Abingdon: Professional Books, 1977); the posthumous fourth edition, as well as the second edition of Howard's *Lazarettos in Europe*, are rpt. in *Prisons and Lazarettos*, ed. Ralph W. England, Jr. 2 vols. (Montclair, N.J.: Patterson Smith, 1973). Informative modern works include Sidney and Beatrice Webb, *English Prisons Under Local Government*, rpt. ed. Leon Radzinowicz (Hamden, Conn.: Archon Books, 1963), pp. 18–37; Leon Radzinowicz, 'The Movement for Reform, 1750–1833,' Vol. I of *A History of English Criminal Law and Its Administration from 1750* (New York: Macmillan, 1948), pp. 165–493; R. W. E. Hinde, *The British Penal System, 1773–1950* (London: Duckworth, 1951), pp. 1–47; Michel Foucault, *Surveiller et punir: Naissance de la prison* (Paris: Gallimard, 1975), trans. Alan Sheridan, *Discipline and Punish: The Birth of Prison* (London: Allen Lane, 1977), especially chs. 2, 3; Michael Ignatieff, *A Just Measure of Pain: The Penitentiary in the Industrial Revolution, 1750–1850* (New York: Pantheon, 1978), pp. 15–113; Sean McConville, *A History of English Prison Administration*, I (London: Routledge and Kegan Paul, 1981), pp. 49–134; and Robin Evans, *The Fabrication of Virtue: English Prison Architecture, 1750–1840* (Cambridge: Cambridge University Press, 1982), pp. 1–236.

5. A few early instances include Geffray Minshull, *Essays and Characters of a Prison and Prisoners* (London, 1618); John Taylor, *The Praise and Virtue of a Jayle and Jaylers* (London, 1623); and John Frith, *Vox Piscis: or, the Book-Fish* (London, 1627).

6. I lay stress here on Turner's initial essay, 'Betwixt and Between: The Liminal Period in *Rites de Passage*,' *Proceedings of the American Ethnological Society* (1964), pp. 4–20; substantially reprinted in his *Forest of Symbols* (Ithaca: Cornell University Press, 1967) and in William A. Lessa and Evon Z. Vogt, eds., *Reader in Comparative Religion: An Anthropological Approach*, 3rd ed. (New York: Harper and Row, 1972), pp. 338–47. The quotation just cited appears on p. 341 of this last edition; subsequent parenthetical references in my text are to this edition unless noted. Turner took inspiration from Arnold van

Gennep, *Les Rites de Passage* (Paris: E. Nourry, 1909), trans. Monika B. Vizedom and Gabrielle L. Caffee (London: Routledge and Kegan Paul, 1960). Subsequently, Turner has developed his ideas in a variety of contexts, but for the sake of clarity I wish to adhere mainly to his original definitions. The later works include *The Ritual Process: Structure and Anti-Structure* (Chicago: Aldine Publishing Co., 1969), especially chs. 3, 5; *Dramas, Fields, and Metaphors: Symbolic Action in Human Society* (Ithaca: Cornell University Press, 1974), especially ch. 6; 'Variations on a Theme of Liminality,' in *Secular Ritual*, eds. Sally F. Moore and Barbara G. Myerhoff (Assen: Van Gorcum, 1977); and 'Process, System, and Symbol: A New Anthropological Synthesis,' *Daedalus*, 106, no. 3 (1977), 61–80; see also his 'Comments and Conclusions,' in Barbara A. Babcock, ed., *The Reversible World: Symbolic Inversion in Art and Society* (Ithaca: Cornell University Press, 1978), pp. 276–96. For an account of Turner's work as intermediary between social science and literary studies, see Clifford Geertz, 'Blurred Genres: The Refiguration of Social Thought,' *The American Scholar*, 49 (Spring 1980), 165–79, especially 172–73.

7. The first two quotations in this paragraph are from *Dramas, Fields, and Metaphors*, pp. 15 and 256.

8. W. Paget, *The Humours of the Fleet* (London, 1749).

9. Ignatieff, *A Just Measure of Pain*, p. 38.

10. See, for example, Robert Darnton, *The Literary Underground of the Old Regime* (Cambridge, Mass.: Harvard University Press, 1982), pp. 159–65 for rites of passage among Continental printers. As Darton notes in 'A Journeyman's Life Under the Old Regime,' *Princeton Alumni Weekly*, 82, no. 1 (September 7, 1981), 13–14, Benjamin Franklin, having refused the second of successive garnishes in the London shop where he apprenticed, suffered from practical jokes. All, says water-drinking Franklin, were 'ascrib'd to the Chapel Ghost, which they said ever haunted those not regularly admitted.' He eventually paid up, but then converted most of the shop to a healthy diet of porridge rather than the beer his garnish or *'Bienvenu'* had been meant to finance. The Chapel was both the printing shop and the body of journeymen, just as Paget's mates in the Fleet formed its College. Franklin's full account appears in his *Autobiography*, ed. Leonard W. Labaree *et al.* (New Haven: Yale University Press, 1964), pp. 100–01. On the revision of old customs governed by tradition in American ideology, where literary representation radically altered paternalistic social forms, see Jay Fliegelman, *Prodigals and Pilgrims: The American Revolution Against Patriarchal Authority, 1750–1800* (Cambridge: Cambridge University Press, 1982), especially pp. 106–13 on Franklin.

11. Jürgen Habermas, *Strukturwandel der Öffentlichkeit* (Neuwied: Hermann Luchterhand, 1962), pp. 45, 64, 73.

12. *The Division of Labor in Society*, trans. George Simpson (New York: The Free Press, 1964), p. 97. Dan Sperber observes more generally that 'the symbolic is not a means of encoding information, but a means of organizing it.' *Rethinking Symbolism*, trans. Alice L. Morton, Cambridge Studies in Social Anthropology, 11 (Cambridge: Cambridge University Press, 1974), p. 70. For a comparable view, elaborated in terms eclectic enough to embrace significant ideas of both Marx and Durkheim, see Pierre Bourdieu, *Outline of a Theory of Practice*, trans. Richard Nice, Cambridge Studies in Social Anthropology, 16 (Cambridge: Cambridge University Press, 1977). I am indebted to Professor David Wellbery for these last two citations, as well as for comments that inspired numbers of substantive changes in this essay.

13. *The Political Unconscious: Narrative as a Socially Symbolic Act* (Ithaca, N.Y.: Cornell University Press). p. 48.

14. On time measurement as a cultural phenomenon, see E. P. Thompson, 'Time, Work-Discipline, and Industrial Capitalism,' *Past and Present*, 38 (1967), 56–97; and Niklas Luhmann, *The Differentiation of Society*, trans. Stephen Holmes and Charles Larmore (New York: Columbia University Press, 1982), pp. 239, 248.

15. 'Introduction to the Structural Analysis of Narratives,' in *Image-Music-Text*, ed. Stephen Heath (New York: Hill & Wang, 1977), pp. 83–84.

16. This change was adumbrated in the technical development of early modern Continental law as traced by John H. Langbein in *Torture and the Law of Proof* (Chicago: University of Chicago Press, 1977). Under Roman-canon law a criminal could be declared guilty and sentenced to death or mutilation only on the basis of 'full-proof,' which had to be founded upon reliable testimony by two eye witnesses or upon confession – thus the use of torture. Historically, the use of torture declined with the emergence of technical devices in law that validated the kind of fine-grained, judicial inquiry (narrative construction) necessary to justify punishment based on circumstantial evidence. Such evidence could sustain only 'half-proof,' and, since no accumulation of half-proofs constituted full-proof, it could not support condemnation, but only time sentences in transient penal institutions. In countries with Mediterranean ports the galleys served conveniently, while in the Low Countries workhouses that originally had been devised for vagrants, beggars, and misdemeanants allowed for punishments measured through time. The famous Amsterdam Rasphuis (opened 1596), for example, inspired a variety of projects during the reformist phase of the Enlightenment – most especially the Maison de Force, a great fortified house of correction opened at Ghent in 1772.

   I join Robin Evans in laying stress on the vital difference between houses of correction and penitentiaries. The houses of correction were demonstrative, emblematic, and theatrical; their impact was corporal, though not final like execution or aggravated like torture. Their aim was *production* of goods through labor. Penitentiaries were psychological, sequential, and introspective; their aim was *reformation* of character through the controlled alteration of material circumstance over time. For this reason, as Evans argues, houses of correction could and did inhabit every variety of building from former royal palaces (London Bridewell) or convents (Amsterdam Rasphuis) to disused chapels or churches (Reading Bridewell), whereas the penitentiary idea brought into being an entirely new architectural type. See *The Fabrication of Virtue*, especially pp. 12–13 and 47–75. Also, Sidney and Beatrice Webb, *English Prisons Under Local Government*, pp. 1–17; Thorsten Sellin, *Pioneering in Penology: The Amsterdam Houses of Correction in the Sixteenth and Seventeenth Centuries* (Philadelphia: University of Pennsylvania Press, 1944); Max Grühut, *Penal Reform, A Comparative Study* (Oxford: Oxford University Press, 1948), pp. 11–22; and Sean McConville, *A History of English Prison Administration*, I, 22–48.

   On the Continent the technical judicial practices described by Langbein had obviated torture well before its much publicized official abandonment during the Enlightenment; these practices appear to have predicated modern, narratively structured conceptions of crime and punishment within a narrow legal sphere. But paradoxically it was in England, where the Bridewells and workhouses, after their establishment during the sixteenth century, quickly subsided into the liminal pattern of the old prisons, and in England where, because of Common Law and the jury system, comparatively few formal strictures governed the judicial process itself, that we find the first concerted institution of penitentiaries along modern lines. It was the English who, during the 1780s, constructed the model penitentiaries that later were reexported from America to Europe during the penal reforms that swept the

Continent throughout the first half of the nineteenth century. The introduction of lawyers (proffering contingent narratives of a case), as well as the subsequent imposition of rules of evidence in English courts, all occurred *after* the period we ordinarily associate with the rise of the novel and after an extended phase of narrative court accounts such as the Old Bailey Sessions Records or the Ordinary's accounts, and later in the *Newgate Calendar*. See Langbein, 'The Criminal Trial Before the Lawyers,' *University of Chicago Law Review*, 45 (1978), 263–316.

17. *Moll Flanders*, ed. G. A. Starr (London: Oxford University Press, 1971), pp. 273–74. Further citations are parenthetical and refer to this edition.

18. On Defoe's representation of Moll's private, individualist consciousness through her self-control during the Newgate episode, see John J. Richetti, *Defoe's Narratives* (Oxford: Clarendon Press, 1975), pp. 133–40.

19. Works that have substantially revised previous estimates of Defoe by placing him in context with the thought of his period include Maximillian E. Novak, *Economics and the Fiction of Daniel Defoe* (Berkeley: University of California Press, 1962) and *Defoe and the Nature of Man* (Oxford: Oxford University Press, 1963); G. A. Starr, *Defoe and Spiritual Autobiography* (Princeton: Princeton University Press, 1965) and *Defoe and Casuistry* (Princeton: Princeton University Press, 1971); and J. Paul Hunter, *The Reluctant Pilgrim* (Baltimore: Johns Hopkins University Press, 1966).

20. See Ian Watt, *The Rise of the Novel* (Berkeley: University of California Press, 1959), ch. 1, 'Realism and the Novel Form,' especially pp. 31–32.

21. On the 'polyglossia' as the essence of the novel – that is, its ability to contain contradictory voices – see Mikhail Bakhtin, 'From the Prehistory of Novelistic Discourse' and 'Discourse in the Novel,' in *The Dialogic Imagination* (Austin: University of Texas Press, 1981), especially pp. 50–60 and 277–84.

22. On shifts of theoretical content within stable terminologies during the Renaissance see Phillip Damon, 'History and Idea in Renaissance Criticism,' in *Literary Criticism and Historical Understanding*, ed. Phillip Damon (New York: Columbia University Press, 1967).

23. The kind of writing we normally call allegorical never quite ran the equation backwards. This was precisely the Puritan objection to icons, fictions, etc: that they were vain and false imitations, not the real thing – that they were self-referential idols, not God-given signs of divine creation.

24. *Serious Reflections During the Life and Surprising Adventures of Robinson Crusoe*, ed. George A. Aitken (London: J. M. Dent, 1895), p. ix; cited parenthetically hereafter.

25. See Watt, *The Rise of the Novel*, pp. 31 and 102; and Novak, 'Defoe's Theory of Fiction,' *SP*, 61 (1964), 650–68, especially 661–62.

26. My terms in this paragraph, like my earlier term 'enabled,' imply causality with all of its problem-laden baggage. I accept the overtones here because I am treating a period in which principles of sequence, perception, character, educational influence, and material causation that emerged in fiction making also permeated mental and cultural institutions, including criticism itself. As Jameson suggests, causation is a trope with a historical life of its own (*The Political Unconscious*, p. 34); therefore, while I may trace its efflorescence, I never can fully separate the restructuration of eighteenth-century culture along the lines of causal narrative from my own methods of inquiry. Even Jameson's acute dialectical self-consciousness ultimately refers itself to a master narrative – that of Marxian history.

27. *Robinson Crusoe*, ed. J. Donald Crowley (London: Oxford University Press, 1972), p. 40. Further references, cited parenthetically, are to this edition.

28. See Douglas Hay, 'Property, Authority and the Criminal Law' in *Albion's Fatal Tree: Crime and Society in Eighteenth-Century England*, ed. Douglas Hay, et al. (New York: Pantheon, 1975), pp. 17–63.

29. *The World Upside-Down: Comedy from Jonson to Fielding* (Oxford: Clarendon Press, 1970), ch. 7.

30. See William Eben Schultz, *Gay's 'Beggar's Opera': Its Content, History & Influence* (New Haven: Yale University Press, 1923), p. 237.

31. Emmett L. Avery, ed., 'Part 2, 1700–1729' of *The London Stage, 1660–1800* (Carbondale: Southern Illinois University Press, 1960), p. cx.

32. See Ronald Paulson, *Hogarth: His Life, Art, and Times*, 2 vols. (New Haven: Yale University Press and Paul Mellon Centre for Studies in British Art, 1971), I, 180–88; Plates 61–62; and Marvin A. Carlson, 'A Fresh Look at Hogarth's *Beggar's Opera*,' *Educational Theatre Journal*, 27 (1975), 31–39.

33. On the Tuscan order, see, for example, William Chambers, *A Treatise on Civil Architecture* (London, 1759), p. 16. For the statues on Old Newgate, see Antony Babington, *The English Bastille* (London: MacDonald, 1971), p. 58. The statues are listed in the caption to item 35.41 in The Museum of London. A modern photograph of 'Liberty' as resituated on Dance's New Newgate appears in Dorothy Stroud, *George Dance, Architect, 1741–1825* (London: Faber and Faber, 1971), Plate 31b.

34. Any interpretation of Hogarth's Progresses along the lines followed here is bound to be indebted to the work of Ronald Paulson. See, in addition to *Hogarth: His Life, Art, and Times*, the detailed entries in *Hogarth's Graphic Works*, 2 vols. (New Haven: Yale University Press, 1965; rev. ed., 1970); *The Art of Hogarth* (London: Phaidon, 1975); *Emblem and Expression: Meaning in English Art of the Eighteenth Century* (Cambridge, Mass.: Harvard University Press, 1975); and *Popular and Polite Art in the Age of Hogarth and Fielding* (Notre Dame: University of Notre Dame Press, 1979).

35. William Ernest Henley, ed. *The Complete Works of Henry Fielding*, 16 vols. (London: Heinemann, 1903), 13, 183–84.

36. For a reproduction of the engraving of 1755 after Dance Sr.'s design, see Dorothy Stroud, *George Dance*, Plate 3a.

6 The Carnivalization of Eighteenth-Century English Narrative

TERRY CASTLE

Terry Castle has written important psychoanalytic and Bakhtinian essays and books on the eighteenth century. She has turned increasingly to gender criticism, with a special interest in lesbian studies. *Masquerade and Civilization* is her most sustained piece of Bakhtinian criticism, in which she argues that masquerade reappears in eighteenth-century novels as a means for refashioning characters' expectations about the world and transforming plot outcomes (see Introduction, pp. 16–17). The essay below presents her basic thesis that the masquerade provides a resistance to conventional ideologies of many different sorts.

'The secret history of a carnival,' wrote Addison in his 1718 *Remarks on Italy*, 'would make a collection of very diverting novels.' One might take such a comment simply as part of the ingenuous discourse of eighteenth-century tourism: like Mary Wortley Montagu, Horace Mann, and many other English visitors, Addison delighted in the masked balls and carnivals of Venice, Rome, and Florence and celebrated the 'great diversion' (as he put it) of dressing 'as a false personage' (*Works* 2: 39).[1] But one might also take his remark, paradoxically, as bearing a certain proleptic relation to English literary history itself. Addison offers what could be called an advertisement for a theme – a theme that the eighteenth-century English novel was subsequently to provide. With the spectacular rise of carnivalesque activity in England in the second and third decades of the eighteenth century – marked by the institutionalization of the public, or subscription, masquerade – the novel took a cue from popular culture: the carnival set piece, or masquerade scene, became a standard, though highly problematic, fictional topos. To the degree that the writers incorporated the novel institution of the masquerade into an existing world of representation, the masquerade became an institution of the novel, making the multifarious body of eighteenth-century English fiction a 'secret history of a carnival' indeed.

One need only recollect some of the eighteenth-century novels in which a masquerade occurs to appreciate the ubiquitousness of the scene: *Roxana, Tom Jones, Amelia, Pamela,* part 2, *Sir Charles Grandison, The Adventures of Peregrine Pickle, Fanny Hill,* Burney's *Cecilia,* Inchbald's *Simple Story,* and Edgeworth's *Belinda.* In addition one can find significant allusions to the world of masquerade and public travesty in *Roderick Random, The Vicar of Wakefield, Evelina,* and a host of minor works of the period.[2] Critics have tended to discount masquerade scenes – in part, one suspects, because such episodes may seem deceptively inconsequential in the novels themselves. Authors like Richardson and Fielding typically try to bracket the masquerade scene – to set it off as merely a brief interlude in some more serious project of mimetic or didactic elucidation – disguising it as a narrative, as well as an existential, 'diversion.' This attempt at circumscription often occurs, oddly enough, while the characters themselves comment on the masquerade's powerful sensuous éclat. Nonetheless, one may still be deceived by a superficial aura of extraneousness or marginality.

But we are inclined to bypass fictional representations of the carnivalesque for deeper reasons too, reasons having to do with our notions of eighteenth-century English fiction itself. True to the masquerade's symbolic role as the exemplary site of mutability, incongruity, and mystery, the episode is often a strangely unrecuperable textual event. It may strike us as uncanny, or as discontinuous with those patterns of didactic or ideological meaning that characterize the work elsewhere. Though subliminally compelling, it may also have a mystifying or chimerical narrative impact. And since the scene often marks a moment in contemporary narrative when otherwise lucid character types, like the adepts of psychosis, suddenly seem to behave conspicuously unlike themselves, as though contaminated by the prevailing instability of the occasion in which they participate, the figure of the masquerade seems subtly linked to the violation of certain cherished critical paradigms – notably, the commonplace that early English fiction is distinguished by its new sense of the integrity of individual psychology and its coherent representation of character over time. The scene is almost invariably an affront to *Bildung*: it offends against those structures of consistency and logical development that we try, consciously or unconsciously, to impose on the classic eighteenth-century text.[3]

In what follows, however, I argue that the masquerade episode is not in fact inconsequential – either for the novel in which it appears or for the theory of eighteenth-century narrative in general. If the role of the masquerade is masked, so to speak, behind a textual facade of moralism and ideological decorum, it is powerfully subversive nonetheless. In particular I am concerned here with the peculiar intimacy between topos and plot, with the ways in which the masquerade, the emblem of universal transformation, is linked to the pleasurable processes of narrative transformation – to intrigue and the working out of larger, often comic fictional destinies. Besides being a symbolic epitome of plot – the embedded imago of a world of metamorphosis and fluidity – the masquerade is typically a perpetrator too: a dense kernel of human relations out of which are born the myriad transactions of the narrative. This plot-engendering function frequently undermines whatever explicit negative didactic or allegorical significance the occasion carries elsewhere – for instance, its conventional inscription as the archetype of a corrupt and hypocritical 'Town.' The scene may thus be considered a master trope of semantic destabilization in eighteenth-century fiction, in that it characteristically precipitates an entire range of thematic as well as narrative changes and discontinuities. Itself a problematic rhetorical event – its own ideological status remains finally unclear – the masquerade episode introduces a curious instability into the would-be orderly cosmos of the eighteenth-century English novel. Its moral indeterminacy is paradigmatic; its saturnalian assault on taxonomies and hierarchies – established 'fixities' of every sort – is the prerequisite, often enough, to a general collapse of decorum in the fictional world.

As Bakhtin has memorably demonstrated, it is possible to make an analogy between the role of the carnivalesque in literary works and its role in culture.[4] Whether rhetorical or actual, the carnivalesque occasion – like the masquerade – is always provocative: it intimates an alternative view of the 'nature of things' and embodies a liberating escape from the status quo. At the end of this essay I return to the comparison between the function of the masquerade in English fiction and that of the institution of masquerade in culture. First, however, a few words are necessary about the diversion itself.

The masked assembly became a popular form of urban entertainment in the mid-teens and early twenties of the eighteenth century, when the first public masquerades were organized in London at the Haymarket under the direction of the Swiss entrepreneur 'Count' John James Heidegger. A nocturnal affair, held in brilliantly illuminated rooms, the 'promiscuous Assembly' (as the *Spectator* called it) was open to anyone who could afford the price of ticket and costume. In many respects the occasion was modeled on the traditional public carnivals of the Continent. Thanks to the general anonymity of the scene, collective behavior was unrestrained: eating, drinking, dancing, and gaming were enjoyed to excess. Costumes were often spectacular and phantasmagoric. Besides the classic black mask and domino, popular masquerade disguises included foreign or exotic 'fancy dress,' transvestite costumes, ecclesiastical parodies (of nuns or priests), picturesque occupational costumes (of shepherds, milkmaids, and the like), as well as costumes representing animals, supernatural beings, and literary, historical, and allegorical personages.[5] The fantastic multiplicity and incongruity of the visual spectacle were to a large degree replicated in the disparate composition of the masquerade crowd itself, which drew on both sexes equally and on all ranks of contemporary English society. Only there, remarked a character in Griffin's 1717 comedy *The Masquerade*, could one meet 'a *Nobleman* [dressed] like a *Cynder-Wench*, a *Colonel of Dragoons* like a *Country Rat-Catcher*, a *Lady of Quality* in *Dutch Trowsers*, and a *Woman of the Town* in a *Ruff* and *Farthingale*' (7; 1.1). Both aesthetically and sociologically the scene was indeed a carnivalesque hodgepodge of promiscuous elements.

From the start, the masquerade occupied a paradoxical place in the symbolic order of eighteenth-century English culture. On the one hand, the new entertainment provoked a cacophony of public criticism – a sizable antimasquerade 'complaint.' Throughout the century, writers of satiric poems, sermons, squibs, and pamphlets, as well as visual artists like Hogarth, reiterated the exemplary dangers of the masquerade: it was an emblem of luxury and excess; it introduced a foreign element of theatricality and vice into English public life; it promoted a potentially inflammatory sense of social equality by allowing the 'lower orders' to consort with their betters. Above all, the masked assembly was seen as the site par excellence for sexual transgression: women – again thanks to disguise – shared the sensual 'freedom' of men; voyeurism and exhibitionism were pervasive; erotic taboos were broken. Adultery, prostitution, homosexuality, incest, and the defloration of virgins were all themes associated with the masquerade: the event became a cultural sign of libertinage itself.[6]

On the other hand, despite this explosion of negative discourse, the masquerade flourished. From the 1720s to the 1780s it was an irrepressible feature of urban public life – not just one among many popular diversions but the emblem of modernity itself, the very signature of fashion, spectacle, and surreptitious excitement. Heidegger's assemblies drew between seven hundred and one thousand persons weekly during the 1720s, while later in the century elaborate subscription masquerades, like those sponsored by Mrs. Cornelys at Carlisle House in the 1760s and 1770s, attracted up to two thousand costumed participants. The spasmodic efforts of civil and religious authorities to put an end to masquerading were generally unsuccessful; for the greater part of the century the masquerade had indeed the status of an established cultural institution, however intense the criticism it inspired.

For all the vociferousness of the opposition, the masked assembly apparently satisfied certain underlying impulses in the culture. Since participants typically adopted the costumes of beings whose natures were antithetical to their own – of a different culture, sex, or sphere of existence – one could conclude that individual masqueraders were acting out repressed fantasies of alterity, symbolically embracing otherness. But the same dialectic applies collectively too. By allowing manifold breaches of decorum, the carnivalization of social roles, and parodic symbolic reversals, the masquerade offered eighteenth-century culture an anti-image of itself: a kind of licensed topsy-turvydom, or *Spielraum*, in which the very principles of order and distinction might be challenged. In a rigidly taxonomic, conceptually polarized society, it opened up a temporary space of transformation, mutability, and fluidity. It embodied, one might say, a gratifying fantasy of change in a world that sanctioned few changes – metaphysical or otherwise.

I call attention here to the conflicting responses to the masquerade because the same contradictions inform fictional representation. Eighteenth-century English culture inscribed the masquerade simultaneously in a code of danger and in a code of pleasure: though preeminently distinguished by its 'pernicious' consequences (in the phrase of one critic), it was also a scene of ecstasy and euphoria – a site of atavistic 'liberties' and golden-age delights. It was at once part of the topography of vice – a place where no one should go – and part of the topography of enjoyment – a place where everyone went.[7]

In the eighteenth-century masquerade novel, too, the masked assembly is a place where everyone goes – eventually. Which is not to say – at the outset at least – that it is not also part of a (textual) code of danger. The occasion figures notably in a larger theme of initiation: 'going to the masquerade' is an exemplary part of the charged confrontation with urbanity, or 'introduction to the Town,' conventionally dramatized in eighteenth-century English novels. Yet initially the masquerade novel characteristically registers, as it were, an 'official' resistance to its own carnivalesque topos – as though it wishes to domesticate, or neutralize in advance, the very scene it will later represent. Some form of embedded negative comment or warning almost always precedes that problematic event, serving as a kind of anticipatory didactic gloss, usually by a character already invested in the fictional world with a certain moral prestige or authority. With such prefacing – a not so subtle attempt to shape the reader's subsequent interpretation of the episode – the writers signal the superficial didactic orthodoxy of their histories, even as these histories turn, ineluctably, toward this least orthodox of diversions.

The modes of stylized resistance are surprisingly uniform. In particular, the masquerade's association with sexual impurity – and consequent danger to heroines – is almost always enunciated. In *Pamela*, part 2, for example, when Richardson's paragon hears that Mr. B. plans to take her to a masked assembly, she expresses her distaste for such entertainments, condemns the 'freedoms' taken with women at these events, and wishes she didn't have to go (262; letter 55). Similarly, despite claiming that she 'never had any notion of Masquerades,' Harriet Byron, in Richardson's *Sir Charles Grandison*, admits to her friend Miss Selby that she wishes the night of the masquerade were over, adding, somewhat ominously, that she fears the evening's party will be 'the last diversion of this kind I shall ever be at' (vol. I, 116; letter 22). In Inchbald's *Simple Story*, Miss Milner's honorable guardian, Mr. Dorriforth, objects to the loose morals of the masked assembly and implicitly forbids her to go (151; vol. 2, ch. 8). Even Defoe's *Roxana*, where the didactic pattern is unstable from the outset, contains hints of the classic encoded warning: when the heroine hears that some 'Gentlemen in Masquerade' are to visit her apartments, she immediately fears a 'Disturbance' and balks at receiving them. She has to be assured that 'a Party of Guards' will prevent any 'Rudeness' of the sort found at the Haymarket masquerade (173).

And finally – befitting the author of one of the first and most virulent poetic satires against the masquerade, *The Masquerade* (1728) – Fielding's novels offer striking examples of the embedded antimasquerade gloss. In book 13 of *Tom Jones*, after Tom offers to take Mrs. Miller and her daughter to a masquerade, his landlady animadverts on the danger of such 'extravagant Diversions,' particularly for innocent young women. When Mr. Nightingale disagrees, she reminds him that when her daughter went to the Haymarket with him the year before, 'it almost turned her Head; and she did not return to herself, or to her Needle, in a month afterwards' (543). But it is in *Amelia*, the most complex of masquerade novels, that one finds the most severe strictures – an initial chorus of warnings so intense as to suggest that a masquerade is not to figure in the heroine's destiny at all. When the sinister Noble Peer presents Amelia with masquerade tickets, his gesture elicits a flood of preventive discourse. Booth fears aloud 'what a wicked and voluptuous man, resolved to sacrifice every thing to the gratification of a sensual appetite, with the most delicious repast' might attempt on such an occasion and forbids his wife to go (301; bk. 6, ch. 6), while Amelia's friend, the wan Mrs. Bennet, is moved to divulge her own horrific experiences at the masked assembly (11–59; bk. 7, chs. 2–9). She too has gone with the Peer to a masquerade, and with catastrophic consequence: after being overcome by the hallucinatory 'intoxications' of the place, she tells Amelia, she unwittingly allowed herself to be drugged and raped by him. The 'fatal masquerade' indeed seems to have been that: Mrs. Bennet subsequently causes the death of her husband by infecting him with the Peer's venereal disease, and her child succumbs to a mysteriously related 'fever.' This exemplary tale recounted, Amelia promptly rejects the gift of tickets, leaving the reader to conclude, logically enough, that a masquerade will play no part, except in this displaced form, in Fielding's novel.

Such embedded commentary seems intended, obviously, to limit the symbolic range of the masquerade to that of the moral emblem. Even before the event occurs, we are invited to comprehend it as a transparent epitome of vice, as part of the moralized topography of the corrupt 'Town.' The masquerade itself masquerades, the gloss warns: ostensibly the scene of pleasure, it is actually the scene of 'snares' – a region of manipulation, disequilibrium, and sexual threat. It disguises itself as exquisite delight, yet degrades all who enter its estranging spaces. This initial treatment of the masquerade topos almost always coincides, not surprisingly, with a larger critique of a deceptive or hypocritical human society. Besides being the icon of a debauched world of 'Fashion,' the allegory of urban disorder, as in Fielding and Richardson, the diversion often seems to intimate a kind of global dysphoria – a universal inauthenticity, obfuscation, and brutality. Thus the internalized attack on the masquerade confirms the didactic pretensions of the larger fiction and establishes – for a time at least – the stereotypically 'virtuous' persona of the novelist, the unmasker of vice.

Yet it is precisely this kind of emblematic transparency that is obscured by the actual representation of masquerade. For despite the encoded resistance, the event, if mentioned at all, always does seem to take place. Indeed, one may take it as a rule that if the possibility of attending a masquerade arises in an eighteenth-century English novel, at some point the characters will go, as though under a peculiar narrative compulsion. This turn toward the carnival world often violates didactic economy, since the 'perniciousness' of the occasion has already been sufficiently established, and the textual switch into saturnalia frequently seems strangely unmotivated or irrational. In the sequel to *Pamela*, one cannot quite grasp, for instance, why a reformed B. should force his pregnant wife (she gives birth a day or two later) to attend this scene of riot against her will, but he does. Similarly in *Amelia*, though Booth strenuously opposes Amelia's accepting masquerade tickets from the Peer, he later insists, surprisingly, that she accept a set of tickets from the equally lustful and devious Colonel James. And in *A Simple Story*, Miss Milner's decision to thwart her fiancé, Dorriforth, and venture out to a masquerade is likewise baffling – a seemingly perverse affront to the emotional bond that she has earlier worked so passionately to establish. Thus this crucial spatial shift from domestic salon to assembly room, from the predictable scenery of 'everyday' life to the estranging realm of the carnivalesque, is almost always accompanied by a certain logical discontinuity, an incursion of irrationalism into the ordered cosmos of eighteenth-century psychologistic, as well as topographic, representation.

With the 'entry' into the masquerade scene itself – for the characters a literal entry into a novel space of estrangement and moral instability – the sense of discontinuity and paradox may be intensified to a hallucinatory degree. However brief the scene and however much the narrator may try to circumscribe its problematic features, it remains a charged textual occasion, productive of unexampled pleasures for characters and readers alike. I do not mean merely the pleasures of local color, though the representation of the carnivalesque obviously entails supplemental interest of this sort, particularly for twentieth-century readers. To be sure, the typical masquerade episode contains some allusion to the spectacular delights of the scene: some rendering of masquerade *adynata* – the marvelous visual incongruities embodied in the costumed crowd itself. The representation of the carnivalesque 'diversion' conventionally diverts in this way: it adds an element of spectacle, in the ancient sense, to the ordinarily quotidian landscape of the realistic novel. Thus in Burney's *Cecilia*, the reader may take vicarious pleasure in the manifold and dreamlike aspects of the entertainment depicted there, where men turn into 'Spaniards, chimneysweepers, Turks, watchmen, conjurers, and old women' and women into 'shepherdesses, orange girls, Circassians, gipseys, haymakers, and sultanas' (169; vol. 1, bk. 2, ch. 3).

But the masquerade diverts in a more important sense too. The verbal allusion to a rich and variegated phenomenological realm – a world of endless, enchanting metamorphosis – coincides always with an even more gratifying pattern of transformation: a proliferation of intrigue. Besides thematizing mutability through image, the masquerade episode serves as a nodal point for narrative transformation – the privileged site of plot. Above all, the masquerade represents that place in the novel at which significant events take place – a classic locale out of which the requisite mysteries of 'story' may be elaborated.

This plot-developing function follows from the very nature
of the diversion. In life as in fiction, the eighteenth-century masked
assembly was a cultural 'locus of intimacy.' There persons otherwise
rigidly segregated by class and sex distinctions might come together
in unprecedented, sometimes disruptive combinations. Satiric
references, like Addison's, to the 'promiscuity' of the masquerade
suggested not only the characteristic sensual excess of the scene
but also the scandalous heterogeneity of the community temporarily
constituted within its confines.[8] Constantly confronting 'strangers'
(with the mask the quintessential visual emblem of estrangement)
was part of the masquerade's appeal: it substituted randomness and
novelty – prerequisites of imbroglio – for the familiar, highly stylized
patterns of contemporary public and private exchange.

This open-endedness, one realizes, is perfectly adapted to the
elaboration of plot, whose existence depends, as Todorov has pointed
out, on an initial destabilization of the ordinary, a disequilibrium at
the heart of things. In his study of the fantastic, Todorov defines the
minimum requirement for narrative – that 'nucleus without which
we cannot say there is any narrative at all' – as 'a movement between
two equilibriums which are similar but not identical' (163). In the
genre of the fantastic – including fantastic eighteenth-century tales
like *The Castle of Otranto* and *Vathek* – that which precipitates
'movement,' the necessary catalyst for narrative, is usually the
supernatural intervention, a mysterious or extralogical incursion that
radically disrupts the stable modes of ordinary fictional existence.
'Habitually linked to the narrative of an action,' writes Todorov,
the marvelous element 'proves to be the narrative raw material
which best fills this specific function: to afford a modification of the
preceding situation, and to break the established equilibrium' of the
fantastic text. Social and literary operations here coincide, for 'in both
cases, we are concerned with a transgression of the law.' 'Whether it
is in social life or in narrative,' he concludes, 'the intervention of the
supernatural element always constitutes a break in the system of
pre-established rules, and in so doing finds its justification' (165–66).

An analogy might be made, however, between the role of the
supernatural in fantastic literature and that of the masquerade
in certain putatively 'realistic' or secularized eighteenth-century
narratives. The carnivalesque episode likewise transgresses the law,
though not a transcendental one; it deranges the orderly world of
human relations elsewhere intimate in classic eighteenth-century
fiction, introducing an imbalance, a fundamental strangeness. The
masquerade typically engenders a series of problematic *liaisons
dangereuses* by throwing characters into proximity who, if an
exhaustive cosmological decorum were truly the goal, would never

meet; the high and the low, the virtuous and the vicious, the attached and the unattached. But by the same token, the episode may also bring about, for a time at least, the alienation of characters who *should* be together by virtue of established conjugal or familial ties: husbands and wives, parents and children, guardians and wards. Out of the masquerade's surplus of scandalous dialectical transactions, a multitude of intrigues develop. These localized complications characteristically infiltrate the larger fiction, shaping – either implicitly or explicitly – the remainder of the story. As a transgressive agent, the carnivalesque episode also provides that necessary mimetic disequilibrium on which plot depends.

The atavistic textual association between the masquerade episode and supernatural agency is typically inscribed in the imagery of costume: the characters often either disguise themselves as supernatural beings or meet others dressed in such costumes. In Inchbald's *Simple Story*, for example, Miss Milner chooses the costume of the goddess Diana – somewhat ironically, it turns out, for the masquerade is subsequently instrumental in bringing about her marriage to Dorriforth. In *Tom Jones*, Lady Bellaston disguises herself as the queen of the fairies, while in *Cecilia*, the heroine's problematic suitor, Mr. Monckton, dresses as a fiend. Since each of these characters is a perpetrator of masquerade intrigue and an instrument in later plot developments, the sartorial hints of supernatural power might be taken as symbolic of his or her *narrative* influence.

The reader, to be sure, may enjoy the hyperelaboration of incident. The immediate puzzles of the masquerade episode (who is talking to whom? who wears what costume? what do the mystifying encounters signify?) are nicely calculated to promote the reader's engagement, and they soon lead to others. The masquerade scene almost always intimates a host of further plot developments and mysteries to be solved. But – and this is perhaps its most paradoxical function in eighteenth-century English narrative – the carnivalesque topos is often peculiarly implicated in the pleasure of characters as well as of readers. Often the masquerade is the instrument not just of plot but of a comic plot in particular. It characteristically precipitates a larger euphoric, or 'rewarding,' pattern of narrative transformation – even for those characters, like the beleaguered heroines, whom one would not expect to benefit from its disarming travesties. This subterranean comic agency is seldom if ever acknowledged; indeed, the narrator or the characters, like Richardson's Pamela, may describe the masquerade, before and after the fact, as the exemplary site of moral danger. Yet the association with a comic telos, a range of ultimately happy 'consequences,' is subtly insistent nonetheless.

Instead of destroying, the masquerade seems finally to reward those who enter its chaotic midnight spaces.

The paradox is worth noting because, as we shall see in a moment, it suggests much about the contradictory and often compromising imaginative role played by the carnivalesque, not just in eighteenth-century fiction, but in eighteenth-century society itself. Granted, the beneficent instrumentality of the occasion may not seem immediately obvious: the narrative repercussions of masquerade can appear sinister, sometimes in highly melodramatic ways. But frequently these seemingly disastrous 'consequences' are in fact a necessary prelude to something else: the ameliorization of a central character's fortunes, the 'Providential' rewarding of the heroine. Like the Fortunate Fall (with which the carnivalesque has strong symbolic resonances), the masquerade episode typically stands out in the narrative as an indispensable event, as that temporary plunge into difficulty and enigma without which the characters could not realize their comic destinies.

Thus in *Sir Charles Grandison* – to take a schematic instance of the pattern – the 'cursed masquerade' bears all the conventional hallmarks of an evil narrative agency: Harriet Byron is there abducted by the odious Sir Hargrave, and everyone fears that her sexual ruin is inevitable. On hearing the 'fatal news' of Harriet's kidnapping, her distraught Uncle Selby exclaims that while he formerly believed public masquerades 'more silly than wicked' he is now convinced that they are 'the most profligate of all diversions' (vol. I, 119; letter 24). But one soon learns that Harriet has not been ruined; rather, the paragon Sir Charles, fortuitously riding past the coach in which she is held after the masquerade, hears her muffled screams for help and, in 'a glorious action,' liberates her from her abductor. Such is the happy accidental meeting on which Richardson's heterosexual romance depends, for of course Harriet and Charles later fall in love and marry. Yet one might argue that it is Harriet's initial movement into the world of sexual danger, represented by the masked assembly, that diverts her toward her ultimate sexual reward: for without the masquerade, she would neither have entered the beatific Grandison household (which takes her in after her ordeal) nor have come to know her 'god-like' benefactor intimately. The masquerade excursion is perversely responsible for all her subsequent happiness and the essential erotic comedy of Richardson's novel. Again, the fiction obscures this almost magical plot function: Harriet's relieved relations afterward revile the occasion that caused such 'barbarous' suffering. But the disguised blessing is inscribed subliminally, in comments like Mr. Reeves's remark that Harriet's experience represents 'a common case' heightened into 'the marvelous' (vol. I, 137; letter 27). Harriet too has the sense of supernatural agency: 'How shall I bear this goodness!' – she exclaims after her adventure – 'This is indeed bringing good out of evil! Did I not say, my cousin, that I was fallen into the company of angels?' (vol. I, 145; letter 27).

One might multiply cases in which the heroine's masquerade venture affirms or reconstitutes the comic plot of heterosexual romance. Roxana meets her most powerful financial and erotic patron, the 'Duke of M—,' at the masquerade, attracting him with her lubricious 'Turkish dance.' Likewise, though in a somewhat more sedate manner, Burney's Cecilia attracts a lover at the masquerade – Delvile, the man who will become her husband. In *A Simple Story*, though the masquerade episode at first appears to estrange Miss Milner and Dorriforth, it actually sets up an ecstatic reconciliation and their subsequent marriage. And in the sequel to *Pamela*, Mr. B.'s masquerade flirtation with the Countess is not the disaster for the heroine it seems to be: it too produces a transporting moment of 'éclaircissement,' when B. renounces the Countess, begs his wife's forgiveness, and 'redoubles' his love for her.

The masquerade episode, then, is not only a narrative crux; it is characteristically implicated in the larger comic patterns of eighteenth-century English fiction. Without it, many apparently 'Providential' turns in contemporary narratives are difficult to imagine. Yet such instrumentality, one may notice, also undermines the conventional moral significance of the topos and threatens the didactic coherence of the work as a whole. By its very comic agency the carnivalesque episode contradicts its superficial negative inscription within the text, revealing itself instead as part of the paradoxical machinery of narrative pleasure. It ceases to be merely an emblem – of hypocrisy or anything else – at the moment that it facilitates, like a covert deus ex machina, the ultimate reward of character and reader alike.

This 'scrambling' of emblematic significance, it turns out, is often paradigmatic; it can signal a collapse of didactic accountability in the fictional world. The masquerade scene typically leaves in its wake what might be called a world upside down. That is, it marks a moment in the narrative at which ordinarily sanctioned social or metaphysical hierarchies may suddenly weaken or show signs of being overthrown altogether. Following the representation of masquerade intrigue, the reader may experience a sense of ideological topsy-turvydom – as though the dramatic transformations in the narrative had somehow precipitated thematic changes too. To use Bakhtin's term, one might say that the fictional world itself suddenly appears 'carnivalized.'

Something of this effect is already obvious in the association just educed between the scene and the comic destiny of heroines. The masquerade frequently coincides with a peculiar reversal of those conventional male–female power relations encoded elsewhere in eighteenth-century fiction. Male characters may abruptly lose their authority following the masquerade, while female characters acquire unprecedented intellectual and emotional influence over them. As the symbolic theater of female power (women masqueraders, we recollect, usurped not only the costumes but the social and behavioral 'freedoms' of the opposite sex), the assembly room engenders patterns of sexual reversal that subsequently pervade, as it were, the rest of the novel. Thus the heroine typically eludes her immediate masquerade persecutors – witness Harriet in *Sir Charles Grandison* or Mrs. Atkinson in *Amelia*, who outwits the evil Noble Peer at the masked conclave in that novel. And often she also derives more lasting powers of sexual control from the occasion. She is particularly likely, as we have seen, to gain psychological sway here over a future lover or husband. A parodic example occurs in *Tom Jones*, when Lady Bellaston, disguised as the queen of the fairies (her very dress a blazon of female authority), seduces Tom at the Haymarket masquerade and thus establishes a brief erotic and economic ascendancy over him. Even here, however, the effect of ideological destabilization remains potent: though Tom later escapes Bellaston's lascivious influence, the masquerade scene introduces an important thematic disturbance into Fielding's otherwise highly conservative fiction – one that both threatens the novel's patriarchal logic and temporarily subverts its normative vision of male–female relations.[9]

While the masquerade precipitates controversy in sexual relations – and is particularly linked to scenarios of female desire and authority – it is also associated with the disruption of class relations. (The two forms of inversion sometimes overlap in interesting structural and thematic ways.) Again it may seem as though the saturnalian reversals of the masked assembly – where 'low' becomes 'high' and vice versa – somehow work their way into the larger fiction. Just as women characters achieve a carnivalesque hegemony following the invocation of masquerade, so 'low' characters may gain new status or importance from this powerful textual event.

Sometimes a directly subversive narrative causation is at work. In *Amelia*, for example, when Amelia's masquerade surrogate, Mrs. Atkinson, tricks the Noble Peer (who has mistaken her for the heroine) into granting her husband an officer's commission, she brings about a radical and lasting sociological change in Fielding's rigidly hierarchical fictional world. Through her ruse, which elegantly exploits the masquerade's requisite sartorial confusions, a carnivalesque transformation, from low into high, becomes permanent. The 'humble' Sergeant Atkinson, who before has served as Booth's valet, indeed receives his commission a few days after the masquerade, thus abruptly rising to Booth's own rank and achieving the coveted status of gentleman (Vol. I, 227; bk. 10, ch. 8). Once again, one might say, the masquerade episode has permitted a breach in the social order and in the underlying ideological structure of Fielding's novel.

But the scandalous consequences of masquerade may occur at a symbolic remove too, as in the second part of *Pamela*. There, a seemingly sinister masquerade adventure – during which B. becomes estranged from the heroine and begins his 'Platonick' affair with the Countess – ultimately produces a scene of ecstatic repetition, in which Pamela symbolically reenacts her own highly transgressive history. This reenactment is implicit in the language of emotion: when B. belatedly expresses his remorse and reaffirms his love for his wife, Pamela – who has taken to dressing again in the plain garments of a servant and asserting that she is not a true 'lady' like the Countess – blissfully declares herself 'lifted up' once more. B.'s transporting demonstration, she tells Lady Davers, has 'exalted' her, and she reassumes her rich garments and her place by his side (320; letter 74). Yet in this 'happy turn,' the melodramatic climax of Richardson's narrative, one recognizes a displaced recapitulation of precisely that problematic change recorded in *Pamela*, part 1: the heroine's original (and revolutionary) 'exaltation' from humble to genteel status. By precipitating this charged repetition, the masquerade episode again betrays its subliminal thematic link with fantasies of mutability and with the subversion of class and sexual distinctions.

Finally, the patterns of ideological destabilization associated with the masquerade are microcosmically reinscribed on the level of character. Just as the personae of eighteenth-century English fiction are likely to transcend supposedly 'given' social or sexual categories following the representation of masquerade, so they are likely to display certain unaccountable moral or emotional traits, as though temporarily estranged, or 'different' from themselves in basic psychological ways. The gesture of self-alienation implicit in the act of masquerading – where one indeed 'becomes' the other – would seem to be exemplary. It heralds additional, more intimate transformations and an incursion of instability into the realm of human nature itself.

The phenomenon is particularly noticeable, as one might expect, in novels like Fielding's, where the allegorical representation of character predominates and the fictional world is ordinarily composed of fixed, even caricatured moral types. Here, true to its antitaxonomic function, the masquerade scene disrupts stereotypical distinctions, such as those between paragons and knaves, the virtuous and the vicious. Supposedly lucid moral types may suddenly behave like their opposites, intensifying the reader's sense of didactic confusion. In *Tom Jones*, for example, the masquerade in book 13 marks the point at which the hero seems, to many readers, to behave in ways notably unlike himself – displaying a venality and opportunism, manifest in his somewhat sordid dealings with Lady Bellaston, not previously associated with his usually open and good-natured character. It is as though, by donning the mask and domino supplied by his secret patron, he temporarily diverges also from a stereotypical mode of being. The schematic code of character structuring Fielding's novel – with its underlying essentialist distinction between good and evil natures – is suddenly thrown into question. Though Tom later recollects himself and becomes the same transparent, even banal moral type he was before, his peculiar opacity and inconsistency on this occasion have troubled *Tom Jones*'s critics. Likewise, the masquerade sequence as a whole has sometimes been educed as an 'unsuccessful' or incongruous element in Fielding's larger artistic and thematic design.[10]

In *Amelia*, too, the masquerade episode marks enigmatic psychological as well as narrative transformations. The crude emblematic dichotomy established early in the fiction between paragons and hypocrites here tends to dissolve, even as Fielding's narrative pattern itself becomes more intricate and mysterious. Antithetical moral types merge in disarming ways. In particular, Amelia herself – elsewhere a model of uncomplicated virtue – reveals new and problematic depths to her character. Her ruse on the night of the masquerade, when she allows Mrs. Atkinson to take her place, unbeknownst to Booth or anyone else, is symptomatic: her complicity is technically a kind of hypocrisy, linking her with the role players and double-dealers vilified earlier by Fielding's moralizing narrator. Though perhaps justifiable on the grounds of prudence, Amelia's gesture is still a compromising one, and for the first time her supposedly immaculate character is shaded with a subtle admixture of deviousness and theatricality. But there are other puzzling shifts in behavior following the masquerade: Amelia is not the only paragon to show signs of lapsing from moral uniformity (Sergeant Atkinson, for example, turns out to harbor an adulterous passion for the heroine, and confesses to the theft of her 'lost' miniature), while the villains of the novel, the Noble Peer and Colonel James among them, are somewhat mystifyingly rehabilitated. Despite having been tricked into granting the sergeant an officer's commission, the Peer charitably permits him to retain it, and both the Peer and James inexplicably cease their lustful machinations against Amelia. The masquerade scene is not only a crux in Fielding's extremely convoluted plot, it marks a chiasmus on the level of character: Fielding's implicit moral typology itself is, for a time at least, turned upside down. With this confusion of types, *Amelia* loses much of its allegorical legibility. To be sure, it becomes in many ways a more compelling fiction at this point, but it is hardly any longer the simplistic didactic exemplum Fielding seems to have conceived.[11]

Thus, to speak of the 'carnivalization' of eighteenth-century fiction is to speak of a multifaceted textual phenomenon. Though the process may begin with a localized, or strictly anecdotal, representation of masquerade – the discrete scene or set piece – it does not end there. The invocation of the masquerade almost invariably coincides with an elaboration of plot, in particular with comic plots of sexual consummation and social mutability. Yet this transgressive narrative agency, the masquerade's privileged relation to intrigue itself, offends against the prevailing didactic economy of eighteenth-century English fiction. The pleasurable consequences of masquerade negate its superficial textual inscription as an emblem of vice, inauthenticity, and corrupt urbanity. The topos cannot be recuperated simply as a version of the *carnaval moralisé*; it conditions powerful transformations in the fictional world.

One may describe these transformations in thematic as well as narrative terms. As we have seen, the allusion to the scandals of masquerade typically engenders, as though by contagion, a larger ideological scandal in the fiction – the subversion of existing distinctions, the reversal of normative moral and social hierarchies. By injecting an enigmatic, destabilizing energy into the orderly cosmos of the eighteenth-century English novel, the carnivalesque episode alters the literary artifact itself, which seldom retains its claim to didactic purity following the representation of this least purifying of diversions. Its imaginative structure may suddenly appear contradictory or hybrid – 'double' in potential significance, unrecuperable according to any straightforward didactic logic. Though it may have advertised itself as allegory, it ceases here to be merely that. With the turn toward the irrationality of masquerade, one might say, the novel itself becomes unlike itself; it diverges from its putative moral project and reshapes itself as phantasmagoria and dream.

Implicit in my argument here, of course, is Bakhtin's notion of 'carnivalization,' which means not just the invocation of a thematic but also a process of generic destabilization. The carnivalized work, Bakhtin suggests, resists generic classification and instead combines, like Rabelais's *Pantagruel*, a multiplicity of literary modes in a single increasingly 'promiscuous' form. Interestingly enough, eighteenth-century English novels containing masquerade scenes often also display generic uncertainty. The masquerade may at times even seem to condition a formal 'shifting' or ambiguity in the work. In *Amelia*, for example, the scene coincides with a general shift from satiric to mimetic modes: it marks the point at which Fielding's fiction lapses from a primarily 'anatomizing' method – characterized by a ridiculing exposure of the 'glaring evils' of society – and assumes more and more of the conventional features of realistic narrative. In Richardson's sequel to *Pamela*, the pattern of generic destabilization is even more obvious: after the masquerade intrigue in that novel, the work becomes a true hodgepodge of discourses – a mixture of embedded exempla, 'table talk' (the symposia of the B. and Darnford households), and miscellaneous items, such as Pamela's lengthy commentary on Locke's treatise on education. Just as the masquerade episode precipitates transformation in the narrative, then, it appears to precipitate a transformation of the genre itself: it instigates a lapse in consistency on every textual stratum.

It may seem, at this point, that I have skirted an obvious epistemological problem by speaking elliptically of the manner in which the representation of masquerade engenders or precipitates a host of transformations in a novel. I have treated the carnivalesque episode as a kind of 'ghost in the machine' in eighteenth-century English fiction – almost as a transcendental agency that provokes an irruption of narrative fluidity and didactic ambiguity. To identify the typical masquerade scene as a subversive textual crux is to sidestep larger matters of authorial intention and literary dynamics. Indeed, one might ask, what conditions the representation of masquerade itself?

The question returns us to the realm of cultural history and the role of the carnivalesque, not just in the literary imagination, but in eighteenth-century English society. Granted, it is always possible to treat the contradictory literary inscription of masquerade simply as a function of idiosyncratic authorial intentions. In Fielding and Richardson, for example, the complex invocation of the carnivalesque can always be seen as a symptom of individual imaginative ambivalence – as the outward sign of a deeper private debate on the questions of order and disorder, restraint and indulgence, decorum and transgression. I do not wish to imply that either Fielding or Richardson *consciously* manipulates the topos to build, as it were, a certain ideological paradox into his fiction – or that the thematic imbroglio precipitated by the masquerade scene is part of any explicitly premeditated design. English novelists of the eighteenth century show little of that intentionally heuristic use of the carnivalesque that occurs later – say, in highly self-conscious writers like Flaubert.[12] Still, the masquerade episode does seem to satisfy diverse conscious and unconscious imperatives. It can express an underlying authorial ambivalence regarding the didactic project itself. For the eighteenth-century novelist, invoking the world of masquerade is typically a way of indulging in the scenery of transgression while seeming to maintain didactic probity. The occasion may be condemned in conventional terms, yet its very representation permits the novelist, like the characters, to assume a different role: to cast off the persona of the moralist and turn instead to the pleasures of intrigue. The writer may become at this point the purveyor of seductive fantasies rather than staid instruction. In novelists like Fielding and Richardson, in whom the conflict between moralism and subversion is intense, the masquerade functions as a figure for ambiguous authorial intentions – the textual sign of an inward tension regarding the author's role.

But it is perhaps more compelling, as I suggested at the start, to make the larger argument: that the paradoxes implicit in the fictional allusion to masquerade mirrored paradoxes in the cultural response to the carnivalesque. The masked assembly institutionalized dreams of disorder not just for its literary adherents but for the real world. Even as eighteenth-century English society preserved, on the face of it, a host of distinctions and hierarchies, reinforced by repressive dictates of one sort or another, the masquerade, like a theater of doubt, dramatized the possibility of change. It expressed collective fantasies of metamorphosis; it intimated that prevailing moral, social, and metaphysical categories were mere artifacts. It may seem an obvious enough point to make, but the way the masquerade functions in eighteenth-century English narrative – as an episode at once diverting and threatening to the implicit taxonomies of the fictional world – is roughly analogous to the way it functioned in the culture: as a discontinuous, estranging, sometimes even hallucinatory event that nonetheless carried with it a powerfully cathartic and disruptive cognitive éclat.

The argument might be embellished in various ways. A proponent of Bakhtin's lyrical theory of carnival, for instance, might favor a historical interpretation of some of the contradictions in the literary masquerade, seeing them as symptomatic of that shift away from the carnivalesque spirit which, Bakhtin has suggested, characterizes the modern period. He claims that the great traditions of European carnival were already in decline by the eighteenth century – a fact he attributes to increasing secularization and the rise of philosophies of rational individualism. The traditional carnival, he argues – the masked fête, charivari, and sotie – celebrated a fluid metaphysics:

an archaic popular belief in the underlying unity of opposites and the 'organic' wholeness of experience. Folk spectacle emphasized union over separation, changing over 'finished' forms, and the 'ever incompleted character of being' itself (32–33). With the development of modern notions of the subject, however – what Bakhtin calls the 'completed atomized being' of rationalism – this popular metaphysics was superseded. A world of discrete individuals, without resemblance or dialectical connection to one another, took its place. Thus, in the eighteenth century one finds a 'gradual narrowing down of the ritual, spectacle, and carnival forms of folk culture, which became small and trivial.' Literature mirrors the change: while the themes and imagery of carnival are central to Rabelais and other writers of the Renaissance, they have become circumscribed and problematic in the literature of the Enlightenment (117–19).

Of course the eighteenth-century masquerade itself might be described as a late or decadent form of the carnivalesque: particularly in England, where festive tradition was already far more attenuated than on the Continent, the masked assembly rapidly became an almost entirely secularized and commercial phenomenon.[13] Its philosophic dimension was somewhat paradoxical from the start, almost a vestigial effect. It is not surprising, therefore, that the contemporary novel of masquerade should also be peculiarly ambiguous. Even while the masquerade scene marks an atavistic incursion of mutability and flux into the symbolic world of representation, its moralistic bracketing – the suspicion and disavowal that surround the occasion – might be taken as the sign of a growing uneasiness and skepticism regarding the fluid epistemology of the older popular tradition. Seen in the elegiac Bakhtinian context, the masquerade novel of this period emerges as a penultimate moment in the literary history of the carnivalesque: it expresses larger philosophic and conceptual conflicts in an especially condensed and ambivalent way.

Certainly, with the exception of a few minor revivals in Regency literature, the masquerade set piece has all but vanished from the topography of the English novel by the late eighteenth century.[14] Yet this absence too reflected cultural reality: the public masquerade itself had virtually disappeared in England by the time of the French Revolution. To be sure, especially in the light of the growing moral and social conservatism of the upper classes in the last decades of the century, one might explain this disappearance politically as well as purely philosophically: in that period of pervasive rebellion and unrest, the utopian reversals of masquerade may have seemed altogether too inflammatory – too threatening to the somewhat precariously maintained balance of English society. During the

unsettled 1770s and 1780s, the stylized chaos of the carnival world
seemed everywhere to be giving way to unmediated scenarios of
active political insurgency.

But the basic connection here – between the literary theme and the
cultural institution – remains a compelling one. It may suggest
something too, finally, about the history of the novel and about the
genre's own complex negotiation with human realities. Tony Tanner
has argued that the novel, since its beginnings, has been subliminally
concerned with representing transgression, even while asserting itself
as the embodiment of bourgeois values and vindicator of the moral
and social status quo. It has harbored dreams of a world upside
down while seeming to validate prevailing ideology (3–4). For the
English novelists of the eighteenth century, popular entertainments
and diversions – the still extant realm of the carnivalesque – offered
a convenient tropology of scandal, a way of figuring such dreams.
The masquerade, one could say, was simply part of a larger
preoccupation with disruption.

As society itself changed, however, so did the novel, and so did
the characteristic scenery of transgression. The carnival topos may
be typical of the novel in its infancy, the period when proponents of
the genre are concerned most intensely with establishing the novel's
claim to didactic authority. So powerful is the overt moralistic
imperative in early fiction that the transgressive element appears, as
it were, by accident; it is figured more or less unself-consciously. The
particular appeal of the masquerade scene, as we have seen, was that
it allowed for just such a 'naive' elaboration of the transgressive plot,
while permitting the novelist to maintain the appearance of moral
orthodoxy. Presumably the writer could justify the episode, however
logically discontinuous, by prefacing it with an obvious negative
commentary. In contrast – it is tempting to speculate – novelists
of the late eighteenth and nineteenth centuries had little need for
ambiguously mediating figures like the masquerade; as the impulse
toward crude didacticism weakened and the writer's absorption
in transgressive modes became more integrated and self-conscious,
scandal – whether sexual, social, or political – could be represented
more directly. Tanner suggests that the plot of private erotic
transgression – for example, adultery – has a new moral neutrality
and imaginative centrality in the novels of Rousseau, Goethe, and
Flaubert; unlike Richardson and Fielding, these writers rely less and
less on devices of ideological or psychological mediation, such as the
carnivalesque intrigue, to set the story in motion. Similarly, collective
transgression seems to be depicted in increasingly unmediated forms
in the nineteenth-century novel, often through a representation of the
politicized divagations of the crowd or mob. Just as the masquerade

scene loses its currency as the primary fictional topos of collective disorder, the crowd scene, or scene of urban riot, seems to take its place: witness the complex use of such episodes in Scott, Hugo, Dickens, Eliot, Flaubert, and Zola. The nineteenth-century crowd scene serves many of the same narrative and thematic functions as the earlier masquerade scene, but it is usually far more integrated, in imaginative terms, into the mimetic and ideological structure in which it occurs. For the nineteenth-century novelist, unlike his or her eighteenth-century counterpart, transgression no longer has the shape of a discontinuous or naive diversion. One might indeed ask whether it has not become the central, self-conscious concern of the fictional enterprise itself.

The classic masquerade scene, then, is to a great extent a temporary phenomenon in the history of the novel – and perhaps a somewhat primitive one at that. In contrast with the topoi of nineteenth-century fiction, the masquerade episode functions in a curiously automatic way; it has the aspect at times of a piece of unconscious or unintegrated textual machinery. Yet its importance in eighteenth-century English fiction, as I have tried to show, is indisputable. The scene is typically a crux; it engenders a host of pleasurable fictional transformations. One might even call the carnivalesque episode an epitome of the seductive power of narrative: it introduces a surprising and gratifying potentiality into the static world of eighteenth-century representation, giving shape to that fantasy of change which lies at the heart of contemporary narrative. That this potentiality conflicts with the emblematic meaning of the scene – its inscription within the conventional moral allegory of the 'Town' – represents a contradiction, of course, yet one with which the eighteenth century itself was at home. By turning to the spectacular, secretive figures of carnival, the novelists of the period reenacted a larger collective flight into theatricality. The novel of masquerade is also, finally, an epitome of the culture in which it flourished – a mark of eighteenth-century England's own ambivalent escape from consistency, transparency, and the claims of an otherwise pervasive decorum.

Notes

1. On Mary Wortley Montagu's fondness for masks and masquerades, see Halsband 185. Writing to Horace Walpole in 1741, Horace Mann speaks enthusiastically of the outdoor carnivals of Florence (1: 97).

2. Typical masquerade tales include Eliza Haywood's *Masqueraders; or, Fatal Curiosity* (London, 1724), her history of Erminia in *The Female Spectator*, 3rd ed. (London, 1750), 32–35, and an anonymous 'Affecting Masquerade

Adventure' (*Gentleman's Magazine* Dec. 1754). The masquerade was also a popular dramatic topos: Benjamin Griffin's *Masquerade; or, An Evening's Intrigue* (1717), Charles Johnson's *Masquerade: A Comedy* (1719), the anonymous *The Masquerade; or, The Devil's Nursery* (1732), Fielding's *Miss Lucy in Town* (1742), Francis Gentleman's *Pantheonites* (1773), and Hannah Cowley's *Belle's Stratagem* (1781) are representative masquerade plays and farces.

3. Only two recent critics have looked in any detail at eighteenth-century masquerade scenes – David Blewett, in his chapter on *Roxana*, and Robert Folkenflik. Both take a somewhat limited and unproblematic view of the episode, however, and discuss only its emblematic significance – as a trope for the corrupt 'Town.' They pass over its peculiar narrative functions as well as its ultimately destabilizing thematic effects.

4. This argument pervades *Rabelais and His World*, but see in particular the introduction and chapter 1, 'Rabelais in the History of Laughter.'

5. On the varieties of masquerade dress, see the dissertation by Aileen Ribeiro, the costume historian, and her illustrated essay in *An Elegant Art*. *Horace Walpole's Correspondence* contains numerous descriptions of costumes worn at contemporary masquerades; see also the *Weekly Journal* 25 Jan., 8 Feb., and 18 April 1724; the *Universal Spectator* 5 April 1729; *Gentleman's Magazine* June 1769, Feb. 1771, Jan. 1773, and April 1774; and *Lady's Magazine* Feb. 1773.

6. On the persistent association between the masquerade and illicit forms of sexual behavior see my essay 'Eros and Liberty.' The moralistic diatribe against the masquerade lasted throughout the century. Typical of the attacks were the Bishop of London's *Sermon Preached to the Societies for the Reformation of Manners* (London, 1724), Fielding's poetic satire *The Masquerade* (London, 1728) and *Charge to the Grand Jury* (1749), and the anonymous pamphlets *The Conduct of the Stage Consider'd, with Short Remarks upon the Original and Pernicious Consequences of Masquerades* (London, 1721) and *Essay on Plays and Masquerades* (London, 1724).

7. According to contemporary accounts, attendance at Heidegger's weekly masquerades at the Haymarket averaged about seven hundred persons. Later in the century masquerades became larger still: *Town and Country Magazine* for May 1770 reports that twelve hundred gathered for a masquerade at Carlisle House on 7 May and that 'near two thousand persons' had attended an assembly at the Pantheon the month before. Besides Horace Walpole and Mary Wortley Montagu, celebrated devotees included George II and numerous members of the English aristocracy and, later in the century, Garrick, Goldsmith, Burney, and Boswell.

8. For Addison's satiric comments on masquerade 'promiscuity' see the *Spectator* 8 and 101 (Addison and Steele 1: 35–38, 1: 423–26) and the *Guardian* 154 (*Tatler and Guardian* 225–26).

9. Grete Ek comments on this subversion of sex roles (though without specifically connecting it with the masquerade).

10. R. S. Crane's comments in his classic essay on *Tom Jones* typify critical displeasure: he suggests that it is impossible not to be 'shocked' by Tom's entanglement with Lady Bellaston and that the masquerade episode as a whole represents one of the 'faults' of Fielding's novel. Crane complains in particular about the inconsistency in the characterization. 'It is necessary, no doubt,' he writes, 'that [Tom] should now fall lower than ever before, but surely not so low as to make it hard to infer his act from our previous knowledge of his character . . . ; for the moment at least, a different Tom is before our eyes' (127).

11. In the preface to *Amelia*, Fielding announces that his work is 'sincerely designed to promote the cause of virtue, and to expose some of the most glaring evils, as well public as private, which at present infest the country' (12). J. Paul Hunter, among others, has commented on the hypertrophy of didactic intention in *Amelia* (see ch. 9 of his book).

12. Barbara Babcock discusses the complex role of the carnivalesque in *Madame Bovary*.

13. On the increasing commercialization of the world of popular entertainment in the eighteenth century, see J. H. Plumb and Peter Burke.

14. Late set pieces include the masquerade scenes in Edgeworth's *Belinda* (1801) and Pierce Egan's *Life in London* (1821). On the Continent, where carnival tradition itself had a longer life, the masquerade remains a fictional topos well into the nineteenth century: notable scenes occur in Balzac, in *La Peau de chagrin* (1831) and *Splendeurs et misères des courtisanes* (1843), and in Flaubert, in *L'Education sentimentale* (1869). The masquerade scene makes interesting vestigial appearances too in nineteenth-century operas. Verdi's *Un Ballo in maschera* (1859) remains the best-known 'masquerade opera,' but other works also invoke the topos – Johann Strauss's *Der Carneval in Rom* (1873), *Die Fledermaus* (1874), and *Eine Nacht in Venedig* (1883); Heuberger's *Der Opernball* (1898); and Neilsen's *Maskarade* (1906). Twentieth-century writers return to the masquerade scene primarily in the context of exoticism or self-conscious nostalgia. A striking costume ball occurs in Lawrence Durrell's *Balthazar*, in *The Alexandria Quartet* (1962), while in Brigid Brophy's *The Snow Ball* (1964), characters attend a sixties London masquerade party, dressed in eighteenth-century (Mozartean) costume. In Isak Dinesen's posthumously published 'Carnival' (1977), erotic intrigues develop among eight persons on the night of the Copenhagen opera masquerade ball.

Works cited

Addison, Joseph. *The Tatler and Guardian*. Edinburgh, 1880.

—— *The Works of Joseph Addison*. Ed. Richard Hurd. 6 vols. London, 1811.

Addison, Joseph, and Richard Steele. *The Spectator*. Ed. Donald F. Bond. 5 vols. Oxford: Clarendon, 1965.

Babcock, Barbara. 'The Novel and the Carnival World.' *Modern Language Notes* 89 (1974): 911–37.

Bakhtin, M. *Rabelais and His World*. Trans. Helene Iswolsky. Cambridge, Mass.: MIT Press, 1968.

Blewett, David. *Defoe's Art of Fiction*. Toronto: University of Toronto Press, 1979.

Burke, Peter. *Popular Culture in Early Modern Europe*. New York: Harper, 1978.

Burney, Fanny. *Cecilia; or, Memoirs of an Heiress*. 5 vols. London, 1784.

Castle, Terry. 'Eros and Liberty at the English Masquerade 1710–1790.' *Eighteenth-Century Studies* 17 (1983–84): 156–76.

Crane, R. S. 'The Plot of *Tom Jones*.' *Journal of General Education* 4 (1950): 112–30.

Defoe, Daniel. *Roxana: The Fortunate Mistress*. Ed. Jane Jack. London: Oxford University Press, 1964.

Ek, Grete. 'Glory, Jest, and Riddle: The Masque of Tom Jones in London.' *English Studies* 60 (1979): 148–58.

Fielding, Henry. *Amelia*. Ed. William Ernest Henley. 2 vols. New York: Cass, 1967.

—— *Tom Jones*. Ed. Sheridan Baker. New York: Norton, 1973.

Folkenflik, Robert. 'Tom Jones, the Gypsies, and the Masquerade.' *University of Toronto Quarterly* 44 (1975): 224–37.

Griffin, Benjamin. *The Masquerade; or, An Evening's Intrigue*. London, 1717.

Halsband, Robert. *The Life of Lady Mary Wortley Montagu*. Oxford: Clarendon, 1956.

Horace Walpole's Correspondence. Ed. W. S. Lewis *et al.* 48 vols. New Haven: Yale University Press, 1937–83.

Hunter, J. Paul. *Occasional Form: Henry Fielding and the Chains of Circumstance*. Baltimore: Johns Hopkins University Press, 1975.

Inchbald, Elizabeth. *A Simple Story*. Ed. J. M. S. Tompkins. London: Oxford University Press, 1967.

Mann, Horace. Letter to Horace Walpole, 30 July 1741. In *Horace Walpole's Correspondence*.

Plumb, J. H. *The Commercialisation of Leisure in Eighteenth-Century England*. Reading, UK: University of Reading Press, 1973.

Ribeiro, Aileen. 'The Dress Worn at Masquerades in England, 1730 to 1790, and Its Relation to Fancy Dress in Portraiture.' Diss. University of London, Courtauld Institute, 1975.

—— 'The Elegant Art of Fancy Dress.' In *An Elegant Art: Fashion and Fantasy in the Eighteenth Century*. Ed. Edward Maeder. New York: Abrams and Los Angeles County Museum of Art, 1983.

Richardson, Samuel. *Pamela*. 2 vols. London: Dent, 1914.

—— *Sir Charles Grandison*. Ed. Jocelyn Harris. 2 vols. London: Oxford University Press, 1972.

Tanner, Tony. *Adultery in the Novel: Contract and Transgression*. Baltimore: Johns Hopkins University Press, 1979.

Todorov, Tzvetan. *The Fantastic: A Structural Approach to a Literary Genre*. Trans. Richard Howard. Ithaca: Cornell University Press, 1975.

Part II
Defoe

7 The Displaced Self in the Novels of Daniel Defoe

HOMER O. BROWN

Influenced by the post-structuralist questions about the stability of individual character or identity, Homer Brown's essay is an early version of a chapter appearing in his latest book, *Institutions of the English Novel from Defoe to Scott* (see Introduction, pp. 13–15). Brown argues that it is a mistake to think of the 'new' novel as defined by a seamless form of psychological realism or coherence. Rather, he stresses that Defoe is writing at a period when personal experience had difficulty finding a corollary in traditional means of making sense of it. At a revealing point, Brown uses Augustine's autobiography as a foil to Robinson's. Whereas Augustine's account of the self ultimately finds a place in some larger interpretive scheme, Defoe's protagonists are alienated from themselves. They regularly encounter strange and uncanny versions of the 'other,' standing in for equally disturbing and hitherto unrecognized aspects of themselves.

I Names

'A fine Story!' says the Governess, 'you would see the Child,
and you would not see the Child; you would be conceal'd and
discover'd both together.'

(Moll Flanders)[1]

Names, false names, absence of names seem to have special importance for Daniel Defoe's novels. None of his fictional narrators, with the exception of Robinson Crusoe,[2] tell their stories under the name he or she was born with. The narrator of *A Journal of the Plague Year* is anonymous, signing his account at the end with the initials 'H. F.' In the other novels, the narrators receive their names in something like a special christening. Bob Singleton is given his name by one of the series of 'mothers' through whose hands he passes after being kidnapped from his true parents. Colonel Jack receives the name 'John' from the nurse who is paid to take him by his real

161

parents, who are unmarried 'people of quality.' Unfortunately, all three of the nurse's 'sons,' one of them really hers and the other two paid for, are named 'John.'

Moll Flanders' real name is too 'well known in the records, or registers, at Newgate and in the Old Bailey,' so she chooses to write under the alias 'Moll Flanders' and begs the reader's patience 'till I dare own who I have been, as well as who I am.' It is by the revelation of this true name (to Moll but not the reader) that Moll recognizes her real mother, who had also adopted an alias, and discovers that she has married her own brother. 'Moll Flanders' is the name she takes during her time as a thief in London, when, though already a middle-aged woman, she falls under the tutelage of a woman who refers to her as 'child' and whom Moll calls 'mother.' The title page of *Roxana* is a veritable catalog of her aliases throughout her career. Curiously, the name 'Roxana' is the name she bears for the shortest time and one she did not give herself. She received it, in the presence of the king, from the spontaneous cry of a group of men at a masked ball in appreciation of the costume she was wearing. But *Roxana* is a special case, for the reader does learn at least her true Christian name because it is also the name of her daughter, who pursues her through the last part of the book.

At the moment of narration few of Defoe's narrators are living under the name by which they 'sign' their stories. Secrecy seems to be an absolute precondition of self-revelation. Or, to put it in a less perversely contradictory way, these narrators seem under a double compulsion to expose and to conceal themselves. Certainly it is a literary convention, a premise of fictional narration, aimed at convincing the reader of their veracity, since Defoe published all these books as the 'real' memoirs of their narrators. But it is a curious convention, since it goes beyond a mere premise of narration and becomes an important theme in the narration, an event in the story itself.

Moreover, literary convention cannot explain this practice of concealment in the life of the true author of these fake memoirs, Daniel Defoe, which was not, incidentally, his real name. Before and even after he took up the writing of these books at the age of sixty, Daniel *Foe* served as the agent of various interests, parties, governments, writing and acting under innumerable assumed names and points of view, to the extent that it is difficult to separate fact from fiction in our knowledge of his own life and impossible to go beyond certain limits in ascertaining what he actually wrote.

Robinson Crusoe is a somewhat special instance of Defoe's habit of concealing the true name of his narrators. Robinson has purportedly related the events of his own life under his own name through two volumes – *he* at least has committed no crime and requires no secrecy. In the Preface to the third volume, however, Robinson hints that if the events he has narrated are not strictly true they are allegorically true and that perhaps Robinson Crusoe is not his real name. Many readers have taken this hint to mean that Defoe had written his own spiritual autobiography under the metaphor of the shipwrecked and isolated Crusoe. The question has never been decided. The double project of revelation and concealment of this least sophisticated of novelists was successful. The 'real' Daniel Defoe has disappeared into the absence of an irrecoverable time.

We can only probe for the meaning of the double compulsion in the written world of his novel and perhaps ponder the relationship of that compulsion to the project of writing lies that look like truth. Our hopes are limited: if on the one hand we are reduced to a search for the meaning of the name he withheld from us, we know that in the end we will have to content ourselves with no more than the name alone.

What will we find to explain this curious game of names? In a sense it cannot be completely explained or understood because the only real evidence lies in the books themselves and also because, since it is a literary convention, we are touching upon a cultural symptom as well as a personal one and all such symptoms are overdetermined. Two provisional explanations, however, will emerge from an examination of Defoe's fiction. One has to do with a strong fear of the menace of other wills, a pervasive fear in these novels. Another explanation has to do with the way the self becomes somebody else in conversion. In this discussion I will place special weight on *Robinson Crusoe*, for while it provides less mystery about names than the other novels, it offers itself as a kind of myth to explain the fear of exposure, detailing the consequent strategies of the self. In order to discuss this impulse at the source of Defoe's fiction, I will have to defer consideration of the intense fascination with the factual, the most pervasive and already much discussed characteristic of Defoe's writing – defer it, I would hope, only to recover it in a new light.

These provisional explanations might help also to illuminate what is involved in the constitution of imaginary novelistic characters.

II The myth of singleness

In my youth, I wandered away, too far from your sustaining hand, and created of myself a barren waste.

(Augustine, *Confessions*)[3]

Defoe's novels are based on a notion of radical egocentricity. Robinson wonders why his isolation on the island was 'any grievance or affliction' since 'it seems to me that life in general is, or ought to be, but one universal act of solitude':

> The world, I say, is nothing to us but as it is more or less to our relish. All reflection is carried home, and our dear self is, in one respect, the end of living. Hence man may be properly said to be alone in the midst of the crowds and hurry of men and business. All the reflections which he makes are to himself; all that is pleasant he embraces for himself; all that is irksome and grievous is tasted but by his own palate.
>
> What are the sorrows of other men to us, and what their joy? Something we may be touched indeed with by the power of sympathy, and a secret turn of the affections; but all the solid reflection is directed to ourselves. Our meditations are all solitude in perfection; our passions are all exercised in retirement; we love, we hate, we covet, we enjoy, all in privacy and solitude. All that we communicate of those things to any other is but for their assistance in the pursuit of our desires; the end is at home; the enjoyment, the contemplation, is all solitude and retirement; it is for ourselves we enjoy, and for ourselves we suffer.
>
> (*Serious Reflections*, pp. 2–3)

Robinson's thirty years of solitude on a desert island is the metaphor of this selfishness. In fact, his story is based on the etymological metaphor 'islanded' – isolated. When Robinson was in Brazil, he 'used to say, I lived just like a man cast away upon some desolate island that had nobody there but himself' (VII, 39). The whole book has to do with the progressive materialization of spiritual metaphors for what is implicit in Robinson's condition from the beginning, in the same way that the book itself is a factualization of the metaphors of the whole tradition of spiritual autobiographies.[4]

Selfish, isolated, but is he really alone? Other Defoe narrators are just as solitary in the midst of society. Robinson's island isolation is after all only a metaphor for the solitary selfishness of all men. This seemingly impenetrable selfishness, however, is a Hobbesian 'state of nature,' transposed into a social world, atomistic, volatile, where the mere existence of another person, for Robinson even the *possibility* of the existence of another person, is a threat to the self. Even Robinson in his wilderness, through all those years of never encountering another human being, is constantly haunted by a sense of menacing otherness. He must always be on guard. He never loses the agonizing sense of being watched. Far from only being a representation of

Robinson's egocentric isolation, the book is peopled by *signs* of the constant presence of the other – Robinson's fear, the footprint of a man, the Hand of God, the constant presence of the older Robinson in the double perspective of the narration, the presence of the spectator-reader before whom Robinson rehearses his solitude. In a sense, no Defoe character, not even Robinson, is ever alone.

The need for secrecy at the moment of narration for most of Defoe's 'autobiographers' is no mystery. With the exception of Robinson and H. F., they have committed crimes for which they can be called to justice. Near the beginnings of their stories, however, they also are all bereft of family and protection and are thrown into a harsh and dangerous world of deceptive appearances, whose inhabitants are indifferent, conniving, menacing. Some, like Robinson or H. F., orphan themselves seemingly by choice. Others, like Colonel Jack and Bob Singleton, are virtually cut off from their origins, and so, from their true names. Roxana, even as a young girl, long before she is deserted by her husband and left to protect herself and her family, is removed from France and her childhood, bringing with her nothing 'but the Language.' The separation from any guardian structure is sharp. Their isolation is complete.

No wonder, then, that Defoe has been said to have discounted the importance of personal relationships in his novels.[5] There is no richly complex conflict between wills more or less equal in strength in his fictional world. The Defoe character has to struggle against all the others, against a harsh necessity.[6] There is no sense of an individualized other consciousness confronting the protagonist as there is in Richardson's world or Austen's or George Eliot's. The paradigm is Moll in a crowded London street; her survival depends on her ability to take 'the advantages of other people's mistakes' while remaining unseen herself. The value of her story for the reader will be in its warning 'to Guard against the like Surprizes, and to have their Eyes about them when they have to do with Strangers of any kind, for 'tis very seldom that some Snare or other is not in their way' (II, 92). Otherness for a Defoe character is generic, anonymous. Individual antagonists like Roxana's landlord, or even her Amy, Moll's various men, Robinson's Moorish captor or Friday can be tricked or subordinated without much apparent difficulty, but a single, anonymous footprint in the sand seizes Crusoe's mind with uncontrollable terror. However easily any Defoe 'I' can deal with any individual menace, the unnamed dread remains. Perhaps the most striking example is the London of the plague. The 'others' of the *Journal* are anonymous numbers of dead and dying. Any conversation, even the slightest human contact, carries the risk of death.

When Robinson finds himself shipwrecked, almost his first act is to begin to build a wall around himself. He further insulates himself; he creates an island within the island. His action is obsessive. He spends almost three and a half months building the wall – 'I thought I should never be perfectly secure 'till this Wall was finish'd' (VII, 87). Although he longs for deliverance from his solitude, he is compelled to hide his presence so 'that if any People were to come on Shore there, they would not perceive any Thing like a Habitation' (VII, 87). So, in the midst of a threatening and unknown space, Robinson creates for himself an ordered interior, crowded with things which can be listed and enumerated to his satisfaction. He 'furnishes' himself 'with many things,' as a chapter title phrases it. Like the fallen angels, Robinson sets about to build and secure his own Pandemonium, following the advice of Mammon to 'seek / Our own good from ourselves, and from our own / Live to ourselves, though in this vast recess, / Free, and to none accountable' (*Paradise Lost* II, 252–55). But, of course, their self-reliance is a sham, their Pandemonium is a parody of Heaven, founded upon denial of the divine Other, whose power they can never escape. Like the angels, Robinson's concern with things is a symptom of his fall. Robinson's brave statement 'I build my fortress' echoes ironically Luther's famous hymn based on the Ninety-first Psalm (cf. *A Journal*, pp. 12–13).

Moll Flanders in disguise in the middle of a crowded London street, H. F. in his 'safe' house surrounded by the plague, Robinson in his fort – the image is a recurrent one. Earlier in Robinson's account, in Brazil he carves out a plantation 'among Strangers and Savages in a Wilderness, and at such a Distance, as never to hear from any Part of the World that had the least Knowledge of me' (VII, 39). Still earlier, there is Robinson quavering in the hold of the ship that takes him from home, surrounded by a raging sea.

At the beginning of the book Robinson's father points out to him that his 'was the middle State, or what might be called the upper Station of *Low Life*, . . . that this was the State of Life which all other People envied' because

the middle Station had the fewest Disasters, and was not expos'd to so many Vicissitudes as the higher or lower Part of Mankind . . . that this Way Men went silently and smoothly thro' the World, and comfortably out of it, not embarrass'd with the Labours of the Hands or of the Head, not sold to the Life of Slavery for daily Bread, or harasst with perplex'd Circumstances, which rob the Soul of Peace and the Body of Rest; not enrag'd with the Passion of Envy, or secret burning Lust of Ambition for great things; but in easy Circumstances sliding gently thro' the World, and sensibly tasting the Sweets of living, without the bitter, feeling that they are happy, and learning by every Day's Experience to know it more sensibly.

(VII, 2–4)

Then, at the outset, Robinson already possesses the kind of security, freedom from exposure, that most other Defoe narrators and later even Robinson himself long for. What is given to Robinson is suddenly taken from other Defoe protagonists by circumstances over which they have no control. Moll Flanders and even H. F. must expose themselves to danger in order to survive. Why does Robinson give up so easily what the others have to struggle so hard to gain? In a sense, this is the same question implicit in the beginning of this essay: expressing so strong a desire for concealment, why do they offer their confessions at all? This is as difficult a question as asking why Defoe wrote novels. The desire for concealment could have been easily satisfied by silence, by writing or publishing no books at all.[7] The obvious answer to so manifestly impossible a question – that Defoe wrote books to make money, that is to say, like Moll or H. F., to survive – is less satisfactory than it might at first appear. There were other ways to make money, many of which Defoe tried. Much of the other writing Defoe did involved the need for secrecy or masking.

Defoe's narrators seem obsessed with concealing themselves, but the impulse leading them towards exposure appears equally strong. Complete concealment is impossible, perhaps not even desirable. On the one hand there is the insistence on building a faceless shelter around the self, but, on the other, a recurring compulsion to move out into the open. This double compulsion can be expressed as a double fear. When an earthquake makes him fear the security of his cave, Robinson writes that 'the fear of being swallow'd up alive, made me that I never slept in quiet, and yet the Apprehensions of lying abroad without any Fence was almost equal to it' (VII, 94). These two fears, however – fear of being swallowed up by the earth, fear of lying in the open – are the same at bottom. Why does Robinson fear sleeping without the protection of a wall? He is afraid of ravenous beasts and cannibals. If one is caught abroad with one's guard down, unconscious (sleeping), one risks loss of self. But the dangers are as great apparently if one never ventures out. Both fears are basically fears of engulfment: one, the fear of being lost in the recesses of one's own nature (the earth), fear of solipsism and anonymity; alternately, fear of being captured, 'eaten' by the other. Perhaps behind both, Defoe's fear of imprisonment.[8] Fear of forms, equally strong fears of the formless. The fear of being devoured

167

recurs throughout Robinson's narrative. At the beginning, he is afraid of being swallowed alive by the sea. Near the end, he defends himself against the devouring wolves.[9]

Besides fear or biological need, there are other reasons apparently for venturing abroad. Curiosity forces H. F. constantly to risk infection. Moll learns that the others betray moments of unconsciousness from which she can profit: 'a Thief being a Creature that Watches the Advantages of other Peoples mistakes' (II, 92). Why does Robinson surrender his initial security? The reasons are intentionally vague to point to the fact that his motivation is beyond his understanding and ambiguously beyond personal choice, for the reasons are generic and at the same time subject to his accountability. His motivation or lack of justifiable motivation, involving disobedience of the father, is a restlessness of spirit which is simultaneously culpability and its own punishment. He describes the sources of his 'meer wandering Inclination' as 'something fatal,' a 'Propension of Nature,' symptoms of what he shares with general man, the heritage of the fall. 'Design'd' by his father 'for the Law,' he 'would be satisfied with nothing but going to Sea,' great symbol of the unformed. The opposition could not be more clear. What is most threatening is also most alluring. Throughout his life, even after his conversion, Robinson will feel the compulsion to leave behind the preformed, the already-given world of law, and face the unknown and undifferentiated, full of menace for the self and simultaneously full of promise. Unable to accept the given definition of himself, the will and legacy of his father, the world of law, Robinson experiences himself as incomplete and searches mistakenly for completion in the world outside. He does not possess himself but is scattered among a world of things. He must externalize himself in the world. He must create a self out of the formless sea of pure possibility, out of the surrounding, anonymous wilderness. The world is for him to make something of – his own.

Here is the source of his egocentricity. His feeling of loneliness in Brazil at being 'at such a Distance as never to hear from any Part of the World that had the least Knowledge of me' (VII, 39) suggests that this distance is an alienation from a part of himself held in thrall by the world outside. This alienation and his longing for companionship through his years of isolation on the 'Island of Despair' and his fear of the other all testify to his continuing sense of incompleteness but also reveal the lie behind the way he has sought fulfillment.

Fear of the other, determining need for concealment; necessity, allurement of the world offering some form of completion to the self, determining the impulse to risk exposure. This is the explanation of the concealment and exposure or guarded exposure of Defoe's narrators that is revealed by the play of names. Hiding behind the disguise of Robinson and his factual-seeming narrative, Defoe is doing what Robinson does – constructing and hiding inside a 'natural' fortification which cannot be perceived as a 'habitation' from the outside. In a sense this is as close as we can get to an answer to the problem formulated at the beginning. Pursuit of the mystery might, however, give a fuller sense of the implications of this strategy for the development of the novel.

III   The necessity of becoming other

> I preferred to excuse myself and blame this unknown thing which was in me but was not part of me. The truth, of course, was that it was all my own self, and my own impiety had divided me against myself.
>
> (Augustine, *Confessions*, p. 103 [Bk. V, Sec. 10])

After fifteen years, after his material and spiritual security has seemed complete, and his only confrontation has been hearing unexpectedly his own name pronounced by his parrot, Robinson experiences the incredible shock of seeing the 'naked footprint of a man.' The hidden self–other structure of the book is brought into the open. The footprint is the merest sign of the *near* presence of another human being – yet shouting significance for Robinson in the very fact of its inadequacy of signification.

It is the sheerest kind of accident, almost miraculous, as he realizes, that he has seen it. Characteristically he sums up the odds: ''twas Ten Thousand to one whether I should see it or not, and in the Sand too, which the first Surge of the Sea upon a high Wind would have defac'd entirely' (VII, 179). A footprint in the sand – a partial signature whose power lies in its mystery and ambiguity. A sign of transience – in both the sense that it is the mark of action and also that it is temporary, contingent; it is the static trace of a human movement and a recent movement at that. But rather than being any signal to Crusoe's hopes – of company or of deliverance – in a flash the footprint destroys all his hopes and all his security.

The contradiction between Robinson's desire to externalize himself and his fear of being seen receives sharp definition:

> The first Thing I propos'd to my self, was, to throw down my Enclosures, and turn all my tame Cattle wild into the Woods, that the Enemy might not find them; and then frequent the Island in Prospect of the same, or the like Booty: Then to the simple Thing

169

of Digging up my two Corn Fields, that they might not find such
a Grain there, and still be prompted to frequent the Island; then
to demolish my Bower, and Tent, that they might not see any
Vestiges of Habitation, and be prompted to look farther, in order
to find out the Persons inhabiting.

(VII, 184)

Seized by this terror at the possible presence of another human being,
Robinson wants to remove all traces of himself from the island at the
cost of destroying all that he has worked for, all that he has created
of himself in things. He wants to disappear, to be invisible, to see
without being seen. When he recovers his reason, he will try to
accomplish this same end by more practical means. He will build a
second wall, further enclosing himself; he will go out of it only
rarely, when it is necessary, and then only with the greatest caution
and circumspection; and he will go to great lengths to provide armed
vantage points, hiding places where he can spy on intruders without
himself being seen.

Before he conceives of the idea of erasing all trace of himself
from the island by destroying his possessions, he imagines more
reasonably such destruction by those who left the footprint:

Then terrible Thoughts rack'd my Imagination about their having
found my Boat, and that there were People here; and that if so, I
should certainly have them come here again in greater Numbers,
and devour me; that if it should happen so that they should not
find me, yet they would find my Enclosure, destroy all my Corn,
carry away all my Flock of tame Goats, and I should perish at last
for meer Want.

(VII, 180)

When he considers doing the same thing to himself, it is almost as if
he would be acting in place of the others, doing to himself what he
most fears at their hands. At this point in his narrative, in a confused
way, a dialectic between self and other begins to emerge.

At first Robinson thinks the footprint must have been made by
the Devil to frighten him. This idea removes the element of the
contingent from the sign, gives it purpose *for* him. Curiously, his idea
also mitigates the otherness of the sign. Later, when he is frightened
by the dying 'he-goat' in the cave, he comments 'that he that was
afraid to see the Devil, was not fit to live twenty Years in an Island
all alone; and that I durst to believe there was nothing in this Cave
that was more frightful than my self' (VII, 205). In the *Serious
Reflections*, he notes the old proverb 'that every solitary person must
be an angel or a devil.' Here the same association is implicit, for he

moves from the idea that it is the Devil's footprint to the persuasion
that it is a 'meer Chimera of my own; and that this Foot might be the
Print of my own Foot' (VII, 182). If this is true, 'I might be truly said
to start at my own Shadow,' but he is unable to convince himself
completely of this solution. He records his terrors when he leaves his
shelter as if he were seen by someone else: 'But to see with what Fear
I went forward, how often I look'd behind me, how I was ready
every now and then to lay down my Basket, and run for my Life, it
would have made any one have thought I was haunted with an evil
Conscience' (VII, 183). Roxana also thinks of herself as being haunted
by her own evil conscience when the daughter named after her
reappears in her life.

All these speculations – the chimera, his own foot, his own
shadow, an evil conscience, the curious ability to see himself as
another would see him – amount to a confusion between the self and
the other. The island, which is an extension of himself, has dark areas
Robinson has never explored; he is constantly startled by versions of
himself, the voice of the parrot, the dying goat. In the same way, the
other holds a dimension of himself which Robinson has ignored, a
reflection of himself that in his selfishness he has not recognized,
and more, the other holds a part of himself in thrall, in an
interdependence to which he has been blind. There is also an
otherness *in* him. At this point, a brief comparison with an earlier
autobiographer might be illuminating. The young Augustine was
alienated from himself in his acceptance of the Manichean belief that
evil was a foreign substance in the soul: 'The truth, of course, was
that it was all my own self, and my own impiety had divided me
against myself' (*Confessions*, p. 103 [Bk. V, Sec. 10]). As a result of
this blindness toward the true location of himself, he had fragmented
and scattered himself among the objects of the world.[10] Similarly,
Robinson is unable to account for whatever it is in him that constantly
leads him to his own misery and destruction, his 'foolish inclination
of wandering abroad' (VII, 42), which leads to his scattering of self
among the objects of his desire and fear.

Recognition of the nature of this otherness and its relation to
himself comes gradually as he is exposed to the other in a series of
very strange stages over a number of years: first, the footprint, then
human bones – 'all my Apprehensions were bury'd in the Thoughts
of such a Pitch of inhuman, hellish Brutality, and the Horror of the
Degeneracy of Humane Nature' (VII, 191) – and then finally the sight
of the cannibals themselves from a distance. He is so horrified by
them that he thinks of slaughtering them, making himself God's
agent of justice, but he realizes both the presumption of this notion
and its dangers for himself, so he decides to hold himself hidden and

apart from them. To attack the cannibals without direct provocation to himself would not only question the design of God's providence for all creatures but it would also mean that he would be matching their barbarity with his own. Such an action on his part, he realizes, would be like the cruelty shown by the Spaniards in America, 'a meer Butchery, a bloody and unnatural Piece of Cruelty, unjustifiable either to God or Man; and such, as for which the very Name of a *Spaniard* is reckon'd to be frightful and terrible to all People of Humanity, or of Christian Compassion' (VII, 199). The irony of this identification of the enemy as Spaniards and cannibals, both outside the pale of what is human, should be apparent, for Crusoe's first friends on his island, the first human subjects of his 'commonwealth,' are two cannibals and a Spaniard. He will not only be forced to recognize their humanity, but also will be driven to acknowledge their barbarity in himself or at least in those with whom he identifies.

For the moment, Robinson's two fears of exposure and of being devoured are now focused on this one representative of a cannibalistic nature which is ambiguously human. When another ship wrecks off his island and the entire crew is apparently lost, Robinson is given a strong sense of the possibilities in his own condition. One of his fantasies about the fate of these men is that they might have tried to make the shore in their boat but instead were carried out by the current 'into the great Ocean, where there was nothing but Misery and Perishing; and that perhaps they might by this Time think of starving, and of being in a Condition to eat one another' (VII, 216). So, there are circumstances which could turn shipwrecked sailors like Robinson into cannibals. This possibility is reinforced when he and Friday witness the treacherous cruelty of the English mutineers – 'O Master!' Friday says, *'You see* English *Mans eat Prisoner as well as* Savage *Mans'* (VII, 42).

On the other hand, it is the humanity of Friday and later of the Spaniard that Crusoe comes to know. The discovery of Friday's loyalty and devotion causes Robinson to reflect that even on savages God has bestowed

the same Powers, the same Reason, the same Affections, the same Sentiments of Kindness and Obligation, the same Passions and Resentments of Wrongs; the same Sense of Gratitude, Sincerity, Fidelity, and all the Capacities of doing Good, and receiving Good, that he has given to us; and that when he pleases to offer to them Occasions of exerting these, they are as ready, nay, more ready to apply them to the right Uses for which they were bestow'd, than we are.

(VII, 243)

Robinson must come to see himself in the other and the other in himself. His 'social contract,' the statement of his subjects' dependence on him, is his covert admission of dependence on them since it is he who insists on it. He also comes to a greater self-knowledge by seeing himself and his works reflected in their eyes. Earlier he had seen himself from the outside as another, totally unsympathetic and possibly hostile, might have seen him. Now he sees himself from the perspective of a friendly providence in the misery of the English seamen who are about to be beached by the mutineers: 'This put me in Mind of the first Time I came on Shore, and began to look about me; How I gave my self over for lost; How wildly I look'd round me: What dreadful Apprehensions I had: And how I lodg'd in the Tree all Night for fear of being devour'd by wild Beasts' (VIII, 43). This time he sees his despair in some one else and from the point of view of their and his deliverance. He reflects that just as he did not know that first night that the storm would drive the ship close enough to land for him to receive supply for his needs 'so these three poor desolate Men knew nothing how certain of Deliverance and Supply they were, how near it was to them, and how effectually and really they were in a Condition of Safety, at the same Time that they thought themselves lost, and their Case desperate' (VIII, 43). Now, more than twenty-five years after Robinson's shipwreck, he knows that the same thing had been true of him, that he had been 'in a Condition of Safety' when he had thought himself lost.

IV   The conversion of conversion

The good which I now sought was not outside myself. I did not look for it in things which are seen with the eye of the flesh by the light of the sun. For those who try to find joy in things outside themselves easily vanish away into emptiness. . . . But it was in my inmost heart where I had grown angry with myself, where I had been stung with remorse, where I had slain my old self and offered it in sacrifice, where I had first purposed to renew my life and had placed my hope in you, it was there that you had begun to make me love you and had made me glad at heart.

(*Confessions*, p. 188 [Bk. IX, Sec. 4])

Crusoe's ability to stand outside himself is related here to his understanding of the providential meaning of experience. That he is able to see the other Englishmen from the standpoint of a providence of which he is now the agent results from his discovery of the plan of his own life much earlier in the book, when he was still alone on the island. This 'objectivity' of the self and the corresponding vision of time's plan, transcending the experience of the isolated self, are the consequences of a conversion which in Defoe never seems a single moment, a sudden and total turning which restructures the self for all time, as it is, for example, in Augustine's *Confessions*. Crusoe does experience something like that moment – there are the misunderstood providential warnings, the despair about his isolation, the new warnings in the storm, earthquake, and dream, the sickness that is symbolic of death, the discovery of the biblical message, the prayer and conviction of spiritual deliverance. But in time his certainty is dissipated as if by time itself. And each discovery of a new danger, for example, Crusoe's discovery of the footprint, at least temporarily wrecks all certainty.

Conversion is a recurrent need, a revelation followed each time by another lapse, a forgetting that is like an absence, requiring a new dialectical struggle. Not a completely new conversion, actually – Crusoe must be brought back to the self discovered in the initial conversion and by that movement freed from self-deception, freed in a sense from self. And this must happen again and again. He will suffer the consequences of the original fall, the restlessness, the 'foolish inclination to wander abroad,' as long as he lives. He must constantly refound himself in Christ and His providence, placing all his reliance on Him.

It is just here that resides buried the curious message of the episode of the corn, curious because it never became completely explicit and because it holds great meaning for Crusoe's egoism. When the corn sprouts first appeared, Robinson thought them miraculous, divine suspension of the laws of nature for his benefit. When he remembered that he had shaken out a bag of chicken feed in the place where the barley and rice were growing, 'the Wonder began to cease; and I must confess, my religious Thankfulness on God's Providence began to abate too upon the Discovering that this was nothing but what was common' (VII, 89–90). In the perspective of the narration, Robinson's judgment on the vacillations is that

> I ought to have been as thankful for so strange and unforeseen Providence, as if it had been miraculous; for it was really the Work of Providence as to me, that should order or appoint, that 10 or 12 Grains of Corn should remain unspoil'd (when the Rats had destroy'd all the rest,) as if it had been dropt from Heaven; as also, that I should throw it out in that particular Place where it being in the Shade of a high Rock, it sprang up immediately; whereas, if I had thrown it anywhere else, at that Time, it had been burnt up and destroy'd.

(VII, 90)

Critics who, like Robinson, attribute spiritual significance to his experience regard the episode as symbolic of the 'seeds' of Grace. In this context of Robinson's egoistic blindness against which the episode renders judgment the implications of the passage seem to be more probing. Surely the scriptural reference is to John 12: 24–25: 'Except a corn of wheat fall into the ground and die, it abideth alone: but if it die, it bringeth forth much fruit. He that loveth his life shall lose it; and he that hateth his life in his world shall keep it unto life eternal.' Robinson must die to himself and place all his reliance on God.

Radical individualism in all its isolated inwardness was implicit in Christianity from its beginning; in its emphasis on the brotherhood of all men, the message of Christ explicitly cut across the limits of family, tribe, or nation. One expression of the subjectivist implications of Christianity was in the intense self-exploration of Augustine's *Confessions*, a work which informs Defoe's fictional project.[11] The implications of this individualism were worked out in the Renaissance and in a more radical way in the Reformation, of whose Puritan strain Robinson is a well-known representative. Yet Christianity was also provided with this antidote to the narcissism that threatened it – the notion of the symbolic death of the self. Robinson's resistance to God's call manifested itself in one way in his obsessive fear of the loss or death of self involved in being 'swallowed up' or devoured by his beginnings, by the unformed chaos of the sea, by the other. Robinson does undergo a sickness unto death, literally and figuratively, a symbolic death of the self from which he emerges with a truer if temporary understanding of God's plan for him. And as the text from John suggests, and as it was for Augustine, in his sacrifice of self Robinson is given himself for the first time.

The nature of this gift is expressed more explicitly in Moll's conversion in Newgate. Her experience is at first wayward fluctuation between repentance and selfishness. When she discovers that her Lancashire husband is bound to be hanged for a highwayman, she is so overwhelmed by grief for him and by reflections on her own previous life that 'in a Word, I was perfectly chang'd, and become another Body' (II, 107). But this transformation is a return to self: 'The wretched Boldness of Spirit, which I had acquired, abated, and conscious Guilt began to flow in my Mind: In short, I began to think, and to think indeed is one real Advance from Hell to Heaven; all that harden'd State and Temper of Soul, which I said so much of before, is but a Deprivation of Thought; he that is restor'd to his Thinking, is restor'd to himself' (II, 107). In as much as she is still concerned about her own fate, she is still selfish and the Moll who narrates doubts the sincerity of her repentance at this point. Finally, when she receives the condemnation of this court it is 'a Sentence to me like Death itself' (II, 112) and she feels 'real Signs of Repentance' (II, 113). Like Augustine and Robinson, she sees the things of this life in a new way: 'I now began to look back upon my past Life with abhorrence, and having a kind of View into the other Side of Time, the Things of Life, as I believe they do with every Body at such a Time, began to look with a different Aspect, and quite another Shape, than they did before' (II, 113).

In his conversion, Augustine is also given a 'view into the other side of time.' He also is transformed into 'another body,' which paradoxically is a matter of being 'restored to himself.' Restored to himself first in this sense, as he says: 'O Lord, you were turning me around to look at myself. For I had placed myself behind my own back, refusing to see myself. You were setting me before my own eyes so that I could see how sordid I was, how deformed and squalid, how tainted with ulcers and sores' (169 [Bk. VIII, Sec. 7]). But he is also restored to himself in a larger sense. Augustine's last doubts before giving himself over to Christ were his doubts concerning his ability to accept continence. For this, he must throw himself on Christ's strength, not try to rely on his own. By being made capable of continence by God, Augustine is given himself, for as he explains: 'By continence we are made as one and regain that unity of self which we lost by falling apart in the search for a variety of pleasures' (233 [Bk. X, Sec. 29]).

The similarities between Defoe's fictional memoirs, particularly Robinson's, and their ultimate model, Augustine's *Confessions*, are striking, but their differences are of signal importance. Both Augustine and Robinson have relied upon themselves, upon their own strength and reason, in important, though differing, ways. Each experienced himself initially as incomplete. The early life of each was a wandering, yet for each, every erring step was guided by Providence bringing him to the moment of salvation. To each the command of God comes by discovery of a chance word in a Sortes Biblicae. Each is brought by the symbolic death of conversion to an understanding of time and to a self-knowledge, the 'proof' of which lies in the act of confession or narration.

For Defoe, however, the gift of self is as 'symbolic' as the sacrificial death. Self will continue to reassert itself and be lost consequently in distraction. For it is Defoe's insight that the essential characteristic of a symbolic death is that it is only symbolic and must be repeated *endlessly. All* solutions in this life are symbolic, perhaps 'figural' is a better word, and fallen man is never free of the consequences of Adam's sin until he suffers its original punishment, actual death. If he can be 'justified' only by God, the promise figured by Providence can be fulfilled only in Heaven. From this point of view, providence is sight cast forward, into the not yet. Is it too commonplace to say that modern realism is born in the split between the symbolic and the actual, in the despair over the real efficacy of the symbolic?

One consequence is that there is a necessary discrepancy between the allegorical truth and the fact of the story. For example, Tom Jones calls 'father' a man named Allworthy, who is squire of Paradise Hall from which he evicts Tom for his wrongdoing. But Allworthy is not omniscient and Tom has not done what he has been accused of. Instead he is a victim of deceit, treachery, and misunderstanding – certainly no orthodox allegory of man's fall. Moreover, in the course of the novel, Tom must acquire worldly wisdom and aspires to Sophia who is not (at least in this novel) wise. Similarly, Richardson's Clarissa disobeys an inexplicable demand of her father and is seduced from her garden by the serpent-like Lovelace. Of course, in this case, the demand of the father is not only inexplicable, it is also patently unjust and Clarissa runs away with Lovelace to escape that injustice. The pattern is there, however, but from this point of view, the realistic story, life in this world, is an incomplete, distorted shadow of its spiritual truth. Hence the traditional dissatisfaction with the 'allegory' of *Robinson Crusoe*. The point is not that these writers tried and failed to write novelistic allegories but that life could not be reduced or raised to a spiritual meaning.

The experiences of both Augustine and Robinson find their clear focus against a scriptural and sacred background. For example, the pear tree of Augustine's adolescence, the garden where his struggle with salvation takes place, and the fig tree under which he is saved are types of Adam's tree of forbidden fruit, the garden of Gethsemane, and Christ's 'tree' or cross under which man is redeemed. Robinson's story is the story of Jonah and of the Prodigal Son. But it is the 'real' Augustine who is offered in the *Confessions* by way of these stories, the real Augustine purged of the accidents of a purely personal life and revealed in the figural patterns of the Scriptures. On the other hand, Robinson is not a real person – the fact of his memoirs is their factitiousness. If, as Robinson insinuates in his *Serious Reflections*, his story is only allegorically true, then it is either true as some have thought of Defoe's own life or the truth of the story is offered as the general truth of everyman's life. If it is Defoe's truth, then the accidents of his own life are given in what is *essentially* true in Robinson's adventures. If it is a general truth, then another reversal has taken place, for this universal essence is offered as the *actuality* of a very eccentric individual life. Symbol and fact are united in Augustine's *Confessions* but forever divided in Robinson's.

This split is demonstrated in a striking way when Robinson appears to the English mutineers 'as another Person': 'So that as we never suffered them to see me as Governour, so I now appear'd as another Person, and spoke of the Governour, the Garrison, the Castle, and the like, upon all Occasions' (VIII, 65). Here it is his metaphoric or spiritual condition (as 'governor' of the island, 'viceroy to the King of all the earth' [*Serious Reflections*, p. 179]), which is held aside, while his disguise, the *other* person he becomes, is his *actuality*, in all the fantastic garb of an eccentricity which has survived almost thirty years of isolation. His disguise is almost like the lies of Odysseus – more plausible than the fantastic adventures he has undergone in the *Odyssey*. I have said that the split is between the symbolic-essential and the accidental-actual, but here the value of these poles has been reversed and the actual has become 'other' than the truth. The split in Robinson's being in this passage is also, and not incidentally, the same as the split between the bourgeois *legal person* and the unique individual.

Through his conversion Augustine gains both the true order of life and his true self – one and the same thing in confession, which is the *full* giving of self in speech whose truth is guaranteed by the presence of the Divine omniscient Other. The 'real' self of Defoe's various 'memoirs,' however, is a fictive self. Defoe's confessions are not *his* confessions at all. The pattern of Christian truth has become the design of a lie masked as actuality, the plot of a novel. The symbolic death of the Christian pattern has become truly symbolic on another level, in as much as even actual death in fiction is still a symbolic death. And the symbolic deaths of Robinson's or Moll's conversions are the doubly symbolic deaths of surrogate selves.

The full implications of this death by proxy are revealed in the story of Roxana, where the death is carried a step more distant and conversion is either impossible or no longer necessary. Roxana makes her escape into the curious oblivion of the end of that book disguised by the clothes and sanctimonious speech of a Quaker, symbols of a conversion she cannot attain. The split in Roxana, indicated by disguise, is more complicated than Robinson's self-division. She appears as the self she would like to be (her 'spiritual truth') at the same time she is confronted by her past self projected onto the form of her daughter who bears Roxana's true name, whom she deserted as a child, and who later appeared again as her servant at the moment she became the notorious Roxana. Now, it is this poor scapegoat of a daughter, the alter ego of a fictional character, yet the only truly individualized 'other' of any of Defoe's fictions, who is made to suffer a sacrificial death for which Roxana will never be forgiven.

The death is brought about in a curious way – curious, in the light of the dialectic between self and other in Defoe's novels. The witness to Roxana's first crime against morality was her servant Amy. Roxana felt compelled to force Amy to sleep with her seducer: 'As I thought myself a Whore, I cannot say but that it was something design'd in my Thoughts, that my Maid should be a Whore too, and should not reproach me with it' (47). As witness to her crime, Amy would become the dangerous other – seducers or seducees never seem to have enough self-consciousness to appear as threats to the self in Defoe. The witness is the dangerous other. Roxana, by watching Amy's seduction by the same man who has ruined her, has rendered Amy 'safe.' She has made her an accomplice, an adjunct to her own will. When, at the end of the book, Amy does away with the daughter by some means that Roxana can't bear to think about, Amy has become like an element of Roxana's personality capable of acting autonomously (somewhat like the daughter herself). That Amy is enacting Roxana's secret will is proved by Roxana's overwhelming sense of guilt. The book ends in the uncertainty of the unspeakable. It is either the most resolved of all the dialectical struggles between self and other in Defoe's fiction or the most unresolvable.

What is certain is that the symbolic death has been moved a step farther away from the 'I' who narrated all of Defoe's books. The conversion has disappeared completely, although Roxana, beyond her Quaker costume, does become another person. Near the beginning of her account of her life, but speaking from the obscurity into which she disappears at the end, Roxana says: 'Being to give my own Character, I must be excus'd to give it as impartially as possible, and as if I was speaking of another body' (6). What has replaced the conversion is the act of narration itself.

And what can be said of Defoe? In the Preface to *Roxana*, he describes himself as the 'Relator' who will 'speak' the words of the Beautiful Lady. Unable to give a true account of the self, he is doomed to speak the words of 'another-body' as if they were his own, putting on the disguise of one fictive self after another.

V Providence and writing: a natural habitation

Roxana's maxim, 'That Secrets should never be open'd, without evident Utility.' Robinson's maxim, 'The prudent man forseeth the evil and hideth himself.'
'Speech was given to man to disguise his thoughts.'

(Talleyrand)

When Robinson began to ponder the mystery of the footprint found on the beach, he discovered that he could not be certain that he had not left the print himself. Like the mystery of causality itself, the footprint is a trace of an intentional act seen from the outside: 'Again, I consider'd also that I could by no Means tell for certain where I had trod, and where I had not; and that if at last this was only the Print of my own Foot, I had play'd the Part of those Fools, who strive to make stories of Spectres, and Apparitions; and then are frighted at them more than any body' (VII, 182). The enigmatic footprint is like a ghost story, a genre most interesting to Defoe, whose power is great enough to deceive even its own teller. The footprint then is similar to a myth, told by an individual who yet cannot claim authorship, like the dream barred from its source by disavowal. In short, the footprint is a figure for the book of Robinson's adventures. Did Robinson leave the footprint or was it left by the threatening other? Are the adventures authored by Defoe, who disavowed them, by the Robinson who signed them, or by the other in whose constant presence they are structured and who is their destination?

Perhaps there is already on Defoe's part a glimmer of that suspicion of the concept of the unified and identifiable 'subject' with which it has been seen by later thinkers, particularly by Nietzsche and Freud and more recently by Derrida. For Defoe's project seems to have involved the creation of more or less autonomous voices, themselves without a center, that is to say, irredeemably ec-centric voices. Or, rather, voices whose center is a felt lack of center, the absence of which could be explained by the *insertion* of the myth of fallen man, yet voices created without the distance or structure of a consistent irony, a fact which has troubled the criticism of Defoe's books. Voices calculating a world of facts but who are themselves fictions after all. Books whose ambiguity is deep, thorough, and finally unresolvable.

The problem of Defoe criticism is well stated by the title of an early twentieth-century study, William Trent's *Daniel Defoe: How to Know Him*. My strategy has been to chip away at the hard flint of that ultimately unanswerable question in the hope that the sparks would illuminate, if only slightly, the surrounding terrain.

How can Robinson tell for certain where 'I had trod and where I had not'? Time, the shifting sand on the beach, how indeed can they afford a true history or a stable identity to a mind isolated in a subjectivity, the subject of which is so elusive? An heir of Adam, Robinson has lost the opportunity of 'sensibly tasting the sweets of living, without the bitter' offered by his father at the beginning of the book. He can only come to knowledge dialectically, by contraries. He can only know good, his good, by experience of evil. Robinson's obsession with reason as *ratio*, measurement, his sometimes comical 'accounting' point not only to his empiricism but also to the curse of

fallen man. All evaluations of his condition are relative. When he
considers himself ruined, he must acknowledge that there are others
who are worse, just as in the beginning when his father tried to
convince him he was set up for life, he thought he could become
better. In order to account for his condition after the shipwreck, he
has to draw up the famous profit and loss sheet, the spiritual book-
keeping for which he (and Defoe with him) has been so often
derided. The curiosity of this debit–credit sheet lies in its slipperiness.
One *fact* is not registered against another. The facts are the same on
both sides of the sheet; each side merely interprets the fact in a
different way. There are no true alternatives present. Instead of
representing Robinson's ingenuous calculation, the sheet does give a
true account of the flux of moods, moods considered as facts, the
dizzying back and forth of a subjectivity deprived of an external
gauge of truth.

Robinson's journal itself is another form of this spiritual book-
keeping. If one cannot gauge the meaning or portent of each
moment, perhaps the pattern formed over longer periods of time
would reveal the truth. Such an accounting might provide a true
profit and loss tally of the spirit. Crusoe's journal not only documents
his recall of day by day events as he recounts them more than thirty
years later, it also represents an attempt to give the shifting moments
of a subjective time something like a spatial ordering in the same
way that he carves notches into a post to mark each day he is on the
island. The journal is an attempt to define a situation by ordering
the present as it becomes the past. Writing also means to Robinson
a deliverance from the agonizing and confusing impact from
momentary impressions about his condition: 'I now began to consider
seriously my Condition, and the Circumstance I was reduc'd to, and
I drew up the State of my Affairs in Writing, not so much to leave
them to any that were to come after me, for I was like to have but
few Heirs, as to deliver my Thoughts from daily poring upon them,
and afflicting my Mind' (VII, 74).

Robinson wants what Sartre's Roquentin, one of his heirs, desires:
'I wanted the moments of my life to follow and order themselves like
those of a life remembered. You might as well try and catch time by
the tail.'[12] Crusoe's journal, like the greater account of which it is a
part, is an attempt to do precisely that – catch time by the tail. The
events of each day are recorded into the journal, already culled
and selected, already abolished by the past tense of language and
presented to us, a legacy to heirs that the Crusoe *living* each moment
could not expect. We can never, however, get close to the lived
moment and neither can Robinson capture it. Even the journal shows
signs of a later editing, at the time of the principal narration, from

the perspective of a story already closed. Moreover, such a perspective inheres in the narrative past tense. As Roquentin observes, 'You have started at the end . . . and the story goes on in the reverse: instants have stopped piling themselves in a lighthearted way one on top of the other, they are snapped up by the end of the story which draws them and each one of them in turn, draws out the preceding instant' (57–58). The whole book is caught up on a past tense suggesting an end which renders significant each sentence.

Crusoe's story, however, goes backwards in more obvious senses than that meant by Roquentin and Sartre. We are given no fewer than four accounts of Robinson's first days on the island, each differing in some small detail: the main account in Robinson's narrative, *two* journal accounts, and finally when Robinson relives his plight as he watches the English mutineers and their victims. First, we have the account in the chronological course of Crusoe's narrative, written years later, long after even his return from the island to civilization.

The second version is composed at the same time. This is the journal that might have been, if he had started it when he first landed on the island and it curiously is the one most different although it is ostensibly contemporaneous with the narration of the book. The reason that he did not begin the journal the first days was that he was too busy then making himself secure but also that he was 'in too much discomposure of mind, and my journal would have been full of many dull things.' The writing of the journal then is the result of the *composition* of his mind and although it has precedence in time over the other two versions, it is still separated from the event by an extensive period of time, for Robinson doesn't begin it until he is more or less settled on the island – perhaps six weeks after the shipwreck, after he finished the table and chair, probably November 12 according to the journal itself.

The differences between these accounts of his first days, mainly concerning whether he wept with joy or with terror, despair or thanksgiving, whether he slept on the ground or in a tree, are less significant than the fact that there *are* differences. What are we to make of this confusion, other than to see it as an emphasis on the elusiveness of even the facts of this narrative and an admission of an irreparable tear between the written account and the naked, lived moment? The journal – trace of the event – is vacant like the footprint. In fact, it is marked by a double absence. The writing of the account releases Robinson from the pain and confusion of experiencing – 'to deliver my thoughts from daily poring upon them, and afflicting my mind.' The journal serves the same purpose. And it is also removed from the event. It objectifies and orders both Robinson's thoughts and his daily experiences.

The gap cannot be closed. Narrative language removes the contingency and absurd inconsequence of the lived moment by abstracting that moment from the field of open possibility and directing it toward a certain outcome which will define it and give it significance. As Roquentin comments, ' "It was night, the street was deserted." The phrase is cast out negligently, it seems superfluous; but we do not let ourselves be caught and we put it aside: this is a piece of information whose value we shall subsequently appreciate. And we feel that the hero has lived all the details of this night like annunciations, promises, or even that he lived only those that were promises, blind and deaf to all that did not herald adventure' (58).

Annunciations, promises, and one might add, portents and warnings – for that is precisely the way Crusoe lives, or rather relives in his narrative, each event of his experience. What in the already realized end guarantees the significance of each event is identical with the ordering of written narrative and the opposite of the subjective flux of the lived moment – the discovery of God's plot, His Providence. The point of view of narrative is precisely a providence. In God's plan, Robinson's end *is* in his beginning – each step along the way is either a promise or a warning, but always an annunciation of a divine structure which exists outside of time, but which operates in and through time. Sartre's argument with narrative is that the foundation of the passing moment in narrative language bestows on it a privilege, robes it with a destiny, that is altogether false to experience, but Robinson's discovery of a special providence saves the moment, placing on each moment a heavy burden of significance.

Providence not only underwrites Robinson's narrative, it is also discovered by means of the writing of the journal. The subject caught in the flow of time is blind to the providential meaning of his experience. Crusoe suffers the flickering onrush of momentary sensations and is driven by selfish appetites and fears which change as rapidly as circumstances change: 'Everything revolves in our minds by innumerable circular motions, all centering in ourselves' (*Serious Reflections*, p. 2): 'And by what secret differing Springs are the Affections hurry'd about as differing Circumstances present! To Day we love what to Morrow we hate; to Day we seek what to Morrow we shun; to Day we desire what to Morrow we fear; nay even tremble at the Apprehensions of' (*Robinson Crusoe*, VII, 180).

Though Crusoe is given many warnings, many chances for repentance, as soon as the warning danger has passed, so dissolve Robinson's resolutions and promises. The Defoe self in isolation is the self of Hobbesian sensationalism. The order revealed one moment is obliterated by the new sensations crowding in the next. It is the function of narrative, with its double perspective, to remember.

By means of his journal, Robinson discovers the startling concurrence of his 'fortunate and fatal days':

> As long as it [the ink] lasted, I made use of it to minute down the Days of the Month on which any remarkable Thing happened to me, and first by casting up Times past: I remember that there was a strange Concurrence of Days, in the various Providences which befel me; and which, if I had been superstitiously inclin'd to observe Days as Fatal or Fortunate, I might have had Reason to have look'd upon with a great deal of Curiosity.
>
> First, I had observed, that the same Day that I broke away from my Father and my Friends, and ran away to *Hull*, in order to go to Sea; the same Day afterwards I was taken by the *Sallee* Man of War, and made a Slave.
>
> The same Day of the Year that I escaped out of the Wreck of that Ship in *Yarmouth* Roads, that same Day – Years afterwards I made my escape from *Sallee* in the boat.
>
> The same Day of the Year I was born on (*viz.*) the 30*th* of *September*, that same Day, I had my Life so saved 26 Years after, when I was cast on Shore in this Island, so that my wicked Life, and my solitary Life begun both on a Day.
>
> (VII, 153–54)

Later, when Robinson leaves the Island of Despair, he is 'deliver'd from this second Captivity, the same Day of the Month, that I first made my Escape in the *Barco-Longo*, from among the *Moors of Sallee*' (VIII, 74). Robinson will justify our belief in such amazing coincidences by detailing examples in his essay on Providence from the long tradition of such concurrences, beginning with the Scriptures and continuing into modern political history. The scriptural example alone marks the meaning of this pattern in Robinson's life. It is in Exodus 12: 41–42 and has to do with the children of Israel leaving their exile and imprisonment in Egypt the same day of the year, 430 years after they entered into it. Robinson's isolation has also been an exile and imprisonment, but the justification has a larger meaning as do all the scriptural parallels. Robinson's exile from himself and from the truth has been a type of the exile of the chosen people and of everyman, but as the real history of a man, as it is presented, it represents a figural truth. In the Preface to his *Serious Reflections* when he admits the story is allegorical, Robinson does not give up the claim to its authenticity. He simply claims to have 'displaced' its literal truth:

> All these reflections are just history of a state of forced confinement, which in my real history is represented by a confined retreat in an

island; and it is as reasonable to represent one kind of imprisonment by another, as it is to represent anything that really exists by that which exists not. The story of my fright with something on my bed was word for word a history of what happened, and indeed all those things received very little alteration, except what necessarily attends removing the scene from one place to another.

(xii)

One is reminded that among the earliest meanings of *figura* was its usage in rhetoric to conceal the truth (in a figure of speech).[13] It usually had to do with suggesting without actually expressing a truth which for political or tactical reasons or simply for effect could not be expressed openly. This was precisely Defoe's purpose.

Any discussion of the question necessarily collapses into the ambiguity Defoe left surrounding it.[14] No sooner are we satisfied with his admission of allegorical truth in the Preface to Robinson's *Serious Reflections* than we discover that among the reflections it prefaces is 'An Essay upon Honesty' and another on 'the Immorality of Conversation,' which contains a section about 'Talking Falsely.' No oversight on Defoe's part. In case we miss the point, he at first distinguished from the lying tales he is attacking such 'historical parables' as those in the Holy Scripture, *Pilgrim's Progress*, or, 'in a word, the adventures of your fugitive friend, "Robinson Crusoe"' (101). But then he makes the standard Puritan attack on realistic fiction: any fiction that offers itself as historical truth is a dangerous and damning lie. Lest we dismiss the discrepancy as mere ingenuousness on the part of Defoe, he adds the following disclaimer: 'If any man object here that the preceding volumes of this work seem to be hereby condemned, and the history which I have therein published of myself censured, I demand in justice such objector stay his censure till he sees the end of the scene, when all that mystery shall discover itself, and I doubt not but the work shall abundantly justify the design, and the design abundantly justify the work' (103). Does that settle the issue?

Ambiguity aside, it is possible to say that while Defoe is impersonating Robinson Crusoe, he is also impersonating on another level Providence itself. Just as the double vision made possible by the Christian conversion is replaced by the double vision of narration, the structure of narration has stood in place of Providence.

It is no accident (and may in fact be 'the end of the scene' Robinson alluded to earlier) that the last story he tells in his *Serious Reflections* concerns a young man who speaks to an atheist in the voice of a mutual friend and is taken instead for the voice of a spirit, messenger of God and medium of His Providence, by the disbeliever who is thereby saved.

Defoe's fortress is complete, constructed according to the laws of nature and concealing the plot of Providence. It is a natural habitation, in which like Robinson, Defoe can live in the open but unseen and unmolested by devouring eyes. In his essay on 'Solitude' Robinson countered the voluntary withdrawal into the desert wilderness of the religious hermit by the voluntary exile in the midst of society by means of something like disguise. Peaceful solitude 'would every way as well be supplied by removing from a place where a man is known to a place where he is not known, and there accustom himself to a retired life, making no new acquaintances, and only making the use of mankind which I have already spoken of, namely, for convenience and supply of necessary food; and I think of the two that such a man, or a man so retired, may have more opportunity to be an entire recluse, and may enjoy more real solitude than a man in a desert' (13–14). Defoe's fiction has provided him with such a hermitage.

Many novelists who followed Defoe were strangers in a strange land and found means of both concealing and exposing themselves in their novels. Pseudonymity and anonymity haunt the novel throughout the eighteenth and nineteenth centuries. Perhaps these novelists too confronted the necessity of becoming other persons in their narrators. There was Richardson's 'editorship,' for example, and while Jane Austen's and George Eliot's concealment of their names was perhaps only conventional for lady writers, Stendhal's need for pseudonyms was obsessional. Scott, already a famous author, concealed himself behind the tag of 'the author of Waverley' and became the most visible 'great unknown' of his day. Defoe's discoveries about the nature of narrative and its plots made the novel an apt genre for a society of isolated and mutually suspicious individuals. Perhaps all novelists begin in anonymity and construct for themselves the personality of their works.

Notes

1. Shakespeare Head edition (Oxford and New York, 1927), I, 188. All citations of *Moll Flanders* and *Robinson Crusoe* refer to this edition and are identified by volume and page number in my text. Quotations from the third volume of *Robinson Crusoe, Serious Reflections*, are taken from the George A. Aitken edition (London, 1895) and are identified by title and page number. Quotations from *Roxana* and from *A Journal of the Plague Year* are taken from the Oxford English Novels series: *Roxana*, ed. Jane Jack (London, 1964), and *A Journal*, ed. Louis Landa (London, 1969), and are identified in my text by page number. The writing of this paper was made possible by a grant from the Center for Advanced Study, University of Illinois.

2. Actually, Robinson was born under the name *Kreutznaer*, 'but by the usual Corruption of Words in *England*, we are now called, nay we call our selves, and write our Name *Crusoe*.'

3. Trans. R. S. Pine-Coffin (Baltimore, 1961), p. 53 (Bk. II, Sec. 10). All further quotations of the *Confessions* are taken from this edition.

4. See G. A. Starr's *Defoe and Spiritual Autobiography* (Princeton, 1965) and J. Paul Hunter's *The Reluctant Pilgrim* (Baltimore, 1966).

5. Ian Watt, *The Rise of the Novel* (Berkeley, 1959), p. 133.

6. At least part of the impulse behind Defoe's fiction is the desire to explore human possibilities in the face of a necessity so harsh as to suspend normal laws. The whole question of natural right has been examined in Maximillian E. Novak's *Defoe and the Nature of Man* (Oxford, 1963).

7. The pressures against Defoe's writing these novels seem multiplied when one remembers that Defoe was violating the Puritan ban against realistic fictions. For a discussion of this problem, see Hunter, *The Reluctant Pilgrim*, pp. 114–24. For other accounts of Defoe's ambivalence about 'feign'd Histories,' see Maximillian Novak's 'Defoe's Theory of Fiction,' *SP*, 61 (1964), 650–68, and the chapter on Defoe in Alan McKillop's *The Early Masters of English Fiction* (Lawrence, 1956). For a discussion of the background of this problem, see William Nelson's 'The Boundaries of Fiction in the Renaissance: A Treaty Between Truth and Falsehood,' *ELH*, 36 (1969), 30–58.

8. See James Sutherland, *Defoe* (London, 1950), p. 91.

9. Frank H. Ellis has revealed in the Introduction to his *Twentieth-Century Interpretations of Robinson Crusoe* (Englewood Cliffs, 1969), pp. 12 ff., the extent to which Defoe organized this book on the basis of images of devouring.

10. I make a more extensive comparison with Augustine's *Confessions* later on. Augustine's influence on the Puritans is well known. In addition, however, there are structural similarities between Augustine's *Confessions* and Defoe's 'autobiographies.' This influence was conveyed, if not directly, by way of the confessions and spiritual autobiographies of the seventeenth century, as Starr and Hunter have shown. On this point, see also Paul Delaney's *British Autobiography in the Seventeenth Century* (London and New York, 1969).

11. See n. 10.

12. Jean-Paul Sartre, *Nausea*, trans. Lloyd Alexander (New York, n.d.), p. 58. Further quotations refer to this edition and are identified by page number in my text.

13. See Erich Auerbach's essay on 'Figura' in his *Scenes From the Drama of European Literature* (New York, 1959), p. 45.

14. See n. 7.

8 Crusoe's Island Exile

MICHAEL SEIDEL

In this essay, Michael Seidel discusses two related features of *Robinson Crusoe*. On the one hand, he exploits the post-structuralist view that knowledge and language are always in some sense divided against themselves. Crusoe's displacement on the island away from his original home is a way of thinking about many other kinds of dyadic and doubling structures in Defoe's classic, not least its tendency to invite allegory. On the other hand, Seidel reveals that Crusoe's displaced experience runs in parallel to an entire history that is lived out in England during the period of his exile, which Defoe is careful to date precisely. Robinson's alternative experience signifies the extent of Defoe's distrust of the late Stuarts, and alignment with figures of dissent.

Homemade

In *Ulysses*, Leopold Bloom, the Irish Odysseus, poses an exile's question to another exile whom Joyce called the English Ulysses: '*O, poor Robinson Crusoe! | How could you possibly do so?*'[1] Bloom's lilting refrain comes from a popular turn-of-the-century song that recalls a haunting moment in *Robinson Crusoe* when Defoe's castaway, alone at that time for six years, hears the disembodied voice of his previously trained wild parrot, Poll, ask, '*Robin, Robin, Robin Crusoe*, poor *Robin Crusoe*, where are you *Robin Crusoe*? Where are you? Where have you been?*'[2]

Before Crusoe was startled by the parrot's words he had been on a reconnaissance mission, or *periplous*, sailing around part of his island in a small canoe, or *periagua*. He had almost been carried beyond the island by ocean currents, at which point he looked back on the place of his exile as a kind of paradisaic home.

Now I look'd back upon my desolate solitary Island, as the most pleasant Place in the World, and all the happiness my Heart could wish for, was to be but there again. I stretch'd out my Hands to

it with eager Wishes. O happy Desart, said I, I shall never see thee
more. O miserable Creature, said I, whither am I going: Then I
reproach'd my self with my unthankful Temper, and how I had
repin'd at my solitary Condition; and now what would I give to
be on Shore there again. Thus we never see the true State of our
Condition, till it is illustrated to us by its Contraries; nor know
how to value what we enjoy, but by the want of it.

(p. 139)

Exile for Crusoe is now anywhere *but* his island, including the
great sea whence he came. Fortunately, he negotiates the treacherous
currents, beaches the canoe, and heads on foot toward his inland
bower, or country house, for a miniature homecoming of sorts. His
trek exhausts him, and he is half asleep when he hears the parrot's
baffling questions. Poll, having flown in on its own accord from
Crusoe's seaward settlement, chooses this occasion to repeat, by
imprint, the sounds it has recorded during the early, more trying
years of Crusoe's exile. So in the same sense that a loner's experience
is rather like talking to other versions of himself, the questions the
parrot asks of Crusoe are the same as those asked earlier by Crusoe.
The questions themselves possess a double structure, hinting at two
times and two places, at the Crusoe who hears them (where *are* you?)
and the Crusoe who asked them (where have you *been*?).[3] The exile
faces the dilemma that he is, indeed, of two places. Or, to put it
another way, where he is displaced becomes his home place.
Paradoxically, the answers to both the parrot's questions are in a
generic sense the same: home. Home is where Crusoe now is, and
home is where he had been. It is as Elizabeth Bishop puts it in her
poem, 'Crusoe in England': 'Home-made, home-made! But aren't
we all?'

Crusoe himself recognizes the mental and territorial transformation
when he comments much earlier on the first night he ever spent
away from his original settlement, the seaward hutch, after exploring
the inland savannas: 'I spent all that Evening there, and went not
back to my Habitation, which by the Way was the first Night, as I
might say, I had lain from Home' (p. 99). The locution 'as I might
say' makes the condition figurative but no less real for Crusoe in
exile. Several months later, he undertakes an exploration of the island
by foot and, after about thirty days, gets homesick.

I cannot express what a Satisfaction it was to me, to come into my
old Hutch, and lye down in my Hamock-Bed: This little wandring
Journey, without settled Place of Abode, had been so unpleasant to
me, that my own House, as I call'd it to my self, was a perfect

Settlement to me, compar'd to that; and it rendred every Thing
about me so comfortable, that I resolv'd I would never go a great
Way from it again, while it should be my Lot to stay on the Island.

(p. 111)

Of course, it is in Crusoe's wandering nature to abjure this
particular promise or any like it upon the shortest possible notice,
but of more immediate interest is the psychological appropriation of
exilic space entailed by his coming 'home.' Crusoe refers to his island
exile as 'my Reign, or my Captivity, which you please' (p. 137). By
whatever principle of abundant or redundant locution we do please,
that place from which the exile is blocked becomes the model for the
place in which he resettles his imagination. Crusoe's habit of mind
has been 'made' permanently binary, a process or, more accurately,
a figuration represented in Crusoe's ledger 'Accompt,' where the
tension between the anxieties of separation and the activities of
resettlement are represented in graphic (or written) shape in double
columns on the page.[4] He records on the side of separation: '*I am
divided from Mankind, a Solitaire, one banish'd from humane Society*'; and
on the side of resettlement (in every sense): '*But I am not starv'd and
perishing on a barren Place, affording no Sustenance*' (p. 66). Crusoe's
ledger conforms to his condition as exile: displacement and
replacement are something of the same phenomenon.

The way Crusoe thinks in exile affects the way Defoe writes
him up. Language mimics perception as the horror of isolation turns
into the relief of deliverance: 'as my Life was a Life of Sorrow, one
way, so it was a Life of Mercy, another' (p. 132). Crusoe's way of
articulating his condition reinforces the pattern that courses through
the entire narrative, the double-entry accounting that transvalues
experience. In his initial despair, Crusoe's hutch was but a hovel.
Later, in full pride of place, his shelter becomes an estate; his estate,
a kingdom; his kingdom, a paradise. When, and for whatever
reasons, Crusoe's insecurities return, his paradise shrinks to his cave.
If he feels fearful or hostile, his cave becomes his fortification.
Crusoe's exile is an invitation to conversion, not simply a turning or
movement from place to place but a transformation – imaginative
and psychological – of one place or state of mind *into* another. This
is, of course, also at the heart of the fictional record that makes up his
exilic story.

'My brain bred islands'

It is precisely the exilic doubleness of Crusoe's situation or placement
that accounts for the generative and allegorical texture of the

narrative. When Defoe got around to commenting, seriously or otherwise, on his fictional strategies in *Crusoe*, he recognized that, however great his urge to substantiate a particular story, any sequence of narrative carries with it the pattern for interchangeability or duplication. Such a notion finds its way into the text of *Robinson Crusoe*, and Crusoe himself articulates it on his Brazilian plantation before he had any way of knowing about his subsequent island exile: 'I used to say, I liv'd just like a Man cast away upon some desolate island, that had no body there but himself.' Crusoe points out that those who utter such words may have heaven 'oblige them to make the Exchange' (p. 35). Indeed, both heaven and Defoe so oblige.

Defoe writes at greater length of narrative interchangeability in his extended commentary on the story of the exiled Crusoe, *Serious Reflections during the Life and Surprizing Adventures of Robinson Crusoe* (1720). His voice is nominally that of Crusoe as a fictional being but actually that of himself as an authorial being: 'In a word, there is not a circumstance in the imaginary story but has its just allusion to a real story, and chimes part for part and step for step with the inimitable Life of Robinson Crusoe.'[5] Defoe cites as an example of what he means an illustration chosen not from the original narrative but from a later section of *Serious Reflections*.

> For example, in the latter part of this work called the Vision, I begin thus: 'When I was in my island-kingdom I had abundance of strange notions of my seeing apparitions,' &c. All these reflections are just history of a state of forced confinement, which in my real history is represented by a confined retreat in an island; and it is as reasonable to represent one kind of imprisonment by another, as it is to represent any thing that really exists by that which exists not.
>
> (3: xiii)

Fable achieves a kind of reality by calling to mind replicative sets of experience.[6] 'My brain bred islands,' as Bishop puts it in 'Crusoe in England.' In *Serious Reflections*, Defoe makes a claim for what he calls the allegorical historical method of narration while defending himself (in the guise of Crusoe) from those who have charged him with lying.

> I Robinson Crusoe, being at this Time in perfect and sound mind and memory, thanks be to God therefor, do hereby declare their objection is an invention scandalous in design, and false in fact; and do affirm that the story, though allegorical, is also historical; and that it is the beautiful representation of a life of unexampled misfortunes, and of a variety not to be met with in the world,

sincerely adapted to and intended for the common good of
mankind, and designed first, as it is now farther applied, to the
most serious uses possible.

(3: ix)

Defoe writes in Crusoe's name but leaves the possibility open
that what is described as Crusoe's life happened to someone else:
Crusoe's story is the fabrication of other 'real' events. This much is,
at least, half true. Crusoe's story is a fabrication. Defoe, still in
Crusoe's voice, suggests that the process of reading is naturally
allegorical – that the mind makes one thing stand for comparable
things no matter what the real or invented status of the events
narrated. In essence, Defoe is trying very hard to shift the grounds
of the argument surrounding fictional invention from verifiability to
application.[7] Now we have before us the possibility that the island
adventure did not take place but that its writing makes it real for
those reading it. The book is, after all, read and experienced. Its
contents empty into one's brain. Crusoe had less wittingly already
offered a similar argument during his actual island adventure when,
after an ague-inspired vision, he saw before him a terrifying
Avenging Angel: 'No one, that shall ever read this Account, will
expect that I should be able to describe the Horrors of my Soul at
this terrible Vision, I mean, that even while it was a Dream, I even
dreamed of those Horrors; nor is it any more possible to describe
the impression that remain'd upon my Mind when I awak'd and
found it was but a Dream' (p. 88). The phrase 'that even while it was
a Dream, I even dreamed of those Horrors' can mean only that the
unreal action of dream *as dream* left a real impression. On just such
terms would Defoe defend the validity of fictional event as 'real.'
It is *made* real to the reader and therefore takes on tangible status
in regard to the uses to which it might be put.

'There are a great many sorts of those people who make it their
business to go about telling stories' (3: 106), Defoe writes in *Serious
Reflections*. Among them are those who, out of the forge of invention,
'hammer out the very person, man or woman, and begin, "I knew
the man," or "I knew the woman"' (3: 106). But the

> selling or writing a parable or an allusive allegoric history, is quite
> a different case, and is always distinguished from this other jesting
> with truth, that it is designed and effectually turned for instructive
> and upright ends, and has its moral justly applied. Such are the
> historical parables in the Holy Scripture, such 'The Pilgrim's
> Progress,' and such, in a word, the adventures of your fugitive
> friend, 'Robinson Crusoe.'

(3: 107)

Once relieved of justifying fiction merely by verifying the occurrence of its events, it becomes possible for Defoe to encourage his readers to think about the significance and design of events relayed as narrative sequence, so that, for example, a reader might expand allegorically upon the idea of solitude from that 'which I have represented to the world, and of which you must have formed some ideas from the life of a man in an island' (3: 3). As Defoe writes in another context: 'Things seem to appear more lively to the Understanding, and to make a stronger Impression upon the Mind, when they are insinuated under the cover of some Symbol or Allegory, especially when the Moral is good, and the Application easy.'[8] Allegory always represents one thing *in* another, and this representation, as we have seen, is very close to what the word *allegory* means: a speaking otherwise where difference itself becomes a form of duplication. Crusoe is more conscious than most fictional characters that an allegory of one kind or another has been going on around him. He even begins a journal that repeats the allegorical shape of the adventure he is in by mirroring its key word and recurrent theme, deliverance, in terms of his impulse to write it up. He writes, as he puts it, in order to 'deliver my Thoughts from daily poring upon them, and afflicting my Mind' (p. 65).[9]

Defoe understands that writing serves to intensify action, imbue it with calculated strangeness, remoteness, liminality that engages as it expands one's interest. The adventures of Crusoe in the original volume are both *Strange* and *Surprizing*. In *Serious Reflections*, Defoe as Crusoe – or Crusoe as Defoe – compares himself to 'the teacher, like a greater [Christ], having no honour in his own country.' Such a teacher knows that 'Facts that are formed to touch the mind, must be done a great way off, and by somebody never heard of' (3: xiii). Familiarity breeds contempt; strangeness or remoteness attracts attention. Crusoe hedges a bit as to whether the adventures he has experienced happened where he represented them, on an island near the mouth of the Orinoco, or somewhere much closer to home. Having raised the allegorical stakes, Defoe wonders whether his readers would lose interest 'when you are supposing the scene, which is placed so far off, had its original so near home?' (3: xiii). The question comports with Defoe's notion that a unique metaphoric configuration makes a greater impression on the mind than a familiar literal one, but it also opens up the territory of the imagination as an exilic supplement.

Home, of course, is a key word in the text of *Crusoe* itself and around it is organized the potential for allegory. To strike home is to startle into realization: 'The world, I say, is nothing to us, but as it is more or less to our relish. All reflection is carried home, and our dear self is, in one respect, the end of living' (3: 4). The self-discovery that is the object of the interpreting mind is imaged constantly in the allegorical discovery that takes place in the sequence of narrative duplications. The allegorical self is a homebody. Crusoe's discovery of an old goat in his cave is perhaps an apposite example. He need not even know exactly what he means when he says it, but when he comes upon the goat he comes upon Crusoe allegorized: 'I durst to believe there was nothing in this Cave that was more frightful than my self' (p. 177). Crusoe in exile is always discovering himself.

In a more general sense, ten months into his stay Crusoe hits upon the principle that rules the narrative: 'Having now secur'd my Habitation, as I thought, fully to my Mind, I had a great Desire to make a more perfect Discovery of the Island, and to see what other Productions I might find, which I yet knew nothing of' (p. 98). This not only repeats the central pattern of action, the narrative and psychological temptation to enlarge the perimeters of experience, but it provides a resource for the analyzing, performing, and, in the final analysis, the imagining mind. It is as 'Discovery' that the status of the island encourages the generous range of allegorical propensities that seem given over to it. The island is located in the fantasy of its own sovereign imagining, that 'true' space, as Melville says of Queequeg's island in *Moby Dick*, that 'is not down in any map; true places never are.'[10] Elizabeth Bishop's 'Crusoe in England' makes the same point.

> . . . but my poor old island's still
> un-rediscovered, un-renamable.
> None of the books has ever got it right.

Robinson Crusoe is the only book that does get it right. It proliferates meaning from its island exile: linguistic, temporal, psychological, spiritual, political. Crusoe himself participates in and encourages the process, reading and misreading[11] the nature of his experience, supplementing his adventure by creating other versions of it that, in narrative terms, never happened: 'I spent whole Hours, I may say whole Days, in representing to my self in the most lively Colours, how I must have acted, if I had got nothing out of the Ship. How I could not have so much as got any Food, except Fish and Turtles; and that as it was long before I found any of them, I must have perish'd first. That I should have liv'd, if I Had not perish'd, like a meer Savage' (p. 130). Robinson Crusoe's story is so allegorically bountiful that it supplements its own island supplement.

'Why did you leave your father's house?'
'To seek misfortune.'

Defoe does not presume a single, privileged allegorical reading
for Crusoe's adventures at the expense of the narrative's general
power as a saga of adaptation and endurance, as a study of isolation
and fear, and as a tale of the mobile fantasy and transforming
imagination. But from the beginning of the action it seems clear that
the pattern of separation and exile is at the heart of the narrative no
matter how we would read it, and that the initiating event of all the
action, Crusoe's disobedience to the wishes of his father that he stay
at home, is complexly implicated in the run of the adventure abroad.

Crusoe steadfastly disobeys despite, perhaps even because of,
his father's proposal to settle him: 'In a word, that as he would do
very kind things for me if I would stay and settle at Home as he
directed, so he would not have so much hand in my Misfortunes,
as to give me any Encouragement to go away' (p. 5). Every word
here is rich, from the hint of originating authority, the 'word,' to the
countercommand of adventure, 'stay,' to the multivalent 'settle,' to
the allegorical 'Home,' to the archetypal 'Misfortunes.' The last plays
on the paradigm of the prodigal son as Joyce plays on it in *Ulysses* –
leaving the father's land or motherland 'to seek misfortune' (*Ulysses*,
p. 619) – and becomes the essence of exilic alienation.

In one sense, perhaps a political one, Crusoe's spirit during his
years of exile represents the antithesis to patriarchal home rule;[12]
in another, Crusoe's anguish at his original disobedience (he calls it
his original sin) is genuine, though most severe when he feels least
secure. Crusoe never does quite sort out the difference in motive
between sin and impulse, and the question for the narrative action
is whether resistance to his father's demands serves him better than
had he succumbed to them. Crusoe is positioned so that his initial
resistance to his home is the prelude to a crisis or series of crises that
are themselves steps in a process of self-substantiation and return.
The measure of Crusoe's hard-won settlement is the degree to which
his impulses force him to avoid too easy a settlement too soon.
This process, I will later argue, provides the political basis of
the narrative's exilic structure. Crusoe's father's advice has to be
tempered by the exclusionary nature of its focus. Some obvious
courses of action cost more in anguish to follow than to resist, and
there are times when the secure and complacent life he recommends
is worse than the necessary errantry of a liberated soul. 'I broke
loose' (p. 7), Crusoe says of his initial sea voyage, and he is always
doing so. His island exile is the final project of his 'rambling Designs'
(p. 40).

At one point in the *Farther Adventures of Robinson Crusoe,* a merchant in the Bay of Bengal tries to talk Crusoe into a sailing expedition. His argument reflects back on the initiating scene of the first volume: 'For what should we stand still for? The whole world is in motion, rolling round and round; all the creatures of God, heavenly bodies and earthly, are busy and diligent; why should we be idle?' (2: 214). The notion of rootedness is associated with the buzzword *idleness.* Defoe's narratives count on the principle of mobility, self-propulsion, and self-extension. Motion is fate. Near the beginning of Defoe's *Memoirs of a Cavalier,* the hero's mother dreams that she wanders out into the middle of a field in order to give birth to a son who, in half an hour's time, sprouts a pair of wings and flies away. The incipient cavalier is dreamed up as one of narrative's bird signs; his is an inborn tendency to fly the coop. As is the case for Crusoe's 'wandring Inclination' (p. 4),[13] the cavalier has elsewhere built into his nature.

Defoe's fiction gains its power by playing the mobile self off the desiring self.[14] Moll Flanders, for example, whose mobility is class-inspired, and whose energies are sexually keen – a better word might be *smart* – seeks the security of the sobriquet *gentlewoman,* but finds herself removed to the very borders of the English-speaking world in America to attain it. Moll tests the status of gentility, which she seems to think means enterprising but which her first employer knew meant flesh peddling, with a set of prodigal relations in Virginia. Because of the exigencies of bourgeois fate, her new husband turns out to be her brother, and her mother-in-law her mother *in deed.* If on Crusoe's faraway island the values of hard-won sovereignty come up against the threat of cannibalism, in *Moll Flanders* newfangled gentility contests with a primordial taboo, incest. Moll's New World interlude is a paradigm of limits; it sets the contours of activity not merely in the simple sense of casting a character to the extremes but in the more complex sense of reaccommodating that character to his or her sense of center once the extremes are subsumed as part of experience. The mobile fantasy entails negotiation at the boundary between extreme circumstance and the formation of character. Usually, matters are turned to profit. As appalled as Moll was at what she called her undoing in Virginia, her brother/husband's estate eventually stakes her future. By the end of the narrative she literally 'capitalizes' the incest taboo, which works for her the way Crusoe's Brazilian plantation worked for him as a land bank in exile.

The voyage out for Defoe is the sovereignty the self establishes over contingency. This is part of the reason that Crusoe first frames his 'irresistible Reluctance . . . to going home' (p. 16) as a negative power: 'I had several times loud Calls from my Reason and my more

composed Judgment to go home, yet I had no Power to do it' (p. 14).
He knows that settlement brings its own rewards, but he operates
under a different imperative. Even when his reason tells him to stay
put in Brazil and he is willing to admit, given his previous ill luck,
that his voyaging scheme is 'the most preposterous Thing that ever
Man in such Circumstances could be guilty of' (p. 40), he feels
compelled to undertake it. Later, when his rhetorical and religious
guard is down on the island, he tells us what really drives him: 'I
seldom gave any Thing over without accomplishing it, when I once
had it in my Head enough to begin it' (p. 168). He refers to his
conviction that in time he would have figured a way to brew beer,
but his sentiment applies to almost all his actions and it resides at the
center of his sometimes mercurial character.

'Freedom lives hence, and banishment is here'

When Defoe speaks, as he does at length in *Serious Reflections*, of
Crusoe's adventure acting the role of allegory to bring the remote
nearer home, he means by home any and all familiar mental territory.
But he also has an exilic fable in mind that makes Crusoe's island, as
a home away from home, politically allusive. Crusoe's displacement
overlaps a time in English history near, if not dear, to Defoe's heart.
It does not tax the imagination, beyond the levy Defoe has already
allowed it, to consider the interplay between the narrative's temporal
configuration and the fold of years 'at home' that coincide with
Crusoe's time on his island. Defoe placed Crusoe in 'banishment,' as
he calls it, from 1659 to 1686 (he returns to England a year later in
1687), a period of twenty-eight years that virtually parallels the years
of the Stuart Restoration in England.[15] In a deliberate and calculated
sense, Defoe makes of Crusoe's reign a government in exile.

For reasons that Defoe never forgot, the Stuart Restoration seemed
apostolic to him.[16] Crusoe is cast ashore on the island a year before
the return of Charles II, and he does not set foot on English soil until
over a quarter century later just as arrangements for the Williamite
succession are under way, a succession that would follow a Glorious
Revolution Defoe considered foundational. As is characteristic of
the exilic reflex in narrative, Defoe represents on Crusoe's island an
ideological supplement separated from home but effectively replacing
the regime in power. Crusoe, without any real political awareness of
his own, sustains, like so many exiles, the values of his original land
during a time when that land seemed incapable, at least in Defoe's
view, of sustaining them properly itself. Defoe felt about the Stuarts
at home in England what Kent felt about Lear's daughters: 'Freedom

lives hence, and banishment is here' (1.1.180). Subsequently, just prior to the time James II and his Stuart supporters are exiled, Defoe ushers his island sovereign home to forecast England's renewed legitimacy or its return to its senses.

Again, I am making an argument not for Crusoe's awareness of the temporal politics of his exilic fable but for Defoe's. He felt that the important gap in the continuity of English history was not the dramatic parliamentary revolution from 1641 through the Cromwellian Protectorate but those alien years from 1660 to 1688, coincidental also with the first twenty-eight years of his own life, during which his family was victimized, at least early in the Restoration, by the oppressive Clarendon codes.[17] *Robinson Crusoe* takes its place alongside traditional narratives where exilic duration is a kind of test until national history is, in a way, ready to legitimize itself. Individuals and peoples best represent themselves by metaphorically standing outside their land.[18]

The Stuarts, in Defoe's view, had two-timed the home island, enshrined a legitimacy founded on worn-out principles of Divine Right and Passive Obedience, and secured the safety of the realm in its later years by the swiftness and exigency of the executioner's ax. It is possible to say that the Restoration, in which most of Defoe's narratives are set, is the epoch that most haunted his imagination, and the notion of the period as a kind of *trou*, lapse, or hiatus is not one to which Defoe turns for the first time in *Robinson Crusoe*. He began his career with a pamphlet attack on the Stuarts, and his major early works capped, so to speak, the alien politics of the previous century. *The Consolidator* (1705) and *Jure Divino* (1706) are both relentless, detailed indictments of Stuart tyranny. Defoe specifically called *The Consolidator*, his first sustained fictional narrative, an 'allegorick Relation,' and the action sets a lunar philosopher on the moon to talk out and act out the precepts of the 1688 Glorious Revolution while explicitly attacking 'lunar' (or lunatic) politics, the much less glorious practices of the Stuart kings, or any who would follow Stuart policies into the eighteenth century.

From the beginning of his career, Defoe had a countermyth in mind, one that depicted the true course of English history not as passive obedience in the face of *jure divino* but as a project or speculative adventure. It is in this sense that many readers have intuited that Crusoe stands for something central in the English experience, even if he does so without a sense of national mission.[19] His exile is a kind of blind trust, a metaphorical account that earns its interest not only as a new kind of sovereignty but as a new national enterprise. In his first full-length work in the 1690s, *Essay upon Projects*, Defoe offers up the Crusoe type and symbol in incipient form, the merchant adventurer with practical vision who, in the face of all manner of risk, is still 'the most intelligent Man in the World, and consequently the most capable, when urg'd by Necessity, to Contrive New Ways to live.'[20] He repeats the essence of this notion much later in his career, after *Robinson Crusoe*, when he refers to the English merchant as a kind of cycle of redemption in and of himself, an allegory of risk, endurance, and profit: 'The English tradesman is a kind of phoenix, who rises out of his own ashes, and makes the ruin of his fortunes be a firm foundation to build his recovery.'[21]

The inauguration of Crusoe's trials always involve risk devolving from capital venture. His island exile proper begins after several intervening commercial years that include imprisonment after capture by pirates and, upon his escape from North Africa, the establishment of a plantation in Brazil.[22] Crusoe claims that setting up the plantation puts him in the same settled stay-at-home condition his father recommended to him 'and which if I resolved to go on with, I might as well ha' staid at Home, and never have fatigu'd my self in the World as I had done' (p. 35). It is not so much Crusoe's conviction speaking here that events such as his earlier capture by the Moors, his escape to the African coast, and his hacking a plantation out of the wilds of South America are the equivalent of taking a law degree – to which his father was willing to stake him – as it is his conviction that he is destined for a more risk-filled life than he happens to be living at the time.

Crusoe departs Brazil 1 September 1659 and he comes to ruin on 30 September 1659.[23] The prelude to his island adventure, as death stares him in the face aboard a foundering ship, previews the ultimate exilic fate, the crossing into another world: 'In a word, we sat looking upon one another, and expecting Death every Moment, and every Man acting accordingly, as preparing for another World, for there was little or nothing more for us to do in this' (p. 43). Crusoe is thrust on his island, and his very survival is a rebirth into a new condition or 'state,' which seems to repeat the scene near the beginning of the narrative when the young Robinson swoons during his first shipwreck only to awake 'with Horror of Mind and the Thoughts of what was yet before me' (p. 13). In this earlier scene the future plot of the whole plays out in its adverbial part; what is later 'before' Crusoe after his second wreck is the battle for life that becomes his restoration.

> Nothing can describe the Confusion of Thought which I felt when I sunk into the Water; for tho' I swam very well, yet I could not deliver my self from the Waves so as to draw Breath, till that Wave having driven me, or rather carried me a vast Way on towards the

Shore, and having spent it self, went back, and left me upon the
Land almost dry, but half-dead with the Water I took in.

(p. 44)

The sea comes at Crusoe, again as a landed form and then as an
enemy: 'for I saw the Sea come after me as high as a great Hill, and
as furious as an Enemy which I had no Means or Strength to contend
with' (p. 44). Crusoe's business, at least in the metaphoric language
with which he relays his experience, is to serve as his own self-
regulator or governor: '[to] Pilot my self toward the Shore' (p. 45).
Later, when the wrecked ship appears for his salvaging and Crusoe
loads a raft with booty, he steers toward a cove near the mouth of an
island creek to moor his vessel and, in an almost symbolic gesture,
marks his sovereignty by 'sticking my two broken Oars into the
Ground' (p. 52). When he considers future trips to the wrecked ship
for salvaging, his self-sovereignty becomes participatory: 'I call'd a
Council, that is to say, in my Thoughts' (p. 54). From disaster comes
a plan, or council, for the beginnings of a new order of things. Of
course, if we credit the possibility of a temporal juxtaposition with
English home rule, we also credit Crusoe's language of resettlement
as conventional to a fault. We have seen its metaphoric equivalent
with every crucial change of government in England, particularly
with the host of encomia for the Stuart beachhead in 1660 that figure
the return of Charles II as the restoration of calm after a storm at sea.
Dryden, for example, compresses the king's exile and return in the
following lines:

> To all the Sea-Gods *Charles* an Off ring owes:
> A Bull to thee *Portunus* shall be slain,
> A Lamb to you the Tempests of the Main:
> For those loud stormes that did against him rore
> Have cast his shipwrack'd Vessel on the shore.
>
> ('Astraea Redux,' lines 120–24)

Defoe need not have remembered the specific Dryden passage
here – that is not the point I am making. What is significant is the
antithetical nature of Crusoe's beachhead in 1659; his new estate
signals what Defoe always believed, that the true Englishman was
compromised when the Stuarts were in his 'home' and he was, so to
speak, 'out of it.' Restoration means resupply or restocking, literally
laying away for the future. Crusoe is as well established, in this
sense, as his temporal sovereign rival; in fact, one of the plus items
on his ledger sheet of miseries and comforts is that from the ship he

has *'gotten out so many necessary things as will either supply my Wants, or enable me to supply my self even as long as I live'* (p. 66). He repeats this comfort a few paragraphs later, commenting on the 'store' in his cave: 'it look'd like a general Magazine of all Necessary things, and I had every thing so ready at my Hand, that it was a great Pleasure to me to see all my Goods in such Order, and especially to find my Stock of all Necessaries so great' (pp. 68–69). Crusoe landed is Crusoe restored.

Oppositions

Timing is no accident in *Robinson Crusoe*. Both Defoe and his 'fugitive hero' are sensitive to coincidence, Crusoe, for example, noticing that 'there was a strange Concurrence of Days, in the various Providences which befel me; and which, if I had been superstitiously inclin'd to observe Days as Fatal or Fortunate, I might have had Reason to have look'd upon with a great deal of Curiosity' (p. 133). That Defoe sets the adventure when he does becomes yet another element of the narrative's readable potential. The politics of the island exile are live issues for Defoe: sovereignty, property, natural law, and toleration. Crusoe reinvents what the Stuarts abused, though in the instance of toleration it requires a few years' worth of taxing conversation between Crusoe's self and soul on the subject of cannibalism to sort out the issues involved.[24]

Crusoe's adventures on the island are such that they conform to the standard exigencies of exilic experience. During the earlier years on the island, he is trapped between his desire for settlement and his readiness to depart an uninhabited, strange, and lonely place. He is vaguely aware that he must organize his territory on what he comes to call 'my beloved Island' so that he can both transform it as a new home and keep paramount any opportunity to leave it. To place himself any distance from the seaward part of the island, from which he could be more easily rescued if circumstance permitted, would, as he puts it, 'anticipate my Bondage' (p. 101). But until the time is ready in the larger scheme of things that Crusoe calls Providence, he is tethered. Crusoe may plan an escape by carving a huge canoe out of a felled tree, but to his dismay he realizes that he has no way of hauling the finished craft to the sea. Poor Crusoe tries to make too much of opportunity before opportunity is ready to make something of him.

The turning point of Crusoe's stay on the island, the point at which the slow process of opportunity begins to shape the necessity for departure, is also the point at which the idea of sovereignty begins to take on different dimensions. This process begins with the famous footprint episode, during the fifteenth year of Crusoe's isolation. Crusoe himself recognizes the moment as an incursion that is also a turning or transition point in his exile: 'But now I come to a new Scene in my Life' (p. 153). Perhaps no scene in fiction better illustrates the subtle workings of surface and depth patternings that narrative has available to it.[25] Crusoe, wandering over now familiar territory, comes on a startling sight, the image of a single footprint in the sand. This stark impression provides his hard-won resettlement – his recessed allegorical history – its most dramatic surface test. At the appearance of the print, Crusoe's lingering despair at his separation from the world he once knew turns into an absolute and immanent fear of having his sovereignty violated, his settlement in exile penetrated. The paradox of the exilic condition is fully realized in a single narrative incident: the necessitous strength of character that allows Crusoe to re-create a version of home abroad also inhibits and distorts the exile's traditional *Drang nach Hause*, his will to return to his original place.

The footprint episode recalls Crusoe's earlier shock at the sudden greeting of his wild parrot, when the sound of another voice so rattled him that it took him 'a good while before I could compose my self' (p. 143). But Crusoe is not so fortunate after sighting the print which, even years later, still 'discompos'd me very much' (p. 157). He is at first thunderstruck 'as if I had seen an Apparition' (p. 153), and his recidivistic response is to wander up and down the beach just as he had done when he set his own foot on the island nearly fifteen years before. He immediately adjusts his language to suit his material circumstances; homecoming now becomes a form of self-defense: 'like a Man perfectly confus'd and out of my self, I came Home to my Fortification, not feeling, as we say, the Ground I went on' (p. 154). Out of himself, he is like the apparition he thinks he has just seen, but his supposed apparition has a very tangible quality to it – it makes a real impression or, at least, a footprint – whereas Crusoe is so scared his feet barely touch the ground.

The confusion here of Crusoe's self with sign – later he hopes the footprint, like the imprint of the parrot's voice, would turn out to be his own – derives from the strength of his desire that his settlement, once so separable from all he had known, now be integral as all he has left.[26] The print in the sand is both an image of trespass on the exile's territory and a strong but necessary reminder that the exile's isolated condition is an unnatural one. Crusoe's fear initially renders him as wild as any being who might have made the print, that is, renders him too native an inhabitant – one with no civilized history other than his island life. He ran home

terrify'd to the last Degree, looking behind me at every two or
three Steps, mistaking every Bush and Tree, and fancying every
Stump at a Distance to be a Man; nor is it possible to describe how
many various Shapes affrighted Imagination represented Things to
me in, how many wild Ideas were found every Moment in my
Fancy, and what strange unaccountable Whimsies came into my
Thoughts by the Way.

(p. 154)

When Crusoe tries to soothe himself with the hope that the
footprint might, after all, be his own, that hope is dashed in an
appropriate externalization of internal apprehension: the print turns
out to be too large. For the fearful Crusoe, the mysterious impression
on the beach assumes in size a power opposite to the self-
diminishment he experiences on seeing it.[27] The print is even more
threatening in its singleness: one print suggests its complement, its
'other.' To put its significance differently, Crusoe learns from the
surface appearance of the footprint a deeper exilic lesson he ought
never to have forgotten and will remember for the rest of his stay on
the island: one simply cannot go it alone forever. By its singleness,
which is to say its incompleteness, the one print in the sand is both a
complement to Crusoe's condition and a corrective to any permanent
historical notion about the possibility or desirability of the exile's
lone sovereignty. By the habit of abundant years, Crusoe had already
begun to cultivate permanent thoughts that ought to have remained
provisional: 'when I began to regret the want of Conversation,
I would ask my self whether thus conversing mutually with my
own Thoughts, and, as I hope I may say, with even God himself by
Ejaculations, was not better than the utmost Enjoyment of humane
Society in the World' (pp. 135–36).

An earlier passage in which Crusoe, aware of the hyperbole,
describes the nature of his supposed sovereignty suggests why
the appearance of the print on the beach is so crucial a point in the
narrative: 'I was Lord of the whole Mannor; or if I pleas'd, I might
call my self King, or Emperor[28] over the whole Country which I had
Possession of. There were no Rivals. I had no Competitor, none
to dispute Sovereignty or Command with me' (p. 128). 'Rivals,'
'Competitor,' and 'Sovereignty' are key words here, and the sighting
of the footprint signals the imposition of new circumstances for
Crusoe, circumstances that are, willy-nilly, political. If Defoe chose
to represent Crusoe's island reign as coincidentally 'occupying' the
Restoration hiatus in England, he also gave considerable thought to
what sort of action affects the alteration of historical circumstance.
In the exilic state, rivalry is opportunity; in the usurped state, rivalry

is disaster. The two possibilities conform to the status of narrative as sovereign on the one hand, sufficient unto its made-up self, and representational on the other, reflecting the contingencies and necessities of the supposed real world it imitates. [. . .]

The footprint in Defoe's narrative is incontestably a sign of opposition to Crusoe – surely he reads it that way – and, given the care Defoe takes in marking its appearance in the fifteenth year of Crusoe's reign, the historically temporal parallel at 'home' is intriguing. Crusoe sees the footprint in 1674, assuming he lands on the island in 1659, as he originally says, and not in 1658, as he later seems to think.[29] Nearly every observer of the course of Stuart history pointed to a different set of circumstances after the first fifteen years of Charles II's reign. Those actively involved in the politics of the period such as Andrew Marvell, Anthony Ashley Cooper, Algernon Sidney, and John Locke, and those that were to write of it in the next generation, Laurence Echard, John Oldmixon, and Daniel Defoe, marked 1674 as a transition from the earlier monarchical consolidation of power to the emergence, within the context of plots and conspiracies, of a newly named opposition party and a new crisis in national sovereignty. In his *Growth of Popery and Arbitrary Power* (1678), Marvell wrote that after 1674 the king's new party, the Tories, tried to stir the old royalist antirevolutionary fervor against the new Whigs: 'They begun therefore after fifteen years to remember that there were such a sort of men in England as the old Cavalier party; and reckoned, that by how much the more generous, they were more credulous than others, and so more fit to be again abused.'[30]

For the Stuarts, the emergence of a powerful opposition after 1674 plotted the beginning of a long road to the end; for Crusoe, the end to his unviolated hegemony during 1674 plotted the beginning of a long road to a new beginning. The potential represented by the footprint is what is required to get Crusoe back to his first home, his 'real' home, the one on the map. In the oft-cited 'Chequer Work of Providence' passage, Crusoe admits the absurdity of having feared as violation what he ought better to have welcomed as possible salvation.

> For I whose only Affliction was, that I seem'd banished from human Society, that I was alone, circumscrib'd by the boundless Ocean, cut off from Mankind, and condemn'd to what I call'd silent Life; that I was as one who Heaven thought not worthy to be number'd among the Living, or to appear among the rest of his Creatures; that to have seen one of my own Species, would have seem'd to me a Raising me from Death to Life, and the greatest

blessing that Heaven it self, next to the supreme Blessing of
Salvation, could bestow: *I say*, that I should now tremble at the
very Apprehensions of seeing a Man, and was ready to sink into
the Ground at but the Shadow or silent Appearance of a Man's
having set his Foot in the Island.

(p. 156)

Crusoe may be ready to recognize the irony of his initial reaction,
but he is not yet prepared to alter his behavior. He has the exilic
terms reversed, if his desire is historical reprise: 'In my Reflections
upon the State of my Case, since I came on Shore on this Island, I
was comparing the happy Posture of My Affairs, in the first Years of
my Habitation here, compar'd to the Life of Anxiety, Fear and Care,
which I had liv'd ever since I had seen the Print of a Foot in the
Sand' (p. 196). Someone made that print and Crusoe is unready to
deem that someone savior or friend. In fact, for years he reacts to his
opposition, real or presumed, as would the worst of tyrants securing
the safety of his tyranny: 'these Anxieties, these constant Dangers I
liv'd in, and the Concern that was now upon me, put an End to all
Invention, and to all the Contrivances that I had laid for my Future
Accommodations and Conveniences' (p. 176). In the political pattern
of the action, Defoe ironically endows his governor in exile with
the most oppressive features of the Stuart regime whose reign he
temporally counters. In the strictly narrative pattern, Crusoe's
exaggerated fears for his own security obsessively protect a 'created'
realm by putting an end to its invention, by ceasing to create it: 'I
had the Care of my Safety more now upon my Hands, than that of
my Food. I car'd not to drive a Nail, or chop a Stick of Wood now,
for fear the Noise I should make should be heard; much less would
I fire a Gun, for the same Reason' (p. 176).

'At this hour lie at my mercy all mine enemies'

It takes Crusoe several years of paranoid defensiveness to get used
to the notion that what seems to be his opposition might actually be
the means by which he can alter his condition as exile. The sighting
of the print refocuses the exilic dilemma – that which had been
appropriated as a substitute has become for Crusoe a necessity.
Something has gone wrong in ways that even Crusoe comes to
recognize, and in the latter years of his stay he begins the process
of reconversion and recivilization. He makes positive again what his
father, in overstressing security at home, had so many years before
envisaged as strictly negative: 'I could not satisfy my self in my

Station, but was continually poring upon the Means, and Possibility of my Escape from this Place' (p. 195). The neutral, indeed, almost scathing 'Place' tells much of the story. Like Odysseus's renewed urge for home while tethered on Calypso's island, or like Prospero's homeward turn after burying his staff on his magical isle, Crusoe reexperiences the exile's original desire: any place but home for him now is undifferentiated. Once Crusoe's counterturn is set in motion things move, if not as quickly as he would choose, at least decisively. He readies himself for actual homecoming by planning a preliminary beachhead on the cannibal mainland.

> All my Calm of Mind in my Resignation to Providence, and waiting the Issue of the Dispositions of Heaven, seem'd to be suspended; and I had, as it were, no Power to turn my Thoughts to any thing, but to the Project of a Voyage to the Main, which came upon me with such Force, and such an Impetuosity of Desire, that it was not to be resisted.
>
> (p. 198)

Crusoe gives up his scheme to go to the cannibal Main only when one very useful cannibal comes to him. Friday's companionship during the last few years of Crusoe's exile provides an actual other who becomes a second self in initiating the strength of will toward repatriation. Friday sees his own land from a vantage point on the high side of Crusoe's island: '*O joy!* Says he, *O glad! There see my Country, there my Nation!*' (p. 223). These stirring words are voiced just after Crusoe anticipates the spatial collapse of the distance between the place of exile and his own home island nation by referring to himself and Friday as 'comforted restor'd Penitents; we had here the Word of God to read, and no farther off from his Spirit to instruct, than if we had been in *England*' (p. 221). The solace of one land for Friday and the mention of another by Crusoe prime the narrative for what is about to happen.

After Friday's arrival, and without precisely knowing why, Crusoe assumes his deliverance is again providentially opportune, telling of 'the great Hopes I had of being effectually, and speedily deliver'd; for I Had an invincible Impression upon my Thoughts, that my Deliverance was at hand, and that I should not be another Year in this Place' (p. 229). The impression that the times are ready for him to return seems as telling in its way as the impression of the footprint years before. Crusoe loses his fear of having his island penetrated when he loses the desire to remain isolated.

In the interim between Crusoe's thoughts about redirecting his efforts toward home and his opportunity to make the break, he begins to revise his notions of what sovereignty ought to mean to him in historical rather than fictional terms. He turns to the law of civilized nations,[31] and he does so by readjusting his view of those cannibals whose intermittent presence on the island had so reduced him to quivering paranoia and unaccountable bloodlust.[32] Divine Right, Crusoe decides, ought to be in the hands of a Divinity, not in the hands of a self-appointed vice-regent. God has not called on him, Crusoe says, 'to take upon me to be a Judge of their Actions, much less an Executioner of his Justice; that whenever he thought fit, he would take the Cause into his own Hands, and by national Vengeance punish them as a People, for national Crimes; but that in the mean time, it was none of my Business' (p. 232).[33] Any one individual, namely Crusoe in this instance, cannot afford to be a scourge on an entire nation, and at the end of his stay, his energies are better employed against those few who have falsely usurped a power that they have no right to hold, that is, against the English mutineers who run riot in conspiracy and betrayal.

At the original sighting of the mutineers and their unfortunate captives, matters come to a head.[34] Crusoe approaches the captives with the mutineers out of earshot and chooses to ally himself with those who face either an exile like his own or, worse, death. That is, he allies himself with historical legitimacy, with the rightful captain of the English vessel. As soon as matters indeed 'right' themselves, the English usurpers and mutineers are cast out from that which they have misappropriated. Later we learn that their fate, too, becomes exilic: 'they would much rather venture to stay there, than to be carry'd to *England* to be hang'd; so I left it on that Issue' (p. 276). The politics of Crusoe's narrative are played out in miniature by the scoundrels suffering what they would have wished upon the forces of legitimacy.

While still in dire straits, the English captain contemplates the bizarre figure of Crusoe as ally coming toward him, a bedraggled version of the mythical stranger-savior figure of legendary tales.[35] Crusoe says to the captain: 'But can you put a Stranger in the way how to help you, for you seem to me to be in some great Distress? I saw you when you landed, and when you seem'd to make Applications to the Brutes that came with you, I saw one of them lift up his Sword to kill you' (p. 254). The captain looks at this apparition and elevates Crusoe beyond or, as Crusoe's father would see it, higher than his merits: '*Am I talking to God, or Man! Is it a real Man, or an Angel!*' (p. 254). Crusoe's self-identification is significant here after twenty-eight years on the island and nearly thirty-seven years away from home: 'I am a Man, an *Englishman*, and dispos'd to assist you' (pp. 254–55). The island sovereign now names himself citizen of his

207

native country, bringing his alien status and resettling impulse into alignment. Again, like Prospero, Crusoe is a magic (or imagined) island recluse willing to become a national subject once certain conditions are met, certain contracts arranged, certain powers displayed. Friday, as commentators have noticed, is Crusoe's Ariel.

> Let them be hunted soundly. At this hour
> Lie at my mercy all mine enemies.
> Shortly shall all my labors end, and thou
> Shalt have the airs at freedom. For a little,
> Follow, and do me service.
>
> (*Tempest*, 4. 1. 262–66)

Crusoe's actions at the end reveal a homeward turn of mind and a set of principles based on necessity. His advice about firing on, and possibly killing, the mutineers justifies violence for legal, not tyrannical, ends: '*Necessity* legitimates my Advice' (p. 256).[36] And Crusoe's forces advance in the name of rightful authority: 'At the Noise of the Fire, I immediately advanc'd with my whole Army, which was now 8 Men, *viz.* my self *Generalissimo*, Friday, my Lieutenant-General, the Captain and his two Men, and the three Prisoners of War, who we had trusted with Arms' (p. 267). Perhaps this force is not so impressive as the advance guard of William III riding into England, but it is surely more effective than the hopeless army in which Defoe may have fought that suffered ignominious earlier defeat at Sedgemoor against the forces of James II in 1685.

Crusoe arrives back in England on 11 June 1687.[37] He comes home truly substantiated, both in status – as returned wanderer, a man of archetypal value – and in funds from his Brazilian plantation, which Defoe totals later at 'above a thousand Pounds a Year, as sure as an Estate of Lands in *England*' (p. 285). Defoe's analogy exceeds even the wishes of Crusoe's father: his exile progresses metaphorically as adventurer from the merchant class to the settled gentry. Crusoe's accumulated property allows him to return, in a sense, properly islanded. Perhaps in a broader sense, Crusoe's substantial return to his native place allows Defoe to realize the full potential of an action in which the exile, abroad and restored, is always sovereign.

Notes

1. *Ulysses* (New York, 1961), p. 109. All references are to this edition, emended, when necessary, in accord with the new Garland Edition (New York, 1984).

2. *The Life and Strange Surprizing Adventures of Robinson Crusoe*, ed. J. Donald Crowley (London, 1972), p. 142. All references are to this edition.

3. In his essay, 'The Displaced Self in the Novels of Daniel Defoe,' *ELH* 38 (1971):562–90, Homer O. Brown makes a similar point about temporal doubling in Crusoe's journal: 'The journal is an attempt to define a situation by ordering the present as it becomes the past' (p. 585). The present 'becomes' the past in the sense that it will both revert to the past in time and reflect the past's essence.

4. David Blewett discusses the action of *Robinson Crusoe* in terms of what he sees as the paradox at its center: 'The island expresses the central paradox of the novel. There Crusoe is both imprisoned and set free, and in ways more complex than he at first grasps' (*Defoe's Art of Fiction: Robinson Crusoe, Moll Flanders, Colonel Jack, and Roxana* [Toronto, 1979], p. 31).

5. *Serious Reflections during the Life and Surprizing Adventures of Robinson Crusoe*, in *The Works of Daniel Defoe*, ed. G. H. Maynadier, 16 vols. (New York, 1903), 3: xi. All references are to this edition, as are references to *The Farther Adventures of Robinson Crusoe*.

6. In '*Robinson Crusoe*: "Allusive Allegorick History,"' *PMLA* 82 (1967): 399–407, Robert W. Ayers neatly defines the process as 'a story whose literal meaning is augmented by a second meaning which is the construct of allusions in the literal narrative' (p. 400).

7. In his recent *Factual Fictions, the Origins of the English Novel* (Columbia, 1983), Lennard Davis argues that Defoe's position is hopelessly confused on the issue of truth telling. At the heart of Davis's presentation is a rather innocently framed question of why 'one man's life should be the allegory of another's' (p. 160), as if Defoe were limited in what he could do with narrative invention because he takes on Crusoe's voice to defend Crusoe's story. But Defoe was playing on the notion that truth 'sells'; his defense, after all, was part of the advertising paraphernalia for the Crusoe saga. John Richetti senses as much in *Defoe's Narratives: Situations and Structures* (Oxford, 1975) when he recognizes the art of advertising in the various commentaries on the story: 'It is, obviously, being sold as an extravaganza to people who like all of us value the exotic and the various as a pleasurable relief from the humdrum and uniform quality of daily life' (p. 24). Richetti's use of the word 'extravaganza' is calculated; the remote wandering beyond bounds makes this feigned truth stranger than romance fiction.

8. Defoe, *A Collection of Miscellany Letters out of Mists's Weekly Journal* (London, 1722–27), 4: 210. See Maximillian E. Novak, 'Defoe's Theory of Fiction,' *Studies in Philology* 61 (1964): 650–68. This seminal essay goes far in addressing the entire matter of fiction, romance, and lying in Defoe's conceptual sense of narrative. Novak maintains, among other things, that Defoe took a traditionally Aristotelian position in privileging probability over verified actuality. What is probable in terms of what might be called the fictional contract is what is useful in extracting the meaning from any fable. Of course Novak knows, as all Defoe's readers ought, that in representing what looks to be probable in fiction Defoe also opens veins of complex narrative psychology that sustain an interest in his work beyond the theory of usefulness Defoe none too modestly advances for it.

9. In a panoramic sense, Robinson Crusoe's allusive allegoric history fulfills a traditional narrative pattern of sustained risk, trauma, and return, a pattern allegorically analogous to biblical history, various national histories, and spiritual and personal lives. See J. Paul Hunter, *The Reluctant Pilgrim: Defoe's Emblematic Method and Quest for Form in Robinson Crusoe* (Baltimore, 1966); George Starr, *Defoe and Spiritual Autobiography* (Princeton, 1965); and, most recently, Leopold Damrosch, Jr., *God's Plot and Man's Stories: Studies in the Fictional Imagination from Milton to Fielding* (Chicago, 1985).

10. *Moby Dick*, chap. 12, 'Biographical' (New York, 1964), p. 88. Of course, an opposite argument has been made with a considerable array of facts to back it up. Defoe's biographer, John Robert Moore, in *Daniel Defoe: Citizen of the Modern World* (Chicago, 1958), claims that Defoe set the island specifically near the region of the Orinoco river basin in order to stimulate a scheme he favored for negotiating with Spain for trade rights in that area. Maximillian Novak takes up the thread of that argument in his chapter 'Imaginary Island and Real Beasts: The Imaginative Genesis of *Robinson Crusoe,*' in *Realism, Myth, and History in Defoe's Fiction* (Lincoln, Neb., 1983), pp. 23–46. Novak points to a scheme that appeared in Defoe's *Weekly Journal*, 7 February 1719, for the South Sea Company to colonize territory at the mouth of the Orinoco in order to build ships and initiate massive trading operations. Defoe's imagination was, in a way, directed toward the region.

11. When W. Bliss Carnochan describes Crusoe's propensity to read into his island, he addresses one of the central ironies of the novel's allegorical dispensation: 'By figuring his island allegorically in his journal he tries to distill its meaning. But the meaning he assigns it jars with the narrative rendering of his experience' (*Confinement and Flight: An Essay on English Literature of the Eighteenth Century* [Berkeley, 1977], p. 30). One of the points to make about allegorical interpretation, whether it takes place as part of the action within a text or part of the experience of reading it, is that it tends to be overdetermined. In its need to make sense of something 'other,' allegory almost by design surpasses the range of the material about which it tries to make sense.

12. Defoe's notion of disobedience has a political cast to it that runs counter to the familial disobedience of Crusoe's presumed original sin. Like Locke, he does not confuse patriarchy and patriarchal politics. In fact, the abused doctrine of passive obedience on the patriarchal model stands at the center of Defoe's antagonism toward the Stuarts. In *Jure Divino* (1706), he points out that his long poetic satire against tyranny 'had never been Publish'd, tho' some of it has been a long time in being, had not the World seem'd to be going mad a second Time with the Error of Passive Obedience and Non-Resistance' (p. i). The first time was in the latter days of an increasingly desperate James II, and an argument could be mounted that the Jacobite turn of mind existed right through the first several decades of the eighteenth century. For a different development of this notion centering on an economic reading of the fable, see Maximillian Novak's chapter, 'Robinson Crusoe's Original Sin,' in *Economics and the Fiction of Daniel Defoe* (Berkeley, 1962), pp. 32–48.

13. Crusoe's very name implies a species of wanderer. Robert W. Ayers ('"Allusive Allegorick History"') ponders the original name of the Crusoe family, Kreutznaer. He suggests various possibilities: *Kreutz* = cross, 'to cross, to cruise' (a religious version would be a *Kreutzzug* or 'crusade'); *naer* or *naher* = comparative of near; *nähren* = 'to journey, to approach.' Crusoe's name, as befits the double exilic pattern, seems to mean both 'to wander' and 'to come home.'

14. If one simply follows Defoe's major heroes and heroines around the globe (discounting sundry pirates and one lunar philosopher, who ascends 250,000 miles up but neglects to come down), one would travel the equivalent of ten times the circumference of the earth. Captain Singleton, the ocean's very waif, is the sweepstakes winner, logging over 100,000 miles. Crusoe places second with over 85,000 miles. Colonel Jack charts in at half that, over 40,000 miles. And Moll Flanders, with a bit of the original gypsy still in her soul, travels close to 20,000 miles.

15. In many attempts to trace the allegorical import of Crusoe's history, commentators have made scant mention of the historical or national coincidence in its timing. J. Paul Hunter is one of the few to notice the temporal parallel of the island exile: 'Crusoe's twenty-eight years of isolation and suffering, for example, parallel the Puritan alienation between the Restoration and the accession of William and Mary; the allusion intensifies the sense of Crusoe's alienation from society and suggests the thematic implications of the Puritan emblematic reading of events' (*The Reluctant Pilgrim*, p. 204). Douglas Brooks acknowledges Hunter and makes the same point briefly in his *Number and Pattern in the Eighteenth-Century Novel* (London, 1972), p. 25. I have developed the notion in an earlier version of this chapter, 'Crusoe in Exile,' *PMLA* 96 (1981):363–74; and, most recently, Maximillian Novak suggests that the allegory of a nation in exile touches on Defoe's pronounced sympathy for the Scottish covenanters under the reign of the original and restored Stuarts ('Imaginary Islands and Real Beasts,' pp. 39 ff.). Of course, the idea of resettling in the New World to sustain values threatened in the old is at the heart of the Dissenters' exodus to New England.

16. In his one sustained autobiographical pamphlet, *An Appeal to Honour and Justice* (London, 1715), Defoe writes in the third person of his reaction to the Stuart cause past and present: 'No Man in this Nation ever had a more riveted Aversion to the *Pretender*, and to all the Family he pretended to come of, *than he*' (p. 28). He goes on to write that he came to maturity opposing the Stuart kings, first Charles II and then James II as 'A Man that had been in Arms under the Duke of *Monmouth*, against the Cruelty and Arbitrary Government of his pretended Father; That for twenty Years had, to my utmost, opposed him (King *James*), and his Party after his Abdication; That had serv'd King *William* to his Satisfaction, and the Friends of the Revolution after his Death, at all Hazards, and upon all Occasions; That had suffer'd and been ruin'd under the Administration of *High-flyers* and *Jacobites*' (p. 28).

17. In *Daniel Defoe and Middle-Class Gentility* (Cambridge, Mass., 1968), Michael Shinagel remarks on the antagonism Defoe, as Dissenter, felt toward the Stuarts: 'The persecutions suffered by the Dissenters during the 1660s served to unite rather than disperse them. They found comfort and succor in their shared afflictions. They felt themselves being tested for their religious beliefs, if not also on trial for their souls' (p. 37).

18. In his *Life and Adventures of Mr. D——Def——* (1719), Charles Gildon was the first to pick up the possible allegorical identification of Crusoe's exile with Defoe's life: 'You are the true Allegorick Image of thy tender Father D——l' (p. x). And Gildon also sensed that there was a political message in the narrative for which Defoe required the protection of fiction: 'But honest D- - --l, I am afraid with all your Sagaciousness, you do not sufficiently distinguish between the Fear of God, and the Fear of Danger to your own dear Carcass' (p. 18). A detailed account of the personal and public events possibly allegorized in *Robinson Crusoe* is offered by George Parker, 'The Allegory of Robinson Crusoe,' *History* 10 (1925): 11–25. Parker concentrates on Defoe's entrepreneurial and political career, citing as the basis for his own speculation Defoe's comment in his *Appeal to Honour and Justice*: 'I have gone through a life of wonders, and am the subject of a vast variety of Providences.'

19. John Richetti, with little mention of the specific political events of the seventeenth and eighteenth centuries, understands as well as any of Defoe's commentators what he calls the 'official ideology' of the narrative, one running absolutely counter to the absolutist position: 'Indeed, the deep fantasy that Crusoe and his story serve is the dream of freedom perfectly

reconciled with necessity, the self using necessity to promote its freedom' (*Defoe's Narratives: Situations and Structures*, pp. 54–55). In *Moby Dick*, Melville makes a similar ideological argument based on extremes of self-sovereignty and cooperative capacity in regard to islanders who make up most of the crew of the *Pequod*. His remarks have allegorical potential for the constitutional structure of American government just as Defoe's might for English rule: 'They were nearly all Islanders in the Pequod, *Isolatoes* too, I call such, not acknowledging the common continent of men, but each *Isolato* living on a separate continent of his own. Yet now, federated along one keel, what a set these Isolatoes were!' (chap. 27, 'Knights and Squires,' p. 166).

20. *Essay upon Projects* (London, 1697), p. 8.

21. *The Compleat English Tradesman* (London, 1726), 2: 198–99.

22. Crusoe is on the seas when Oliver Cromwell defeats the remaining royalist forces at Worcester and the future Charles II flees to France. Defoe held no brief for Cromwell the militarist. Crusoe's gradual eclipse from England seems to coincide, at least in terms of Defoe's politics, with worsening stages of English rule. Crusoe is in a Moorish prison and on a plantation in Brazil for the Protectorate and in island exile for the Restoration.

23. In September of 1659 Lambert dismissed the ineffective Rump Parliament as a ruling body, thus leading to the series of events that ushered in the Restoration of Charles II.

24. If the difficult part of Crusoe's working through toward toleration involves the cannibals, the spirited part involves his own political commentary on his reign once he has accommodated himself to its mechanisms: 'My Man *Friday* was a Protestant, his *Father* was a *Pagan* and a *Cannibal*, and the *Spaniard* was a Papist: However, I allow'd Liberty of Conscience throughout my Dominions: But this is by the Way' (p. 241). One of Defoe's severest complaints against the Stuarts in his assessment of state politics in *The Consolidator* is that they used and misused toleration as a hypocritical tool to ease into a Catholic succession in England.

25. In the classic first chapter, 'Odysseus' Scar,' of *Mimesis* (Princeton, 1953), Erich Auerbach considers the polarities of narrative in terms of surface and background (or depth) sequences, arguing that a sense of immediacy is associated with the Homeric epic, an immanent mode of narration where all things are brought to the fore as stark presence. Background narration is associated with the teleological perspective of the Old Testament where sequences of action recede into a much wider panorama of allegorical history and historical promise. Implicit in Auerbach's summary of narrative potential is the notion that the Western tradition of prose fiction has, in various ways, worked toward bringing foreground and background closer together. Defoe certainly centers his own discussion of *Robinson Crusoe* and allegory on just such a notion in his *Serious Reflections*.

26. John Richetti, recognizing both the irony and the scope of the footprint episode, writes: 'And it is precisely at this point in the narrative, when the island has been totally possessed by Crusoe, when it is fully an extension of himself, that he discovers the footprint on the beach' (*Defoe's Narratives*, p. 50). David Blewett sees the print as the bifurcating point in a bifurcated novel: 'It shatters Crusoe's tranquil existence and opens the movement of the second half of the novel' (*Defoe's Art of Fiction*, p. 39).

27. Because of his fear of the print and its unknown maker, Crusoe later says he lived 'like one of the ancient Giants, which are said to live in Caves, and Holes, in the Rocks, where none could come at them' (p. 179). If he were like

a Cyclopean giant, the print he sees ought to be smaller, not larger, than his own. As Rousseau argues in his *Essay on the Origin of Languages*, size and its perception are often a metaphoric adjustment to fear.

28. Maximillian Novak ('Imaginary Islands: Real Beasts') suggests that readers interested in some of Defoe's seemingly offhand remarks in *Crusoe* refer to his journalistic efforts while at work on the novel. In a *Weekly Journal* for 19 April 1718, Defoe presents a scheme to make all kings emperors and all men with political control of an area kings. Either this occurred to him as a result of his work on *Crusoe* or in conjunction with it.

29. Crusoe claims he leaves the island on 19 December 1686 after twenty-eight years, two months, and nineteen days. These calculations would bring the date of arrival back to 30 September 1658, which is a year earlier than he says when he lands. But we ought to credit the 1659 date because, even admitting the fictional status of the whole saga, that is the year he gives us while in the middle of it. To get to 1658 we have to count backward. Defoe makes a number of hopeless chronological mistakes toward the end of the narrative, and to get himself off the hook he has Crusoe say 'nor had I kept even the Number of Years so punctually, as to be sure that I was right, tho' as it prov'd, when I afterwards examin'd my Account, I found I had kept a true Reckoning of Years' (p. 249).

30. *Account of the Growth of Popery and Arbitrary Government in England* (1678), in *Works*, ed. Alexander B. Grosart (London, 1875), 4: 303–04. A modern authority on the Restoration writes of 1674 as the year in which 'an opposition now national in character' appeared in English life (David Ogg, *England in the Reign of Charles II*, 2nd ed. [London, 1956], 2: 544).

31. For the full context of Crusoe's experience and the principles of natural law, see Maximillian E. Novak, *Defoe and the Nature of Man* (Oxford, 1963). Cannibalism, of course, is one of the supreme challenges to natural law. And, as Everett Zimmerman points out, it is a charged subject and symbol for Defoe: 'The ubiquitous references to being devoured point to a generalized fear: of being dematerialized – the reversal of the desire to accumulate. It is a fear shared by author and character' (*Defoe and the Novel* [Berkeley, 1975], p. 32). [. . .]

32. What Crusoe works out in his response to the persecution of the cannibals touches on the natural propensity toward tyrannical violence that exists in mankind without the check of law and contractual restraint. Defoe observes in *Jure Divino* (1706): 'Nature has left *this Tincture in the Blood*/That all *Men would be Tyrants if they cou'd*./If they forbear their Neighbors to devour,/'Tis not for want of *Will*, but want of Power' ('Introductory Verses,' p. 1). Melville again makes a comparable point with more savage wit in *Moby Dick*: 'Go to the meatmarket of a Saturday night and see the crowds of live bipeds staring up at the long rows of dead quadrupeds. Does not that sight take a tooth out of the cannibal's jaw? Cannibals? who is not a cannibal?' (chap. 65, 'The Whale As a Dish,' p. 393).

33. This conclusion is obviously important for Defoe; he repeats it virtually word for word from an earlier passage in *Crusoe*: 'I ought to leave them to the Justice of God, who is the Governour of Nations, and knows how by National Punishments to make a just Retribution for National Offences; and to bring publick judgments upon those who offend in a publick Manner, by such Ways as best please him' (p. 173).

34. In the same sense that Crusoe thinks, incorrectly it turns out, that there may have been a Dutchman with the English crew (and a Dutchman, indeed, helped the English cause in 1688), all the illegitimate shenanigans at the end

of the narrative may reflect, in part, on the desperate last days of James II and his Cabal fighting to hold on to a realm that was more and more ready to expel them.

35. We have an idea from an earlier passage what Crusoe must have looked like and how he might affect an Englishman: 'My Beard I had once suffer'd to grow till it was about a Quarter of a yard long; but as I had both Scissars and Razors sufficient, I had cut it pretty short, except what grew on my upper Lip, which I had trimm'd into a large Pair of *Mahometan* Whiskers, such as I had seen worn by some *Turks*, who I saw at *Sallee*; for the *Moors* did not wear such, tho' the *Turks* did; of these Muschatoes or Whiskers, I will not say they were long enough to hang my Hat upon them; but they were of a Length and Shape monstrous enough, and such as in *England* would have pass'd for frightful' (p. 150).

36. Again, it seems to me that John Richetti expresses the implicit ideology of the exilic allegory with precision: 'The elaborate games that Crusoe plays as he ends his story are not only strategies for managing the mutineers; they represent an awareness in the narrative of the nature of freedom. They repeat on that trickiest and most difficult level of reality – the social and political – the games that Crusoe has had to master all through his story in order to "survive," that is, to achieve a special kind of autonomy' (*Defoe's Narratives*, p. 61).

37. Not only is this date of historical importance to Defoe as the second anniversary of Monmouth's Rebellion against James II, in which he may have taken some small part, but it was precisely at this time that leading national figures in England invited the Protestant Prince of Orange to mount an invasion and wrest the British Crown from James II.

Part III

Richardson

9 Strategies of Self-Production: *Pamela*

NANCY ARMSTRONG

In this section from her book *Desire and Domestic Fiction* (see Introduction, pp. 20–21), Nancy Armstrong applies her thesis about the
making of gender ideology and fiction to *Pamela*, which she sees as
setting a precedent for the ideological program she describes. By
framing a tale of seduction within the framework of the conduct-
book tradition, Richardson was able to reveal two things at once:
how a woman could be defined as distinctly feminine, and how a
woman could be made to seem desirable. Moreover, through the
vehicle of his fiction Richardson insinuates that debate into numerous different social venues. Armstrong argues however that the
success of that project did not necessarily amount to the oppression
of women. For in her resistance to Mr. B., Pamela helped to define a
crucial ideological distinction between men and women, where
women could strategically assert their difference from men.

Every language has its anomalies, which, though inconvenient,
and in themselves once unnecessary, must be tolerated among the
imperfections of human things, and which require only to be
registered, that they may not be increased, and ascertained, that
they may not be confounded: but every language has likewise its
improprieties and absurdities, which it is the duty of the
lexicographer to correct or proscribe.
                    (Samuel Johnson, Preface to the *Dictionary*)

Definitions could be useful if we didn't use words to make them.
                    (Jean-Jacques Rousseau, *Émile*)

By the mid-eighteenth century, new forms of writing were
contending with those that had long dominated English thinking,
each claiming the right to declare what features made a woman
most desirable. The sheer volume of print already devoted to the
project of redefining the female indicates that by that time a massive
ideological struggle was underway. But in addition to conduct books,
ladies magazines, and such newspapers as the *Tatler*, whose title
was supposedly coined out of deference to its female readership,

some authors created their idea of womankind out of the most unpromising material of all, namely, the novel. The novel had a reputation for displaying not only the seamy undersides of English political life, but also sexual behavior of a semi-pornographic nature. On both counts, it was considered a vulgar form of writing.[1] As late as 1810, a well-known conduct-book author could say of his readers, 'While cultivating a refined taste for the admirable productions of the classic British authors, I may venture to predict, that you will find neither time nor leisure nor much inclination for writing of *an inferior rank*' (italics mine). By this he means 'to include in one undistinguishing censure, all the various productions which come under the name of novels.'[2]

In shaping an ideal woman out of the stuff of novels, then, novelists did not appear to be assaulting the dominant culture so much as rescuing both the female and the domestic life she superintended from their fate at the hands of degenerate authors. It was this strategy that Richardson set in motion when, after declaring he was not actually writing a novel, he used fiction for redefining the desirable woman. Such an event helped to change both the terms of cultural conflict and the nature of the victory that would be won. But I want to stress that *Pamela* was not so much about this struggle as quite literally part of it. As I shall demonstrate, the strategies of the larger conflict gave Richardson's first novel its peculiar form. One can observe his strategies with particular clarity in those places that are usually considered clumsy or tedious within the framework of 'the art of the novel.' To speak of the qualities of the text that resist modern aesthetics, however, is to identify the role of the text in the far more extensive process I call feminization, whereby certain areas of aristocratic culture were appropriated for the emergent social group.[3]

By the end of the eighteenth century, conduct books had settled on one kind of fiction as truly safe for young women to read. This was a non-aristocratic kind of writing that was both polite and particularly suitable for a female readership. It also had the virtue of dramatizing the same principles sketched out in the conduct books. Burney's *Evelina* is only one of the better-known examples of the fiction by lady novelists, as the women who wrote polite novels were called. So well established did this kind of writing become, so thoroughly did the literate classes grant it approval over the other, older, and more prevalent varieties of fiction, that it eventually supplanted everything the novel had formerly been. In this manner, a relatively new form of writing came to define the genre within a remarkably few number of years. Austen could write *Northanger Abbey* and the rest of her fiction knowing full well what a novel had to do in order to be considered a novel. She never pursued the direction in which she began her writing career. Her *Lady Susan* was a work of fiction, to be sure, but it was certainly no novel in the polite sense of the term, for the heroine appeared to be a successful adventuress in the mode of Restoration drama. When by the middle of the nineteenth century the new middle classes were entrenched and the British economy had stabilized, the novel was already known as a female form of writing, and the conflict between fiction and the polite tradition of letters had all but been resolved. By this point, such fictions as Richardson's and Burney's were brought within the realm of the normative, and a continuous tradition of the novel could be written backward as well as forward in time. As the novel was written into a literary history, however, the process of its production disappeared. Only the novels themselves preserved the struggle between writing that only later became known as the novel and another kind of fiction – once referred to as novels or romances – that has since been consigned to the attics and storerooms of cultural history.

Beginning with Richardson's *Pamela*, then, one can observe the process by which novels rose to a position of respectability among the genres of writing. This process created a private domain of culture that was independent of the political world and overseen by a woman. Such a cultural fantasy held forth the promise that individuals could realize a new and more fundamental identity and thus free themselves of the status distinctions organizing the old society. In this respect, the novel provided a mighty weapon in the arsenal of Enlightenment rhetoric, which aimed at liberating individuals from their political chains. Richardson demonstrated how fiction could deploy strategies that reorganized the country house around a woman who had nothing but a gendered form of literacy to offer. But as much as his strategies may have resembled those which Rousseau put to use in writing *The Social Contract*, they nevertheless offered an important variation on familiar Enlightenment themes: they constituted the female subject as she became an object of knowledge in and through her own writing. Richardson was probably only trying to gain the authority to create this woman, and most likely he only sought to control the interpretive strategies that readers brought to bear on her behavior. But fiction itself demonstrates that by the end of the eighteenth century the same strategies which laid claim to the rights of the individual underwent a form of mutation and acquired the power to control the individual on whose behalf they continued to argue. [*Pamela* inaugurates] the history of certain political strategies that first offered the theory and rationale for modern social institutions, but that later came to be used as techniques of social control.

[. . .]

Strategies of self-production: *Pamela*

Richardson has been accused of all the faults for which Austen
ridicules Mary Bennet, and not without reason. But it is also because
he used the feminizing strategies of conduct-book literature in his
first work of fiction that it was received with such acclaim and
even recommended from the pulpit in a time when novels were
considered morally dangerous. We know that Richardson took great
pains to distinguish his 'pretty novel' from the 'horrid romancing'
of others and that he tried to control the interpretation of *Pamela* by
calling together ladies for the purpose of discussing his fiction.[4] In
addition to making numerous revisions, he drew upon this and his
later fiction to compile a book of moral homilies for publication.
He even published and revised his correspondence in a compulsive
effort to reclassify his fiction as something other than common
fiction. But if, as Richardson insisted, *Pamela* is not a novel according
to the standards of his day, then neither is it a conduct book. As
Richardson obviously knew, conduct books never represented the
female body at all, except to mention the particularities of dressing or
to recommend a modest bearing when a woman presented herself to
the public view. Nor did they value the body as a female body, even
in those passages that describe procedures for health and hygiene.
Although they frequently declared that fiction would somehow
prevent a woman from performing her domestic duties, these books
also refused to say what exactly was so threatening about fiction that
women had to shun it above all other reading.

In writing *Pamela*, Richardson struck upon a double maneuver that
ensured his novel was not a novel in the derogatory sense of the
word, even though it was indeed a work of fiction. He deployed the
strategies of conduct-book literature within fiction, and he contained
the strategies of the most deleterious fiction – a tale of seduction –
within the framework of a conduct book. To domesticate fiction, he
thematically represented both modes of writing – fiction that aimed
at producing the new domestic world and fiction that reinforced the
stratifying strategies identified with the old society – as the struggle
between a female servant and her aristocratic master. He represented
their struggle for possession of the female body in scene after scene
of seduction, which he elaborated in minute detail. Thus he provided
a local habitation and a name for the very sexual behavior against
which the conduct books had pitted their rhetoric. But Richardson
also used fiction to enter into a struggle with fiction. And he saw to it
that this struggle was one which other fiction would lose, for sexual
relations would be contained within the categories of domestic

economy. Indeed, the last third of *Pamela* deals with little else but the details of household management [. . .]

Once again, I want to stress the fact that the struggle Pamela wages against the advances of Mr. B does not point to some order of events going on outside of language; it records a struggle that actually took place within fiction. On the outcome of this struggle hinged the right to determine not only what made a female desirable, but also what made her female in the first place. By having Pamela gain the power of self-representation, Richardson enclosed the tale of her seduction within a framework that, like the conduct book, redirected male desire at a woman who embodied the domestic virtues. Richardson thus carried on the project of the conduct book, but by doing so in and through fiction, he carried it into the symbolic heart of the old society – the aristocratic country house – where it engaged in a mortal dialectic with the dominant political categories. Pamela's successful struggle against the sexual advances of Mr. B transformed the rules of an earlier model of kinship relations into a sexual contract that suppressed their difference in station. Rather than that of a master and servant, then, the relationship between the protagonists of these competing kinds of fiction may be understood as that of male and female. There can be no better illustration than this of how the discourse of sexuality worked and of what political goal was achieved as it suppressed the political categories that until then had dominated writing.

To make my point, let me first recall the relationship between male and female as it appears in an early seventeenth century Puritan marriage pamphlet:[5]

Husband	*Wife*
Get goods	Gather them together and save them
Travel, seek a living	Keep the house
Get money and provisions	Do not vainly spend it
Deal with many men	Talk with few
Be 'entertaining'	Be solitary and withdrawn
Be skillful in talk	Boast of silence
Be a giver	Be a saver
Apparel yourself as you may	Apparel yourself as it becomes you
Dispatch all things outdoors	Oversee and give order within

As much as its principle of gender differentiation resembles that organizing modern households, and even though its Puritan heritage certainly distinguishes British fiction from the fiction of other capitalist nations, the domestic ideal illustrated above did not pass through the centuries unmodified. By so enclosing the family, the static and binary model of Puritan handbooks and sermons sought to establish an alternative basis for political power and represented the family as a little commonwealth in whose government the larger state could not interfere. As such, the domestic unit resisted the dominant notion of kinship relations at two crucial points. First, it represented the state within the state as independent and as containing relationships that were based on gender rather than on family or fortune. In thus contesting the dominant notion of power relations, however, the Puritan household organized the state within the state in terms of the radically disymmetrical relations of monarch and subject. As Robert Cleaver explains, the household was a commonwealth made up of two sorts, 'The Governor' and 'those who must be ruled.'[6] This direct assault on the principle of monarchy never succeeded in transforming the political organization of England.

But the Puritan version of the household contained another point of resistance, which came into play later on in the history of the family. Post-Enlightenment versions of the household appeared to leave the political world alone as they avoided the language of government that runs through seventeenth century handbooks of marriage. Eighteenth century conduct books in particular presumed to tamper exclusively with sexual relations and then solely with the female component. At the same time, however, they claimed to represent all households as the natural domain of a woman who was dedicated to making the place into a happy middle-class home. By representing only the household, these later conduct books accomplished what earlier and avowedly political representations of the family had not been able to do. Although theirs was very much a minority view, the conduct books detached the household from the larger political order and made it a world of its own, a world where status distinctions were suspended.

Pamela demonstrates perhaps more clearly than any other single example that to transform one party of the sexual contract effectively transforms the relationship between the two sexes and therefore the contract itself. To explain how *Pamela* turns the minority representation of sexual relations into an instrument of hegemony, I offer below an example from a section of the sexual contract in which Mr. B attempts to negotiate with the servant girl who has steadfastly resisted all his sexual advances. Particularly important is the form in which Richardson presents this contract to his readers. He counterpoints Mr. B's demands with Pamela's responses and inserts them side by side in this paradigmatic fashion about midway through the narrative.[7]

To Mrs. Pamela Andrews.	This is my Answer.
II: I will directly make you a present of 500 *guineas*, for your own use, which you may dispose of to any purpose you please: and will give it absolutely into the hands of any person you shall appoint to receive it; and expect no favour in return, till you are satisfied in the possession of it.	II. As to your second proposal, let the consequence be what it will I reject it with all my soul. Money, sire, is not my chief good: May God Almighty desert me, whenever it is! and whenever, for the sake of that, I can give up my title to that blessed hope which will stand me in stead, at a time when millions of gold will not purchase one happy moment of reflection on a past misspent life!
IV. Now, Pamela, will you see by this, what a value I set upon the free-will of a person *already* in my power; and who, if these proposals are not accepted, shall find, that I have not taken all these pains, and risked my reputation, as I have done, without solving to gratify my passion for you, at all adventures; and if you refuse, without making any terms at all.	IV. I know, sir, by woful experience that I am in your power: I know all the resistance I can make will be poor and weak, and, perhaps, stand me in little stead: I dread your *will* to ruin me is as great as your *power*: yet, sir, will I dare to tell you, that I will make no free-will offering of my virtue. All that I *can* do, poor as it is, I *will* do, to convince you that your offers shall have no part in my choice; and if I cannot escape the violence of man, I hope, by God's grace, I shall have nothing to reproach myself, for not doing all in my power to avoid my disgrace; and then I can safely appeal to the great God, my only refuge and protector, with this consolation,

Simply by inserting Pamela's voice into the field dominated by Mr. B's contract, Richardson empowers the subject of aristocratic power with speech. In allowing her the grounds for negotiating such a contract, furthermore, he modifies the presupposition of all previous contracts, namely, that the male defined and valorized the female as

223

a form of currency in an exchange among men. This is to say that Richardson's version of consensual exchange empowers the female to give herself in exchange with the male. Although this novel claims to deal only with the sexual contract, doing so in this instance also revises the way in which political relationships are imagined.[8]

The male party of this exchange is a member of the older landed gentry. It is perhaps curious that someone of such high yet untitled status should provide the target of Richardson's reformist rhetoric. Still, one finds it consistently true that – from Richardson's Mr. B to Austen's Mr. Knightley to Brontë's Mr. Rochester – the male of the dominant class, as represented in fiction, is likely to occupy precisely such a social position. He is likely to bear certain features of the ruling class that inhibit the operations of genuine love. To a certain degree, however, domestic fiction remakes this figure in the image of a new ruling class. The gentry was permeable, a class one could enter through marriage, and its features as a group, like those of the manor house, could be remodeled to the specifications of the middle-class family.[9]

It is worth noting that the male of the dominant class, though he may bear certain features of the libertine or of the snob, is capable of going either way socially, but his female counterpart is generally not. Such women as Mr. B's sister Lady Davers, or Darcy's aunt Lady Catherine de Bourgh, or Rochester's fiancée Blanche Ingram are hopelessly devoid of feelings and concerned only with displaying their position. They embody the features of the dominant class that, in contrast with a fine pair of eyes or a genteel education, cannot be included among those of the domestic woman. What I am suggesting by making this comparison is that Richardson endows Mr. B with certain political features that can be transformed by the thematics of gender. Within the gendered framework, the male is indeed defined in political terms, for this is precisely what it means to be male. Only those features of the aristocratic woman that testify to her development of certain psychological qualities can go into the making of the new domestic ideal. Through marriage to someone of a lower station, the male but not the female of the upper gentry can be redeemed. I do not mean to imply that this class of people really behaved in so paradoxical a manner as fiction depicted them, but rather that such a representation of the upper gentry offered the rhetorical means for redistributing certain attributes, along with corresponding powers and privileges, according to the principle of gender.

As a man of significantly higher station than his own servant, Mr. B is initially disposed to consider that his offer to grant Pamela economic independence in return for sexual pleasure is a gesture of pure generosity. He could claim such pleasure as his to enjoy without entering into a consensual exchange at all. By virtue of being master of the estate and thus of all the personnel and objects therein, Mr. B already possesses – as he reminds Pamela – the thing he most desires. Had Richardson endowed Pamela with wealth or station, Mr. B would be perfectly within the rules of his caste to marry her, for she would then not only possess an erotic body but an estate and bloodline as well. The fact that Mr. B tries and fails to seduce Pamela on so many occasions tells us that this woman possesses some kind of power other than that inhering in either the body of a servant or in that of a prominent family. By making the female party to the contract, Richardson implies an independent party with whom the male has to negotiate, a female self who exists outside and prior to the relationships under the male's control.

When in the history of writing before *Pamela*, we might ask ourselves, did a female, let alone a female servant, have the authority to define herself so? To understand the power Richardson embodies in the non-aristocratic woman, one need only observe how he endows her with subjective qualities. In her response to Article II of Mr. B's proposition, Pamela asserts an alternative form of value to that of his money and rank. This value is called into being as she rejects what Mr. B offers in exchange for the pleasure of using her body. At all costs, even that of life itself, she resolves to preserve an essential self that the male of the dominant class does not and cannot possess by virtue of his wealth and monopoly on violence. In both Articles II and IV, we can see Richardson counter the power available in the aristocratic tradition by drawing on the language of theological tradition for the terms of Pamela's resistance. 'Hope,' 'reflection,' 'reproach,' as well as 'soul' describe the feelings of a woman bent on preserving control over her body in the face of a system that gives license to sexual assault. Richardson does not settle on this language because he is particularly interested in representing the condition of her soul. He uses this terminology to give her value as a partner in marriage.

The term 'will' is especially revealing in this respect. By the time Richardson is through with it, it no longer has anything to do with the grand tradition of theological debate. It has everything to do with a new concern for personal motivation.[10] Caught up and redefined within the figure of the contract, the whole idea of will becomes individuated, sexual, and internalized; it becomes, in other words, the volition required before any consensual contract can take place. In acquiring a modern psychological meaning, furthermore, 'will' also adheres to a principle of economy. To accept Mr. B's money would cause Pamela to suffer a loss that she describes in spiritual

terms but that she also identifies as bad business; if she accepts his
money, she will have to look back upon a 'misspent' life. To refuse
Mr. B on these grounds makes the integrity of the female body,
regardless of birth and station, worth more than money and defines
that body within a system of values that cannot be translated into
economic value per se. Richardson's heroines embody a contrary
principle of economy that is founded on the sexual contract or gender
relations and that is to be understood as distinct and apart from the
social contract or relations among social groups. The female in this
exchange is thus constituted as a form of resistance, or 'will,' which
poses an alternative moral economy to that of the dominant class.

Her power *not* to consent redefines the nature of the contract
between man and woman as it had been represented by a Puritan
tradition, according to which a woman voluntarily entered into
master–servant relationship when she consented to marriage. Rather
than enter into a sexual contract that replicates the economic contract
of master and servant, Pamela holds out for an exchange between
parties whose difference is determined only by gender. Ironically
enough, in making a romance that sought to unite the extremes
of the social hierarchy, Richardson had to erase virtually all
socioeconomic markings before the male and female could enter into
an exchange. What chance did Richardson have of overthrowing the
centuries-old notion of contractual relations that bound one to submit
to those of superior rank? Fielding thought Pamela's resistance silly;
a man of Mr. B's station would never have been willing to 'risk his
reputation' (as Mr. B himself explains in the contract quoted above)
in order to enjoy such a woman's sexual favors. But simply by
introducing the figure of the female with a capacity to say 'no'
and then providing a basis on which she could find such refusal
advantageous, Richardson overthrew the longstanding tradition of
thinking about courtship and kinship relations. Fielding as much
as conceded this point when he drew upon these strategies to write
fiction that sought to expose Richardson's total misrepresentation
of political circumstances. It should be understood that I am using
Richardson's name in a strictly rhetorical sense when I say this, for of
course Pamela's 'no' would have meant very little had she not been
speaking with the voice of thousands who by then knew the conduct-
book philosophy of reading. Nor, for that matter, would her denial
have reverberated through time had it not addressed millions who
came to understand themselves as basically the same kind of
individual first described in these female conduct books.

The effect of inserting Pamela's written presence into Mr. B's
text as if she were equal to the dominant class is the effect of
supplementation. Paired with the words of her master, her response

displaces the master–servant relationship onto a battle between the sexes, where the value of the politically subordinate party arises from an alternative source, her gender, rather than from her place in a political hierarchy. While Mr. B offers money in exchange for her body, she maintains that her real value does not derive from her body; she is not, in other words, currency in a system of exchange among men. Saying this, as Pamela does on more than one occasion, only raises the question of why, if Richardson meant to locate value in a site other than the woman's material body, did he produce a long and unremitting tale of seduction. Pamela insists that her identity depends on her sexual purity, for in her words, 'to rob a person of her virtue is worse than cutting her throat' (p. 111). If the male's forcible penetration of her body assaults the very life of the non-aristocratic woman herself, then the master's exercise of his power over the bodies of those within his household amounts to murder. It destroys their value. Thus with a stroke Richardson forces his reader to condemn the political system that authorizes the exercise of such power.

By rewriting the female body in this fashion, Richardson overturned the basis on which political relationships were understood as natural and right. Whether he meant to do this or not, it is clear that his tale of seduction participates in a much larger cultural project. Pamela fights to possess her body in a world where the necessity of doing so is a minority view. Over and against her claim that sexual penetration of the body is tantamount to murder, Mrs. Jewkes, Pamela's custodian, delivers the verdict of common sense – 'how strangely you talk!' – and then proceeds to put her charge through a catechism concerning the laws of sexuality: 'Are not the two sexes made for one another? And is it not natural for a gentleman to love a pretty woman? And suppose he can obtain his desires, is that so bad as cutting her throat?' (p. 111). If we turn to one of the two central scenes in the novel where Mr. B succeeds in gaining control over Pamela's body, it soon becomes clear that even without much of a struggle Pamela's own definition of her body triumphs over his common sense. To the woman he has pinned naked on her bed beneath him, Mr. B delivers these lines: 'You see now you are in my power! – You cannot get from me, nor help yourself' (p. 213). Rather than possess her in this violent manner, however, he would prefer to release her unmolested upon her consent to exchange her body for money. At the very moment when the terms of that contract seem impossible for the woman to refuse – when it means her submission by force if not by consent – Richardson suddenly changes the terms of sexual relations in the novel. That is, he changes what it is the male must possess in order to possess the woman, for it is not a creature of flesh and blood that Mr. B encounters in the body naked and supine upon the bed, but a proliferation of female words and feelings.

Pamela successfully resists Mr. B's attempts to exercise traditional forms of power – money and force – because she possesses herself through the exertions of her own emotions. She swoons. She returns to consciousness to hear her assailant vow 'that he had not offered the least indecency; that he was frightened at the terrible manner I was taken with the fit; that he should desist from his attempt, and begged but to see me easy and quiet, and he would leave me directly, and go to his own bed' (p. 213). Thus Richardson stages a scene of rape that transforms an erotic and permeable body into a self-enclosed body of words. Mr. B's repeated failures suggest that Pamela cannot be raped because she is nothing but words. As such, she demonstrates the productive power of the trope of the contract. Presuming to rescue the pure and original Pamela, Richardson creates a distinction between the Pamela Mr. B desires and the female who exists prior to becoming this object of desire and who can therefore claim the right of first property to herself. By means of a curious splitting of the female, Richardson represents the two of them – male and female – struggling for possession of Pamela: 'He came up to me, and took me by the hand, and said, Whose pretty maiden are you? – I dare say you are Pamela's *sister*, you are so like her. So neat, so clean, so pretty! . . . I would not be so free with your sister, you may believe; but I must kiss *you.*' In characteristically Richardsonian style, the splitting that occurs whenever Mr. B tries to possess Pamela has a doubling effect by producing a subject who can claim possession of herself as an object. 'O sir,' she replies, 'I am Pamela, indeed I am: indeed I am Pamela, *her own self*' (p. 53). As it provides occasion for her to resist Mr. B's attempts to possess her body, seduction becomes the means to dislocate female identity from the body and to define it as a metaphysical object.

Significantly, Pamela's transformation from an object of desire into a female sensibility also transforms Mr. B. He once desired only the surface of her body and found her resistance annoyingly 'saucy' and 'pert.' After the rape scene, however, Mr. B comes full circle to desire the same female qualities that formerly obstructed his advances. His assessment of these qualities reveals how Richardson uses the figure of sexual exchange to produce a modern concept of gender:

You have a good deal of wit, a great deal of penetration, much beyond your *years*, and, as I thought, your *opportunities*. You are possessed of an open, frank, and generous mind; and a person so lovely, that you excel all your sex, in my eyes. All these

accomplishments have engaged my affection so deeply, that, as I
have often said, I cannot live without you; and I would divide,
with all my soul, my estate with you, to make you mine upon my
own terms. These you have absolutely rejected; and that, though
in saucy terms enough, yet in such a manner as makes me admire
you the more. . . . And I see you so watchful over your virtue,
that though I hoped to find it otherwise, I cannot but confess
my passion for you is increased by it. But now, what shall I say
farther, Pamela? – I will make you, though a party, my adviser in
this matter, though not, perhaps, my definitive judge.

(p. 223)

Even though Mr. B still lacks the language to rationalize marrying
someone of a position so far beneath him, a language which Pamela's
letters will eventually supply, the contract has nevertheless done its
work effectively.

If we compare this statement to the dialogue between male and
female that Richardson pairs off to dramatize their contractual
negotiations, we find that the dialogue takes on a dialectical force.
Even as it dramatizes the failure of the male party to effect an
exchange in economic and political terms, Mr. B's ridiculously
protracted seduction of an otherwise unnoteworthy servant girl
redefines the two parties of the contract. At this moment, Richardson
creates the possibility for an exchange that violates neither the
integrity of the female body nor the conditions of female subjectivity.
Theirs can no longer be understood as an exchange of his money for
erotic pleasure once Mr. B acquires all the qualities of the prosperous
male who – as the conduct books promise – desires nothing so much
as the female accomplishments that conduct books describe in
glowing terms. Upon his transformation, Mr. B enjoys an entirely
different form of pleasure from Pamela than he formerly sought:
'Said he, I hope my present temper will hold; for I tell you frankly,
that I have known in this agreeable hour, more *sincere pleasure* than
I have experienced in all the guilty tumults that my desiring soul
compelled me into, in the hopes of possessing you in my own terms'
(p. 229, italics mine). Now seemingly heedless of his 'reputation,' or
of the violations of his class codes that he might be committing by
privileging the abstract virtues of his maid, Mr. B understands the
benefits he reaps from his relationship with Pamela in terms that
must have sounded a familiar economic note:

My beloved wants no language, nor sentiments neither; and her
charming thoughts, so sweetly expressed, would *grace* any
language; and this is a *blessing* almost peculiar to my fairest. – Your

229

so kind acceptance, my Pamela, added he, *repays* the *benefit* with *interest* and leaves me under *obligation* to your *goodness*.

(p. 387, italics mine)

Although the dominant discourse now encompasses that of the female, it has been thoroughly infiltrated by a terminology that is utterly hostile to an earlier model of exchange. Accordingly, one finds the terms of Christian theology ('grace,' 'blessing') mingled with those of nascent capitalism ('benefit,' 'interest') to form a distinctively modern discourse of sexuality.

It is important to see that what happens in this novel could never happen in a conduct book, much as the two kinds of writing shared a single strategic intention. To be sure, *Pamela* carried on the same struggle to define the female that was being waged wherever writing invoked the need for female education and for the reform of sexual practices. Represented as the struggle between a master and his female servant, *Pamela* contained this struggle first within the household and then within the writing that transformed Pamela herself into a distinctively female form of subjectivity. The differentiation and enclosure of a female self was nothing short of a victory for the modern self over the political system that was authorized by a household which a male governed and sustained by his patronage. If a servant girl could claim possession of herself as her own first property, then virtually any individual must similarly have a self to withhold or give in a modern form of exchange with the state. We know Pamela has such a self only because she acquires the power to withhold it. *Pamela* can dramatize, as no other kind of writing can, the triumph of this sexual self over traditional forms of political identity because the novel arose out of the struggle between modes of writing to define sexuality. To put it quite crudely, this novel is a struggle in which one fiction captures and translates the other into its terms. More than likely, the writing of normal sexuality did not proceed with the intention of dismantling the hierarchical world, or it would not have concentrated so much effort on the female. Nevertheless, Richardson's strategy of enclosing subjectivity and then endowing it with power in its own right was also an aggressive act of reclassification; it was the means by which all manner of political information could be turned into features of gender.

This political dimension to Richardson's sexual theme constantly threatens to overturn the psychological hermeneutics of Pamela's writing and to place the text among the common sort of novels and romances. Against the threat of semiotic inversion, Richardson marshalled not only all manner of extratextual precautions, but also –

and more importantly from a historical perspective – the strategies conduct books had devised in their own effort to control meaning. Such strategies shift the struggle for meaning from the level of political force to that of language. *Pamela* reminds us at every turn that we are witnessing a process of writing. Even as she records her emotional responses to a world governed by an unscrupulous man, Pamela worries that the daily record will turn out to be a romance. Mr. B tells her they are making 'a pretty story in a romance' (p. 26), and she discovers that his plots have the power to turn her record into 'horrid romancing' despite all her attempts to evade them. When he finally hands her the authority to author their history, she exclaims, 'my story would furnish out a surprising kind of novel if it was to be well told' (p. 258). It is fair to say the act of writing becomes so obtrusive that the purity of her language seems to matter more than that of her body.

On her language alone depends the power of her resistance. As she puts it, 'How then, sir, can I act but by shewing my abhorrence of every step that makes towards my undoing? And what is left me but words?' (p. 220). 'Words' are indeed all Pamela has to exert against the coercion of rank and a large fortune, but her 'words' prove the more powerful for being the only power she has. The more Mr. B persists in his attempts to possess her, the more he subjects his behavior to Pamela's view, and the deeper she penetrates into the heart of the dominant culture to appropriate its material as the stuff of her own subjectivity. Even before her letters are publicly aired and authorized, Richardson grants them a reformist power that is actually the power to form desire. Mr. B feels compelled to censor the letters lest they damage his reputation, but by confiscating them, he has not really escaped the classificatory power of Pamela's pen. Quite the contrary, he finds himself taken up within and converted to her mode of narration.

It is no ordinary moment in political history when a male novelist imagines a woman whose writing has power to reform the male of the dominant class. Surely, if this had been an ordinary novel, the scene where Richardson situates Mr. B astride Pamela's naked body would qualify as the most erotic scene in a narrative made of his fruitless efforts at surmounting her discourse. But this is hardly the case; Mr. B's attempt to seize pleasure from her body only engenders fear on his part as well as on hers. When he reads Pamela's letters, on the other hand, such male aggression suddenly achieves its traditional objective and gratifies sexual desire. Although he could not penetrate her body, Mr. B has Richardson's permission to pry at will into the secrets of her written self, to spy on her every act of writing, to intercept her letters, and finally to force her to divulge the whereabouts of even more writing. Strange to say, by far the most and perhaps the only genuinely erotic scene in the novel occurs when Mr. B takes possession of a thoroughly self-inscribed Pamela.[11] It is as if, having displaced the conventionally desirable female onto a written one, Richardson at last allows novelistic convention to have its way with this woman:

> Artful slut! said he, What's this to my question? – Are they [Pamela's letters] not *about* you? – If, said I, I must pluck them out of my hiding-place behind the wainscot, won't you see me? – Still more and more artful! said he – Is this an answer to my question? – I have searched every place above, and in your closet, for them, and cannot find them; so I *will* know where they are. Now, said he, it is my opinion they are about you; and I never undressed a girl in my life; but I will now begin to strip my pretty Pamela; and I hope I shall not go far before I find them.
>
> (p. 245)

Only by so deflecting eroticism away from the material body and onto writing could Richardson develop procedures for reforming libertine desire. He represented this change as a process of reading.

Such reading provided a new object of pleasure that was supposed to redirect male desire away from the surface of the female body and into its depths. When Mr. B finally removes her dress, he no longer finds an erotic body to be possessed at all, but a body of sentiments having no reality other than words. Pamela's writing, Mr. B admits at last, 'has made me desirous of reading all you write; though a great deal of it is against myself' (p. 242). The letters about Pamela's body not only succeed in transforming that body into a body of words, they also offer Mr. B a self that has been represented and evaluated in feminine terms, a purely sexual and psychological phenomenon that challenges the codes of his class. To her he surrenders mastery over sexual relations, which he then allows to dominate the rest of the novel: 'There is such a pretty air of romance as you relate them, in your plots, and my plots, that I shall be better directed in what manner to wind up the catastrophe of the pretty novel' (p. 242). Along with the authority to write their story, he hands the regulation of the household over to her, and the novel becomes little more than the conduct book it has passed through so much peril to resemble.

By representing relationships within the traditional country house as a struggle between competing interest groups, Richardson challenged the dominant cultural ideal. By casting this struggle as a sexual relationship, he concealed the politics of such representation. This may, as a number of readers have claimed, be attributed to his personal ambivalence both toward those of higher station in eighteenth century society and toward women.[12] But what retrospectively appears as ambivalence can, I believe, be better explained as the artfulness of the middle-class intellectual reworking certain cultural materials to aim desire away from the aristocratic body and into a world of private gratification that anyone by implication could enjoy. Richardson indicates a more acute consciousness of the politics of writing than we are usually willing to grant someone of his unsubtle psychological understanding. At crucial instances throughout his narrative, he takes pains to connect the struggle over writing, the struggle to control interpretation, with the struggle for political power. I have already referred to the way in which he has Pamela reject Mr. B's generous offer of an economic contract, and I have explained how the narrative of seduction enables Richardson to produce female subjectivity as a form of resistance. But he also uses turns of phrase that openly acknowledge the political dimension of sexual conflict. Mr. B says of Pamela, for example, 'the artful *creature* is enough to corrupt a nation by her seeming innocence and simplicity' (p. 169). Because the point is to do away with political categories, however, this potential for interpreting Pamela's behavior as subversion is there chiefly to be contained and transformed within her letters. The language of power must be ever present as an interpretive possibility if Richardson is to dramatize Mr. B's conversion to Pamela's sentimentality.

To understand all the fuss he makes over the morality of fiction – and whether he is writing a novel or not – it is necessary to understand Richardson's writing as a material reality in its own right. He says as much when he wraps Pamela in her letters, replacing the surface of her body with the depths of her private feelings in a scene that reveals the new – and true – object of Mr. B's desire. Cast in this light as quite literally a struggle between two kinds of self-representation, the Richardsonian text is not *about* a struggle between opposing political groups that achieves mediation in and through writing so much as it is a struggle for control of the very terms in which political conflict will be understood and mediation accomplished. This novel concludes not with a marriage of families or fortunes, but with a message that conjoins different modes of subjectivity to produce the gender-divided world of the conduct books. In triumphing over the other languages of the novel, personal letter writing successfully removes domestic relations from all economic and political considerations as it subjects such relations to a woman's moral scrutiny and emotional response.

That this panoptical conception of authority is the same one Bentham would later represent as a political theory is clear. *Pamela* offers a narrative in which the work of the pen is rivaled only by that of the eyes. In fact, it is fair to say that while Pamela is imprisoned on Mr. B's estate the assaults on her body seem neither so frequent nor so perverse as the 'watchments' she has to endure. It is to establish the power of observation as superior to that of either money or force that Richardson suddenly breaks into the narrative he has entrusted to Pamela on every other occasion:

> Here it is necessary, the reader should know, that the fair Pamela's trials were not yet over; but the worst were to come, at a time when she thought them at an end; and that she was returning to her father: for when her master found her virtue was not to be subdued, and he had in vain tried to conquer his passion for her, being a gentleman of pleasure and intrigue, he had ordered his Lincolnshire coachman to bring his travelling chariot from thence, . . . he drove her five miles on the way to her father's; and then turning off, crossed the country, and carried her onwards toward his Lincolnshire estate.
>
> (p. 91)

If this seems an awkward shifting of rhetorical gears, it is because the change in the direction of Mr. B's coach does indeed effect an abrupt shift in the form of political power that has, up to this point in the narrative, dominated sexual relations. Why else invent another country house if not to have a country house organized according to a new set of rules? In the Lincolnshire estate, Mr. B is significantly invisible in person, but he is omnipresent in the form of vigilant surrogates who do little else but watch Pamela's every move and intercept most of her letters. Pamela, in other words, becomes an object of knowledge. Where he once spied on her undressing from the vantage point of her closet, Mr. B now possesses the means of insinuating himself into the most private recesses of her emotions through reports on her every word and gesture, as well as through the record of her emotional experience contained in her letters. Her isolation and a rigid form of censorship that all but prohibits communication create greater anguish than even the threat of physical assault. For the Lincolnshire estate is represented as a grimly gothic version of the first manor house, replacing, for example, the benign Mrs. Jervis with the malevolent Jewkes and the paternal coachman John with the demonic Colbrand who owes loyalty only to his master. This nightmarish version of the country house leaves no doubt that the threat of self-annihilation intensifies as the assault on Pamela's body becomes more a matter of ocular rape than of physical penetration. Such a shift in the strategy of sexual violation to the violation of psychological depths provides a strategy for discovering more depths within the female to write about, thereby producing more words by which to displace her body.

Pamela wins the struggle to interpret both herself and all domestic relations from the moment the coach swerves off the road to her father's house and delivers her at Mr. B's Lincolnshire estate. The power dominating at the estate is already female power. It is the power of domestic surveillance. The reader of conduct books knows, furthermore, that Mrs. Jewkes will not successfully manage the household because she has 'a huge hand, and an arm as thick as my waist,' 'a hoarse, man-like voice,' and many other masculine features (p. 116). The manor house displays a need, the satisfaction of which requires turning the house into the one represented in conduct books. I am not suggesting that having a mannish woman in charge is what makes the house so different. Rather, the difference lies in the fact that sexuality in this household bears little resemblance to the kind of transaction enabled by the other estate. Lincolnshire does not dramatize a bawdy bedroom comedy ruled by desire that aims to possess the female body; it dramatizes instead the operations of female subjectivity. Such a place establishes essentially the same structure of power as the eighteenth century medical theater where anatomies were performed before an audience. In this characteristically modern theater, as at Lincolnshire, power did not reside in the object of the gaze, whose model and emblem was the docile body of the cadaver undergoing dissection. Instead, it operated through the eye of an observer who discovered truth beneath the surface of that body. This, I have been arguing, was the form of power that would sweep aside an earlier form that inhered in the aristocratic body and depended on that body's power to hold the gaze of the people.

At Lincolnshire, Pamela is released from her servile position as a domestic laborer to spend her hours doing little else but telling a story that resembles an instruction book in how to write the feminine emotions. Mr. B has situated her where she can be observed. Because she spends her time not only observing but also representing herself and others, however, it is here that she seizes the power of surveillance as her own. In other words, as soon as the assault on her body has settled into this form of voyeurism, then her victory over such oppression requires only a shift in the direction and dynamics of gazing.[13] This is the function of Pamela's kind of writing. It turns the gaze back upon itself as a critical mirror of power to establish much the same relationship that Richardson himself establishes with 'other' fiction. As Mr. B reads her letters aloud to her parents and to his neighbors and sister, he makes public the knowledge she

intended to keep strictly between herself and her parents. As he
speaks her writing, then, his speech incorporates its own critique –
a form of resistance to his codes of social identity. By reading her
private communication, then, he internalizes her moral authority,
her conscience becomes his, his speech is indistinguishable from
her writing, and she has achieved a form of power over him. Every
time Mr. B reads one of her letters, he exposes both her innermost
thoughts and the innermost secrets of the country house under his
supervision. Her letters display her capability for self-regulation and
his corresponding need for her supervision. As writing displaces the
exercise of force with the force of surveillance, in other words, it also
shifts the power of the gaze from the male to the female. The ideal
conditions as specified by Pamela in her objection to Mr. B's initial
offer of a contract are therefore met. They marry.

Having ensured the power of her gaze through writing, Pamela
grows tired, she says, 'of their gazing' and retires from public view
into the objects and activities of the household under her control
(p. 299). And after the marriage is solemnized, events come to the
reader as a 'journal of all that passes in these first stages of my
happiness' (p. 475). Who does not question Richardson's wisdom in
furnishing us with almost two hundred pages of this account? All
narrative conflict dissolves into catalogues of household duties and
lists of do's and do not's for prospective housewives; several of these
passages in the novel could have been taken directly from any one of
a number of conduct books. As she takes over the text, furthermore,
Pamela's writing waxes suddenly stuffy, static, and both patronizing
and obsequious, displaying all those qualities, in short, that made
conduct books themselves seem so empty and tedious to read once
their historical moment had passed. No longer a form of resistance,
in other words, the female voice flattens into that of pure ideology.
From a historical perspective, however, it makes perfect sense that
Richardson should feel compelled to transform his first work of
fiction into such a static paradigm. The principle of reading that
governed programs for female education also provided him with
procedures for rewriting the country house in opposition to an
aristocratic tradition of letters.

It is well worth noting how such a reordering of the household
uses certain features of the aristocratic country house in order to
render the existing mode of kinship relations obsolete. One might
remark that Mr. B himself renounces the desire he once found
perfectly appropriate for a master to hold for a servant girl, and he
does so in terms that put such desire in the past: 'O how heartily I
despise all my former pursuits, and headstrong appetites! What joys,
what true joys, flow from virtuous love! joys which the narrow soul

of the libertine cannot take in, nor his thoughts conceive! and which I myself, whilst a libertine, had not the least notion of!' (p. 379). The 'joys' of which he speaks have little to do with the pleasures of the flesh as the bedroom that formerly provided a setting for narrative events disappears entirely from the printed page as it comes to occupy a blank space between two of Pamela's journal entries. The more expansive joys to which Mr. B refers are diffused throughout the household as its time and space are reorganized under Pamela's supervision.

Before Pamela assumes control of the household, its organization resembles nothing so much as a paranoid conspiracy. For as Pamela's writing exposes the secrets of life within the aristocratic household, Richardson turns the place into a theater for sexual intrigue. Household personnel are bound only by the principle of satisfying their master's desire. Time as well as space and human labor are devoted to serving this single end. According to the emergent domestic doctrine, however, this principle of order actually produces disorder. As Pamela observes:

> By this we may see . . . of what force example is, and what is in the power of the heads of families to do: And this shews, that evil examples, in superiors, are doubly pernicious, and doubly culpable, because such persons are bad *themselves*, and not only do no good, but much *harm* to others.
>
> (pp. 399–400)

When Pamela becomes mistress of the household, on the other hand, the servants are ruled by her moral example rather than by the sheer force of political loyalty and economic power. Because a well-regulated household depends entirely on the moral qualities of the female in charge, it cannot succumb to the double tyranny of male desire and aristocratic whim. As Pamela describes the relationship between the order of the household and her own qualities of mind, they are clearly one and the same:

> In short, I will endeavor, as much as I can, that good servants shall find in me a kind encourager; indifferent ones be made better, by inspiring them with a laudable emulation; and bad ones, if not too bad in nature, and quite reclaimable, reformed by kindness, expostulation, and even proper menaces, if necessary; but most by a good example.
>
> (p. 350)

Those who have defended her honor fall into the first category; those who have not fall into the third, and nary a one, not even the odious

237

Mrs. Jewkes, proves to be beyond the power of Pamela's redemptive example. With this, the place ceases to operate in the manner of a paranoid conspiracy and readily converts to rational order.

Several strategies of this order deserve our attention. These strategies develop out of the narrative combat between modes of writing. They constitute a process of feminization that the conduct books, by virtue of their exclusive focus on female matters, do not have to put into force. These are strategies, in other words, that reorganize the manor house according to the principles of domestic economy [. . .] Now a proselytizer of domestic virtue himself, Mr. B explains the reforms that must be effected in a country house such as his. Of women to the manor born, he says, 'they generally act in such a manner, as if they seemed to think it the privilege of birth and fortune, to turn day into night, and night into day, and are seldom stirring till it is time to sit down to dinner; and so all the good old family rules are reversed' (p. 389). Thus to the woman of his own caste he attributes habits that disrupt the natural order of things; to the modern woman, on the other hand, he grants the power to restore order by inverting the patterns established by the idleness and amusement of the aristocratic woman. Even though it is no longer permissible for Pamela to labor, her hours are now more rigidly regulated than before, the principle being that, as Mr. B explains, 'man is as frail a piece of machinery as any clock-work whatever; and, by irregularity, is as subject to be disordered' (p. 390). Indeed each hour of the day well into the evening is accounted for mostly in this way: 'You will then have several useful hours more to employ yourself in, as you shall best like; and I would generally go to supper by eight' (pp. 389–90). This dramatizes nothing else so much as the total reorganization of leisure time toward which the conduct books also aspired.

Curiously enough, such reorganization is accomplished in the name of the old aristocratic ideal of hospitality. If Pamela keeps to a routine, Mr. B explains, then 'whomsoever I bring home with me to my table, you'll be in readiness to receive them; and will not want to make those foolish apologies to unexpected visitors, that carry with them reflection on the conduct of those who make them' (p. 389). The well-ordered house will, in short, be the more able to extend the tradition of hospitality to any and all who require it. But the failure to extend hospitality, we should note, does not point to a man's lack of position and wealth so much as to his wife's lack of domestic virtue; such lapses 'carry with them reflection on the conduct of those who make them.' The same principle dictates Pamela's appearance. She is not to display herself for guests, but always to exhibit 'that sweet ease in your dress or behavior, which you are so happy mistress of' (p. 389). What most clearly distinguishes Mr. B's dress code from that issued by royal proclamation during the Renaissance is the careful attention to facial expression, for there the true qualities of the woman, as opposed to her rank, may be noted.

> I expect from you, whoever comes to my house, that you accustom
> yourself to one even, uniform complaisance: That no frown take
> place on your brow: That however ill or well provided we may
> be for their reception, you shew no flutter or discomposure: That
> whomever you may have in your company at the time, you signify
> not, by the least reserved look, that the stranger is come upon you
> unseasonably, or at a time you wished he had not. But be facetious,
> kind, obliging to all; and, if to one more than another, to such as
> have the least reason to expect it from you, or who are most
> inferior at the table; for thus will you, my Pamela, cheer the
> doubting mind, quiet the uneasy heart, and diffuse ease, pleasure,
> and tranquillity, around my board.
>
> (p. 393)

Richardson's notion of largesse does not dispense with the aristocratic figure of hospitality, that is, the generous patron's table. But its content has indeed been modified along with the woman who oversees the table. To those who congregate around the table, the modern patron yields up copious sentiments rather than either the fruits of his bountiful estate or the wealth of his ample purse. In this way, Richardson transforms the patron's table from a setting that displays traditionally masculine forms of power into a therapeutic setting whose riches are distributed on a purely psychological level – through displays of militant cheerfulness. He accomplishes this simply by transforming Pamela's passive and essentially defensive virtues from nouns into verbs that *'cheer* the doubting mind, *quiet* the uneasy heart, and *diffuse ease, pleasure, and tranquillity,* around my board' (italics mine).

In virtually doing away with traditional patronage rites as the means of distributing wealth, Richardson creates a compensatory form of generosity. His notion of charity filters the economic power of the male through the sympathy of the female, and the excesses of his estate become the overflowing of her heart and trickle down in this form to needy people lower down the social ladder. Thus Pamela enjoins Mr. B to

> look through your poor acquaintances and neighbours, and let me
> have a list of such honest industrious poor, as may be true objects
> of charity, and have no other assistance; particularly such as are

blind, lame, or sickly, with their several cases; and also such poor families and housekeepers as are reduced by misfortunes, as ours was, and where a great number of children may keep them from rising to a state of tolerable comfort: And I will choose as well as I can; for I long to be making a beginning, with the kind quarterly benevolence my dear good benefactor has bestowed upon me for such good purposes.

(pp. 500–501)

We should note how Pamela defines the whole category of who should benefit from wealth that has been diverted from a patronage system into one based on the principle of charity. Only those deserve attention who are unable to provide a subsistence living for themselves, and this mobility must be due to some deficiency in themselves rather than in the conditions under which they must labor. Before they become objects of charity, these people must be listed on a case by case basis, the reason for their poverty so designated, and the amount of money distributed accordingly. This is to say that Richardson represents those who depend on the generosity of the wealthy not as a social group or faction that must be appeased, but as reckless children who require the care of responsible parents. Such a view of the distribution of wealth can make sense only if Richardson detaches the wealth from its source in inherited property, profession, and region. To do so, he again takes a page from the conduct books. To remove the wealth of the estate from the patronage system and distribute it according to the principle of charity, he has the male hand over part of his money to the female. As Mr. B explains,

God has blessed me with a very good estate, and all of it in a prosperous condition, and generally well tenanted. I lay up money every year, and have, besides, large sums in government and other securities; so that you will find, what I have hitherto promised, is very short of that proportion of my substance, which, as my dearest wife, you have a right to.

(p. 387)

By means of these propositions that Mr. B offers Pamela, Richardson constructs a domestic economy that appears to be independent of the political categories maintained by an earlier patronage system.

I call attention to this economic exchange in order to demonstrate how Richardson's first novel revises the sexual contract. In addition to Mr. B's specifications for what he expects in a wife, this offer constitutes his own revision of the contract originally offered to and rejected by Pamela. As he explains in making these demands, 'All that I wish, is to find my proposals agreeable to you; and if my *first* are not, my *second* shall be, if I can know what you want' (p. 386). In the course of negotiating the ideal relationship to which both parties can fully consent, Mr. B makes all the same offers that he put forth in the first contract and that would have made her his mistress. If anything, the first contract was more lucrative for Pamela than the second. We must conclude that Pamela's resistance to the first contract – resistance prompted by nothing short of the need, she implies, to preserve her very existence – was aimed only at revising the nature of the sexual contract. If Pamela is the first to find fault with the spirit in which his first proposal was made, then Mr. B is the first to explain where the source of its error lies: 'We people of fortune, or such as are born to large expectations, of both sexes, are generally educated wrong.' This is one of the lessons, he acknowledges, that may be gleaned from Pamela's journal: 'We are so headstrong, so violent in our wills, that we very little bear control' (p. 470).

With their desires so little constrained, any relationship between a man and woman so poorly educated would be no less tempestuous than each of the parties is in and of itself. When, Mr. B continues,

> a *wife* is looked out for: convenience, or birth, or fortune, are the first motives, affection the last (if it is at all consulted): and two people thus educated, thus trained up, in a course of unnatural gratitude, and who have been headstrong torments to every one who has had a share in their education, as well as to those to whom they owe their being, are brought together; and what can be expected, but that they should pursue, and carry on, the same comfortable conduct in matrimony, and join most heartily to plague one another?
>
> (p. 471)

Given that Mr. B's second proposal resembles his first offer to Pamela, it transforms that first attempt at sexual relations between master and servant – the proposed exchange of money for pleasure – into a model for legitimate monogamy that criticizes the traditional marriage of 'convenience.' We see the modern notion of love emerging in the statement above, as Richardson makes 'convenience,' 'birth,' and 'fortune' equivalent and puts them in a category that excludes 'affection.' Affection cannot coexist, this novel argues, with an economic motive for marriage, and neither fortune nor birth can therefore constitute particularly desirable features in a woman, even though they remain unqualified as such in a man. As Mr. B explains, the exchange between male and female is not primarily an economic one:

I have ample possessions for us both; and you deserve to share them with me; and you shall do it, with as little reserve, as if you had brought me what the world reckons an equivalent: for, as to my own opinion, you bring me what is infinitely more valuable, an experienced truth, a well-tried virtue, and a wit and behaviour more than equal to the state you will be placed in.

(p. 355)

Here the exchange is one between gendered parties – a wedding of her moral authority to his particular economic practices and social place. Together they compose the same domestic world that conduct books were also intent upon making attractive to their readership.

The key to the success of this model resides in the fact that while it requires the female to submit to the male, it does not ask her to adopt the practices of the dominant class. Pamela's adamant refusal to accept the conditions of Mr. B's first offer of a contract establishes this difference, for her submission to the second proposal is as complete as her rejection of the first. The point is to distinguish the unnatural submission of a household servant to her master in an erotic adventure from the natural subordination of female to male in an ideal marriage. While it is good to obey a kind husband, it is no longer acceptable to gratify the libertine desires associated with the old aristocracy. Although the reformed country house is one where a rigid hierarchy has been restored, this principle of hierarchy opposes that which organizes the political world outside. Domestic order is not based on one's relative socioeconomic position so much as on moral qualities of mind. This principle enters into the household through the female and reforms that household by means of her writing. As if the reader did not understand the difference between the two contracts, or how the second one reorganized the whole concept of the domestic domain to situate a woman at its center, Richardson recapitulates this logic of the figure in the encounter between Pamela and Mr. B's sister, Lady Davers.

Lady Davers speaks for an archaic contract that, according to Mr. B, constitutes an economic and political alliance rather than a bond of affection. She feels that the family name has been tarnished by Pamela's claim that Mr. B did not simply take her to bed but actually married his servant. Of Mr. B's letter testifying to this marriage, Lady Davers tells Pamela, 'you shewed it me, to upbraid me with his stooping to such painted dirt, to the disgrace of a family, ancient and untainted beyond most in the kingdom' (p. 417). To convince her that Pamela is not only Mr. B's wife but also the more desirable woman for a man of his station to marry requires nothing short of converting Lady Davers to a way of thinking that contradicts her own interests and very nature as a woman of the ruling class. This is something that does not take place within the pages of the novel but at some later time when Lady Davers has read Pamela's journal. Even while testifying to the recalcitrance of this kind of woman, however, Richardson still has her acknowledge Pamela's superiority by acceding to the terms of Pamela's sentimental writing. Of her successor's entry into polite society, Lady Davers simply says, 'I shall not give you my company when you make your appearance. Let your own merit make all your Bedfordshire neighbours your friends, as it has done here, by your Lincolnshire ones; and you'll have no need of my countenance, nor any body else's' (p. 466).

It is important to note that such an acknowledgment of Pamela's moral authority leaves the old categories untouched when determining the status of the male. For the acknowledgment suggests only that her possession of certain emotional qualities determines the status of the female. Even so, the change of heart on the part of Lady Davers as well as among the polite folk of Bedfordshire and Lincolnshire constitutes an important modification of prevailing kinship relations. The modification alone explains the novel's obsession with the nuances of female subjectivity. Such an obsession is demonstrated as well by the conduct books from which Richardson drew his strategies for replacing the reigning cultural ideal with another. When Lady Davers belligerently inquires where 'can the difference be between a beggar's son married by a lady, or a beggar's daughter made a gentleman's wife,' Mr. B provides a most concise description of the modification in which the entire body of feminine writing conspired: 'Then I'll tell you, replied he; the difference is, a man ennobles the woman he takes, be she *who* she will; and adopts her into his *own* rank, be it *what* it will: but a woman, though ever so nobly born, debases herself by a mean marriage, and descends from her *own* rank to *his* she stoops to' (p. 447). This is the principle of hypergamy, or marriage 'up,' which both cuts the female off from the political power that might inhere in her by birth and, at the same time, enables the family to achieve higher status through her, should she marry into a higher social position. On Pamela's power to effect a marriage that moves her from the bottom of the social ladder to the top depends the conversion of the aristocracy and upper gentry to her domestic values, which is actually the formation of a new ruling class.

In addition to the other chunks of a cultural argument that for modern readers no longer needs to be waged, the last section of the novel contains several bizarre encounters between Pamela and the social world into which marriage has thrust her. As she relates to the company of polite society assembled at Lincolnshire how rudely

Lady Davers had behaved towards her, the spirit of reform ripples outward in circles radiating from her center. After seeing Pamela's willing compliance to her husband's wishes, one lady allows 'that it will be the interest of all the gentlemen to bring their ladies into an intimacy with one that can give them such a good example' (p. 301). But the gentlemen are also instructed by the example of her suffering; in the words of one, they 'are resolved to turn over a new leaf with our wives, and *your* lord shall shew us the way' (p. 426). Furthermore, although contained within the relationship of husband and wife, reform is not without overt political ramifications. A game of cards at this gathering provides an unsubtle means of translating the change in sexual relations into political terms, and thus, one may note, a moral basis for domestic authority is extended into the realm of politics by way of thinly disguised allegory. Mr. B has this to say 'in regard to the ace: . . . by the ace I have always thought the laws of the land denoted; and as the ace is above the king or queen, and wins them, I think the law should be thought so too.' But this, Richardson hastens to add, does not make his reformed hero a Tory, for according to Pamela's master, 'I think the distinction of *whig* and *tory* odious; and love the one or the other only as they are honest and worthy men; and never have (and never shall, hope) given a vote, but according to what I thought was for the public good, let either *whig* or *tory* propose it' (pp. 428–29). Although it has all the earmarks of offering up a mediation between contending social groups, then, the union of Pamela and Mr. B in fact does no such thing. Instead, their marriage calls into being a concept of political authority that is neither Tory nor Whig because it is other than both. Resting on the virtues of honesty and self-worth rather than on 'honours,' such power originates in the female from whom it spills over into the political world. This, we might say, is Richardson imagining the power of a new hegemony, which asserts the good of England in terms that somehow transcend those of social experience as he knew it to be. For his ability to imagine such an ideal political situation depends entirely on men forgetting traditional political categories and understanding all social relationships in domestic terms.

Far from making claims for this power unconsciously, Richardson seems highly aware of the politics of his rhetoric of reform. The last two hundred pages or so of his first novel indicate, if nothing else, that he is playing a sophisticated ideological game that repackages political resistance as the subjectivity of a woman. It does so in order to translate the political strategy of a decided minority into an effective rhetorical tactic. That he has this act of translation very much in mind is as clear as his revision of Mr. B's original offer of a contract to Pamela. In each case, Richardson makes the changes

effected by Pamela as clear as the print on the page. Perhaps
strangest of all the curious rites that he puts Pamela through in his
apotheosis of the housewife is the dinner party that Mr. B stages with
his friends and neighbors and the clergyman Williams. To entertain
the company thus assembled, Mr. B has Williams read the 'common
translation' of the 137th Psalm a verse or two at a time. This is
followed by Mr. B's reading of the same verses as translated in
Pamela's letters. One verse, first from the Bible and then from
Pamela's journal, offers a fair sample of her turn of phrase:

> IV.
> Alas! said we; who can once frame
> His heavy heart to sing
> The praises of our living God,
> Thus under a strange king?

> IV.
> Alas! said I, how can I frame
> My heavy heart to sing,
> Or tune my mind, while thus enthrall'd
> By such a wicked thing?

(pp. 335–36)

If, at an earlier moment in history, the translation of the Bible into
English transferred moral authority from the church to the state,
then here was an equally significant shift in the structure of power
in England. Pamela's verse translates the historical and political
meaning of the 'common translation' of a psalm into terms at once
personal and universal. This is to mark symbolically a shift in moral
authority from the male institutions of state to the head of household.
Furthermore, although it is Mr. B who gives voice to the new
language of morality, he must read Pamela's writing in order to do
so. In contrast with the earlier Puritan, then, this head of household
is authorized by a woman's writing rather than by the word of God.
One might even go so far as to say that the Puritan revolution, which
failed to seize political control through force as well as polemical
writing, in fact succeeded in the eighteenth century sentimental
fiction that delegates control to the female.

Such a shift in gender designates a change not only in the locus
of political power but also – and just as profoundly – in its strategic
target and procedures. The shift in Pamela's verse to the first-person
pronoun transfers moral authority from a domestic framework to
the framework of female subjectivity, which is surely to wrest such
authority from the male institutions of church and state. This is not

only to signal the birth of a new ideology whereby power arises from within the individual. It is also to suggest that such power operates by reconstituting the subject out of words. But to have such political power – as is also made clear by Pamela's act of translation – words must conceal it. They must conceal all signs of operating in the name of a particular interest group and take on the features of the individual. They must work by an example that is at once highly personal, in other words, and yet applicable to virtually everyone. All this Richardson understood perfectly well, and if we deny him such knowledge, it is only because the tradition of literary criticism has not discovered what someone so ordinary as Richardson already knew by reading and writing during the period when this power was emerging but had not yet become the dominant form of social control.

Notes

1. For an account of the early eighteenth century tradition that linked the novel with lowlife, see Lennard Davis, *Factual Fictions: The Origins of the English Novel* (New York: Columbia University Press, 1983), pp. 123–37. For the objection to the novel because of its quasi-erotic appeal, see John Richetti, *Popular Fiction Before Richardson: Narrative Patterns, 1700–1734* (Oxford: Clarendon, 1969). In an issue of Addison and Steele's *Spectator*, for example, Mr. Spectator warns readers about the perils of May, advising that women 'be in a particular Manner how they meddle with Romances, Chocolates, Novels, and the like Inflamers, which I look upon to be very dangerous to be made use of during this great Carnival of Nature,' quoted in *Four Before Richardson: Selected English Novels 1720–1727*, ed. William H. McBurney (Lincoln: University of Nebraska Press, 1963), p. xi. The novel was considered a use of language – often written by women – that was designed to inflame the passions. Modern readers have noted this quality in the language of many of the novels written by women in the first half of the eighteenth century. Patricia Meyer Spacks thus describes several works by Eliza Hayward and Mary Manley as 'semi-pornographic novels,' in 'Every Woman is at Heart a Rake,' *Eighteenth Century Studies*, 8 (1974–75), 32. It was the pornographic element in some of their language that led William Forsyth in 1871 to refrain from quoting examples of pre-Richardsonian fiction for his book *The Novels and Novelists of the Eighteenth Century in Illustration of the Manners and Morals of the Age* (1871; rpt. Port Washington, New York: Kennikat, 1971). He claims that he cannot cite examples of the coarse manners of women novelists before Richardson: 'Necessarily I cannot give quotation to show this for in doing so I should myself offend' (p. 162). See also Jean B. Kear, 'The Fallen Woman from the Perspective of Five Early Eighteenth Century Women Novelists,' *Studies in Eighteenth-Century Culture*, 10 (1981), 457–68, and Ruth Perry, *Women, Letters, and the Novel* (New York: AMS Press, 1980). For a list of what were considered novels before the category was redefined, see William H. McBurney, *A Check List of English Prose Fiction, 1700–1739* (Cambridge: Harvard University Press, 1960).

2. Thomas Broadhurst, *Advice to Young Ladies on the Improvement of the Mind and Conduct of Life* (London, 1810), p. 53.

3. Terry Eagleton has discussed the role of Richardson's fiction in seizing hold of the signs and symbols of the dominant culture and putting them to use on behalf of another set of socioeconomic interests. *The Rape of Clarissa* (Minneapolis: University of Minnesota Press, 1982), pp. 30–39. Ann Douglas has shown how feminization operated as a middle-class strategy within a Protestant culture. *The Feminization of American Culture* (New York: Avon, 1978).

4. For a discussion of the immediate popularity of *Pamela*, see T. C. Duncan Eaves and Ben D. Kimpel, *Samuel Richardson: A Biography* (Oxford: Clarendon, 1971), pp. 119–53.

5. Kathleen M. Davis, 'The Sacred Condition of Equality – How Original were Puritan Doctrines of Marriage?' *Social History*, 5 (1977), 570. Davis quotes this list from John Dod and Robert Cleaver, *A Godly Forme of Householde Gouernment* (London, 1614).

6. Robert Cleaver, *A Godly Forme of Householde Gouernment* (London, 1598), p. 4.

7. Samuel Richardson, *Pamela, or Virtue Rewarded* (New York: W. W. Norton, 1958), pp. 198–99. Citations of the text are to this edition.

8. For this understanding of Richardson's political role, I am indebted to Terry Eagleton's discussion of Richardson as a middle-class intellectual. Borrowing Gramsci's notion of the 'organic intellectual,' Eagleton argues convincingly that Richardson's novels 'are not mere images of conflicts fought out on another terrain, representations of a history which happens elsewhere; they are themselves a material part of those struggles, pitched standards around which battle is joined, instruments which help to constitute social interests rather than lenses which reflect them. These novels are an agent, rather than an account, of the English bourgeoisie's attempt to wrest a degree of ideological hegemony from the aristocracy in the decades which follow the political settlement of 1688.' *The Rape of Clarissa*, p. 4.

9. Lawrence Stone and Jeanne C. Fawtier Stone's *An Open Elite? England 1540–1880* (Oxford: Clarendon, 1984) grants this issue all the complexity it deserves. The gentry was an extremely fluid socioeconomic group, they explain, from which one could decline by necessity to the status of a merchant, and to which tradesmen, on the other hand, could rise given sufficient prosperity. In 1710, Steele apparently claimed, 'as did many others before and after him, that "the best of our peers have often joined themselves to the daughter of very ordinary tradesmen upon . . . valuable considerations"' (p. 20). The Stones isolate three factors contributing to this unstable social situation: 'The first was the alleged fact, that merchants were busy buying landed estates, building seats, and turning themselves into squires or nobles. The second was another alleged fact, that the declining gentry often restored their fortunes by putting their sons, especially their younger sons, into trade. The third was an alleged social attitude, the relatively easy acceptance of self-made men, as companions or marriage partners, by persons of genteel birth and elite status' (p. 20). Later citations of the text are to this edition.

10. On the relation between writing and the 'will' in *Clarissa*, Tony Tanner observes that 'the isolated writer is secure within her writing, whereas the speaker/listener has to negotiate in (Clarissa's case) the always possible dangers of physical propinquity. Thus part of her final triumph is to *write* her *will* (not just the document of bequest, but *will* in all senses of the word), since, physically speaking, she could never live it. *This* will, with all its positives and imperatives, cannot be negated or gainsaid.' *Adultery in the Novel: Contract and Transgression* (Baltimore: Johns Hopkins University Press, 1979), p. 111.

11. Of the various attempts to possess Pamela's writing, Lennard Davis notes, 'Pamela-the-heroine becomes replaced by Pamela-the-linguistic simulacrum.' *Factual Fictions*, p. 184.

12. Eaves and Kimpel's *Samuel Richardson: A Biography* documents both his contacts with people of higher station and his many friendships with women. See William Beatty Warner, *Reading Clarissa: The Struggles of Interpretation* (New Haven: Yale University Press, 1979), pp. 143–218, for an ingenious account of the games Richardson played in making revisions that would tantalize readers.

13. Voyeurism had long been a standard feature of the kind of novel Richardson claimed he was not writing. By shifting the voyeuristic gaze from Pamela's body to her writing, Richardson is quite literally shifting Mr. B out of the narrative world from which he comes and into what Richardson claims is 'a new species of writing.' The shift of the gaze from male to female, as I see it, changes the very nature of the gaze from voyeurism to supervision and, with it, the role of the novel from semi-scandalous tale-telling to demonstrations of exemplary behavior. For discussion of the voyeurism in novels before Richardson, see Ruth Perry, *Women, Letters, and the Novel*, pp. 157–67. 'A new species of writing' is Richardson's phrase in a letter to Aaron Hill, *Selected Letters*, ed. John Carroll (Oxford: Clarendon, 1964), p. 41. On the meaning of the phrase itself, see William Park, 'What was new about the "New Species of Writing"?' *Studies in the Novel*, 2 (1970), 112–30, and his 'Romance and the "New" Novels of Richardson, Fielding, and Smollett,' *Studies in English Literature*, 16 (1976), 437–50.

10 Revelation of the Heart through Entrapment and Trial

Ann Jessie Van Sant

Ann Jessie Van Sant belongs to a strong critical tradition of linking Richardson with the development of a sentimental culture from the mid eighteenth century onwards and she pursues an interdisciplinary approach which links the history of science with literary concerns. In her book, Van Sant argues that sentimentalism must be understood in relation to changing conceptions of human physiology in the eighteenth century, when there was an attempt to taxonomize the physical basis of human feeling. In this chapter, Van Sant also expands on her view that sentimentalism was caught in a paradox: for great feeling and sympathy to be invoked, it was often necessary to indulge in spectacles of others' pain, such as Clarissa's. In some ways, Van Sant suggests, for all his talk about virtue, Richardson's rhetorical implication in scenes of distress and psychological torture anticipates Sade's experiments in sensation.

In one of his *Hypochondriack* papers, James Boswell speculates somewhat wishfully, 'It would truly be very pretty and amusing if our bodies were transparent, so that we could see one anothers sentiments and passions as we see bees in a glass hive.'[1] Boswell's reference to the glass hive suggests that he has taken the idea from Laurence Sterne – were there a '*glass* in the human breast,' Tristram Shandy says, 'nothing more would have been wanting, in order to have taken a man's character, but to have taken a chair and gone softly, as you would to a dioptrical bee-hive, and looked in, – viewed the soul stark naked . . .'[2] Alexander Pope, writing to Charles Jervas, indicates a similar desire for direct access to the heart: 'The old project of a Window on the bosom to render the Soul of Man visible, is what every honest friend has manifold reason to wish for.'[3] Pope uses the same figure in a letter to Lady Mary Wortley Montagu: 'If Momus his project had taken of having Windows in our breasts, I should be for carrying it further and making those windows

Casements: that while a man showd his Heart to all the world, he might do something more for his friends, e'en take it out, and trust it to their handling.'[4]

Fusing the literal and metaphorical meanings of *heart*, the image of a window in the breast makes the soul, or interior being, anatomically accessible. This image for interior revelation originates in satire as an image for interior exposure. In Lucian's *Hermotimus*, Momus is reported to have criticized Hephaestus for creating man without 'a window in his chest, so that it could be opened and everybody could see his thoughts and intentions and whether he was telling the truth or not.'[5] Sterne and Boswell combine Momus's window with a modern scientific contrivance (the dioptrical beehive) while Pope retains the architectural and anatomical suggestiveness of the image. But all three writers use the window-on-the-breast metaphor to convey a sense of predicament on account of the impossibility of direct access to thoughts and emotions. Transparency of body would figuratively solve the problem by transferring to mental and passional experience the sort of substantiality and visibility that belong to physical organs. The uses of this image are one indication of the eighteenth-century interest in interior discovery.

The same metaphor was sufficiently anatomically suggestive to be useful to a medical writer studying the lungs: 'It has not yet been granted to any one,' wrote John Mayow in 1688, 'to fit a *window to the breast* and redeem from darkness the profounder secrets of nature.'[6] Like Pope, Sterne, and Boswell, Mayow expresses the desirability and the difficulty of gaining access to concealed material. The use of the metaphor in physical as well as psychological contexts suggests that interior experience and interior function are conceptually similar because similarly hidden from view. In this chapter, I will continue to draw on the analogy implied in these uses of the window-on-the-heart metaphor. I argue that there are important similarities in the methods used to gain access to the two kinds of interior space, and, further, that the procedures necessary to remedy natural opaqueness are far from benign. That the desire for access to interior experience is not always amiable, Lady Mary intimates when in response to Wortley Montagu's desire 'to see into [her] heart,' she suggests that such a privilege granted to him would be painful to her: 'I am a little surpriz'd at your curiosity to know what passes in my Heart . . . except you propose to your selfe a peice of ill naturd satisfaction in finding me very much disquieted. Pray, *which way* would you see into my Heart?' (emphasis added).[7]

Samuel Richardson's novelistic aims and general talents are frequently described in terms that amount to *the discovery or revelation of the heart*, particularly the heart of women. 'No body, like you,' writes Frances Sheridan, 'has the art to penetrate into the secrets, and unwind the mazes of a female heart.'[8] Samuel Johnson's well-known preference for Richardson over Henry Fielding rests on the former's ability to 'dive into the recesses of the human heart.'[9] And Anna Laetitia Barbauld, in her 'Sketch of Richardson's Life and Writings,' also describes Richardson's ability as a novelist by saying that 'his business was not only with the human heart, but with the female heart' and, in the same essay, that he 'lays open . . . the secret recesses of the heart.'[10] Richardson allows Lovelace to attribute more or less the same propensity to himself (he delights in 'trac[ing] human nature, and more particularly female nature, through its most *secret recesses*'[11]), and Lovelace's overall aim in the novel is to gain access to Clarissa's heart: he says that he will 'enter her heart' (II, 222), that he will 'unlock and open' it (II, 342), and, perhaps more tellingly, that he will '*cut through a rock of ice*' to it (II, 316).[12]

The recesses – or comparable terms for interior spaces – were also used in physical contexts. Mayow says that the lungs are 'placed in a *recess* so sacred and hidden that nature would seem to have specially withdrawn this part both from the eyes and from the intellect' (emphasis added).[13] Oliver Goldsmith, using the term more generally for any of Nature's concealments, writes in his 'Survey of Experimental Philosophy' that the ancients 'were but little employed in thus [by experimentation] diving into the *secret recesses of Nature*' (emphasis added).[14] Similarly, Thomas Willis, in the dedicatory epistle to his *Anatomy of the Brain and Nerves*, declares that he will enter the mind by unlocking it: 'I had resolved to unlock the *secret places* of Man's Mind, and to look into the living and breathing Chapel of the Deity (as far as our weakness was able) . . .' (emphasis added).[15] Physical and nonphysical 'spaces' were then extensively related by the figurative language used to describe them.

Many of the terms used to refer to gaining access to these spaces – *penetrate, unwind, dive, trace, open, enter, unlock* – imply an innocuous mode of entry. Willis, however, while using the word *unlocking*, refers to an anatomy, a procedure that his architectural metaphor conceals.[16] Similarly, the metaphorical diving of Goldsmith's scientists is carried out by experimentation, a process that he compares to torture: 'At length . . . man . . . would set himself down, not only to collect new observations, in order to enlarge his history of Nature, but in a manner to torture Nature by *Experiments*, and oblige her to give up those secrets, which she had hitherto kept concealed.'[17]

As these metaphors fail to delineate processes for scientific discovery, so also the metaphors used by and about Richardson for the discovery of the heart frequently conceal rather than reveal the implicit violence of his method. That violence is, however, suggested

in his own prefatory discussion of the novel: ' "Much more lively
and affecting," ' he says, quoting from one of Belford's letters to
Lovelace, ' "must be the style of those who write in the height of
present distress, the mind tortured by pangs of uncertainty" ' (I, xv).
In her essay 'An Inquiry into Those Kinds of Distress Which Excite
Agreeable Sensations,' Barbauld discusses modern writers' attempts
to give pleasure through the 'representation of distress.' 'An author
of this class sits down, pretty much like an inquisitor,' she writes,
'to compute how much suffering he can inflict upon the hero of his
tale before he makes an end of him; with this difference, indeed, that
the inquisitor only tortures those who are at least reputed criminals;
whereas the writer generally chooses the most excellent character
in his piece for the subject of his persecution.'[18] What I argue here
is that the cruelty of Richardson's method, the computation of pain,
should be seen in the context of investigation. Expressed
metaphorically as diving into the heart's secret recesses, laying it
open, penetrating its secrets, or unwinding its mazes, that method
has much in common with the investigative methods of science,
particularly the sensibility experiments, which, as we have seen,
combine invasive entry with provocation of pain.[19]

By using the term *violence*, I do not mean simply to point to the
cruelty that the novel itself makes explicit ('We begin when boys
with birds,' says Lovelace, 'and, when grown up, go on to women;
and both, perhaps, in turn, experience our sportive cruelty') and that
numerous critics have discussed.[20] Instead, I want to draw attention
to the novel's alignment of sexual cruelty and investigation. Further,
as I hope to show, the issue of novelistic method is of particular
interest in *Clarissa*, since by incorporating it into the novel in
Lovelace's machinations, Richardson brought it onto the same plane,
so to speak, as that on which the characters 'exist.'

The key term for Richardson's method is *trial*, which, whatever
one's reading of *Clarissa*, requires elucidation. In its judicial sense,[21]
it provides the framework for the novel: Clarissa's account originates
from Anna Howe's request that she provide a potential defense,
and the collection and publication of the letters substitute for a legal
prosecution of Lovelace. Furthermore, Clarissa's preparation for
defense coincides with conventional spiritual practices – she lives
defensively, not only to be able to account for herself in the court
of public opinion but to be able to present her case before God. As
defined from within, the novel thus serves as a judicial *demonstration*
of Clarissa's innocence and Lovelace's crime.

In addition to the judicial trial, however, there is a different
sense of trial that generates much of the fiction.[22] Clarissa's need
for a defense, as well as the requests for advice that characterize her

narrative, is subsequent to, and occurs as a result of, Lovelace's inventive activity, which is devoted to her trial. This trial is set up to discover whether Clarissa is capable of unguarded desire, to discover whether she is a woman. Carried out by isolation and provocation and characterized by the creation of suffering, this trial has the rape as its final stage. The originating letter of the fiction is Anna Howe's request for a defense 'lest anything unhappy should fall out,' but the conceptual source of the fiction lies in Lovelace's letters to Belford explaining his presence in the Harlowe house, his romantic devotion to Clarissa, and his intention to *try* her virtue, a project that is both heroizing and investigative.

'Has her virtue ever been *proved*?' Lovelace writes from St. Albans. 'Who has dared to try her virtue? . . . To the test then' (II, 36). The vocabulary of trial as used here by Lovelace – *prove, try, test* – is based principally on a physical, scientific process – the test of metals. A *test* is a pot or vessel, orginally made of earthenware, in which gold or silver alloys and ore are refined. A definition given in Blount's *Glossary* (1674) illustrates the literal meaning from which Lovelace's uses of the terms derive: ' "*Test*," is a broad instrument . . . on which refiners do fine, refine, and part silver and gold from other metals, or as we say, *put them to the test* or trial.'[23]

The refinement of gold or silver has traditionally provided the figurative vocabulary for the persecution on which spiritual heroism depends.[24] Lovelace makes clear that his own trial is a means of heroizing Clarissa, not only by claiming that he wants to 'exalt the sex,' but by making his series of trials parallel to Satan's trial of Job: 'Satan, whom thou mayest, if thou wilt, in this case call my instigator, put the good man of old upon the severest trials. "To his behaviour under these trials that good man owed his honour and his future rewards" ' (II, 40). Lovelace's persecutory trial, dependent on suffering as a process of refinement, works on one level to reinforce the judicial demonstration: Lovelace's heroizing claims are Richardson's means of articulating his own novelistic intention – to demonstrate through her suffering that Clarissa is gold.

Lovelace's claim to use trial for heroizing aims is, however, a thinly veiled justification for an *investigative* trial, also based on the test of metals: '[A]m I not bringing virtue to the touchstone with a view to exalt it?' (II, 36). The touchstone is a dark stone used to test 'gold or silver alloys by the colour of the streak produced by rubbing them upon it.'[25] It is an instrument not of refining or purifying but of discovery. Though potentially heroizing, the figurative meaning of touchstone ('that which serves to test or try the genuineness of anything') remains investigative – and is in fact close to the definition of *experiment*. A comparison with one of Johnson's illustrative quotations in the *Dictionary* reveals the similarity: 'When we are searching out the nature or properties of any being by various methods of trial, this sort of observation is called *experiment*.'[26]

'Lovelace, indeed,' writes Barbauld, 'who has a very bad opinion of women, and thinks that hardly any woman can resist him, talks of trying her virtue, and speaks as if he expected her to fail in the trial. But, surely, the virtue of Clarissa could never have been in the smallest danger . . . It is absurd, therefore, in Lovelace to speak of trying her chastity.'[27] Barbauld is right of course – reading Richardson's demonstrative narrative. That narrative rests, however, on an investigative process. Richardson, having created Clarissa, presumably knew the quality of her chastity, but his demonstration of it to his readers rests on Lovelace's investigation.

The investigation that underlies the heroizing test is intended to discover whether Clarissa is a woman: '[A]llow me,' Lovelace says at St. Albans, 'to try if I cannot awaken the *woman* in her' (II, 42). And just before the rape: 'Is she not a woman?' (III, 190). Not only the aim but the continuing outlines of his project are investigative. It begins with an hypothesis (if Clarissa is a woman, she can be seduced), an hypothesis that requires repeated testing: 'Nor is *one* effort, *one* trial, to be sufficient. Why? Because a woman's heart may be at one time *adamant*, at another *wax*' (II, 41). The test requires not only continual repetition but continual observation: 'Let me begin then, as opportunity presents – I will, and watch her every step to find one sliding one; her every moment, to find the moment critical' (II, 42). And Lovelace himself, immediately after placing his test in a heroizing context, compares it with a proposed test of a woman's chastity in Ariosto, a test that he calls an experiment (II, 40).

Other readers have noticed a similarity between Richardson's narrative and an experiment. In his *Virtue in Distress*, R. F. Brissenden suggests that *Clarissa* is 'both a novel of ideas and something like a programmed experiment,' the purpose of which is

> to test to destruction certain notions – such as man's innate humanity – which are basic to sentimental morality. Almost as a spin-off from this experimental process he produces an account of the inner conflicts of morally sensitive individuals which for dramatic, psychological vividness and minuteness of detail is new in English fiction.[28]

The link between Richardson's novel and an experimental process seems to me more significantly related to method than to thematic content. Rather than an experiment to test sentimental ideas, the novel seems to me to have incorporated an experimental approach to character.[29]

Brissenden further points out that Richardson shares certain commitments with Albrecht von Haller: 'One cannot help being reminded of Richardson, similarly praising God and labouring for the benefit of mankind, as he pressed forward relentlessly to the tragic conclusion of *Clarissa*.'[30] '[I]t was only by insisting that the main purpose of his pathetic stories was a moral one,' Brissenden explains, 'that Richardson was able to justify, both to himself and his readers, the anguish he made them all suffer.'[31] Both novelist and scientist, in other words, reluctantly create suffering for the benefit of society. The similarity between novelist and scientist is not only that both create suffering for what they see as a beneficial purpose. More importantly, in my view, they are both interested in making a discovery through the pain they create. This common aim, rather than the moral intentions of the one and the utilitarian ends of the other, points to the conceptual similarity of their methods.[32]

Richardson's study of psychological sensibility, like Haller's investigation of physical sensibility, is accomplished by provoking pain. Haller located sensibility by touching, cutting, burning, and lacerating; Lovelace tries to locate Clarissa's concealed nature (her unguarded responses) through a psychological provocation of pain. In a letter to Lady Bradshaigh, Richardson implies such a process by using such terms as 'try her, vex her, plague and torment her worthy heart'[33] to describe the treatment Clarissa endures. He is protesting against the possibility of a happy ending and uses these terms not to characterize his own novelistic method but to reflect on would-be Lovelaces. Nevertheless, *trying, vexing, plaguing*, and *tormenting* are the psychological equivalents of Haller's physical procedures. The test of Clarissa derives from the vocabulary of metals, but the method of that test is the provocation of response.

The proposal scene at Mrs. Sorlings's house (II, 135–42), recorded at some length by both Clarissa and Lovelace, illustrates Lovelace's method. The word that reveals the provocative strategy is *tease*. Both their reports speak of his teasing as a method of exposure: it causes a confusion that allows him to 'gaze' upon her 'as if,' Clarissa writes, 'he would have looked me through'; 'My heart struggled violently between resentment and shame to be thus teased'; 'Surely he had not the insolence to *intend* to tease me, to see if I could be brought to speak what became me not to speak. But whether he had or not, it *did* tease me; insomuch that my very heart was fretted, and I broke out at last into fresh tears, and a declaration that I was very unhappy.'[34] Clarissa's language associates teasing not with a harmless and intimate exchange but with a struggle on her part against pain and exposure.

And in saying that Lovelace teased her 'insomuch that my very heart was fretted,' Clarissa uses language similar to the physical language of Robert Whytt: 'But, although the outer surface of the heart . . . ha[s] no great degree of sensibility, it will not follow, that [the] internal surface, where the natural *stimuli* exciting [its] motions act upon [it] is not endowed with a more exquisite feeling.'[35] Lovelace, no less than Whytt and Haller, prods a creature into pain in order to observe the resulting motions. He, too, wants to expose the part 'endowed with a more exquisite feeling.' Teasing intensifies to torment, always with the aim of discovering concealed nature. Lovelace's method of provocative exposure is Richardson's method of revelation.[36]

Richardson, then, not only relies on the origin of heroizing tests in alchemical ones, but develops his novel through an extended investigation comparable in method with the provocative methods of sensibility experiments. In so doing, he also exploits a submerged similarity between various scientific tests and certain traditional narrative forms. That is, his novel depends on *confinement* and *trial*, a pattern shared by some experimental reports on the one hand and traditional spiritual narratives and romances on the other.

An excerpt from Edmund Goodwyn's *The Connection of Life with Respiration; or an Experimental Inquiry into the Effects of Submersion, Strangulation, and several Kinds of noxious Airs, on living Animals* illustrates the pattern of confinement and trial in a scientific report:

> I confined a cat . . . in an erect posture, and made a small opening in the trachea by cutting out one of the cartilaginous rings. Through this opening, I introduced two ounces of water into the lungs. The animal had immediately a difficulty breathing and a feeble pulse.[37]

As this narrative of suffering shows, *confinement* locates an object for close observation, and *trial* produces the material for study. Isolating the creature and making it suffer are the principal means of investigation.

The same pattern – confinement and trial – is no less fundamental to the narratives of the 'persecuted maiden.'[38] Romance writers arrange an entrapment of the heroine in order to set up the conditions for heroic rescue, and then persecute her in order to create pathos or demonstrate her strengths. Along with romance, numerous other forms – narratives of saints and martyrs, heroic drama, fairy tales, contemporary amorous fiction – provided Richardson with models.[39] Trials in such narratives allow their heroines variously to resist temptation or withstand pain, and to demonstrate resilience, courage, purity, fidelity, etc. '[V]irtue is like precious odours, most fragrant when crushed.'[40] Francis Bacon's aphorism, quoted by Barbauld to characterize Clarissa, might be said to outline the writer's task: in order to create pity and admiration, create suffering. Isolating the creature and making it suffer are the methods of dramatist as well as scientist.

Richardson develops the coincidence between the scientific and romantic or spiritual forms of narrative. The Harlowe family's spurious legal confinement and trial function principally to allow Richardson to isolate Clarissa and cause her to suffer heroically. After Clarissa leaves Harlowe Place, the persecutions, only barely removed from the contexts of romance, fairy tale, and potential martyrdom, alternate with trial in its investigative sense, creating the desire for heroic rescue and elevating Clarissa to her singular position but, in addition, providing the condition and method of an experiment to locate her responses. Confinement is essential: 'To such a place then – and where she cannot fly me – and *then* see how my will works, and what can be done by the *amorous see-saw*; now humble; now proud; now expecting, or demanding; now submitting, or acquiescing – till I have tired resistance . . .' (II, 32). Her isolation in Sinclair's infamous house locates Clarissa for study; and trial, though it remains persecutory and thus creates pathos, now also provokes a response for Lovelace's – and our – objective observation. As Lovelace promises, his reader can fully watch his operations: 'Now wilt thou see all my circulation; as in a glass wilt thou see it' (II, 42).

In outlining his project later to Belford, still half protesting and half eager for the report, Lovelace presents his central simile of entrapment:

> Hast thou not observed the charming gradations by which the ensnared volatile has been brought to bear with its new condition? How at first, refusing all sustenance, it beats and bruises itself against its wires, till it makes its gay plumage fly about, and overspread its well-secured cage. Now it gets out its head; sticking only at its beautiful shoulders: then with difficulty, drawing back its head, it gasps for breath, and erectly perched, with meditating eyes, first surveys, and then attempts, its wired canopy. As it gets breath, with renewed rage it beats and bruises again its pretty head and sides, bites the wires, and pecks at the fingers of its delighted tamer . . . After a few days, its struggles to escape still diminishing as it finds it to no purpose to attempt it, its new habitation becomes familiar . . .

Now, Belford, were I to go no further than I have gone with my beloved Miss Harlowe, how shall I know the difference between *her* and *another* bird? . . . How do I know, except I try, whether she may not be brought to sing me a fine song?

(II, 245–7)

This simile is often seen as evidence of Lovelace's 'sadistic' view of relations between men and women. It allows Lovelace to reveal his intentions in concise form, and can be taken as a paradigm for his treatment of Clarissa. We will return to the comparison between the work of Richardson and that of the Marquis de Sade, and to Lovelace's 'Sadean' cruelty, but his statement here also bears comparison with a straightforwardly scientific report. Lovelace's simile can be juxtaposed with a further excerpt from Goodwyn's account of his investigation:

> When an animal is immersed in water, his pulse becomes weak and frequent; he feels an anxiety about his breast, and struggles to relieve it: in these struggles he rises towards the surface of the water, and throws out a quantity of air from his lungs. After this, his anxiety increases; his pulse becomes weaker; the struggles are renewed with more violence; he rises towards the surface again, throws out more air from his lungs, and makes several efforts to inspire; and in some of these efforts a quantity of water commonly passes into his mouth. His skin then becomes blue, particularly about the face and lips; his pulse gradually ceases; the sphincters are relaxed; he falls down without sensation, and without motion.[41]

Both reports are narratives of suffering. Each follows a creature's steady and failing efforts to escape entrapment. Though the confinement described by Lovelace here and elsewhere in the novel depends in part on images of the hunt ('snares,' 'nobler game,' 'joys of the chase'),[42] his interest in the gradual changes brought about in the creature links his narrative to that of the scientist; both writers steadily catalogue a creature's responses and report a situation of extremity designed to allow discovery. Goodwyn's account illustrates the ways that science was 'distressing' or 'tormenting' nature's creatures in order to ferret out nature's secrets, Lovelace's his intention to distress Clarissa in order to expose her nature as a woman.

Not only does the procedure through which Clarissa is to be revealed have an underlying similarity to the procedures of science, but Lovelace's report shares a stylistic feature with Goodwyn's. Both Lovelace's simile and the excerpt from Goodwyn are characterized by a particularity that engages the reader's interest in the results of a test being carried out on a struggling creature. In addition, however, a pathetic narrative is embedded in each of these detached reports. The increasing anxiety of the animal, like that of the 'ensnared volatile,' is reported with a particularity that not only invites detached scrutiny but creates a point of view that potentially calls for pity.

The embedded pathetic narrative in Goodwyn's report has no function except to disturb the detached narrative. In Richardson's novel, on the other hand, both narratives of suffering are essential. Richardson's power as a novelist depends on his being able to alternate between them. Both the investigation of Clarissa's responses and the production of pathos require particularity. When Richardson has Belford write to Lovelace – 'Much more lively and affecting must be the style of those who write in the height of present distress, the mind tortured by the pangs of uncertainty' – a detached, investigative view is submerged in the rhetorical or dramatic intention of affecting the passions of the reader. The particulars of her suffering make Clarissa both an object of sympathy and an object of knowledge. Lovelace alternately objectifies Clarissa and capitulates, overcome by his own sympathy. Similarly, the reader is alternately held at a distance – interested in the responses provoked by her extreme situation – and absorbed in sympathy. Thus Richardson is able, through his delicate managing of antithetical uses of suffering, to intensify pathos and at the same time sustain his investigation.

Belford, as reader, illustrates the responses to these two narratives. After trying to dissuade Lovelace from his test of Clarissa, he asks for a report of it: 'But nevertheless, I should be desirous to know (*if thou wilt proceed*) by what gradations, arts, and contrivances thou effectest thy ingrateful purpose' (II, 254). Belford's alternation between pity and defense of virtue, on the one hand, and curiosity about methods and results, on the other, also characterizes readers' responses; in both cases, the novel elicits an interest in pathetic drama and in the results of an investigation. Richardson steadily creates a model for reading that fuses not only pity and sexual pleasure, as Praz and others have indicated, but pity and curiosity.

In his *Skepsis scientifica; or Confest ignorance the way to science*, Joseph Glanvill speaks of scientific trial in terms that might be applied to *Clarissa*:

And perhaps humane nature meets few more sweetly relishing and cleanly joyes, than those, that derive from the happy issues of successful Tryals: Yet, whether they succeed or not; 'tis . . . a pleasant spectacle to behold the shifts, windings, and unexpected Caprichios of distressed Nature, when pursued by a close and well managed experiment.[43]

This formula works for writer as well as scientist – and in fact, the phrase *pleasant spectacle* sounds rather more like the view of an audience for rhetoric or drama than that of the investigative observer. The aesthetic detachment necessary in order for the creation of suffering to be acceptable as a source of pleasure is analogous to scientific detachment. The novel depends on 'the shifts, windings, and unexpected Caprichios of distressed Nature, when pursued by a close and well managed experiment.' 'Virtue in distress,'[44] to use one of Lady Bradshaigh's particularly resonant phrases, implies Richardson's investigative as well as his pathetic aims.

Sade's *Justine* provides an interesting parallel for the sustained invitation to curiosity and pity. The heroine is a virtuous young woman in distress, enduring assaults with a resilience possible only in the world of the marvelous. In his prefatory letter, Sade firmly aligns his work with the romance tradition by pointing out the novel's interest in the sufferings of the 'persecuted maiden': '[M]y book . . . will acquaint thee with the sweetness of tears Virtue sore beset doth shed and doth cause to flow.'[45] But the continual persecution of the heroine shows that Sade's 'monster' has an intellectual curiosity about his own and his victim's responses. Although Sade's creation of pathos is only minimally engaging, he adopts, and extends into parody, Richardson's fusion of the pathetic and investigative uses of suffering. And by describing Mme. Quesnet, the good friend who is addressed in the prefatory letter, as a woman 'of profoundest sensibility' with 'the most enlightened of minds,'[46] he also suggests the qualities he expects in an appreciative reader – sympathy and intellectual curiosity.

Both in his comments on the novel and in his own work, Sade also illuminates the assaultive method of the novelist studying the heart. 'It is Richardson and Fielding,' Sade wrote in *Idée sur les romans*,

> who have taught us that only the profound study of the heart of man, that veritable labyrinth of nature, can inspire the novelist, whose work must make us see man not only for what he is or what he shows of himself (that is the duty of the historian) but for what he may become, for what he may be made by the modifications of vice and the blows of passion.[47]

The chief element in Sade's formula, and in Richardson's and Sade's practice, is the study of a subject under extreme conditions. Lovelace's plan is to reduce Clarissa's pride and thereby expose her essential being: 'What may not both *man* and *woman* be brought to do in a *mortified state*? . . . Pride is perhaps the principal bulwark of female virtue. Humble a woman, and may she not be *effectually* humbled?' (II, 36). He wants to expose not what she would reveal of herself, to use Sade's formulation, but what she may be made through mortification. The suffering inflicted is part of the revelatory method. Both Sade's and Richardson's novelistic procedures imply that conditions of extremity allow the novelist to be an investigator.

Lady Bradshaigh protests in her correspondence with Richardson against the cruelty she sees as central to Richardson's method. After pleading in vain for Clarissa, she can barely refrain from accusing the author of inflicting suffering in order to portray it: 'I have heard,' she writes,

> that the most lively delineators of cruelties in paintings, were generally esteemed naturally barbarous . . . I have been told of one who crucified a man that he might the better express the attitude and agonies of our blessed and expiring Saviour. I wish I could forbear thinking of these things, because they make against *you*, at least I think they do.[48]

Lady Bradshaigh's failure to distinguish between actual and fictional cruelty will become important to the later part of my analysis, but for now I want to point to the connection she makes between the creation and delineation of suffering – which becomes explicit in *Justine* and leads to an alliance of artist and scientist. Rodin, surgeon and schoolmaster, explains his willingness to anatomize the vaginal tract of his daughter, after making her suffer a cruel death,[49] by referring to the same tradition of painterly cruelty that Lady Bradshaigh describes. Aligning himself with 'great men' committed to the scrutiny of suffering for the sake of knowledge, he asserts his own high aims:

> I find it odious that futile considerations check the progress of science; did great men ever allow themselves to be enslaved by such contemptible chains? And, when Michelangelo wished to render a Christ after Nature, did he make the crucifixion of a young man the occasion for a fit of remorse? Why no: he copied the boy in his death agonies.[50]

The key to Richardson's, as to Rodin's, procedure lies in the fact that the suffering creature reveals itself through its suffering. For Richardson, as for Rodin, in other words, inflicting suffering is part of an investigative method. And for Richardson, it is simultaneously a means of presenting a pathetic drama. His task as a novelist is to present an opportunity for the reader to observe suffering as it is created.

The central episode of suffering in *Clarissa* is the rape. As a dramatic event, it is, in my view, unpersuasive: Clarissa's and Lovelace's bodies exist in different genres. Except in such early Harlowe Place scenes as that in which Solmes presses on her hoop or James causes her to fall, Clarissa's body is almost wholly idealized, the body of romance. Lovelace's body, on the other hand, is quite inconsistently imagined. As changeable as his postures, equally protean, it is sometimes imaginary (his proboscis reaches to the moon [II, 114]), sometimes oddly physiological (he has 'the nerves of a tottering paralytic' [III, 475].[51] He is a fantastical man of feeling.

As a thematic event, however, the rape is central: it is the physicalization of the sustained psychological assault on Clarissa. It is, as Lovelace declares, the 'ultimate trial' (III, 190), the final stage in Lovelace's effort to gain access to the recesses of Clarissa's heart. 'Is not *this* the hour of her trial . . . Whether her frost be frost indeed? . . .' 'Is she not a woman?' (III, 190). The equation of rape with trial illuminates Lovelace's use of the metaphors relating to the discovery of the heart. The trial is now to occur physically rather than psychologically. The rape relocates the scene of the trial from heart to genitals, which that heart has both concealed and represented. The metaphorical and literal centers of women's desire are now identified. Thus Lovelace's declaration that he will enter her heart is 'realized' by the rape.

As the last stage of his trial of Clarissa, the rape fuses sexual with investigative assault and becomes not only a culminating but a parodic event. Its investigative nature is confirmed by the quasi-scientific atmosphere in which it takes place: after the administration of a sedative (laudanum, a drug used in medicine to 'weaken the sentient power of the nerves')[52] and in view of Lovelace's women assistants. The medical context is reinforced by Lovelace's casuistical comparison of himself with a doctor: '[D]o not physicians prescribe opiates in acute cases, where the violence of the disorder would be apt to throw the patient into a fever of delirium? . . . [I]f these somnivolencies (I hate the word *opiates* on this occasion) have turned her head, that is an effect they frequently have upon some constitutions . . .' (III, 214). The scientized rape is doubly parodic. It parodies both sexual event (insensibility makes desire impossible) and the investigation: it allows Lovelace to discover, but only in the most reduced, anatomical sense, that Clarissa is a woman. Further, Lovelace describes the results of his 'inquiry' in the reductive terms of satire, displacing location and gender, but not concealing the anatomical nature of his discovery: '[T]here is no difference to be found between the skull of King Philip and that of another man' (III, 199).

Justine, again, offers a useful comparison. Rodin's proposed
anatomy of his daughter's vaginal tract, a scientific rape, extends
and further distorts the fusion of investigative and sexual assault. In
conjunction with this anatomy, Rodin also plans to vivisect Justine's
heart, thus 'scientizing' Sade's metaphor for the novelist's task –
'the profound study of the heart.' He not only would create a
literal 'window on the breast,' making explicit the unique viewing
opportunities offered by a cruel procedure, but through his double
project would investigate both centers of woman's desire. Sade's
development of the *'gothic* element'[53] in Richardson supplies
exaggerated images of Richardson's fusion of investigation and
sexual violence.

Sexual violence as a means of heroizing women is not unusual.[54]
Richardson's novel is of particular interest, however, because of the
layered interpretation of the rape in the novel itself – and because
of the alliance between author's and character's methods. Sexual
violence is the culmination both of Lovelace's investigation and of
his invention or stratagem. *Trial* and *plot* or *invention* are thus
identified both with rape and with each other. This equivalence can
be used as a guide to the interpretation of the novel: if plot, which
belongs to Richardson as well as to Lovelace, is identified with trial
and rape, then Richardson's method (not just Lovelace's) of getting
at Clarissa's heart is a trial that culminates in rape. From within the
novel, rape is announced as the means of discovering and heroizing
the woman.

The alliance between author's and character's methods is explicit
in the novel,[55] and there are numerous examples of Richardson's
fusion with Lovelace in the creating/writing task. Barbauld, taking a
common-sense approach to interpretation, suggests that 'Belford is a
being, created in order to carry on the story, and must not be made
too strictly the object of criticism.'[56] In that sense, however, Lovelace,
too, is such a being. He is created in order to invent the story.
Richardson's pride in his own manipulation of particularity and in
his 'familiar way of writing' is frequently expressed in Lovelace's
self-promotion: 'The minutest circumstances are often of great service
in matters of the least importance' (III, 251); *'familiar writing* is but
talking, Jack' (III, 241). These moments of Richardson's and Lovelace's
narrative identity, though they frequently create narrative
awkwardness, have more than a 'local' significance. Lovelace's
articulation of his seduction plan – and his method of pursuing it by
trial – belong as much to Richardson the writer as to Lovelace the
character.

Richardson's artistic aim of isolating and trying Clarissa is, in other
words, continually visible in Lovelace's stratagems and provocations.

Richardson frequently gives Lovelace lines about the management of plot that perfectly fuse the latter's skill and aims with Richardson's own. After getting Clarissa to agree to go to London and live at Sinclair's, for example, Lovelace asks for Belford's admiration: 'Well, but how comes all this about, methinks thou askest? – Thou, Lovelace dealest in wonders, yet aimest not at the *marvellous*. – How did all this come about?' (II, 183). Nothing could better express the novelistic problem faced by Richardson. That is, the problem for Richardson's invention – getting Clarissa to London and plausibly set up in a brothel – is also the problem for Lovelace's invention. Were such a statement in Sterne, it would have a liberating effect, something like 'Learned men, brother *Toby*, do not write dialogues upon long noses for nothing.'[57] In *Clarissa*, however, such a double-voiced comment is an index of the pervasive, structural irony of the work, a structural irony that allows Richardson to get his plot wholly achieved through his characters but that also for much of the novel identifies Richardson's getting the story told with the progress of Lovelace's trial. Much of what Lovelace says – and all the inventiveness with which he isolates and tests Clarissa – operate as Richardson's novelistic method.

Because Lovelace's assaultive method continuously outlines the method of the novelist, the novel brings artistic and ethical cruelty onto the same plane. Lady Bradshaigh's hesitation about whether to blame Richardson for his method reveals her perceptive reading. Ethical and aesthetic categories are confused, with two opposing results. The identification of author and character contextualizes Richardson's method in Lovelace's ethical situation. Thus contextualized, the method of trial, which culminates in rape, is itself subject to ethical charges. The ethical confusion that they share is epitomized in Lovelace's report of the circumstances of the rape: 'some *little* art . . . with a *generous* design' (III, 201). Lovelace explains his own generosity as a desire 'to lessen the too quick sense she was likely to have of what she was to suffer' (III, 201–2), and the generosity that Richardson and Lovelace both claim (Lovelace in the text, Richardson in his correspondence) is their intention to *exalt* the sex.[58] Nevertheless, both, as arrangers of plot, equate art with an insensibility drug: to create a heroine by having her reduced to insensibility by laudanum in preparation for rape is the art of Lovelace through which Richardson works. So thoroughly exposed is Richardson's plot in the ethical context, that the heroizing of woman through rape – the traditional pattern itself – becomes offensive. No matter how compelling the pathos created by her responses, such art with a generous design is not free from fundamental ethical objections.

On the other hand, because Lovelace's cruelty is part of a method
– investigative, revelatory, heroizing – the novel detaches cruelty
from its ethical context. Lovelace's ethical abuses seem temporarily
to demand attention as pure inventive skill – and more specifically as
the means by which Richardson is creating his novel. Thus within the
novel torment, vexing, trial, and plaguing lose part of their ethical
offensiveness by becoming recategorized as methods of discovery.[59]
So thoroughly do Lovelace's aims function as Richardson's novelistic
management that the reader is entrapped in an irony as intense as
the plot in which Clarissa is entrapped. The novel destabilizes ethical
and aesthetic categories, and thus creates two continuously opposing
'readings' – one sympathetic, the other detached. The novel teaches
readers to read cruelty not simply as cruelty, but as a method of
revelation, and in so doing provides a psychological training in
conflict with the psychology of pity that the novel aims for as a
whole.

One might think that irony would have made a distinction
between Lovelace's and Richardson's projects, but, instead, the
extended identification works to give an artistic and an ethical
context to each. The separation that for much of the novel Richardson
does not make between Lovelace's project and his own, he makes
decidedly after the rape. The novel loses 'energy,' vividness.
Richardson takes the plot away from Lovelace in the episode of
Clarissa's imprisonment, which, though it follows from Lovelace's
contrivances, is not part of his invention. Beginning at this point in
the novel, her persecution is pathetic, but not investigative. Clarissa
is merely displayed; one can only look on and weep, as Belford
does. Richardson's own artistic invention was animated by the
investigation (and the double level of particularity to which that
investigation contributed), which comes to an end with the rape.

Until the rape the novel is Clarissa's story but Lovelace's plot.[60]
Afterwards, Richardson allows Clarissa to take over plotting her
story and to reshape it as the trial of a Christian martyr. She first
unravels Lovelace's plots, then wrests her story from Lovelace with
the allegorical letter by which she temporarily makes him act in her
plot of the dying daughter of God.[61] And finally, she controls the plot
by her refusal to be anatomized. Had Lovelace been in charge of the
fiction, it would have ended in an anatomy: his last plan is to take
possession of her heart. This exaggerated gesture derives from
romance and heroic tragedy, but is made literal and bizarre by his
announcement that he has a surgeon standing by with the proper
instruments to extract and preserve it. Clarissa has, however, by
implication already anatomized herself – by subjecting herself to
spiritual scrutiny.[62] She thus forestalls Lovelace's management of her

story and determines its end by specifying in her will that 'the occasion of my death not admitting of doubt, I will not, on any account, that it [her body] be opened' (IV, 416). She returns the discovery of the heart from its physical to its psychological meaning.

By making a contriver of rape the source of his plot and rape itself the culmination of his heroizing and revelatory method, Richardson extended the male's heroizing of woman through suffering as far as it would go. After this, there is only repetition or Sade's wholly parodic use of such a heroizing strategy. As if to make up for his assaultive methods of heroizing, Richardson ends the novel not in the investigative mode, but as a saint's life. He turns to instructive dying[63] and hagiography. Though he loses dramatic power with these comparatively static forms, they imply a repudiation of the violence of the novel's provocative method.

As used in *Clarissa*, the vocabulary of sensibility – *sensibility, sensible, insensible, delicacy, niceness* – shows the expected range of meanings from awareness or perception to physical and psychological delicacy, to refined generous feeling, to romantic susceptibility. It is not the recurrence of this vocabulary that marks *Clarissa* as a novel of sensibility, however. It is, instead, Richardson's use of trial as a means of revelation.

In linking scientific ideas of nerve functioning to the general cultural preoccupation with sensibility, George Rousseau comments briefly on *Clarissa*: 'It is impossible to imagine a *Clarissa Harlowe*, whatever else that book may be, without a blow-by-blow description of the exquisite state of the heroine's nerves.'[64] Actually, though Clarissa's delicacy is physical as well as psychological – 'Who would think,' Belford rhetorically asks Lovelace, 'such a delicately-framed person could have sustained what she has sustained?' (III, 435) – her nerves are not a matter of description or discussion. In fact, it is Lovelace who has the visible nerves, fibers, and heart pulses. But Rousseau's suggestion is nevertheless well taken. The novel proceeds by provoking Clarissa at a psychological level comparable to that which would produce an account of her nervous response.

The novel rests on an investigation of desire. As virtue means chastity, woman means a creature in whom desire is natural, virtue a product of pride. Discovering her heart means locating desire, another term for which is sensibility, as Lovelace indicates when he complains that she has 'no love, no sensibility' (II, 188). But sensibility – psychological and physical – also accounts for the delicacy and intensity of her experience. In this sense, Lovelace complains that she has a sensibility he does not understand: the greatest of her sufferings arises from an 'extreme sensibility, I know nothing of that; and cannot, therefore, be answerable for it' (III, 281).

Sensibility is both the delicacy that makes her modest and the susceptibility to romantic or sexual feeling that that modesty conceals. Trial is a means of locating her concealed – and therefore actual – nature. The analogy between Richardson's method of revelation and that of the scientists rests on their comparable uses of provocation. [. . .]

Notes

1. James Boswell, *The Hypochondriack*, I, 143.

2. Laurence Sterne, *The Life and Opinions of Tristram Shandy*, I, 82. In the text of *Tristram Shandy* edited by James A. Work, the citation is I. xxiii. 74. In Bailey's edition of the *Hypochondriack* papers, the editor points out that Boswell was alluding to Sterne and also notes a similar expression used by Samuel Johnson ('the mirror of his breast'), and by Rousseau.

3. Alexander Pope, *The Correspondence of*, ed. George Sherburn, 5 vols. (Oxford: Clarendon Press, 1956), II, 23. Quoted in James Anderson Winn's study of Pope's letters, the title of which he took from this metaphor. *A Window on the Breast* (Hamden, Conn.: Archon Books, 1977), p. 200.

4. *Ibid.*, I, 353 (August 18, 1716). Quoted by Winn.

5. Lucian, 'Hermotimus,' in *Selected Works*, trans. Bryan P. Reardon (Indianapolis: Bobbs-Merrill, 1965), p. 124. In her discussion of Boswell, Bailey points out that the source of this image is Lucian.

6. John Mayow, *Medico-Physical Works*: a translation of the *Tractatus quinque medico-physici* printed in the Sheldonian Theatre in 1674, reissued by permission of the Alembic Club of Edinburgh (Oxford, 1926), p. 183.

7. *The Complete Letters of Lady Mary Wortley Montagu*, 3 vols., ed. Robert Halsband (Oxford: Clarendon Press, 1965–7), I, 63–4. Lady Mary continues: 'You can frame no guesses about it from either my speaking or writeing, and supposeing I should attempt to shew it you, I know no other way.'

8. Samuel Richardson, *The Correspondence of Samuel Richardson*, IV, 162. Further citations will be to *Correspondence*.

9. James Boswell, *The Life of Samuel Johnson, LL.D.*, ed. George Birbeck Hill, rev. by L. F. Powell, 6 vols. (Oxford: Clarendon Press, 1964), II, 49. The expression was also used to describe Sterne's novelistic skills: 'O beloved Sterne! sensitive philosopher, thou art able to solve such enigmas! Thou art the master who penetrates into the *secret recesses* of the heart; thou dost know the reason for Sophia's tears.' Extract from Gavriil Petrovich Kamenev, 'Sofia,' *Muza* (1796), i. 208–9, as quoted in *Sterne, the Critical Heritage*, p. 459 (emphasis added). And Anne Himmelfarb has pointed out to me that Dryden uses the term *recesses* in 'Original and Progress of Satire': Horace 'entered into the inmost recesses of nature' (clearly indicating human nature). *Of Dramatic Poesy and Other Essays*, ed. George Watson, 2 vols. (London: J. M. Dent, 1962), II, 129.

10. *Correspondence*, I, clxxii and xxiv–xxv.

11. Samuel Richardson, *Clarissa or, the History of a Young Lady*, 4 vols. (London: Everyman, 1932, 1968), III, 139. I am using the Everyman edition because it is

commonly available. The new one-volume Penguin edition has, in my view, replaced others as a teaching text, but because it reproduces the first rather than the third edition, it does not have all the necessary material. The new AMS Press facsimile edition of Richardson's eight-volume third edition is preferable to both but is not yet in wide use. All further citations will be included in the text.

12. In his *Reading Clarissa: The Struggles of Interpretation* (New Haven and London: Yale University Press, 1979), William Warner argues that *diving into the recesses of the heart* is the project of the humanist critic, a project that Warner wants to undermine:

> To 'dive into the recesses of the human heart' – this is the adventure the humanist critic urges us to embark upon in reading Richardson. And this journey is charged with significance, because the humanist critic makes man's interiority – his heart, mind, or consciousness – the locus of human value. In humanist criticism the heart becomes an object of delicious mystery, a source of pleasure, and the touchstone to man's nature. Richardson's novel is said to meet the needs of this heart and to teach the reader the secrets that lie buried there. The humanist critic sees himself as the handmaiden who will help deliver these truths and experiences from the book to the reader.

My location of this standard formula, like my overall reading, differs from Warner's.

13. Mayow, *Medico-Physical Works*, p. 183.

14. Oliver Goldsmith, 'A Survey of Experimental Philosophy,' in *Collected Works*, ed. Arthur Friedman, 5 vols. (Oxford: Clarendon Press, 1966), V, 343.

15. Thomas Willis, *The Anatomy of the Brain and the Description and Use of the Nerves*, in *The Remaining Medical Works of that Famous and Renowned Physician Dr. Thomas Willis*, Englished in 1681 by Samuel Pordage (London: Printed for T. Dring, C. Harper, J. Leigh, and S. Martyn, 1681), n.p. (from the 'Authors Epistle Dedicatory to his Grace Gilbert Archbishop of Canterbury). (Facsimile of Thomas Willis, *The Anatomy of the Brain and Nerves*, ed. William Feindel, 2 vols. [Montreal: McGill University Press, 1965], II, n.p.)

16. Willis's language might be compared to Locke's use of *closet* to refer to interior space and to his term *the mind's presence room*.

17. Goldsmith, *Works*, V, 342.

18. *The Works of Anna Laetitia Barbauld*, 2 vols (London, 1825), II, 214–15.

19. For a discussion of Albrecht von Haller's and Robert Whytt's sensibility experiments, see Ann Jessie Van Sant, *Eighteenth-Century Sensibility and the Novel: The Senses in Social Context* (Cambridge: Cambridge University Press, 1993), Chapter 3.

20. Several critics have discussed the cruelty in the novel, frequently with references to the Marquis de Sade. In his *The Romantic Agony*, Mario Praz discusses Richardson in a chapter called 'The Shadow of the Divine Marquis'; Praz says that 'the persecuted maiden . . . was refurbished in the eighteenth century by Richardson' and that Richardson's 'moralizing reveals itself fully for what it was – namely, little more than a veneer – in his French imitators, who sought in the subject of the persecuted woman chiefly an excuse for situations of heightened sensuality' ([Oxford University Press, 1970], pp. 97, 99). John Traugott ('*Clarissa's* Richardson: An Essay to Find the Reader') analyzes Richardson's combination of cruelty and play: 'What Sade finds particularly attractive in Richardson is the torture of Clarissa and the covert

suggestion of the father's complicity in her ruin by his insistence on the ugly toad Solmes as her rightful despoiler. Sade has in short many times intensified what I have called the *gothic* element in *Clarissa*' (*English Literature in the Age of Disguise*, ed. Maximillian Novak [Berkeley, Los Angeles, and London: University of California Press, 1977], pp. 181–2). Ian Watt discusses the metaphor of the hunt as one of the major expressions of the sadistic relation of men to women in the eighteenth century: 'Sadism is, no doubt, the ultimate form which the eighteenth-century view of the masculine role involved: and it makes the female role one in which the woman is, and can only be, the prey' (*The Rise of the Novel* [Berkeley and Los Angeles: University of California Press, 1965], pp. 231 ff.). Leopold Damrosch characterizes the Harlowe family life in similar terms: 'James and Arabella cooperate in sadism until at last Clarissa is goaded to exclaim to her aunt "I see, I see, madam, that I am considered as an animal to be baited, to make sport for my brother and sister, and Mr. Solmes. They are all, all of them, wanton in their cruelty"' (I, 404) (*God's Plot & Man's Stories*, p. 219). And Richardson, in discussing the creation of Grandison, confirms the cruelty but attributes it to women as well: 'And then, to make *sport* for the *tender-hearted* reader as he went along, must we not give him great distresses? only taking care to make him happy at last, as it is called' (*Correspondence*, IV, 12).

21. See Warner for a discussion of the novel as essentially derived from Clarissa's self-defense, a construction of self through self-justification. For a discussion from a different point of view of the deeply embedded significance of legal concepts and language in the novel, see John P. Zomchick, 'Tame Spirits, Brave Fellows, and the Web of Law: Robert Lovelace's Legalistic Conscience,' *ELH*, 53 (1986), 99–120.

22. I understand the 'origin' of the fiction, in other words, to be not in its first letter but in the invention that generates it.

23. Walter Skeat, *An Etymological Dictionary of the English Language* (Oxford, 1953; 1st ed. 1879–82), p. 637.

24. 'That which purifies us is trial.' This quotation from Milton's *Areopagitica* is followed in the *OED* by one from Richardson's *Grandison* – 'How would such a creature . . . have behaved under such tryals?' – to illustrate trial by suffering.

25. *OED*.

26. Samuel Johnson, *A Dictionary of the English Language* (London, 1755), *experiment*.

27. *Correspondence*, I, c. ci.

28. R. F. Brissenden, *Virtue in Distress: Studies in the Novel of Sentiment from Richardson to Sade* (London: Macmillan, 1974), pp. 34–5.

29. See also Ruth Perry, *Women, Letters, and the Novel* (New York: AMS Press, 1980), pp. 22–3. In her brief but suggestive discussion, she mentions Richardson's heroines in particular but makes a more general claim about epistolary fictions:

> Indeed, these epistolary novels are often plotted like experiments performed on isolated individuals. The characters are almost systematically manipulated and their reactions under pressure carefully preserved in their letters or journals. Both Pamela and Clarissa are put through paces to see if they pass the test of virtue. Certainly in a civilization steeped in the Christian tradition of wanderings in the wilderness and of finally finding salvation, stories of trials are no novelty. Yet these references to tests and trials are not so allegorical in tone as they are experimental.

269

30. Brissenden, *Virtue in Distress*, p. 41.

31. *Ibid.*, p. 100.

32. For a discussion of Haller's experimental method, see Van Sant, *Eighteenth-Century Sensibility*, Chapter 3, 'Gazing on Suffering.'

33. *Correspondence*, IV, 189.

34. Lovelace both calls Clarissa a teaser and reports the effects of his teasing her: 'She hemmed twice or thrice; till at last the lovely teaser, teased by my hesitating expectation of her answer, out of all power of articulate speech, burst into tears . . .' (II, 141).

35. *Observations on the Sensibility and Irritability of the Parts of Men and other Animals. Occasioned by the Celebrated M. De Haller's late Treatise on those Subjects*, in *Works of Robert Whytt*, pp. 282–3. See Van Sant, *Eighteenth-Century Sensibility*, Chapter 3, note 15 for a previous reference to Whytt's statement.

36. Such provocation, as many readers have noticed, is common in Richardson's letters. 'Will you forgive me, Madam,' he writes to Lady Bradshaigh, 'if I own that I really have so much cruelty in my nature, that I should wish to provoke you now and then, if I knew what would do it, consistent with respect and decency?' (*Correspondence*, IV, 232–3).

37. A review article in *Analytical Review*, 1 (May to August 1788), I, 459. The reviewer quotes Goodwyn at length.

38. I use Praz's term.

39. I am influenced in my discussion by John Richetti's *Popular Fiction Before Richardson* (Oxford: Clarendon Press, 1969); Margaret Anne Doody's *A Natural Passion: A Study of the Novels of Samuel Richardson* (Oxford: Clarendon Press, 1974); and Carol Houlihan Flynn's *Samuel Richardson: A Man of Letters* (Princeton: Princeton University Press, 1982).

40. *Correspondence*, I, xxi.

41. *Analytical Review*, I, 458.

42. In fact, much of Lovelace's language depends on the metaphor of the hunt and is thus a corruption of the association in romance of the courtly knight's skill in hunting the deer (hart) and in pursuing and engaging the heart of his mistress.

43. Joseph Glanvill, 'An Address to the Royal Society,' in *Skepsis scientifica: or, Confest ignorance the way to science* (London: Printed by E. Cotes, for Henry Eversden, 1665), n.p. (Facsimile edition: *The Vanity of Dogmatizing: The Three 'Versions' by Joseph Glanvill*, with critical introduction by Stephen Medcalf [Hove, Sussex: The Harvester Press, 1970].) Johnson uses part of Glanvill's second sentence to illustrate the meaning of *caprichio*. Elizabeth Hedrick pointed this quotation out to me.

44. Lady Bradshaigh's phrase is, as R. F. Brissenden indicates, the source of the title for his study of the novel of sentiment.

45. The Marquis de Sade, *Justine*, in *Three Complete Novels: Justine, Philosophy in the Bedroom, Eugénie de Franval and other Writings*, compiled and translated by Richard Seaver and Austryn Wainhouse (New York: Grove Press, 1965), p. 455.

46. *Ibid.*

47. Sade, *Idée sur les Romans*, from *Selected Writings of De Sade*, selected and translated by Leonard de Saint-Yves (London: Peter Owen, 1953), p. 284.

While I have found Sade's reference to Richardson suggestive, his inclusion of Fielding is puzzling.

48. *Correspondence*, IV, 208.

49. By way of combining his pleasures in science and libertinage, Rodin makes the following suggestion to his dinner companion and collaborator: 'Anatomy will never reach its ultimate state of perfection until an examination has been performed upon the vaginal canal of a fourteen- or fifteen-year-old child who has expired from a cruel death; it is only from the contingent contraction we can obtain a complete analysis of a so highly interesting part.' Having overheard these plans, Justine then hears of the procedure the two men plan to carry out on her: 'it is nothing less than a question of a vivisection in order to inspect the beating of my heart, and upon this organ to make observations which cannot practicably be made upon a cadaver.' (*Justine*, p. 551 and pp. 555–6.)

50. *Ibid.*, p. 552.

51. Lovelace is here writing before the outcome of the family marriage offer is known. He says that he will spend his time trying 'to brace up, if I can, the relaxed fibres of my mind, which have been twitched and convulsed like the nerves of some tottering paralytic, by means of the tumults she has excited in it.' He sounds a bit like the valetudinarian Richardson and almost in some instances seems to be a foreshadowing parody of the man of feeling, whose physiological body is the location of experience. See Van Sant, *Eighteenth-Century Sensibility*, Chapter 6, for a discussion of the body of sensibility.

52. Whytt, *Observations on the Nature, Causes, and Cure of those Disorders which are Commonly Called Nervous, Hypochondriac, or Hysteric*, in *Works*, p. 502.

53. I use John Traugott's phrase. '*Clarissa*'s Richardson: An Essay to Find the Reader,' p. 182.

54. For a discussion of Clarissa as 'virgin martyr' and for her place in the tradition of 'Lucrece,' see Margaret Doody's 'Tyrannic Love and the Virgin Martyr: Tragic Theme and Dramatic Reference in *Clarissa*,' in *A Natural Passion*.

55. Richardson's dependence on and identification with his libertine has been analyzed by Carol Houlihan Flynn in *Samuel Richardson: A Man of Letters* (Princeton: Princeton University Press, 1982).

56. *Correspondence*, I, cvi.

57. Sterne, *The Life and Opinions of Tristram Shandy, Gentleman*, I, 271. In the Work edition, the citation is III. xxxvii. 229.

58. See Flynn's discussion of Richardson's manner of elevating his women in 'A Delicate Balance: Richardson's Treatment of the Sentimental Woman,' in *Samuel Richardson: A Man of Letters*.

59. They are also recategorized in scientific experiments.

60. This assertion [. . .] may appear to be an allusion to Damrosch's *God's Plot and Man's Stories*. I did not intend the allusion, though the resonance of Damrosch's title no doubt influenced me.

    Control over Clarissa's story is central to Terry Castle's *Clarissa's Cyphers* (Ithaca, NY: Cornell University Press, 1982). Castle argues that the novel is about reading, about the 'problematization of the very notion of "Story" itself' (40). The violence in the text is hermeneutic, and Clarissa is a 'naive exegete' (57). My view of the 'problematization of "Story"' differs from Castle's. As I see it, the novel is about the heroization of women through a violence that is shaped by investigation. 'Story' becomes problematic because of Richardson's fusion and confusion of ethical and aesthetic values, a problem frequently made explicit in discussions of fiction.

61. For a thorough treatment of the death theme in *Clarissa*, see Margaret Anne Doody's 'The Deathbed Theme in *Clarissa*,' in *A Natural Passion*.

62. For an analysis of *Clarissa* as shaped principally by Puritan spiritual self-examination, see Cynthia Griffin Wolff's *Samuel Richardson and the Eighteenth-Century Puritan Character* (Hamden, Conn.: Archon Books, 1972). See also Damrosch's *God's Plot and Man's Stories*: 'Doctrine and Fiction,' 'Puritan Experience and Art,' and '*Clarissa* and the Waning of Puritanism.'

63. See Doody, 'The Deathbed Theme in *Clarissa*,' for instructions on death and death as instruction.

64. 'Science,' in *The Eighteenth Century*, ed. Pat Rogers (London: Methuen, 1978), p. 193.

Part IV

Fielding

11 'The Exact Picture of His Mother': Recognizing Joseph Andrews

JILL CAMPBELL

In this essay, Jill Campbell reflects a post-structural view that oppositions between the two genders are not as fixed as has traditionally been thought. This perception of fluidity Campbell applies to her reading of *Joseph Andrews*, to show the many ways in which Joseph is a peculiarly feminized character. Campbell links this ambiguity to Fielding's own ability to raise questions about proper masculinity in the middle of the eighteenth century, even after having mocked what he thought was a dangerously feminized sensibility in the novels of Richardson. Viewed in this light, *Joseph Andrews* is no simple rejection of *Pamela*.

'O Sir,' cried *Joseph*, 'all this is very true, and very fine; and I could hear you all day, if I was not so grieved at Heart as now I am.'[1]

Joseph's cry, interrupting Adams's long exposition of the comforts of philosophy and Christian submission, at once acknowledges the integrity of Adams's arguments and asserts their irrelevance to the feeling they claim to address – Joseph's present grief at Fanny's abduction by the servants of the Roasting-Squire. The two men have been left together at the inn, tied 'back to back' to a bedpost by Fanny's abductors, and the dialogue between them that constitutes book 3, chapter 11, of *Joseph Andrews* might be said to bring back to back separate human 'truths' of reason and of feeling – to place them in a forced conjunction, but looking off in diverse directions rather than confronting each other face to face. The scene provides an emblem for a quality that a number of critics have admired in Fielding's fiction, his willingness to sustain 'unresolved dualities' or to 'wrestle central contradictions . . . only to a standoff'; Joseph's exclamation, with its twinned acceptance and rejection of offered principles, seems to me the characterizing cry of *Joseph Andrews*.[2]

Henry Knight Miller gives one pair of names to the 'unresolved dualities' in Fielding's work when he cites Joseph's exclamation as evidence of Fielding's willingness to value 'feminine' feeling as well

275

as 'masculine' reason, adapting the gender terms that have
always been used to contrast Fielding's 'masculine' sensibility with
Richardson's 'feminine' sentimentalism to describe a tension he sees
within Fielding's work itself.[3] But critics have not attended to the
extent to which Fielding himself uses the terms of gender to frame
his complex response to Richardson in *Joseph Andrews*. His parody
of Richardson begins, of course, by inverting the genders in *Pamela's*
central situation, and through allusion, description, and narrative
event the novel sustains and extends Joseph's implication in
feminine roles. But the stakes change as the novel goes on: Fielding's
construction of a compromised gender identity for his title character
becomes not just a device of comedy but a vehicle for the imaginative
reconciliation of opposite allegiances traditionally systematized by
gender. The two terms of gender provide *Joseph Andrews* with its
most abiding structure of double response to the kinds of conflicting
claims voiced in Joseph's cry; and the promise represented by
Joseph's 'feminized' heroism suggests unlikely connections between
the problem of gender in the novel, familiar critical issues of
novelistic representation in Fielding's and Richardson's work, and
what Miller has called the 'elegiac undertone' in Fielding's comedies,
that bass note of threatened loss sounded in Joseph's expression
of grief.[4]

I

The twenty-six plays that Fielding wrote before the Stage Licensing
Act turned him out of the theater demonstrate his sustained interest
in the categories of gender and in the more abstract dualisms with
which they might be aligned. He had repeatedly used cross-gender
casting for satiric purposes in his productions of his plays at the
Haymarket, and his plays deal again and again with the gender
inversions represented by 'petticoat government,' the effeminate
beau, or the Italian castrato singer.[5] There he used figures of
compromised gender satirically to dramatize the compromising of
various political and cultural standards associated with masculinity.
But, in the chapter of *Joseph Andrews* in which Joseph rejects Adams's
consolation, thereby committing himself to the conventionally
feminine claims of feeling, Fielding's intention isn't satirical. Here
he allows Joseph to dignify his (potentially Pamelian) position with
a quotation from Shakespeare, one that employs the terms of gender
not to belittle his feelings as feminine, but to place them within a
more expansive definition of the masculine.[6] As if responding to an
unspoken imputation of his manhood, Joseph 'bursts out' at the end
of the chapter, after a period of silence:

Yes, I will bear my Sorrows like a Man,
But I must also feel them as a Man.
I cannot but remember such things were,
And were most dear to me –

(267)

Quoting Macduff's lament at the death of his wife and children on
the occasion of Fanny's abduction, Joseph seems to conflate the threat
of rape with death, implicitly associating mortality with woman's
vulnerability to sexual coercion, or with the particular irreversibility
of her loss of virginity within a code of female chastity. At the same
time, in the face of the problems of loss and of reason and feeling
raised by this scene, Joseph calls on Shakespeare's authority to assert
a definition of the masculine that allows for a double response 'as
a man.'

Joseph's own fitness as a masculine hero, however, has been
thrown into question at the very beginning of the chapter by the
narrator, who comments upon that 'Heart' that would remain
untouched by Joseph's sorrow and adds: 'His own, poor Youth, was
of a softer Composition; and at those Words, *O my dear* Fanny! *O my
Love! shall I never, never see thee more?* his Eyes overflowed with Tears,
which would have become any but a Hero' (264). The narrator's
criticism balances carefully here – it might fall either against Joseph
or against the idea of a hero. On the one hand, the question of
Joseph's fitness as a male hero was raised earlier still, of course, by
the joke that initially generated the novel's plot: we meet Joseph first
in the guise of a cross-dressed Pamela, a man substituted into the
conventionally feminine position of beleaguered chastity. On the
other hand, before we reach the narrator's comment in 3.11, Fielding
has provided some skeptical commentary on the notion of the
masculine hero itself. In the scene in which we first meet Fanny,
Adams's crabstick falls unregarded on the head of Fanny's attacker
only because, as Fielding explains, Nature had

taken a provident Care . . . to make this part of the Head three
times as thick as those of ordinary Men, who are designed to
exercise Talents which are vulgarly called rational, and for whom,
as Brains are necessary, she is obliged to leave some room for them
in the Cavity of the Skull: whereas, those Ingredients being entirely
useless to Persons of the heroic Calling, she hath an Opportunity of
thickening the Bone . . . and indeed, in some who are predestined
to the Command of Armies and Empires, she is supposed
sometimes to make that Part perfectly solid.

(137–38)

Fielding follows up his identification of this thick-skulled rapist with 'Persons of the heroic Calling' with a reference to the 'impenetrable' heads of 'some modern Heroes, of the lower Class,' who can use their heads 'like the Battering-Ram of the Ancients, for a Weapon of Offence' (138). As in *Jonathan Wild*, he equates lower-class criminals with public military and political leaders; as in the *Champion* essays on vanity, male coxcombs, and the present 'Wooden Age,' he suggests that a man's reliance on force – whether a public official's reliance on institutional authority or a poor man's reliance on physical strength – turns him into a kind of solidified puppet, which might as well have been made of straw, brass, or wood, as of guts and skin.[7] In this scene, the aggression of the lignified hero poses a specifically sexual threat to a woman. Perhaps, then, in the next episode in which Fanny is threatened with rape, if Joseph's tears, 'which would have become any but a Hero,' reflect some limitation in his role, they at least distinguish him from one ironically conceived kind of hero, the 'impenetrable' ravishers that surround Fanny.

The question of what kind of puppet or wooden effigy Joseph would make is raised several times in the first book of the novel and linked to the question of his masculinity. One of the oddest moments in Fielding's treatment of Joseph's gender identity occurs when, explaining why Joseph failed in his post as scarecrow in the Boobys' garden, Fielding associates him with those Italian castrato singers he had repeatedly satirized in his plays. Throughout the novel, Fielding emphasizes the sweetness of Joseph's voice, and in summarizing the brief and rather uneventful history of Joseph's life before the action of the novel opens, he reports:

> the young *Andrews* was at first employed in what in the Country they call *keeping Birds*. His Office was to perform the Part the Antients assigned to the God *Priapus*, which Deity the Moderns call by the Name of *Jack-o'-Lent*: but his Voice being so extremely musical, that it rather allured the Birds than terrified them, he was soon transplanted from the Fields into the Dogkennel. . . . For this Place likewise the Sweetness of his Voice disqualified him: the Dogs preferring the Melody of his chiding to all the alluring Notes of the Huntsman.
>
> (21–22)[8]

Fielding refers to Joseph's humble task of scaring birds from the fields as the part of Priapus, a daemon of fertility often represented as a grotesquely misshapen man with a huge and erect phallus, and sometimes represented simply as the phallus itself, 'the other human attributes being incidental.'[9] Coming just before Joseph's refusal of Lady Booby's sexual advances, the allusion is telling: Joseph is found unfit for the 'part of Priapus' by the sweetness of his voice; like the castrati, he combines an alluringly sweet voice with a disqualification from phallic office.

Several chapters later, when Fielding describes Joseph's physical appearance, he carefully denies him certain masculine characteristics, and indicates that their absence is in fact a source of his beauty. He introduces the special nature of Joseph's attraction by alluding to 'the uncommon Variety of Charms, which united in this young Man's Person' (38), and what is uncommon about them is that they bring together, in his person, both qualities associated with masculine beauty and those associated with feminine beauty ('great Elegance and no less Strength,' 'as full of Sweetness as of Fire').[10] Throughout the description, Fielding repeatedly provides a balanced weighting of these qualities, or insists on the distinction between a positive masculine characteristic assigned to Joseph and some negative extension of it ('His Shoulders were broad and brawny, but yet his Arms hung so easily, that he had all the Symptoms of Strength without the least clumsiness'). Even Joseph's beard equivocates: it is rough below, but downy above, in a way that allows the flush of his blood to appear. Finally, Fielding's description of Joseph's hair, 'displayed in wanton Ringlets down his Back,' echoes the passage in *Paradise Lost* in which Milton uses contrasting images of hair to represent the difference in identity created by gender in the first man and woman. Fielding's phrasing associates Joseph with Eve rather than Adam not only by employing Milton's phrase for Eve's hair, 'wanton Ringlets,' but by specifying that Joseph's hair hangs 'down his Back,' while Milton insists that Adam's 'manly' locks hung 'not beneath his shoulders broad.' Though the physical detail is small, Milton goes on to suggest the significance of Eve's curling, pendant locks as a fitting emblem of her female sexuality and her feminine position of 'subjection' and 'submission.'[11] What might it mean for Fielding thus glancingly to suggest that Joseph resembles Milton's original woman?

Joseph's appearance in the conventionally feminine role of 'embattled chastity,' his failure in the part of Priapus, and this description of his combined masculine and feminine beauties all occur early in the novel, when the character of Joseph still serves at least partly as a vehicle for Fielding's ridicule of *Pamela*. But an interchange between Joseph and female identity will prove crucial to the end of the novel as well, when Joseph has left his initial appearance as parodic reduction long behind him. In the scene that provides a comic resolution to the novel's plot, Gammar Andrews reveals the key to Joseph's obscured birth, history, and true family relations: he came into the Andrews family as a boy substituted in the cradle by gypsies for the Andrewses' own girl. Before Joseph's history is revealed, a series of 'curious Night-Adventures' occur among those spending the night at Lady Booby's, and their content prepares us for the importance of gender substitutions in the news that arrives in the morning. The night's events involve both mixups between the occupants of beds and confusions in gender identity: Adams hears a woman's cry for help and runs to defend threatened chastity but mistakes the soft-skinned Beau Didapper for 'the young Woman in danger of ravishing' and the stubble-chinned Slipslop for the male aggressor, and so rescues the man from the woman whose bed he has invaded (332). In these final chapters of the novel the satiric potential of an ambiguous gender identity shifts away from Joseph and onto Beau Didapper, but the revelation of Joseph's history that follows affirms, in a serious key, Joseph's deep connection to female identity. The long-ago exchange of Joseph and Fanny that emerges in *Joseph Andrews*'s recognition scene reasserts as the identifying feature of Joseph's character the substitution of boy for girl that we were aware of in the novel's inaugural joke. That identifying feature, however, has come to have a different meaning.

Even as he deflates the notions of feminine virtue and feminine feeling that Richardson had exploited in *Pamela*, Fielding interrogates traditional notions of the masculine hero in *Joseph Andrews*, suggesting that heroic roles may only aggrandize destructive aggression and may be as void of individual and spontaneous life as public effigies. Fielding renegotiates the conventional idea of a literary hero – seen under pressure in Joseph's cry with which I began and in the narrator's comment upon his tears, as well as in the ironic labelling of Fanny's ravisher – largely through the terms of gender, and specifically through his complicated construction of Joseph's gender identity. And I will argue that the prospect of mortal loss, evoked in Joseph's unheroic cry, suggests some of what is at stake for Fielding in imaginatively reconciling notions of feminine and of masculine identity; it appears repeatedly in the novel as a kind of crisis, or moment of reckoning, for the conflicting loyalties that Fielding customarily holds together in suspension.

II

The scene of apparent loss and offered consolation that prompts Joseph's cry recurs later in the novel, though this time with Adams in the position of the bereaved and Joseph in that of the comforter.

Adams has in fact been delivering another speech to Joseph about submission to Providence in response to Joseph's fears for Fanny's safety when 'one came hastily in and acquainted Mr. *Adams* that his youngest Son was drowned' (309). Joseph attempts to comfort the parson – who begins to 'deplore his Loss with the bitterest Agony' – with arguments from his own discourses, which Adams himself now finds irrelevant to the matter of present personal grief. But when Adams's lament reaches its most pained with a question that closely echoes Joseph's after Fanny's abduction – ' "My poor *Jacky*, shall I never see thee more?" ' – Joseph answers with what seems a spontaneous affirmation, words of consolation not repeated from Adams's lectures: ' "Yes, surely," says *Joseph*, "and in a better Place, you will meet again never to part more." ' The promise of a lasting reunion offered here by Joseph suggests a very different form of comfort from the imperative to accept final partings presented by Adams earlier. In this scene, Joseph must provide his own response to the claims of present feeling rather than simply a rejection of Adams's; and, though the interests have turned from comic to elegiac at this moment in the novel, Joseph's compromised gender position remains crucial to recognizing and understanding the alternative he offers. It is here to function as a means of reconciliation, rather than of comic effect. But how?

The news soon arrives, in the person of Adams's son himself, that the report of his drowning was premature. After a joyful reunion, the parson turns back to Joseph and resumes his lecture on the sin of carnal attachments and on a man's duty not to 'set his Heart on any Person or Thing in this World, but that whenever it shall be required or taken from him in any manner by Divine Providence, he may be able, peaceably, quietly, and contentedly to resign it' (308). Joseph finally loses his patience, protesting the contradiction between Adams's words and conduct, and when Adams insists on a difference between paternal and conjugal love, Joseph refuses to wish to restrain his love for Fanny. Both in this argument and in his much earlier 'deathbed' conversation with Barnabas, Joseph resists the demand that he bow to divine order by resigning the claims of his mortal attachment to a woman. His identification with that woman is so strong, he tells Barnabas, that he loved her 'as tenderly as he did his Heartstrings' (59). Here Fielding delicately suggests, I think, that his hero's relationship to death has something to do with his committed connection to female identity.

We discover at the end of the novel that the fates and identities of Joseph and the woman 'whom he loved as tenderly as he did his Heartstrings' are historically more closely linked than they or we had known: their past literalizes in an odd way that identification created

between them by their love, for in a brief interval they occupy the
same space in the Andrews cradle, and then Joseph takes over
Fanny's place in the Andrews family. The gypsies seem to have left
Joseph in Fanny's place specifically because of his closeness to death:
Mrs. Andrews describes how she returned to the cradle and found
'instead of my own Girl that I had put into the Cradle, who was as
fine a fat thriving Child as you shall see in a Summer's Day, a poor
sickly Boy, that did not seem to have an Hour to live' (337). Suckled
and soon loved by Mrs. Andrews, Joseph returns to life, but even as a
strong and brawny twenty-one-year-old, Joseph is repeatedly seen in
postures of apparent death. I will consider a particularly interesting
example of this pattern later, but it appears most insistently in the
episodes following Joseph's beating by the highwaymen. In chapters
12 through 14 of book I, Joseph is referred to eight or nine times by
different characters as a 'dead man': the postillion who stops the
coach for him says ' "he was certain there was a *dead* Man lying in
the Ditch, for he heard him groan" ' (52); and Joseph, Betty, Mrs.
Tow-wouse, and even Joseph's doctor also refer to him this way.[12]

Timotheus, the keeper of the inn where Joseph has taken shelter
just before his beating, prepares us for this emphasis 'with an
excellent Observation on the Certainty of Death, which his Wife said
was indeed very true' (50). Fielding has attached the *memento mori*
provided by Timotheus more specifically to Joseph when he supplies
him in book 1, chapter 2, with an admittedly imaginary genealogy.
Fielding confesses that he has not been able to trace Joseph's
genealogy farther than his great grandfather, and so offers in place
of ancestors an epitaph, 'which an ingenious Friend of ours hath
communicated':

> Stay Traveller, for underneath this Pew
> Lies fast asleep that merry Man *Andrew*;
> When the last Day's great Sun shall gild the Skies,
> Then he shall from his Tomb get up and rise.
> Be merry while thou can'st: for surely thou
> Shall shortly be as sad as he is now.

(20)

Fielding goes on to discount the epitaph as evidence of Joseph's
ancestry, but nonetheless retains this odd gesture of imagining
Joseph's origins in a generalized figure of the mortality of man.[13]

I have argued elsewhere that in several of his plays Fielding
consigned women to an explicitly ghostly existence as he attempted
to resolve the contradictions in his notions of female identity.
Already in his plays, Fielding began to suggest the costs of a

geography of gender that renders women ghostly, disembodied, and men material puppets.[14] He pointedly asserts in *Joseph Andrews* that his title character is no scarecrow or lignified puppet of heroism. Indeed, as he continually implicates Joseph in feminine roles, he also repeatedly (at least playfully) associates Joseph with the feminine realm of ghostly presence or voice: his groans are those of a 'dead man.' The epitaph that Fielding entertains briefly as a clue to Joseph's identity speaks of the universal inevitability of death, but it also speaks crudely, darkly, of the day of judgment and the final raising of the dead. Curiously, the sickly little boy that Gammar Andrews finds in Fanny's cradle, apparently so near death, comes to represent to her a hope for the restoration of her own child: ' "A Neighbour of mine happening to come in at the same time, and hearing the Case, advised me to take care of this poor Child, and G— would perhaps one day restore me my own" ' (337). As a grown man, Joseph will console Adams for the mortal loss of his son with the promise of a lasting reunion between them in the next life; as an infant, he served as a token to Mrs. Andrews of the hope for a reunion with her daughter in this one. The recurrent fear of mortal loss in the novel and the hope for reunion represented by Joseph may appear to be isolated or discordant elements within Fielding's comic fiction. Yet they suggest complexities within Fielding's attitude towards those novelistic methods that readers have seen as most basic to his difference from Richardson.

III

The hope for a reunion after death heard in Joseph's voice within this novel will reappear at several points in Fielding's other works: Fielding makes it Allworthy's comfort for the loss of his wife in *Tom Jones*, extends it as 'the sweetest, most endearing and ravishing' hope in his own discourse on consolation, and imagines its attainment in the narrator's reunion with his little daughter upon entering Elysium in 'Journey From This World to the Next.'[15] In this last work, the narrator's account links the fantasy of an absolute and lasting reunion with the fantasy of an intuitive recognition of others: 'I saw infinite numbers of spirits, every one of whom I knew, and was known by them (for spirits here know one another by intuition)' (245). Presented here as fantasies about the next world, the fantasies of complete reunion and transparent identity, instantaneous and effortless mutual recognition, nonetheless take their peculiarly poignant power and importance within Fielding's corpus from the way his fictions typically render *this* world. Whether defending or disparaging the characteristic qualities of his fiction, Fielding's readers have agreed that his characters seem separate, present to us only 'externally,' their inner lives opaque to the reader and to each other, their encounters full of misunderstandings and misrecognitions and an obscure or only shorthand sense of individual identity.

Readers have defined this quality of Fielding's fictional world largely through contrasts with the 'interiority' achieved in Richardson's. They have generally understood it as a deliberate choice reflecting different designs or beliefs from Richardson's, though some have emphasized its creative limitations and others its existential veracity. Ian Watt refers to Fielding's intentional 'avoidance of the subjective dimension' and complains that he puts the interests of elaborate plotting above those of character study, noting that the plots of his novels depend on the characters' own lack of access to each other's interior selves: the plot of *Tom Jones*, for instance, 'would be impossible if the characters could share each other's minds and take their fates into their own hands.' But their inability to do so seems to David Marshall exactly Fielding's point in his response to Richardson and in his treatment of character: 'Arguing against Richardson's fictions of immediacy and transparency . . . Fielding maintains that the only knowledge we can have of characters in novels and characters in the world is the knowledge we can construe from the outside.' Ronald Paulson argues that the elaborate plotting observed by Watt itself makes a point about the problem of judging action and character: 'Through the ironic complexity of *Tom Jones* Fielding also says that motive too is so difficult to assign that only much later, by surprise, by accident, can we see behavior as good or evil. . . . the reader as well as the character never knows all he needs to know in a given situation.'[16] Marshall cites Fielding's 'Of the Knowledge of the Characters of Men' as Fielding's expression, outside his fiction, of just how difficult it is to construe from the 'vizors' of outside appearance – just how likely it is that it will be 'only much later, by surprise, by accident,' that we will be able to recognize the true nature of an action or a person. If ever. The afterlife that Fielding imagines as the scene of a 'melting' union of souls and of an intuitive and universal recognition of others might be described as a mythological provision for that 'much later' moment when all could come clear.[17] The interests of the elegiac Fielding that Henry Knight Miller discovers are not unrelated to the features of the more familiar Fielding of critical discourse, and they reveal that Fielding's difference from Richardson is not without thought or wishful ambivalence.

Within the particular fictional world described as Fielding's by Watt, Marshall, and Paulson, an elegiac strain may represent not only mourning for the absence of the dead but some element of mourning for the absence of the living to each other – an absence otherwise accommodated as the comedy of Adams's absent-mindedness, for example, or of slap-stick confusions, an absence treated largely satirically rather than sentimentally. Yet it is as if Joseph's and Adams's question – 'Shall I never, never see thee more?' – took the occasion of a threatened mortal loss to express some sense of privation about living in uncertainty as to whether people ever really do see each other. Joseph's consolation to Adams must express some wish about this life as well as about the next.

In their journey on the road from London to the Booby estate, Adams and Joseph move through a world apparently rigged for misrecognitions of every sort, from Adams's and Fanny's failure to recognize each other at first remeeting, and their apprehension as criminals by the men out bird-batting, to Slipslop's later denial of any recognition of Fanny. In the most extended motif of misrecognition, Adams encounters a series of hypocrites, posted along his route for clearly satiric purposes, and enacts with each a little mistaken drama, an emotional recognition scene with an apparent 'brother' in his beliefs. As if his journey were a quest to discover such soul mates, with tears in his eyes Adams tells the falsely courageous Patriot, the falsely charitable Parson Trulliber, the false promiser, and the Romish priest that he has found a brother in each, and that he 'would have walked many a Mile to have communed with you,' or 'have taken a Pilgrimage to the holy Land to have beheld you' (132, 166, 173, 253).

Among these satiric scenes of hypocrisy's staging of false recognitions, the one possible sentimental scene of true recognition and reunion between blood relatives on this journey remains narrowly averted. The reunion between Joseph and his father that will restore him to his true identity and provide the resolution of the novel's plot first occurs just two-thirds of the way through the novel, but passes unrealized. Joseph, Adams, and Fanny's visit to the Wilsons constitutes a strangely failed recognition scene. Though Wilson tells not only the long story of his own life in London but the story of his lost son, down to that identifying mark by which he 'should know him amongst ten thousand,' Joseph, while present at Wilson's fireside account, might as well be absent, for during its final hours he remains 'buried' in sleep (225–26). When Adams misunderstands Wilson's reference to the loss of his eldest son as a mortal loss and begins to console him that death is 'common to all,' Wilson hastens to explain that Joseph was lost when stolen by gypsies and complains that this uncertain loss has proven even harder to accept than death. Joseph's burial in sleep extends his effective absence from his father by preventing recognition, serving, like his abduction by the gypsies, as a kind of provisional, living equivalent of death, and mixing tragedy with comedy in the small chance by which a destined encounter is missed.

Though both this first, unrealized reunion and the eventual successful restaging of it take place between Joseph and his father, the identifying mark that would have allowed Joseph to recognize himself in Wilson's account had he stayed awake, and that does prove his identity in the end, links him specifically to his mother rather than his father. Remembering the little boy who was taken from him so many years before, Wilson cries, 'Poor Child! he had the sweetest Look, the exact Picture of his Mother,' and, imagining the possibility of a reunion with him in the future, he tells Adams that 'he should know him amongst ten thousand, for he had a Mark on his left Breast, of a Strawberry, which his Mother had given him by longing for that Fruit' (225). Wilson's recollection of a family resemblance between mother and son so strong as to be 'exact' heightens the strangeness of Joseph's presence there among his family, unknown, and makes us wonder about the status of that resemblance: has it passed with age? how is the difference in gender accommodated by an *exact* resemblance between mother and son?

Any sense in which Joseph remains an 'exact picture' of his mother has become complicated enough not to serve, anyway, as a cue to recognition, but his link to her survives as the clue to his true history. The external mark he bears that will make him known memorializes a 'longing' she felt when she bore him within – *pre partum* – before the first of familial partings. He carries this mark on his left breast, over that heart which the narrator makes a vexed subject in the chapter on Joseph's grief; outward yet hidden, physical yet a sign of someone's inner longing, the mark brings together the internal and the external. Wilson's story of its origin fancifully plays upon the strange confusion of inner and outer, and of self and self, in the biological facts of pregnancy and birth. It harks back to a moment in the history of each identity when attachments are palpable, and when physical process provides not an allegory of the absence of one person to another, as in death, but a hyperbolic emblem of continuity between selves.

Wilson's story of the birthmark's origin also draws on a long medical tradition about the cause of birthmarks and deformities that was the subject of great popular controversy from the 1720s to the 1760s. This tradition explained any extraordinary feature with which a child was born as the 'sad Effect of the Mother's irregular Fancy and Imagination,' or, as in Joseph's case, the physical trace of some longing she conceived while she carried him. Cravings for particular fruits were most commonly cited as examples of the phenomenon.[18]

The celebrity of Mary Tofts in 1726 for allegedly giving birth to seventeen rabbits, having craved them throughout her pregnancy, sensationalized the medical issue; a dispute in print between James Augustus Blondel and Daniel Turner in the late '20s and early '30s gave the controversy new currency; and G. S. Rousseau observes that 'throughout the 1740s cases of extraordinary childbirth of every sort continued to interest the English public.'[19] The effects commonly attributed to a pregnant mother's cravings are suggestive for our reading of *Joseph Andrews*: Rousseau reports that, according to Nicholas Culpepper's *Directory for Midwives* (first published in 1651), 'even a single instance of bizarre desire would produce "Hermaphrodites, Dwarfs or Gyants," and this idea was repeated again and again in medical works of the period.'[20] Could Wilson's reference to his wife's desire for strawberries not only explain the identifying mark on Joseph's breast but, within this popularized medical tradition, quietly offer a folk etiology for the ambiguous gender that marks his identity again and again?

The pseudomedical concerns of the 'doctrine of imagination' speak for a fascinating constellation of cultural anxieties: explanations for marked and even monstrous births provide a locus of morbid suspicion of woman's imagination and desire. They express a fear of that spiritual interiority with which she is credited and of the formative influence she is said to exert, here turned to deformation, and a kind of horror of her literal powers of conception, here turned vengeful, or in the service of her own spontaneous desires. The underlying logic of the doctrine is interesting: the intervention of a woman's own illicit desire in reshaping the fetus she and a man have together produced may lead to the creation of a hermaphrodite, reflecting, perhaps, its mother's double and transgressive power to 'conceive,' as if on her own.

But Joseph's ambiguous gender identity, sometimes drawing him into ridiculous positions, sometimes advancing him as a new kind of hero, never seems to partake of the horror often attached to hermaphrodism; and Wilson's mention of the imprint of his wife's longing on his son seems casual and unalarmed, even affectionate.[21] Fielding seems to have been aware of the controversy over the influence of a mother's imagination and desire on a fetus, but he makes the power of Mrs. Wilson's desire neither threatening nor damaging: her desire only marks her child, otherwise lost, as her own.[22] Joseph is marked by female imagination and desire, but not as one of Culpepper's 'monsters.' Fielding even naturalizes the mark magically left on Joseph by Mrs. Wilson's longing when he names the strawberry as the specific fruit she desires, for 'strawberry' is a common slang word for a nevus, a birthmark or a mole.[23] He grafts the highly charged, sensationalized material of this pseudomedical dispute onto the stable and idealizing conventions of romance: the mark left on Joseph by his mother's desire becomes the conventional token or distinguishing sign required by the standard recognition scene in romance, and it leads to the reunion for which they all wish. A female capacity for continuity with other selves – embodied literally in pregnancy and rendered horrific in Fielding's time by the 'doctrine of imagination' 's account of monstrous births – extends a special promise within the world described by *Joseph Andrews*.

IV

When Fielding, at the end of his own life, came to write of what he foresaw would be his final parting from his children, he expressed the power of his resistance to that parting by describing his feelings as those of a mother rather than a father. He opens his *Journal of a Voyage to Lisbon* with this entry:

> On this day . . . I was, in my own opinion, last to behold and take leave of some of those creatures on whom I doated with a mother-like fondness, guided by nature and passion, and uncured and unhardened by all the doctrine of that philosophical school where I had learnt to bear pains and to despise death.
>
> In this situation, as I could not conquer nature, I submitted entirely to her, and she made as great a fool of me as she had ever done of any woman whatsoever: under pretence of giving me leave to enjoy, she drew me in to suffer the company of my little ones, during eight hours; and I doubt not whether, in that time, I did not undergo more than in all my distemper.[24]

In describing his feelings, Fielding makes explicit the association that Miller observes of 'nature and passion' with women and of stoic philosophy's 'reason' with men, and he openly owns the feminine attachment to worldly things heard in Joseph's cry of protest against Adams's urging 'to despise death.' He gives these abstract associations more specific content, however, describing his feelings not just as womanly but as motherlike, and opening the journal, which will self-consciously record his journey towards death, with a scene of wrenching parting not just from worldly things but from loved ones. Joseph's consolation to Adams, his promise of a lasting reunion in the afterlife, might here answer to the initial emphasis of Fielding's anticipation of his own death. Fielding tells us that he suffered not only at the moment of farewell but for the final eight hours he spent in 'the company of my little ones,' for he was drawn in by nature – a female personification – to linger with them; and he presents the period of this parting almost as the grueling labor of parturition which he elsewhere pities as women's fate: 'I doubt not whether, in that time, I did not undergo more than in all my distemper.'[25] This passage from Fielding's account of his own life might encourage us to interpret that birthmark which identifies Joseph and links him to his mother as the sign of his implication in 'feminine' feelings like grief, his motherlike resistance to final partings, his advocacy of hope for reunion rather than resignation to absence in a world characterized not only by violence and death but by separations and mistakings.

Even the title of this novel is a testimony to its world's mistakings. As Homer Obed Brown notes, the title of *Joseph Andrews* memorializes the error about Joseph's identity that is only cleared up in the novel's concluding scenes.[26] Our title-character should be called, we eventually learn, Joseph Wilson, except that to name the book that way would undo its process of revelation – and besides, the novel never seems to become very concerned about establishing that the character we had thought of as Joseph Andrews is really Joseph Wilson. It never forms the whole name for us, just as it never articulates the revision of Fanny Goodwill to Fanny Andrews that its revelations imply. After all, the former Joseph Andrews and the newly christened Fanny Andrews will share one name through the marriage with which the story ends. If Joseph were to take Fanny's family name in marriage, he could keep the name he'd always thought was his: what was his original childhood name and identity in error might be given back to him in fact through his adult union with Fanny (and the novel's title could stand). But that would be for a man to take his wife's name in marriage, and the digressive tale of Horatio and Leonora has reminded us earlier in the novel of the long-standing legal and social convention that the woman take the man's name when they are wed. Horatio proposes to Leonora by declaring to her that ' "there is something belonging to you which is a Bar to my Happiness, and which unless you will part with, I must be miserable. . . . It is your Name, Madam. It is by parting with that, by your Condescension to be for ever mine, which . . . will render me the happiest of Mankind" ' (104).

Horatio's peculiar way of framing his proposal serves to remind us that social conventions, shaping identity differently for men and for women, even determine how one possesses that most basic marker of continuous personal identity, one's own name. The circumstances of the novel's plot resolution arrange that if (influenced by the title of the novel, and by its silence about new names) we are to imagine

Joseph, like a man, retaining always one name, we must imagine him, like a woman, taking on his spouse's name in marriage. The legal practice of name changes expresses, more generally, the greater tenuousness of woman's possession of her own identity (' "It is by parting with that, by your Condescension to be for ever mine" ').[27] Clothing can function, like a name, as a public sign of personal identity, and the way Joseph bears his clothing has the same fluid and relational quality that the way he bears his name shares with conventional feminine identity. Before book 1 has ended, Joseph has lost his clothing twice – stripped of his livery and his professional identity by the authority of his employer, Lady Booby, in 1.10, and stripped 'entirely naked' by the brute force of the highwaymen in 1.12 – and has donned a series of substitute garments on loan.[28] At the end of the novel, he will be married in one of Mr. Booby's suits – which, we are told, 'exactly fitted him' (342). The 'something borrowed' in Joseph's wedding regalia might be at once his name and his whole apparel.

But then Joseph has grown to maturity, without knowing it, as himself something borrowed, dependent for his place in the Andrews family on Mrs. Andrews's willingness to take up, as her own, a merely substitute child. She explains how Joseph became Joseph 'Andrews': ' "I took the Child up, and suckled it to be sure, all the World as if it had been born of my own natural Body. And as true as I am alive, in a little time I loved the Boy all to nothing as if it had been my own Girl" ' (337). The connection between mother and child represented by the child's intimate relation to its mother's 'own natural Body' here appears not as something inherent, essential, truly natural, but as something that depends on an act of hypothetical faith, on an acceptance of a substitution as the token of future restoration. The substitution only becomes 'as if' an original bond. Gammar Andrews did not feel confident that her husband would embrace the same substitution (337), and her fears are borne out by Gaffar Andrews's wariness when she and the Pedlar have told their tales: ' "Well," says Gaffar *Andrews*, who was a comical sly old Fellow, and very likely desired to have no more Children than he could keep, "you have proved, I think, very plainly that this Boy doth not belong to us; but how are you certain that the Girl is ours?" ' (338).

The Andrewses' two attitudes towards the child's 'belonging' might roughly correspond to Hélène Cixous's realms of the Gift and of the Proper as they mark off a feminine willingness to make 'vertiginous crossings' with the other from a masculine obsession with classification, systematization, and property.[29] Parson Adams, however, in his clerical/parental role provides an interesting complication to the scheme: repeatedly, he is characterized by his willingness to regard all his parishioners as his children, while Mrs. Adams insists on a more literal and legalistic definition of family.[30] She reminds Adams that ' "it behoved every Man to take the first Care of his Family; that he had a Wife and six Children, the maintaining and providing for whom would be Business enough for him without intermeddling in other Folks Affairs" ' (306); and she tells Lady Booby, ' "he talks a pack of Nonsense, that the whole Parish are his Children. I am sure I don't understand what he means by it . . . I can read Scripture as well as he; and I never found that the Parson was obliged to provide for other Folks Children" ' (321–22). Adams's pastoral role might be said to feminize him in this respect (the Roasting-Squire's men certainly regard his clerical office as a mitigation of gender, proposing that his cassocks serve as 'petticoats' and refusing to fight with a man in a 'gown'), but Fielding's emphasis on Adams's willingness, like Gammar Andrews's, to accept a substitute or second self as his own makes the point that the quality Fielding is interested in here, expressed largely through the terms of gender, does not inhere only in biology.

Fielding's plays concentrate on exposing the scandal of acquired or borrowed identities, including, prominently, affectations of gender. *Shamela* discloses, through parody, the self-serving dramatizations and mediated desires that underlie Pamela's feminine claims to spontaneous personal expression and identity. So does *Joseph Andrews*. But *Joseph Andrews* also draws a limit to the legitimacy of satire's practice of exposure, which Fielding chooses to express this way in his preface: 'What could exceed the Absurdity of an Author, who should write *the Comedy of Nero with the merry Incident of ripping up his Mother's Belly*; or what would give a greater Shock to Humanity, than an Attempt to expose the Miseries of Poverty and Distress to Ridicule?' (7). In Joseph, marked by his own connection to a mother's belly – by his hidden identification with another self, and a self of the other gender – Fielding imagines a character predicated on the borrowing of identities who yet achieves a kind of autonomous stature. Giving up the implied alternative to satire's exposure of false fronts – that clothing, for instance, might ever 'properly' belong to and express inner identity – Fielding attempts to create a male character whose circumstances are initially borrowed from another book, whose name (that signifier of patrilineal descent) is borrowed from his adoptive mother or from his wife, whose clothes are borrowed from anyone generous enough to lend.[31] In *Joseph Andrews*, Fielding not only moves beyond his earlier treatment of gender's mobility as a betrayal of fixed, natural categories, reinterpreting what had seemed essential as contingent, but imagines a kind of naturalizing of that contingency: he simultaneously insists on an undeluded view of life's uncertainties, 'metonymic' causalities, and substitutions, and conceives of a response to that condition that allows one to embrace life's contingencies 'all to nothing as if' they were naturally one's own.[32] He himself borrows conventionally feminine attitudes to figure this possibility both in the story he tells about Joseph's life and, in *The Journal of a Voyage to Lisbon*, in the one he tells about his own.

Notes

1. Henry Fielding, *Joseph Andrews*, ed. Martin C. Battestin (Middletown, Conn.: Wesleyan University Press, 1967), 265. All subsequent citations will be noted parenthetically.

2. Henry Knight Miller, *Essays on Fielding's Miscellanies. A Commentary on Volume One* (Princeton: Princeton University Press, 1961), 269; and J. Paul Hunter, *Occasional Form: Henry Fielding and the Chains of Circumstance* (Baltimore: The Johns Hopkins University Press, 1975), 45. Dianne Osland argues that a 'moral stalemate' is created by the conjunction between chapters 11 and 12 of book 3 in her essay, 'Tied Back to Back: The Discourse Between the Poet and Player and the Exhortations of Parson Adams in *Joseph Andrews*,' *The Journal of Narrative Technique* 12 (1982): 191–200.

3. Miller, 267–69. The tradition of referring to Richardson as in some sense 'feminine' and to Fielding as representatively 'masculine' began in their own day, and continues to our own among critics as diverse as Martin Battestin and Terry Eagleton. See, for example, Battestin's introduction to *Joseph Andrews* and *Shamela* (Boston: Houghton Mifflin Co., 1961), and Eagleton's *The Rape of Clarissa: Writing, Sexuality, and Class Struggle in Samuel Richardson* (Minneapolis: University of Minnesota Press, 1982), viii. Robert Etheridge Moore provided in 1951 perhaps the boldest statement of the contrast: '[*Tom Jones*,] like its creator, is virile and forthright, qualities which appealed especially to Johnson. Richardson, on the other hand, is fussy and hesitating. Johnson, like Fielding, is a man, and what is more, a man's man. . . . Richardson may be called, in all seriousness, one of our great women' ('Dr Johnson on Fielding and Richardson,' *PMLA* 66 [1951]: 172).

4. Miller, 271.

5. I have argued the importance of gender inversions in Fielding's drama at length in ' "When Men Women Turn": Gender Reversals in Fielding's Plays,' in *The New Eighteenth Century: Theory, Politics, English Literature*, ed. Felicity Nussbaum and Laura Brown (New York: Methuen, 1987), 62–83.

6. Several critics have commented upon the special authority that Fielding grants to Shakespeare. Hunter (note 2) observes that Fielding uses Shakespeare as a 'touchstone for knowledge of human nature' in *Tom Jones*, and that he is 'at one with his age in expressing such strong admiration' for Shakespeare (27); and Maurice Johnson, while underlining the difference in contexts between Macduff's speech and Joseph's quotation of it, concludes that, 'by associating himself with Shakespeare, Joseph dignifies himself above Adams' (*Fielding's Art of Fiction* [Philadelphia: University of Pennsylvania Press, 1961], 68). Note also that Joseph quotes from a play that not only in this passage but throughout has everything to do with a struggle to define proper manly and womanly responses.

7. See the essays of December 20, 1739, and April 8, 15, and 22, 1740, collected in *The Champion* (London: H. Chapelle, 1743), 1: 113 and 2: 80–86, 107, and 128.

8. For other examples of the sweetness of Joseph's voice, see 1.2, 1.4, and 4.6. In 2.12, when Joseph and Fanny are finally reunited in the novel, Fanny recognizes Joseph first 'as a Voice from an inner Room,' overheard singing a song with 'one of the most melodious [voices] that ever was heard' (153–54). Early in the novel, Slipslop reminds us of the focus of Fielding's satiric concern with the opera in his plays when she sharply responds to Lady Booby's censure of 'lewdness' in her house: ' "If you will turn away every Footman," said *Slipslop*, "that is a lover of the Sport, you must soon open the Coach-Door yourself, or get a Sett of *Mophrodites* to wait upon you; and I am sure I hated the Sight of them even singing in an Opera" ' (43).

9. Michael Stapleton, *A Dictionary of Greek and Roman Mythology* (New York: Hamlyn, 1978), 182–83.

10. Several critics have noted how much Fielding's description of Joseph shares with his later description of Fanny. Jean Hagstrum notes the parallel between Fanny's portrait and Fielding's description of Joseph's 'tenderness joined with a sensibility inexpressible' (*Sex and Sensibility: Ideal and Erotic Love from Milton to Mozart* [Chicago: University of Chicago Press, 1980], 179). Thomas E. Maresca, too, notes the shared phrasings in the two descriptions and comments that they make Fanny 'the female counterpart of Joseph,' though he also argues for important differences between the two characters (*Epic to Novel* [Columbus: Ohio State University Press, 1974], 200–201). Hagstrum identifies the sensibility Fielding grants to both Joseph and Fanny as feminine, observing that he grants it to Tom Jones as well, and commenting: 'once again, as if to avoid the implication of effeminacy that sensibility could obviously carry with it, Fielding insists that Tom also possesses a "most masculine person and mien." The whole of *Tom Jones* illustrates abundantly both the vigorously masculine and the delicately feminine qualities of the hero. . . . It may be worth considering that in the spirit of so robustly a heterosexual man as Fielding delicate sensibility loomed larger than we have hitherto realized' (179–80).

11. *Paradise Lost*, 4.295–311, in *The Poems of John Milton*, ed. John Carey and Alastair Fowler (New York: Longman, 1968), 631. In their notes to this passage, the editors cite St. Paul's similar treatment of hair-length as an expression of the hierarchic relation of the sexes (1 Cor. 11: 7, 15).

12. See pages 53, 55, 56, 57, 61, and 63 for examples.

13. Fielding's offer of the epitaph as genealogy for Joseph jokingly plays, of course, upon the name 'merry Andrew' for a clown, and he ultimately dismisses it with the observation 'that *Andrew* here is writ without an *s*, and is besides a Christian Name' (20–21).

14. Campbell (note 5), 77–83.

15. 'Of the Remedy of Affliction for the Loss of our Friends' and 'Journey From This World to the Next,' in *The Complete Works of Henry Fielding*, ed. William Ernest Henley (New York: Croscup and Sterling, 1902), 16: 109 and 2: 245. Fielding's interest in the sentimental wish for reunion in the afterlife appears in his satirical works as well. There, in a different mood, he punctures sentimental expectations by imagining death as a blessed relief from married union, and a reunion in the afterlife as a distressing surprise. See, for example, the puppet show in *The Author's Farce* (act 3) and the central joke of his version of *Eurydice*.

16. Ian Watt, *The Rise of the Novel: Studies in Defoe, Richardson, and Fielding* (Berkeley: University of California Press, 1957), 273–76; David Marshall, *The Figure of Theater: Shaftesbury, Defoe, Adam Smith, and George Eliot* (New York: Columbia University Press, 1986), 236; Ronald Paulson, *Satire and the Novel in 18th-Century England* (New Haven: Yale University Press, 1967), 147–48. Hunter (note 2) concurs with Marshall and Paulson, describing Fielding as 'intrigued by the inherent ambiguities of action,' concerned with the problem 'of knowing how to construe accurately' (69–70).

17. The word 'melting' appears in Fielding's description of such a reunion in 'A Journey From This World to the Next' and 'Of the Remedy of Affliction for the Loss of our Friends.' Entering Elysium in 'A Journey From This World': 'I presently met a little daughter, whom I had lost several years before. Good Gods! what words can describe the raptures, the melting passionate tenderness, with which we kissed each other, continuing in our embrace, with the most ecstatic joy, a space, which if time had been measured here as on earth, could not be less than half a year' (2: 246). Describing 'the hope of again meeting the beloved person' in another world: 'This is a rapture which leaves the warmest imagination at a distance. *Who can conceive* (says Sherlock, in his Discourse on Death) *the melting caresses of two souls in Paradise?*' ('Of the Remedy,' 16: 109).

18. My information on this subject derives from G. S. Rousseau's suggestive essay, 'Pineapples, Pregnancy, Pica, and *Peregrine Pickle*,' in *Tobias Smollett: Bicentennial Essays Presented to Lewis M. Knapp*, ed. G. S. Rousseau and P.-G. Boucé (New York: Oxford University Press, 1971), 79–109. The quoted phrase is from James Augustus Blondel's *The Power of the Mother's Imagination Over the Foetus Examin'd*, published in 1729 (Rousseau, 90); and the observation that cravings for exotic fruits were cited most frequently as sources of birthmarks was made by Daniel Turner in his response to Blondel (Rousseau, 91).

19. Rousseau, 93.

20. Rousseau, 84.

21. Phyllis Rackin has described the historical shift that took place in the course of the seventeenth century from 'the high Renaissance image of the androgyne as a symbol of prelapsarian or mystical perfection' to 'the satirical portrait of the hermaphrodite, a medical monstrosity or social misfit' ('Androgyny, Mimesis, and the Marriage of the Boy Heroine on the English Renaissance Stage,' *PMLA* 102 [1987]: 29). The role of the hermaphrodite in this medical controversy of the eighteenth century seems to be an extension of the trend she traces.

22. Fielding also alludes to the relation between a pregnant woman's longings and her child's nature in *Jonathan Wild*. In leading up to 'the birth of our hero,' Fielding reports that, during her pregnancy with him, the great thief's mother's longings foretold her son's nature: 'Another remarkable incident was, that during her whole pregnancy she constantly longed for everything she saw; nor could be satisfied with her wish unless she enjoyed it clandestinely; . . . so had she at this time a most marvellous glutinous quality attending her fingers, to which, as to birdlime, everything closely adhered that she handled' (in Henley [note 15], 2: 7–8).

23. See John S. Farmer and W. E. Henley, *Slang and its Analogues, Past and Present*, vol. 7 (1904; reprint, Millwood, New York: Kraus Reprint Co., 1974). Farmer and Henley do not give a date for the first slang uses of the word, but they do cite a nineteenth-century example which suggests that the word was by then a clichéd expression for an identifying mole or birthmark:

'c. 1866. Burnand and Sullivan. *Box and Cox*. Have you a STRAWBERRY MARK on your left arm? No! Then you are my long lost brother' (8).

24. Wednesday, June 26, 1754. In *The Journal of a Voyage to Lisbon*, ed. Harold E. Pagliaro (New York: Nardon Press, 1963), 43.

25. In 'Of the Remedy,' he recalls the pain of his wife's labor in the context of the pain of mortal loss: 'I remember the most excellent of women, and tenderest of mothers, when, after a painful and dangerous delivery, she was told she had a daughter, answering; *Good God! have I produced a creature who is to undergo what I have suffered!* Some years afterwards, I heard the same woman, on the death of that very child, then one of the loveliest creatures ever seen, comforting herself with reflecting, that, *her child could never know what it was to feel such a loss as she then lamented.* In reality, she was right in both instances' (16: 108).

26. 'Before addressing larger problems of the relationship of fiction to truth (however it is defined), one might note the curious fact that even within their own respective systems of reference the titles [*The History of the Adventures of Joseph Andrews* and *The History of Tom Jones, a Foundling*] are superficially fictional or fictitious – that is to say, they are erroneous. What the reader learns along with the protagonists at the unravelling of the narrative riddle is among other things the answer to a riddle not even suspected. Joseph Andrews' name is not properly Andrews and Tom's name should not be Jones. On the other hand, if the novels' titles had given the "true" names of their protagonists, the "story" would have been spoiled. . . . In neither case does the narrator or Fielding call attention to those rather obvious facts' (Homer Obed Brown, '*Tom Jones*: The "Bastard" of History,' *Boundary 2* [1979]: 202).

27. *Pamela*, too, had acknowledged the symbolic significance of its heroine's adoption of her husband's name upon marriage. That identity which she has composed and sustained for herself against all external pressures through the act of writing she surrenders, along with her name and her pen, when she confesses herself uncertain how to sign herself after marrying Mr. B.: 'He then took a pen himself, and wrote, after Pamela, his most worthy surname; and I under-wrote thus: "O rejoice with me, my dear Mrs. Jervis, that I am enabled, by God's graciousness, and my dear master's goodness, thus to write myself"' (Samuel Richardson, *Pamela* [New York: Norton, 1958], 332).

28. Namely, a frock and breeches borrowed from one of his fellow servants (1.10), the greatcoat of the generous postillion (1.12), the shirt provided by Betty from her sweetheart, the hostler (1.12), and the shirt provided by Mrs. Tow-wouse from her husband's wardrobe when she thinks Joseph a gentleman (1.15).

29. See Hélène Cixous, 'Castration or Decapitation?,' trans. Annette Kuhn, *Signs* 7 (1981): 41–55; and 'The Laugh of the Medusa,' trans. Kuhn, *Signs* 1 (1976): 875–99.

30. For Parson Adams's clerical/parental role, see, for example, 172, 196, and 277.

31. The narrative of Joseph's and Adams's travels also places an insistent emphasis on the financial question of borrowing (on matters of exchange, debt, loans, and gifts); and the two men who must converge on Adams's parish at the end of the story to reconstruct Joseph's history have either lent or given the travellers money at critical moments.

32. In his reading of *Tom Jones*, Homer Obed Brown (note 26) brilliantly argues for Fielding's interest in 'metonymic' versus 'genealogical' models of causality and history.

Notes on Authors

NANCY ARMSTRONG is Nancy Duke Lewis Professor of Comparative Literature, English, Modern Culture and Media, and Women's Studies at Brown University. Her books include *Desire and Domestic Fiction: A Political History of the Novel* (1987) and (with Leonard Tennenhouse) *The Imaginary Puritan: Literature, Intellectual Labor, and the History of Personal Life* (1992). A book entitled *Fiction in the Age of Photography* is forthcoming. She is at present at work on a book on American sentimentalism.

JOHN BENDER is Professor of English and Comparative Literature at Stanford University. His books include *Spenser and Literary Pictorialism* (1972), and *Imagining the Penitentiary: Fiction and the Architecture of Mind in Eighteenth-Century England* (1987), which won the Louis P. Gottschalk Prize from the American Society for Eighteenth-Century Studies that year. With David Wellbery, he has edited *The Ends of Rhetoric: History, Theory, Practice* (1990) and *Chronotypes: The Construction of Time* (1991), and he has recently completed an edition of *Tom Jones*.

HOMER OBED BROWN has taught at Columbia University, at the State University of New York, Buffalo, and is currently Professor of English and Comparative Literature at the University of California, Irvine. His books include *James Joyce's Early Fiction: The Biography of a Form* (1972) and, most recently, *Institutions of the English Novel from Defoe to Scott* (1997). His essay on Defoe (see Chapter 7) won the prize for the best eighteenth-century essay in its year, awarded by the American Society for Eighteenth-Century Studies.

JILL CAMPBELL is Associate Professor of English at Yale University, and the author of *Natural Masques: Gender and Identity in Fielding's Plays and Novels* (1995). She is currently working on a book about satire and self-representation in Lady Mary Wortley Montagu, Lord Hervey, and Alexander Pope.

TERRY CASTLE is Professor of English at Stanford University, and has written five books including *Masquerade and Civilization: The Carnivalesque in Eighteenth-Century English Culture and Fiction* (1986), *The Apparitional Lesbian: Female Homosexuality and Modern Culture* (1993), and *The Female Thermometer: Eighteenth-Century Culture and the Invention of the Uncanny* (1995). Her scholarly interests include eighteenth-century British fiction, the history of sexuality, and British women's writing to the present. She is currently editing *The Literature of Lesbianism: A Historical Anthology, 1545–1975* for Oxford University Press.

RICHARD KROLL is Associate Professor of English and Comparative Literature at the University of California, Irvine. He is author of *The Material Word: Literate Culture in the Restoration and Early Eighteenth Century* (1991), and co-editor of *Philosophy, Science, and Religion in England, 1640–1700* (1992). He is currently working on a book on Restoration drama provisionally entitled *The Circular Economies of Restoration Drama*.

MICHAEL McKEON teaches literature at Rutgers University. He is author of *Politics and Poetry in Restoration England: The Case of Dryden's 'Annus Mirabilis'* (1975), and *The Origins of the English Novel, 1600–1740* (1987). He is currently working on a study of the separation of the public and private spheres in the seventeenth and eighteenth centuries, entitled *The Secret History of Domesticity: Public, Private, and the Division of Knowledge*.

JOHN RICHETTI is the Leonard Sugarman Professor of English at the University of Pennsylvania. Among his books are *Popular Fiction before Richardson: Narrative Patterns, 1700–1739* (1969), *Defoe's Narratives: Situations and Structures* (1975), and *Philosophical Writing: Locke, Berkeley, Hume* (1983). He has also edited *The Columbia History of the British Novel* (1994) and *The Cambridge Companion to the Eighteenth-Century Novel* (1996).

MICHAEL SEIDEL is Professor of English and Comparative Literature at Columbia University. He has written widely on literary topics, and occasionally on non-literary ones, including the history of baseball. His critical books include *Epic Geography: James Joyce's 'Ulysses'* (1976), *Satiric Inheritance: Rabelais to Sterne* (1979), *Exile and the Narrative Imagination* (1986), and *'Robinson Crusoe': Island Myths and the Novel* (1991). He is at present engaged as an associate volume editor in the revived project to produce *The Works of Daniel Defoe* for AMS Press.

ANN JESSIE VAN SANT teaches at the University of California, Irvine. She is author of *Eighteenth-Century Sensibility and the Novel: The Senses in Social Context* (1993). She is now working on a project tentatively entitled *Women's Bodies, Women's Stories*, which focusses on the complexities that emerge when women are included in, and excluded from, the general cultural pattern of locating experience in the body.

The English Novel Volume I: 1700 to Fielding

WILLIAM WARNER is Professor of English at the University of California, Santa Barbara. He is author of *Reading 'Clarissa': The Struggles of Interpretation* (1979), and *Chance and the Text of Experience: Freud, Nietzsche, and Shakespeare's 'Hamlet'* (1986). His latest book, *Licensing Entertainment: The Elevation of Novel Reading in Britain* will appear in 1998 from the University of California Press.

Further Reading

I have divided the books and articles listed here into seven
categories, to reflect the structure and concerns of this anthology.
Some of these, or their main theses, are discussed in my introduction,
or are summarized by a key article or chapter included in the
collection above. To some extent, any reading list will be arbitrary,
but I have tried to present the student with some sense of the
standard historiography on each topic or author, as well as with
pieces that try new things.

General anthologies of essays

Armistead, J. M. (ed.). *The First English Novelists: Essays in
Understanding*. Knoxville: University of Tennessee Press, 1985.
Richetti, John, *et al.* (eds). *The Columbia History of the British Novel*.
New York: Columbia University Press, 1994.
—— (ed.). *The Cambridge Companion to the Eighteenth-Century Novel*.
Cambridge: Cambridge University Press, 1996.

The origins of the novel and the early novel in England

Brown, Homer Obed. *Institutions of the English Novel from Defoe
to Scott*. Philadelphia: University of Pennsylvania Press, 1997.
Davis, Lennard. *Factual Fictions: The Origins of the English Novel*.
New York: Columbia University Press, 1983.
Doody, Margaret Anne. *The True Story of the Novel*. New Brunswick:
Rutgers University Press, 1996.
Hunter, J. Paul. *Before Novels: The Cultural Contexts of Eighteenth-
Century English Fiction*. New York: Norton, 1990.
McKeon, Michael. *The Origins of the English Novel, 1600–1740*.
Baltimore: The Johns Hopkins University Press, 1987.
McKillop, Alan Dugald. *The Early Masters of English Fiction*. Lawrence:
University of Kansas Press, 1956.
Warner, William. *Licensing Entertainment: The Elevation of Novel
Reading in Britain, 1684–1750*. Berkeley: University of California
Press, (forthcoming).
Watt, Ian. *The Rise of the Novel: Studies in Defoe, Richardson and
Fielding*. 1957; rpt. Harmondsworth: Penguin, 1976.

General readings of the eighteenth-century novel

Armstrong, Nancy. *Desire and Domestic Fiction: A Political History of the Novel*. New York: Oxford University Press, 1987.

Bender, John. *Imagining the Penitentiary: Fiction and the Architecture of Mind in Eighteenth-Century England*. Chicago: University of Chicago Press, 1987.

Castle, Terry. *Masquerade and Civilization: The Carnivalesque in Eighteenth-Century English Culture and Fiction*. Stanford: Stanford University Press, 1986.

Kay, Carol. *Political Constructions: Defoe, Richardson, and Sterne in Relation to Hobbes, Hume, and Burke*. Ithaca: Cornell University Press, 1988.

Keener, Frederick. *The Chain of Becoming: The Philosophical Tale, the Novel, and a Neglected Realism of the Enlightenment: Swift, Montesquieu, Voltaire, Johnson, and Austen*. New York: Columbia University Press, 1983.

New, Melvyn. ' "The Grease of God": The Form of Eighteenth-Century English Fiction.' *PMLA* 91 (1976): 235–44.

Spacks, Patricia M. *Desire and Truth: Functions of Plot in Eighteenth-Century English Novels*. Chicago: University of Chicago Press, 1990.

Early women novelists

Ballaster, Ros. *Seductive Forms: Women's Amatory Fiction from 1684–1740*. Oxford: Clarendon Press, 1992.

Gallagher, Catherine. *Nobody's Story: The Vanishing Acts of Women Writers in the Marketplace, 1670–1820*. Berkeley: University of California Press, 1994.

Gonda, Caroline. *Reading Daughters' Fictions, 1709–1834: Novels and Society from Manley to Edgworth*. Cambridge: Cambridge University Press, 1996.

Perry, Ruth. *Women, Letters, and the Novel*. New York: AMS, 1980.

Richetti, John. *Popular Fiction before Richardson: Narrative Patterns, 1700–1739*. Oxford: Clarendon Press, 1969.

Schofield, Mary Anne. *Masking and Unmasking the Female Mind: Disguising Romances in Female Fiction, 1713–1799*. Newark: University of Delaware Press, 1990.

Spencer, Jane. *The Rise of the Woman Novelist: From Aphra Behn to Jane Austen*. Oxford: Blackwell, 1986.

Spender, Dale. *Mothers of the Novel: 100 Good Writers before Jane Austen*. London: Pandora, 1986.

Todd, Janet. *The Sign of Angellica: Women, Writing and Fiction, 1660–1800*. London: Virago, 1989.

Defoe

Alkon, Paul. *Defoe and Fictional Time*. Athens: University of Georgia Press, 1979.

Backscheider, Paula. *Daniel Defoe: A Life*. Baltimore: The Johns Hopkins University Press, 1990.

Chaber, Lois. 'Matriarchal Mirror: Women and Capital in *Moll Flanders*.' *PMLA* 97 (1982): 212–26.

Faller, Lincoln. *Crime and Defoe: A New Kind of Writing*. Cambridge: Cambridge University Press, 1993.

Hunter, J. Paul. *The Reluctant Pilgrim: Defoe's Emblematic Method and Quest for Form in 'Robinson Crusoe.'* Baltimore: The Johns Hopkins University Press, 1966.

Novak, Maximillian E. *Defoe and the Nature of Man*. Oxford: Oxford University Press, 1965.

—— *Realism, Myth, and History in Defoe's Fiction*. Lincoln: University of Nebraska Press, 1983.

Richetti, John. *Defoe's Narratives: Situation and Structures*. Oxford: Oxford University Press, 1975.

Schaffer, Simon. 'Defoe's Natural Philosophy and the Worlds of Credit.' In John Christie and Sally Shuttleworth (eds) *Nature Transfigured: Science and Literature, 1700–1900*. Manchester: Manchester University Press, 1989, pp. 13–44.

Sherman, Sandra. *Finance and Fictionality in the Early Eighteenth Century: Accounting for Defoe*. Cambridge: Cambridge University Press, 1996.

Starr, George. *Defoe and Spiritual Autobiography*. Princeton: Princeton University Press, 1965.

—— *Defoe and Casuistry*. Princeton: Princeton University Press, 1971.

Sutherland, James. *Defoe: A Critical Study*. Cambridge, MA: Harvard University Press, 1971.

Richardson

Castle, Terry. *Clarissa's Cyphers: Meaning and Disruption in Richardson's 'Clarissa.'* Ithaca: Cornell University Press, 1982.

Doody, Margaret Anne. *A Natural Passion: A Study in the Novels of Samuel Richardson*. Oxford: Clarendon Press, 1974.

Doody, Margaret Anne, and Peter Sabor (eds.). *Samuel Richardson Tercentenary Essays*. Cambridge: Cambridge University Press, 1989.

Eagleton, Terry. *The Rape of Clarissa: Writing, Sexuality and Class Struggle in Samuel Richardson*. Oxford: Blackwell; Minneapolis: University of Minnesota Press, 1982.

Eaves, T. C. Duncan, and Ben D. Kimpel. *Samuel Richardson: A Biography*. Oxford: Clarendon Press, 1971.

Folkenflik, Robert. 'A Room of Pamela's Own.' *ELH* 39 (1972): 585–96.

Hill, Christopher. 'Clarissa Harlowe and Her Times.' In *Puritanism and Revolution: Studies in Interpretation of the English Revolution of the 17th Century*. 1958; rpt. London: Mercury Books, 1962, pp. 367–94.

Kinkead-Weekes, Mark. *Samuel Richardson: Dramatic Novelist*. London: Methuen, 1973.

Warner, William Beatty. *Reading 'Clarissa': The Struggles of Interpretation*. New Haven: Yale University Press, 1979.

Wilt, Judith. '"He Could Go No Farther": A Modest Proposal about Lovelace and Clarissa.' *PMLA* 92 (1977): 10–31.

Fielding

Baker, Sheridan. 'Fielding and the Irony of Form.' *Eighteenth-Century Studies* 2 (1968): 138–54.

Battestin, Martin C., and Ruthe R. Battestin. *Henry Fielding: A Life*. New York: Routledge, 1989.

Braudy, Leo. *Narrative Form in History and Fiction*. Princeton: Princeton University Press, 1970.

Brown, Homer Obed. '*Tom Jones*: The "Bastard" of History.' *Boundary 2* 7 (1979): 201–33.

Campbell, Jill. *Natural Masques: Gender and Identity in Fielding's Plays and Novels*. Stanford: Stanford University Press, 1995.

Hunter, J. Paul. *Occasional Form: Henry Fielding and the Chains of Circumstance*. Baltimore: The Johns Hopkins University Press, 1975.

Paulson, Ronald. *Satire and the Novel in Eighteenth-Century England*. New Haven: Yale University Press, 1967.

Price, Martin. *To the Palace of Wisdom: Studies in Order and Energy from Dryden to Blake*. Garden City, NY: Doubleday, 1964.

Rawson, Claude. *Henry Fielding and the Augustan Ideal under Stress*. London: Routledge, 1972.

—— *Order from Confusion Sprung: Studies in Eighteenth-Century Literature from Swift to Cowper*. London: Allen and Unwin, 1985.

Rogers, Pat. *Henry Fielding: A Biography*. New York: Scribner, 1979.

Sacks, Sheldon. *Fiction and the Shape of Belief: A Study of Henry Fielding with Glances at Swift, Johnson and Richardson*. Berkeley: University of California Press, 1967.

Index